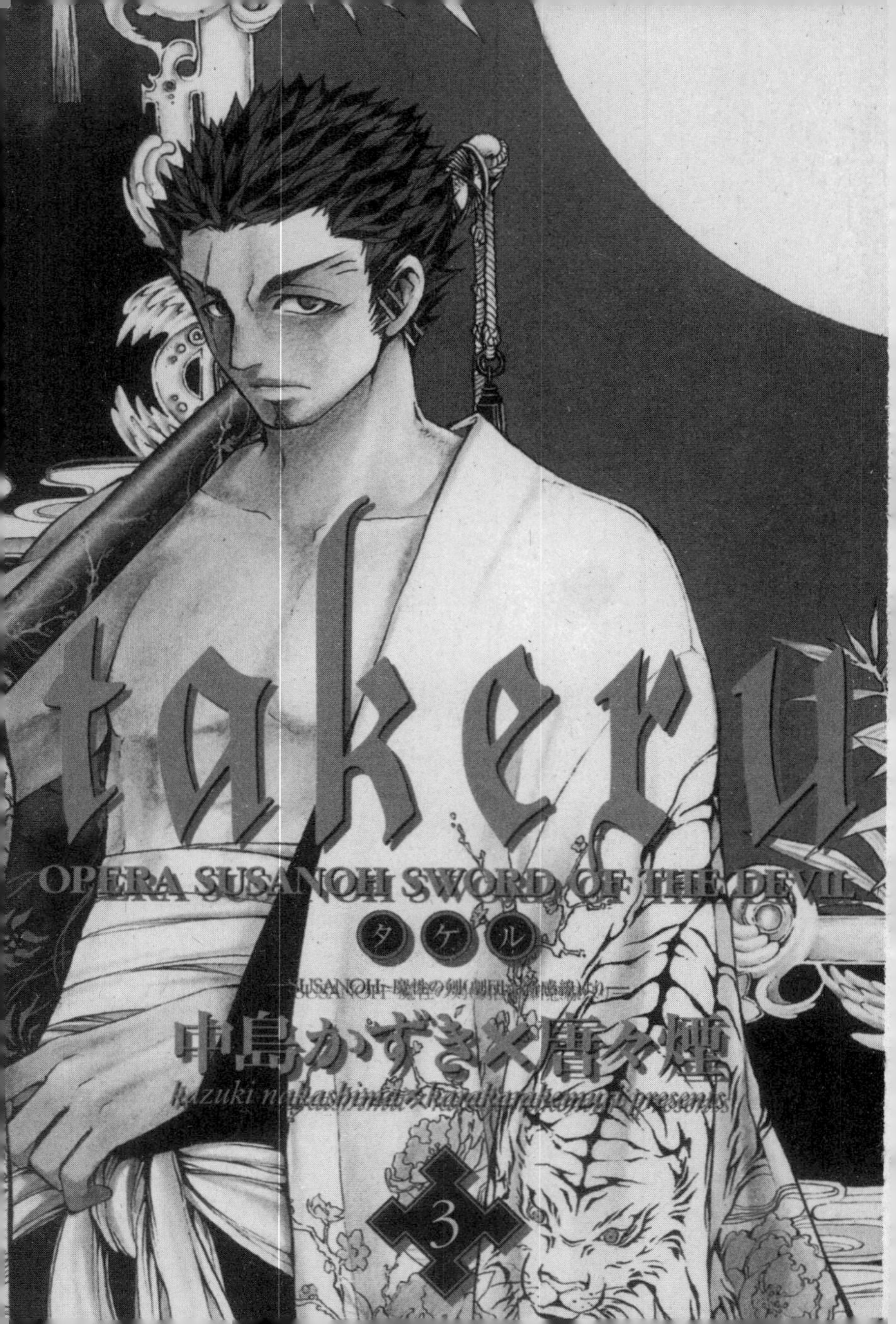
takeru
OPERA SUSANOH SWORD OF THE DEVIL
タケル
中島かずき×唐々煙
kazuki nakashima×karakarakemuri presents
3

takeru: OPERA SUSANOH SWORD OF THE DEVIL 3
Created by Kazuki Nakashima X Karakarakemuri

Translation - Stephen Paul
English Adaptation - Tim Beedle
Copy Editor - Daniella Orihuela-Gruber
Retouch and Lettering - Star Print Brokers
Production Artist - Rui Kyo
Graphic Designer - Louis Csontos

Editor - Lillian Diaz-Przybyl
Print Production Manager - Lucas Rivera
Managing Editor - Vy Nguyen
Senior Designer - Louis Csontos
Art Director - Al-Insan Lashley
Director of Sales and Manufacturing - Allyson De Simone
Associate Publisher - Marco F. Pavia
President and C.O.O. - John Parker
C.E.O. and Chief Creative Officer - Stu Levy

A **TOKYOPOP** Manga

TOKYOPOP and are trademarks or registered trademarks of TOKYOPOP Inc.

TOKYOPOP Inc.
5900 Wilshire Blvd. Suite 2000
Los Angeles, CA 90036

E-mail: info@TOKYOPOP.com
Come visit us online at www.TOKYOPOP.com

ISBN: 978-1-4278-1572-9

First TOKYOPOP printing: December 2009
10 9 8 7 6 5 4 3 2 1
Printed in the USA

Takeru

Opera Susanoh
Sword of the Devil™

SUSANOH～魔性の剣（劇団☆新感線）より

HAMBURG // LONDON // LOS ANGELES // TOKYO

CONTENTS

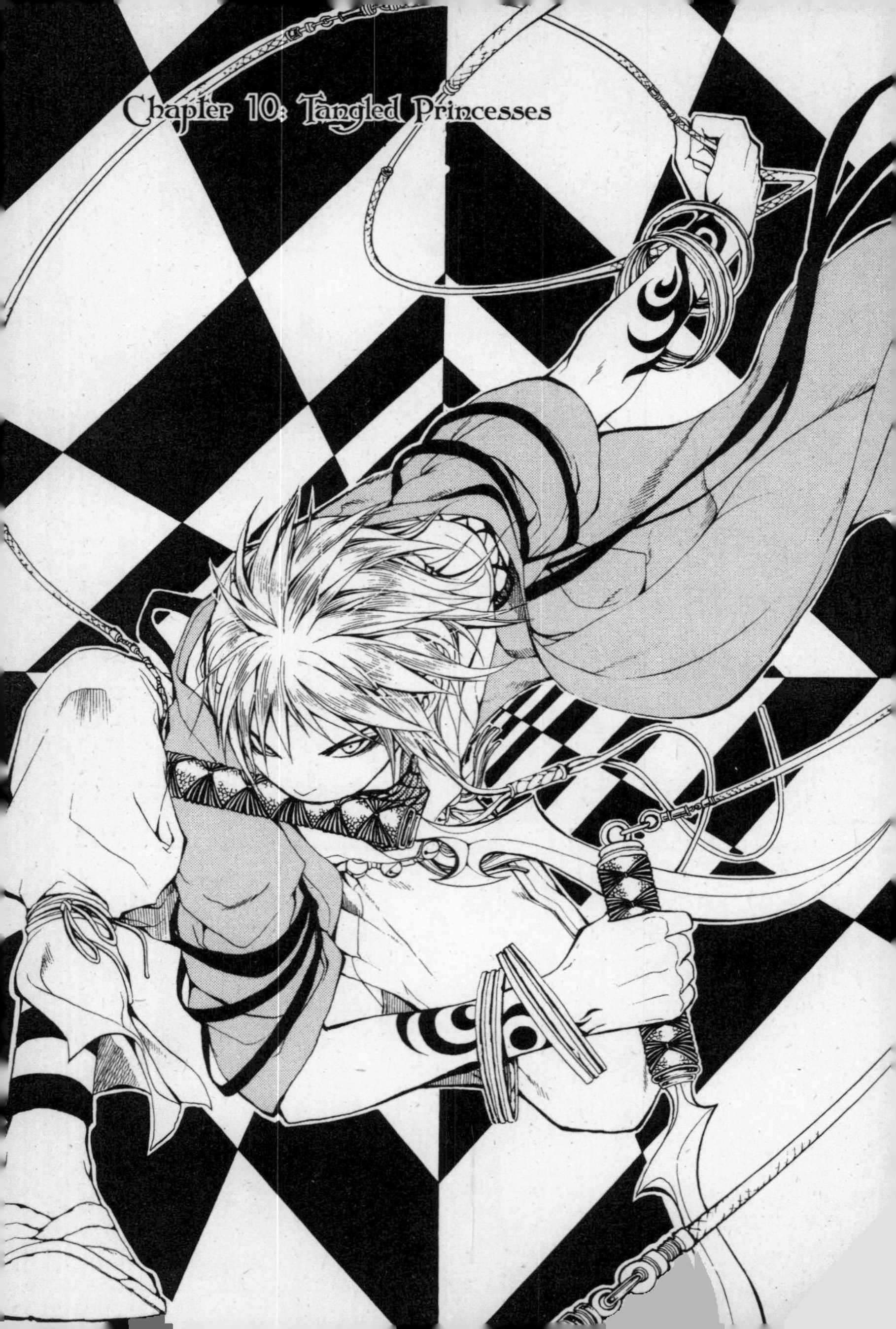
Chapter 10: Tangled Princesses

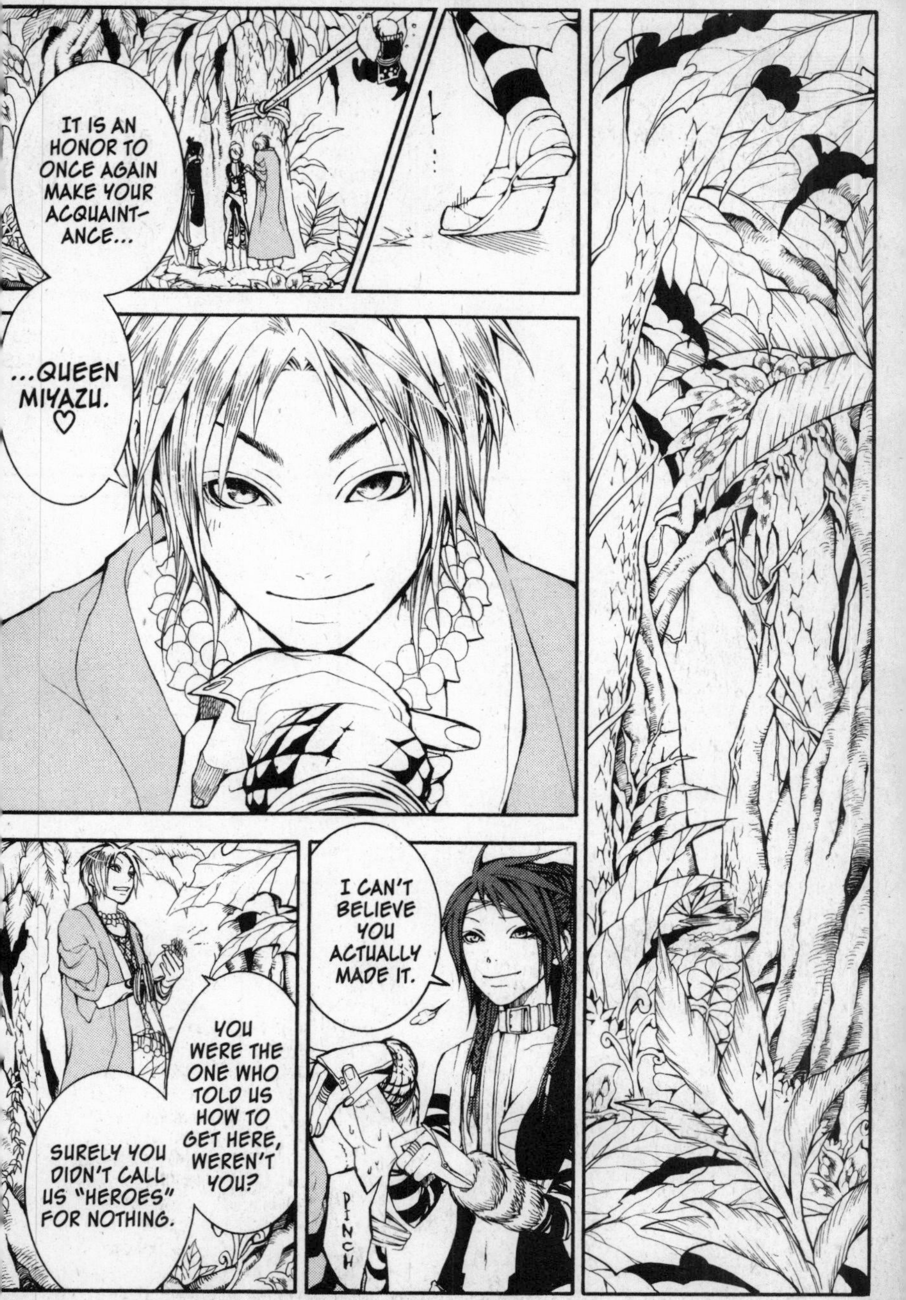
IT IS AN HONOR TO ONCE AGAIN MAKE YOUR ACQUAINT-ANCE...
...QUEEN MIYAZU. ♡
I CAN'T BELIEVE YOU ACTUALLY MADE IT.
PINCH
YOU WERE THE ONE WHO TOLD US HOW TO GET HERE, WEREN'T YOU?
SURELY YOU DIDN'T CALL US "HEROES" FOR NOTHING.

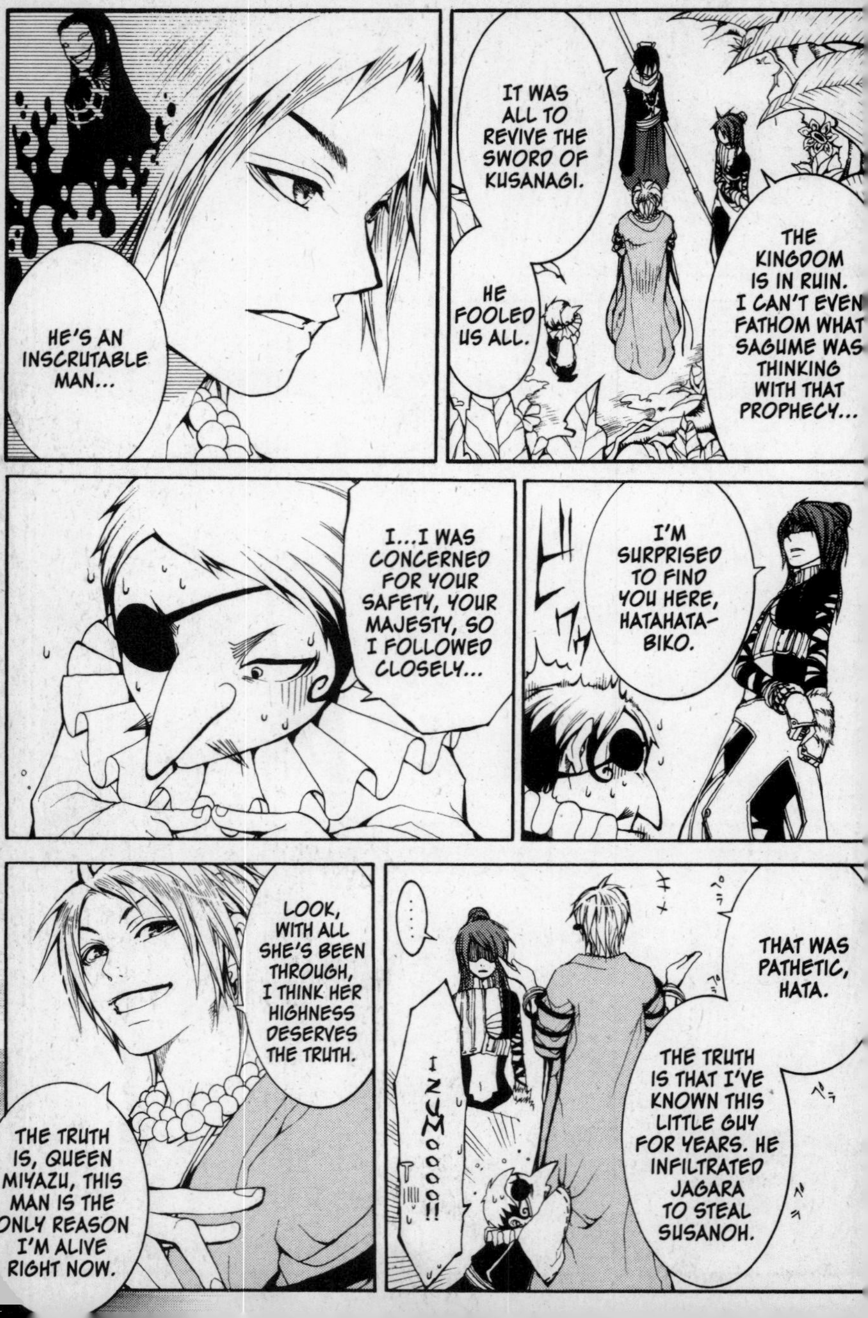
THE KINGDOM IS IN RUIN. I CAN'T EVEN FATHOM WHAT SAGUME WAS THINKING WITH THAT PROPHECY...
IT WAS ALL TO REVIVE THE SWORD OF KUSANAGI.
HE FOOLED US ALL.
HE'S AN INSCRUTABLE MAN...
I'M SURPRISED TO FIND YOU HERE, HATAHATA-BIKO.
I...I WAS CONCERNED FOR YOUR SAFETY, YOUR MAJESTY, SO I FOLLOWED CLOSELY...
THAT WAS PATHETIC, HATA.
THE TRUTH IS THAT I'VE KNOWN THIS LITTLE GUY FOR YEARS. HE INFILTRATED JAGARA TO STEAL SUSANOH.
......
IZUMOOOOO!!
LOOK, WITH ALL SHE'S BEEN THROUGH, I THINK HER HIGHNESS DESERVES THE TRUTH.
THE TRUTH IS, QUEEN MIYAZU, THIS MAN IS THE ONLY REASON I'M ALIVE RIGHT NOW.

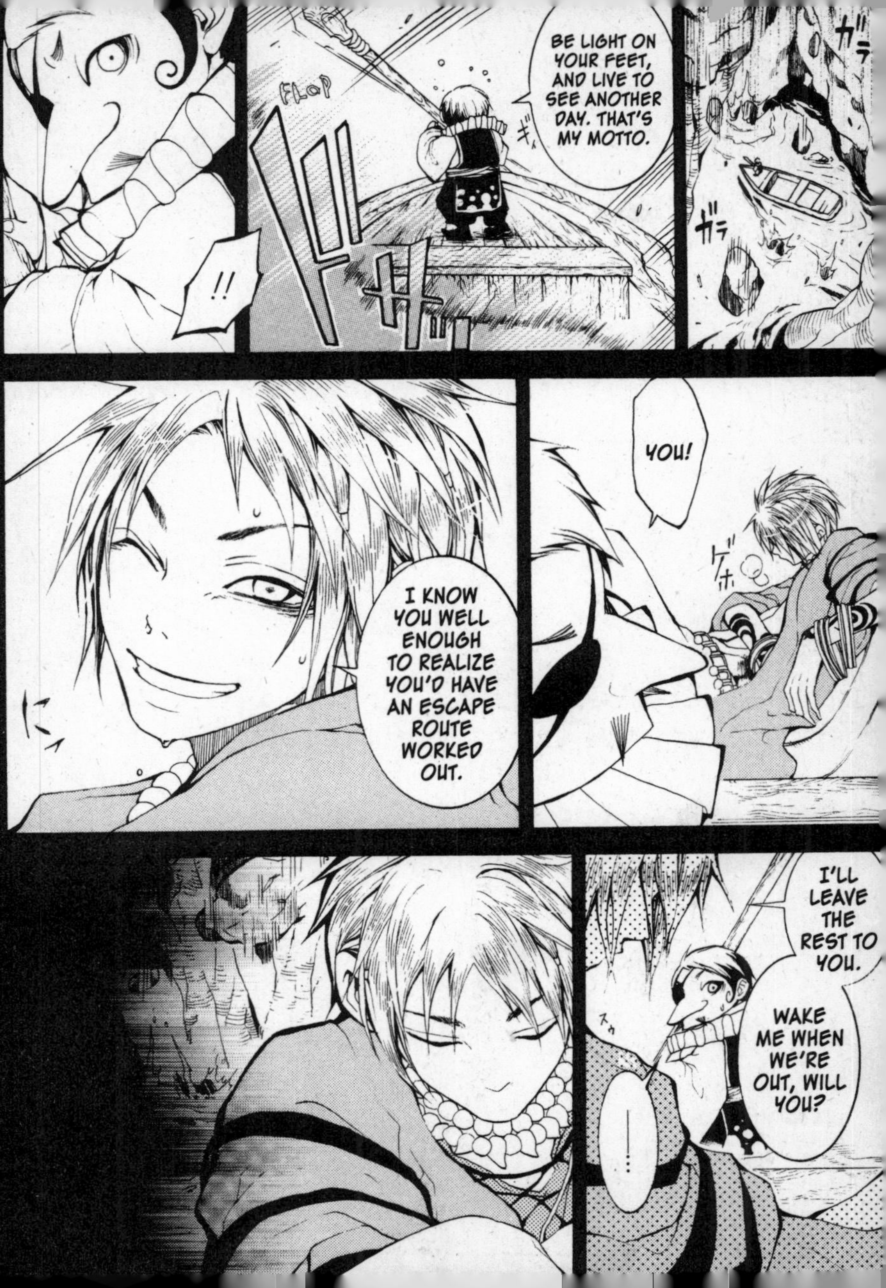
FLAP
BE LIGHT ON YOUR FEET, AND LIVE TO SEE ANOTHER DAY. THAT'S MY MOTTO.
!!
YOU!
I KNOW YOU WELL ENOUGH TO REALIZE YOU'D HAVE AN ESCAPE ROUTE WORKED OUT.
I'LL LEAVE THE REST TO YOU.
WAKE ME WHEN WE'RE OUT, WILL YOU?
......

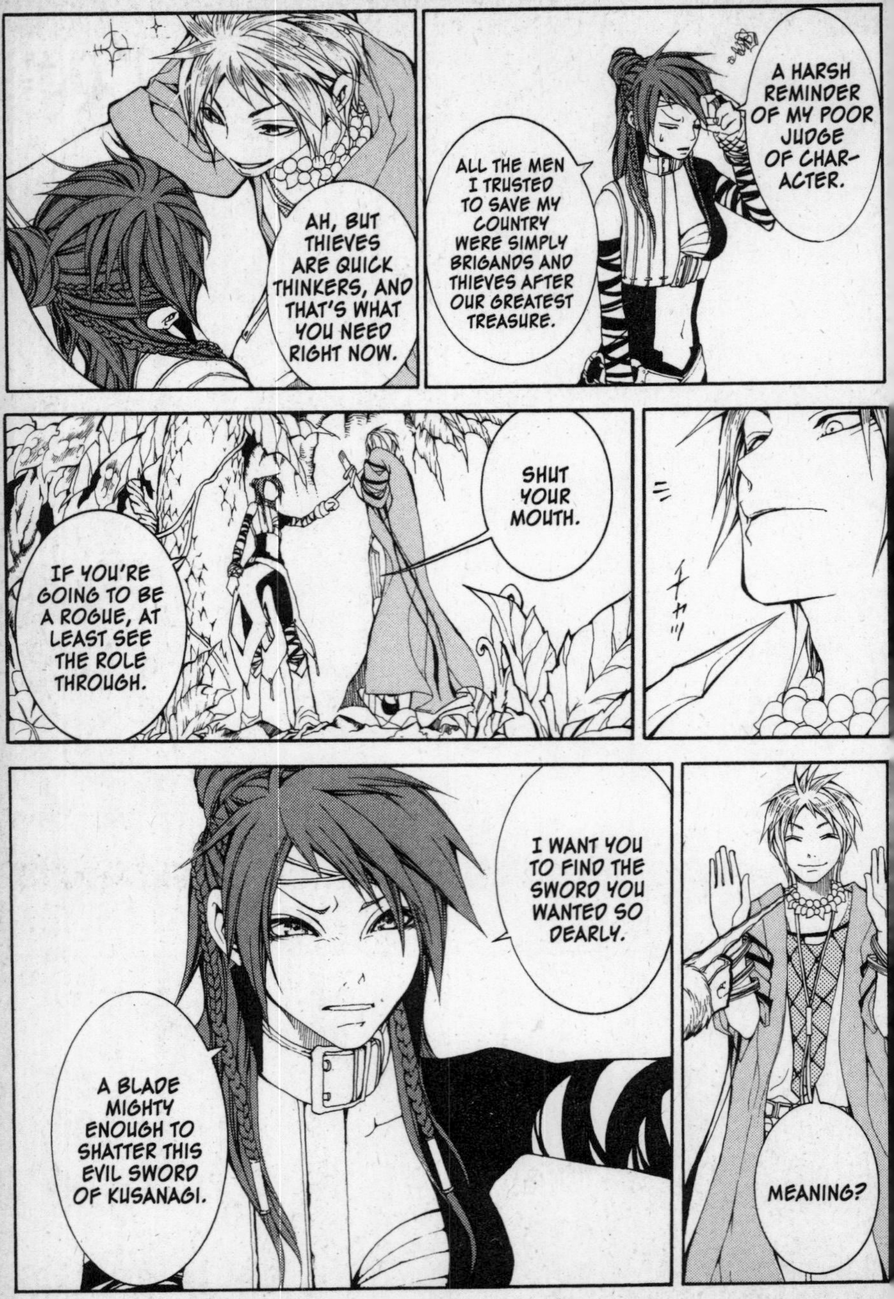
A HARSH REMINDER OF MY POOR JUDGE OF CHAR-ACTER.
ALL THE MEN I TRUSTED TO SAVE MY COUNTRY WERE SIMPLY BRIGANDS AND THIEVES AFTER OUR GREATEST TREASURE.
AH, BUT THIEVES ARE QUICK THINKERS, AND THAT'S WHAT YOU NEED RIGHT NOW.
SHUT YOUR MOUTH.
IF YOU'RE GOING TO BE A ROGUE, AT LEAST SEE THE ROLE THROUGH.
MEANING?
I WANT YOU TO FIND THE SWORD YOU WANTED SO DEARLY.
A BLADE MIGHTY ENOUGH TO SHATTER THIS EVIL SWORD OF KUSANAGI.

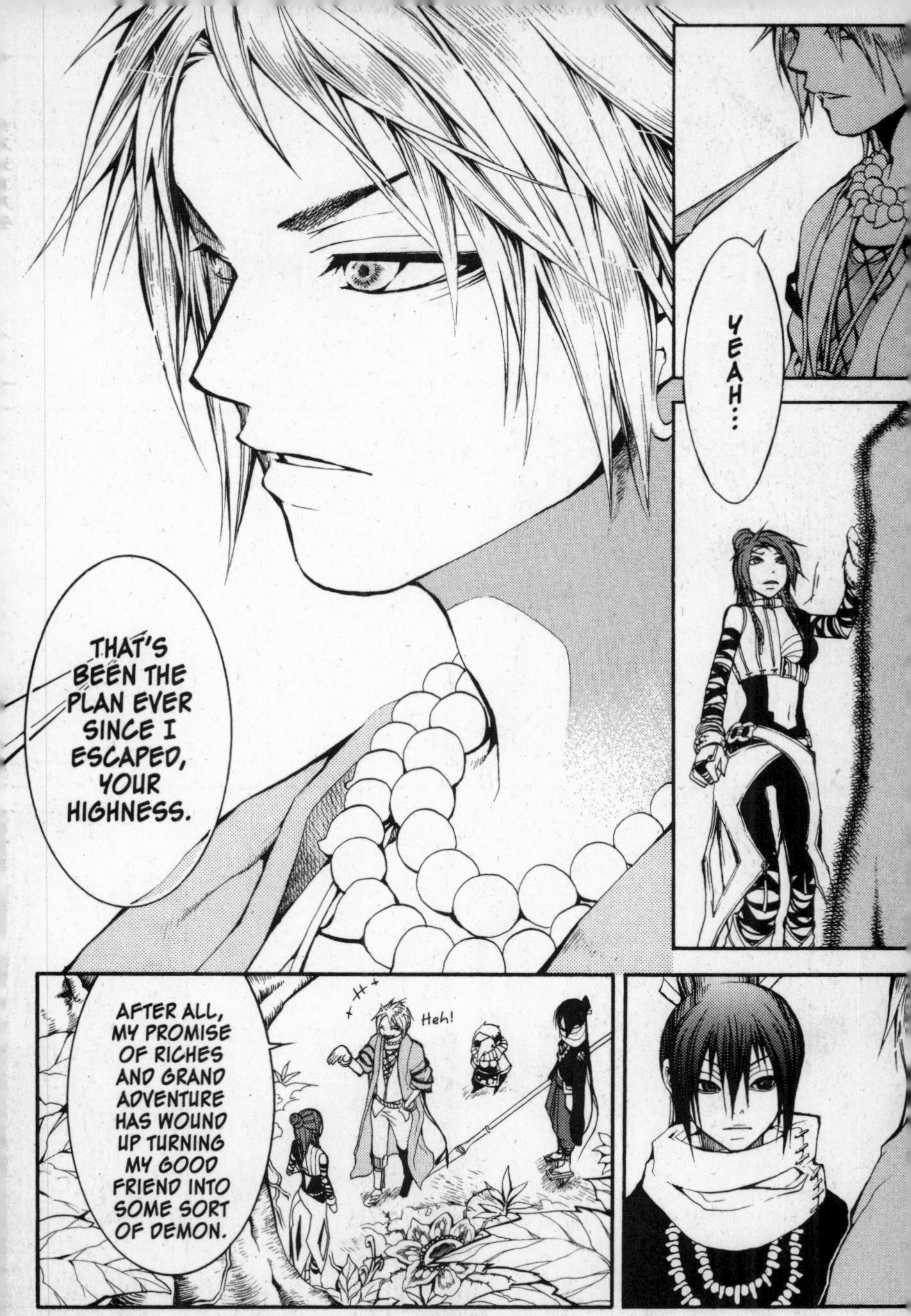
YEAH...
THAT'S BEEN THE PLAN EVER SINCE I ESCAPED, YOUR HIGHNESS.
AFTER ALL, MY PROMISE OF RICHES AND GRAND ADVENTURE HAS WOUND UP TURNING MY GOOD FRIEND INTO SOME SORT OF DEMON.
Heh!

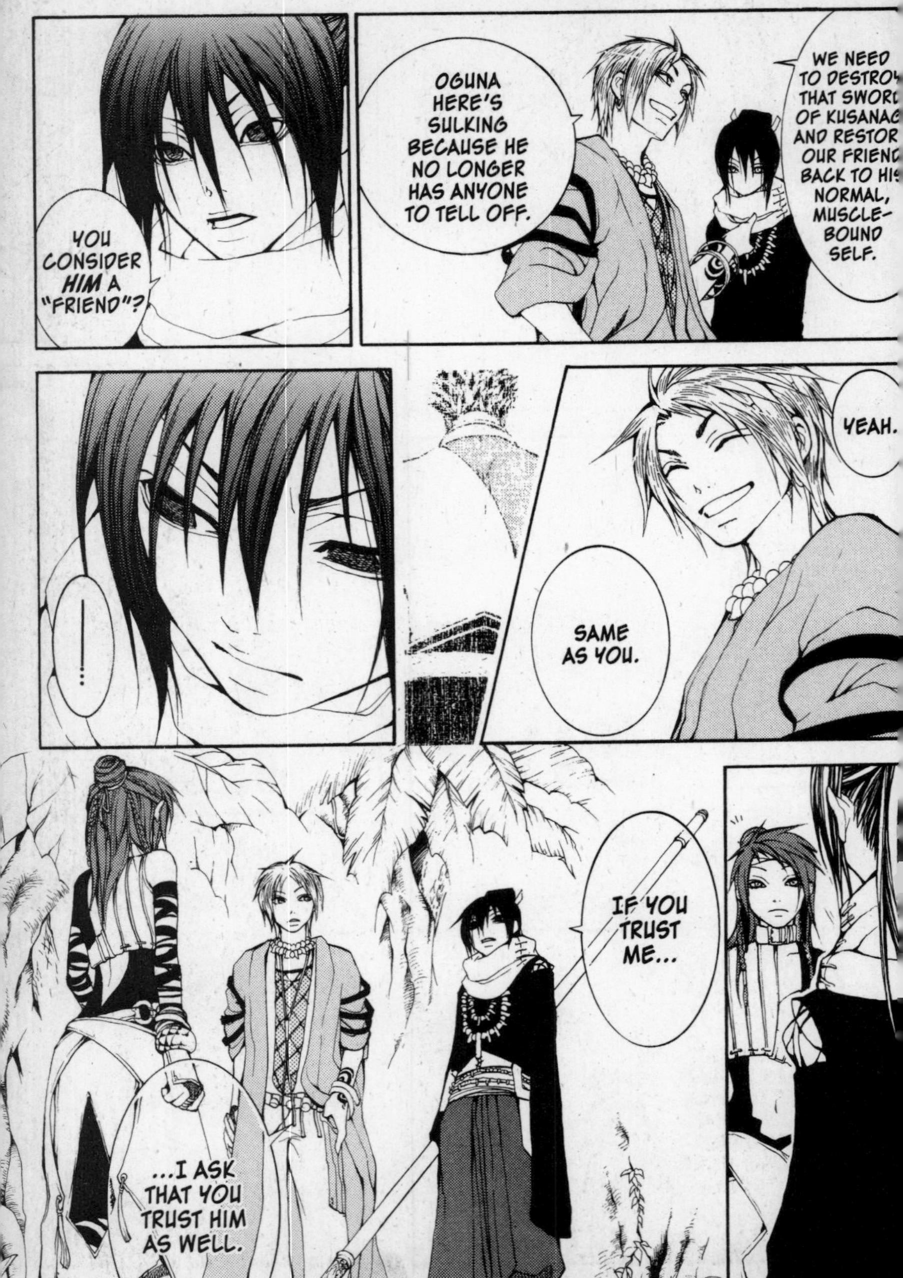
WE NEED TO DESTRO THAT SWORD OF KUSANAG AND RESTOR OUR FRIEND BACK TO HIS NORMAL, MUSCLE-BOUND SELF.
OGUNA HERE'S SULKING BECAUSE HE NO LONGER HAS ANYONE TO TELL OFF.
YOU CONSIDER *HIM* A "FRIEND"?
YEAH.
SAME AS YOU.
...!
IF YOU TRUST ME...
...I ASK THAT YOU TRUST HIM AS WELL.

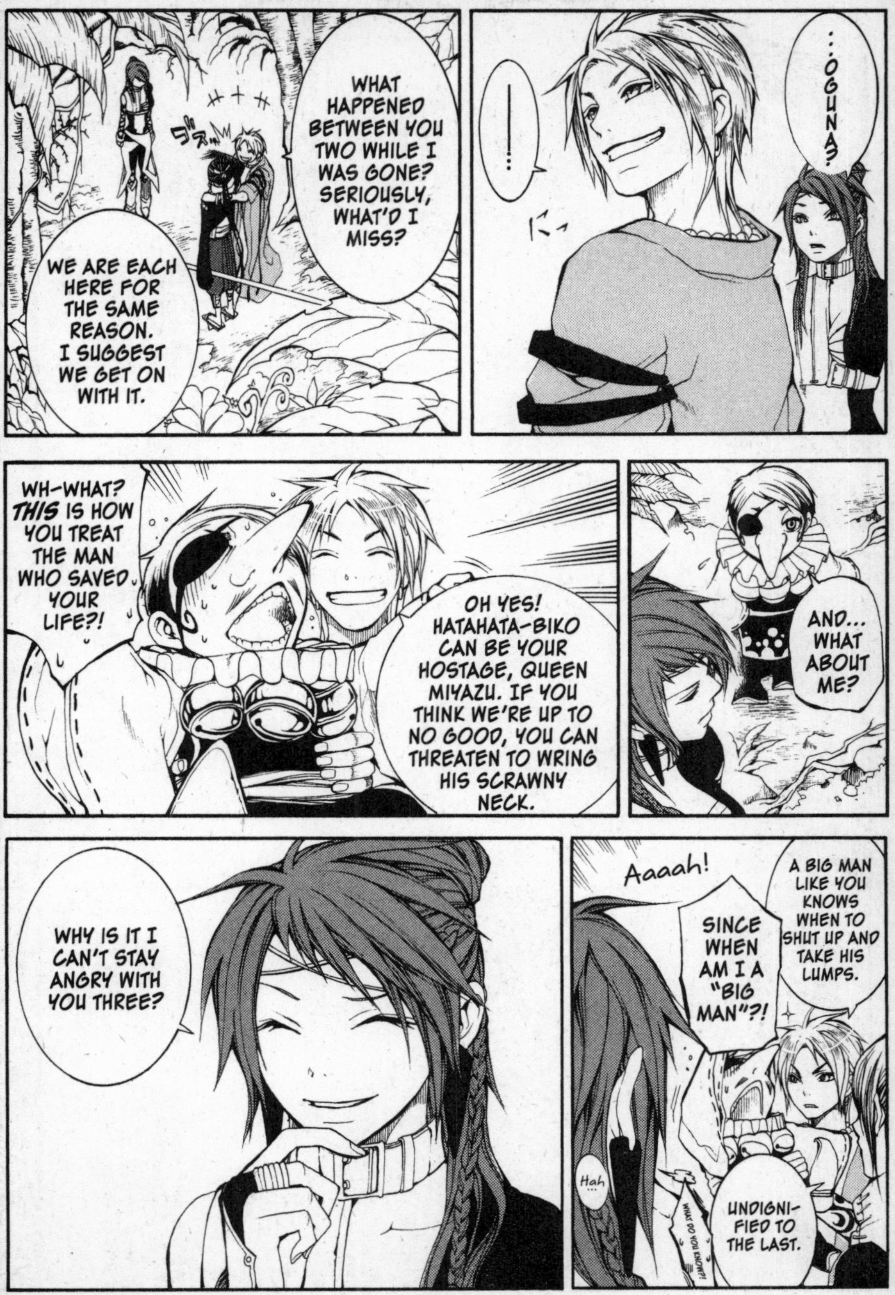
...OGUNA?
!......
WHAT HAPPENED BETWEEN YOU TWO WHILE I WAS GONE? SERIOUSLY, WHAT'D I MISS?
WE ARE EACH HERE FOR THE SAME REASON. I SUGGEST WE GET ON WITH IT.
AND... WHAT ABOUT ME?
OH YES! HATAHATA-BIKO CAN BE YOUR HOSTAGE, QUEEN MIYAZU. IF YOU THINK WE'RE UP TO NO GOOD, YOU CAN THREATEN TO WRING HIS SCRAWNY NECK.
WH-WHAT? *THIS* IS HOW YOU TREAT THE MAN WHO SAVED YOUR LIFE?!
A BIG MAN LIKE YOU KNOWS WHEN TO SHUT UP AND TAKE HIS LUMPS.
Aaaah!
SINCE WHEN AM I A "BIG MAN"?!
Hah...
WHAT DO YOU KNOW?!
UNDIGNI-FIED TO THE LAST.
WHY IS IT I CAN'T STAY ANGRY WITH YOU THREE?

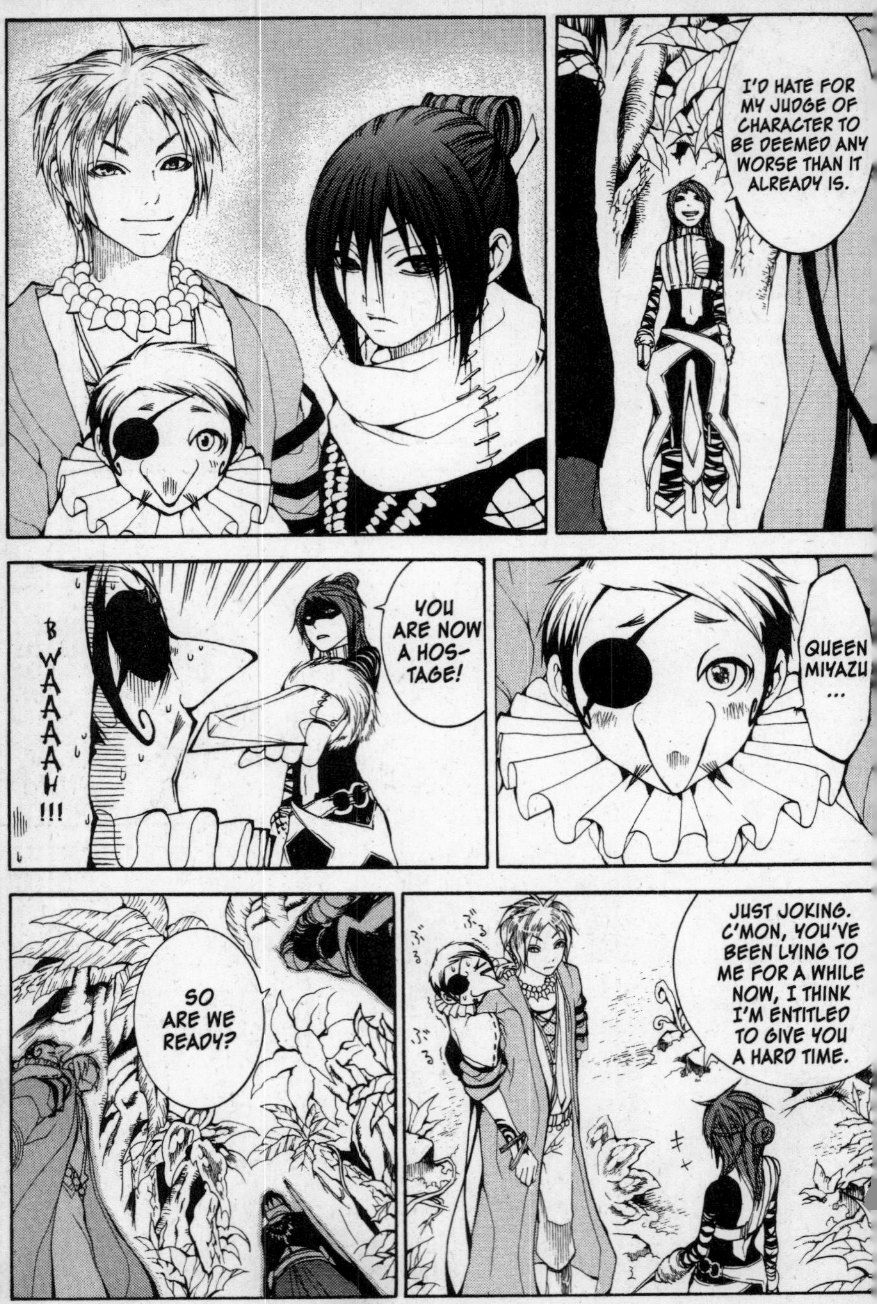
I'D HATE FOR MY JUDGE OF CHARACTER TO BE DEEMED ANY WORSE THAN IT ALREADY IS.
QUEEN MIYAZU ...
YOU ARE NOW A HOS-TAGE!
BWAAAAAH!!!
JUST JOKING. C'MON, YOU'VE BEEN LYING TO ME FOR A WHILE NOW, I THINK I'M ENTITLED TO GIVE YOU A HARD TIME.
ぶる ぶる
ぶる
SO ARE WE READY?

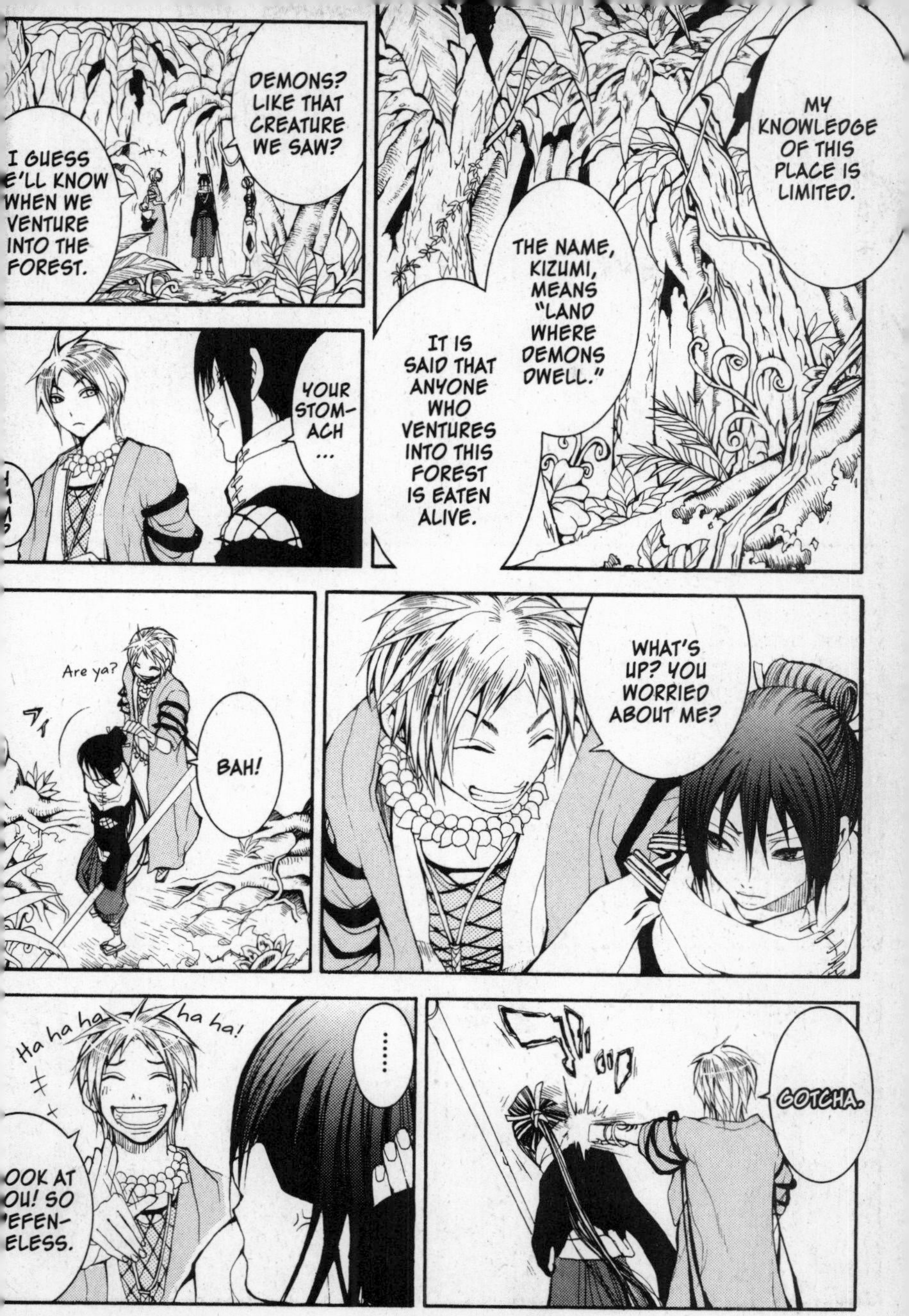
MY KNOWLEDGE OF THIS PLACE IS LIMITED.
THE NAME, KIZUMI, MEANS "LAND WHERE DEMONS DWELL."
IT IS SAID THAT ANYONE WHO VENTURES INTO THIS FOREST IS EATEN ALIVE.
DEMONS? LIKE THAT CREATURE WE SAW?
I GUESS E'LL KNOW WHEN WE VENTURE INTO THE FOREST.
YOUR STOM-ACH ...
WHAT'S UP? YOU WORRIED ABOUT ME?
Are ya?
BAH!
GOTCHA.
......
Ha ha ha ha ha!
OOK AT OU! SO EFEN-ELESS.

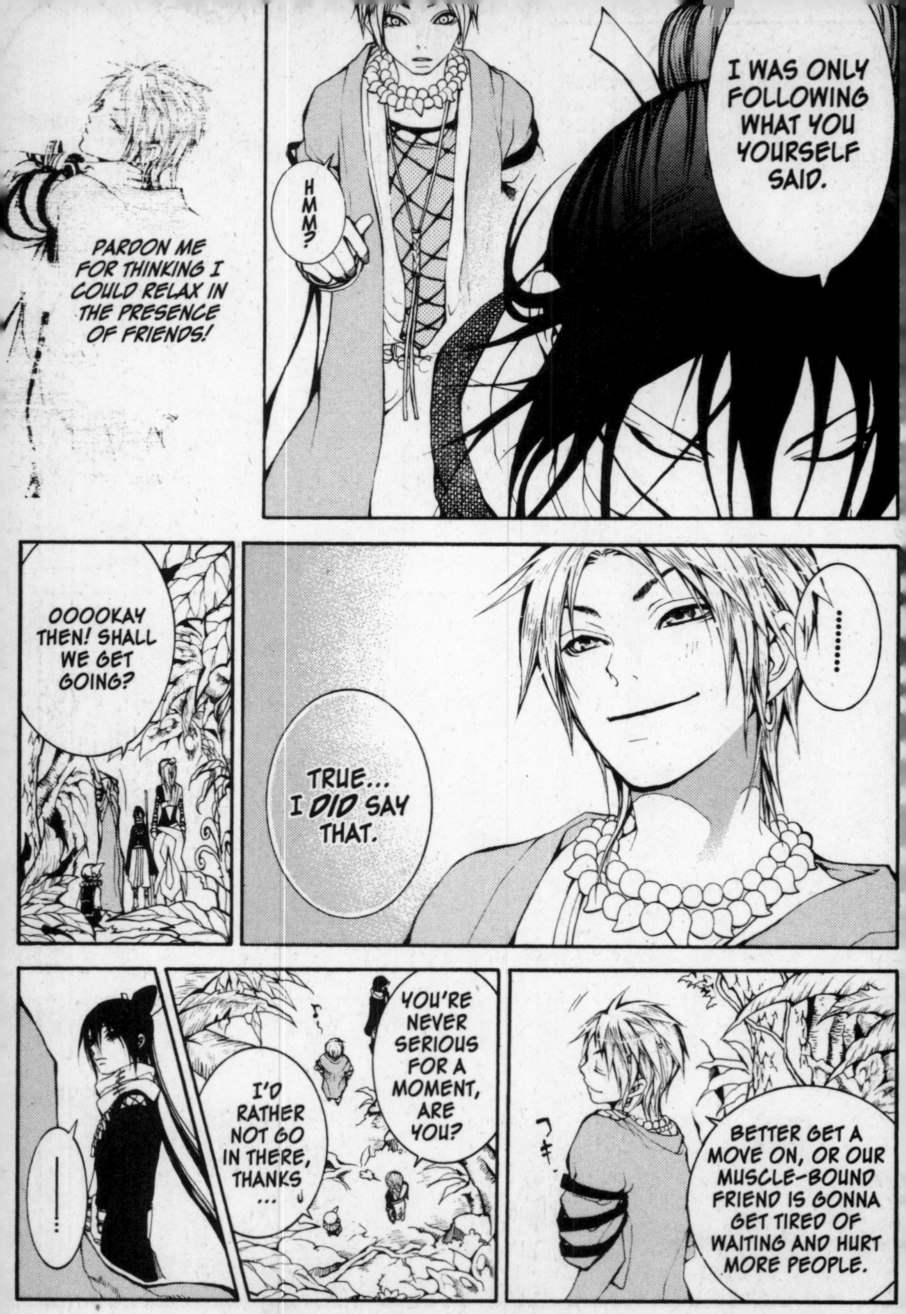
I WAS ONLY FOLLOWING WHAT YOU YOURSELF SAID.
HMM?
PARDON ME FOR THINKING I COULD RELAX IN THE PRESENCE OF FRIENDS!
......
TRUE... I *DID* SAY THAT.
OOOOKAY THEN! SHALL WE GET GOING?
BETTER GET A MOVE ON, OR OUR MUSCLE-BOUND FRIEND IS GONNA GET TIRED OF WAITING AND HURT MORE PEOPLE.
YOU'RE NEVER SERIOUS FOR A MOMENT, ARE YOU?
I'D RATHER NOT GO IN THERE, THANKS...
!...

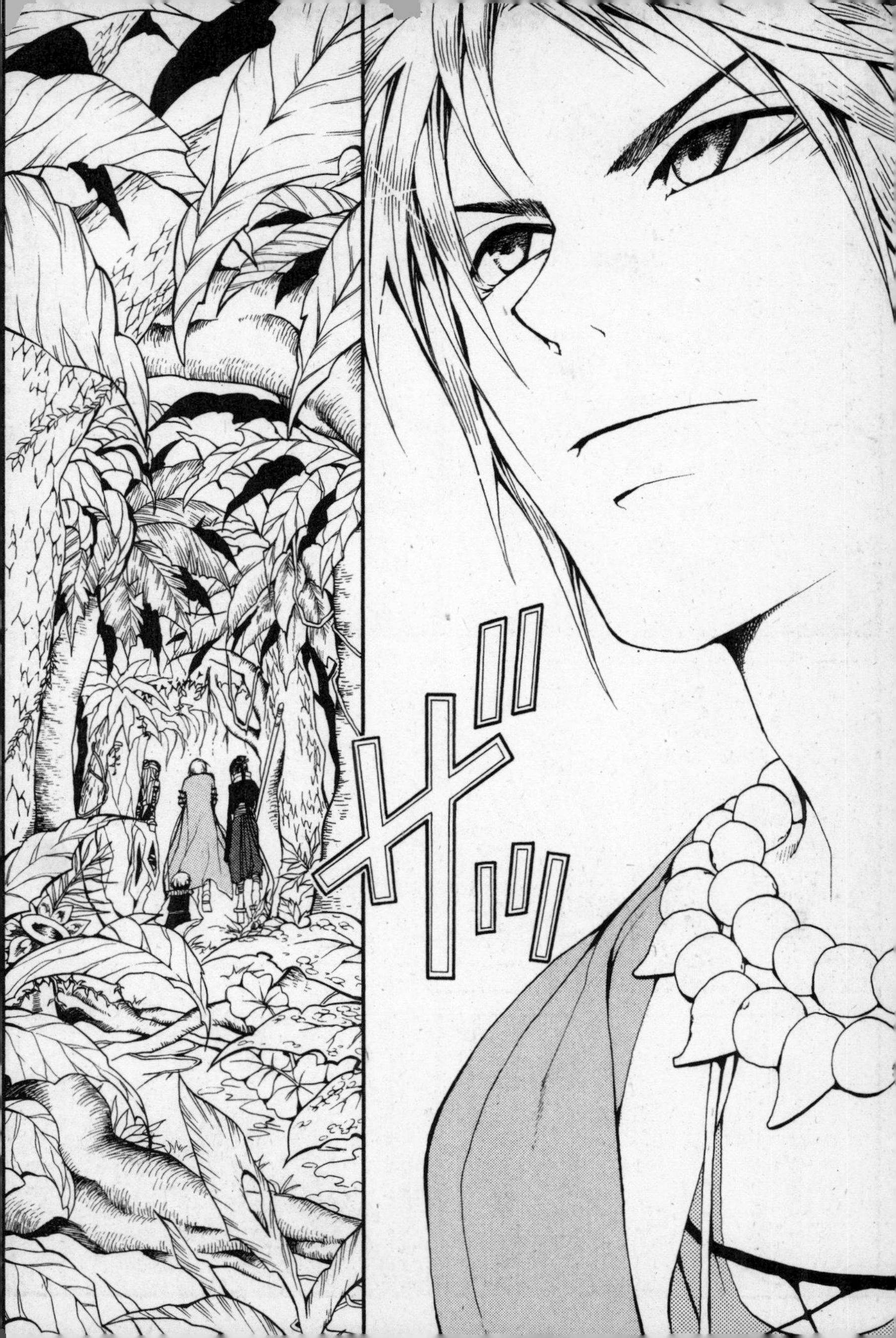
ザッ

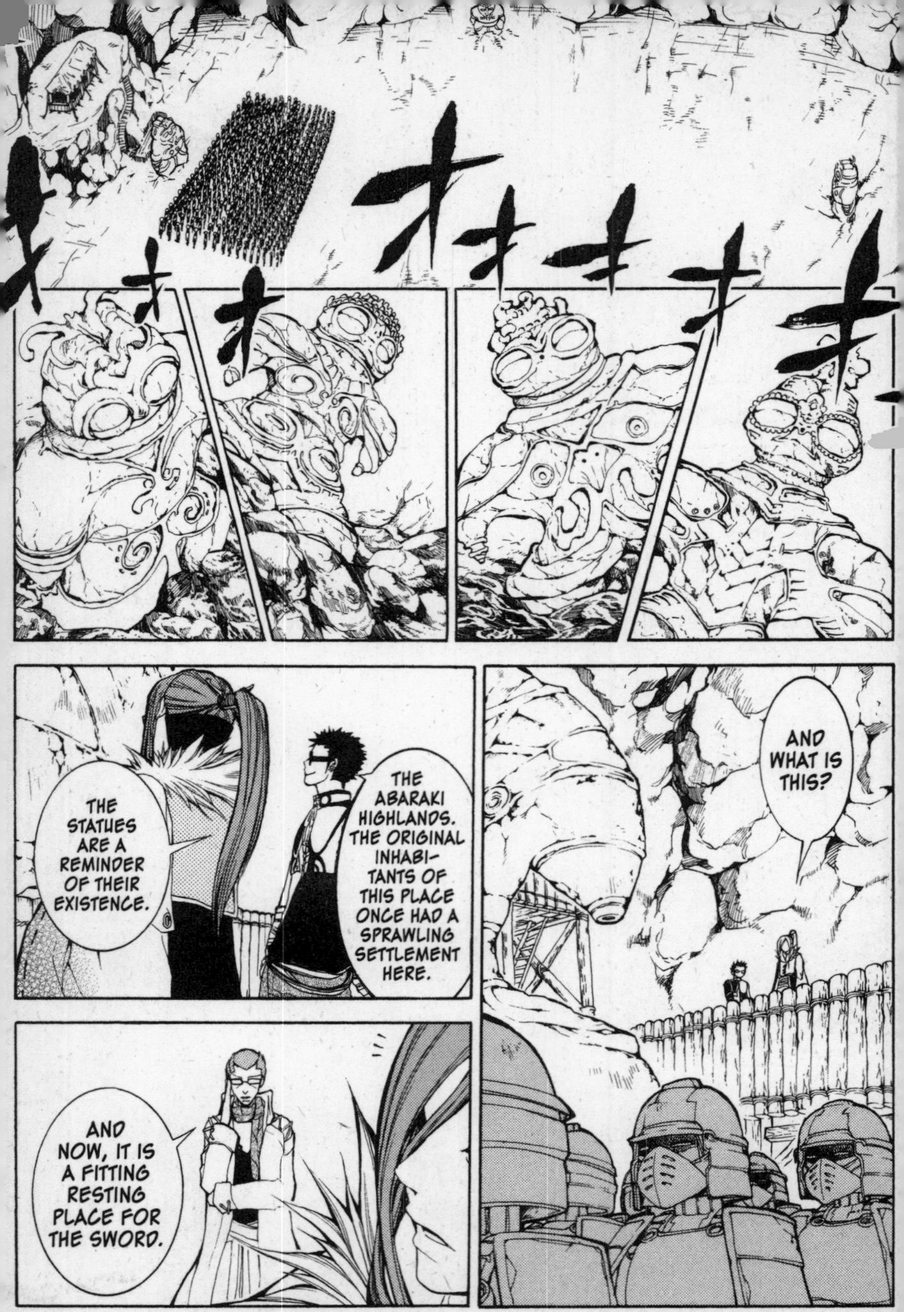
AND WHAT IS THIS?
THE ABARAKI HIGHLANDS. THE ORIGINAL INHABI-TANTS OF THIS PLACE ONCE HAD A SPRAWLING SETTLEMENT HERE.
THE STATUES ARE A REMINDER OF THEIR EXISTENCE.
AND NOW, IT IS A FITTING RESTING PLACE FOR THE SWORD.

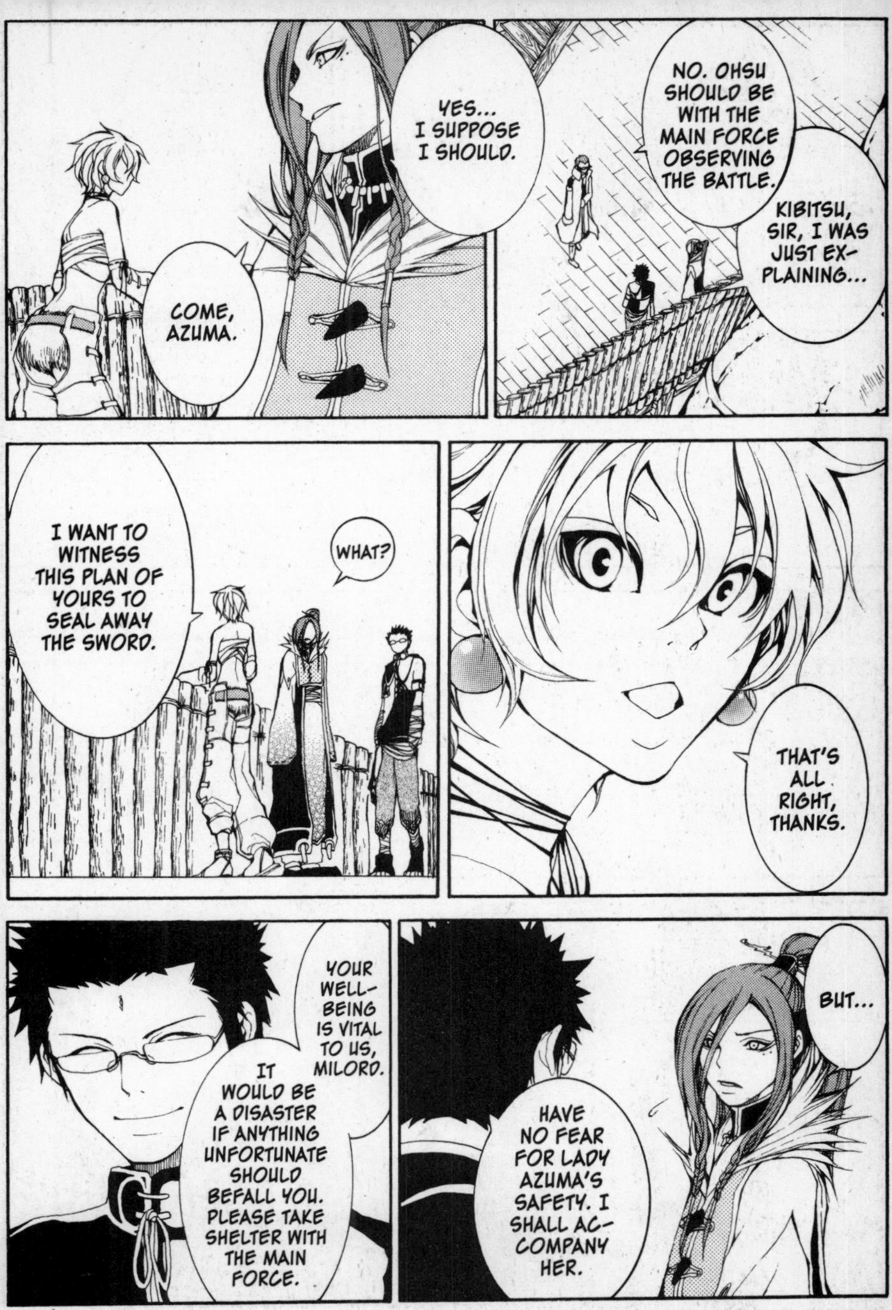
NO. OHSU SHOULD BE WITH THE MAIN FORCE OBSERVING THE BATTLE.
KIBITSU, SIR, I WAS JUST EX-PLAINING...
YES... I SUPPOSE I SHOULD.
COME, AZUMA.
THAT'S ALL RIGHT, THANKS.
WHAT?
I WANT TO WITNESS THIS PLAN OF YOURS TO SEAL AWAY THE SWORD.
BUT...
HAVE NO FEAR FOR LADY AZUMA'S SAFETY. I SHALL AC-COMPANY HER.
YOUR WELL-BEING IS VITAL TO US, MILORD.
IT WOULD BE A DISASTER IF ANYTHING UNFORTUNATE SHOULD BEFALL YOU. PLEASE TAKE SHELTER WITH THE MAIN FORCE.

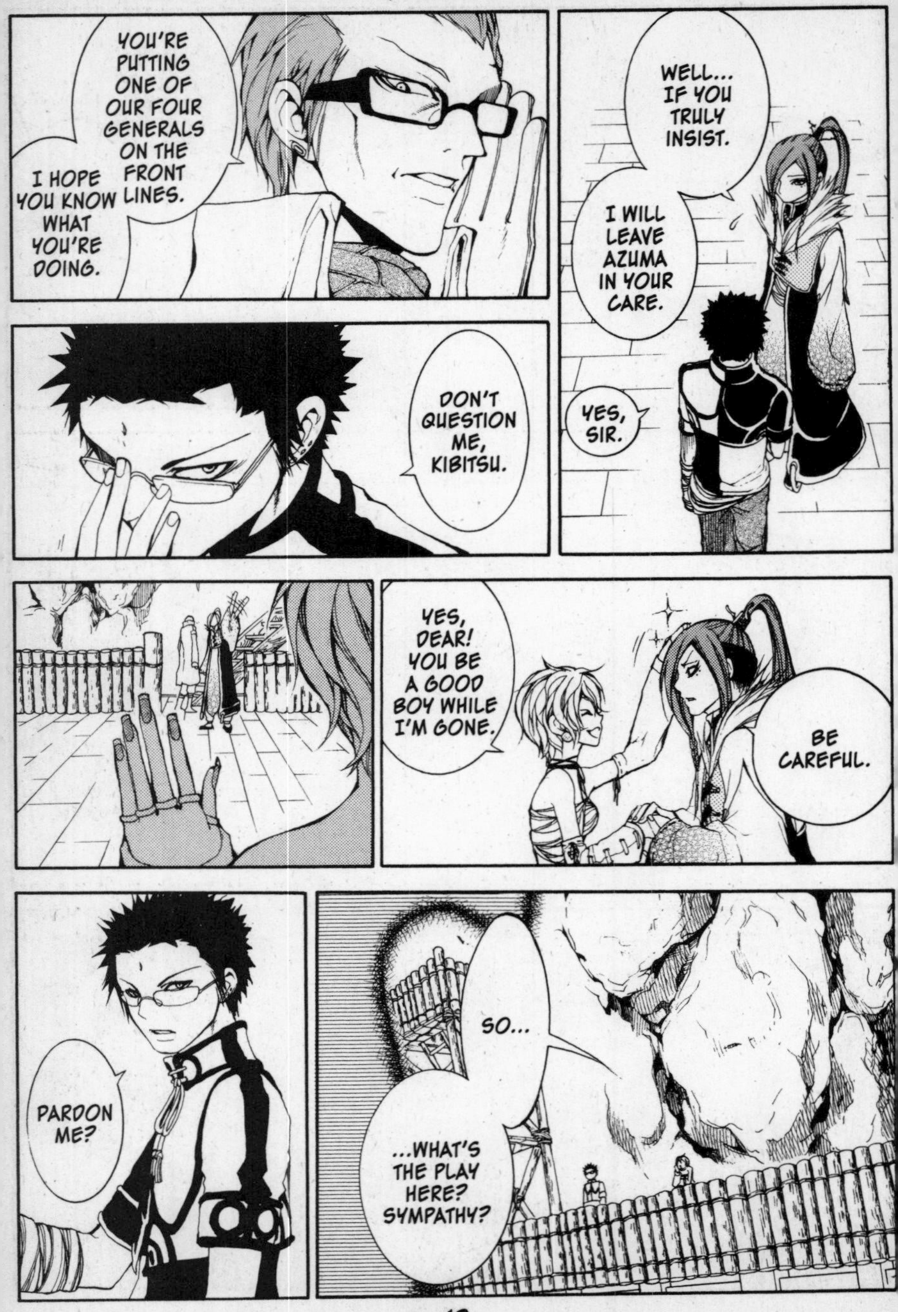
WELL... IF YOU TRULY INSIST.
I WILL LEAVE AZUMA IN YOUR CARE.
YES, SIR.
YOU'RE PUTTING ONE OF OUR FOUR GENERALS ON THE FRONT LINES.
I HOPE YOU KNOW WHAT YOU'RE DOING.
DON'T QUESTION ME, KIBITSU.
BE CAREFUL.
YES, DEAR! YOU BE A GOOD BOY WHILE I'M GONE.
SO...
...WHAT'S THE PLAY HERE? SYMPATHY?
PARDON ME?

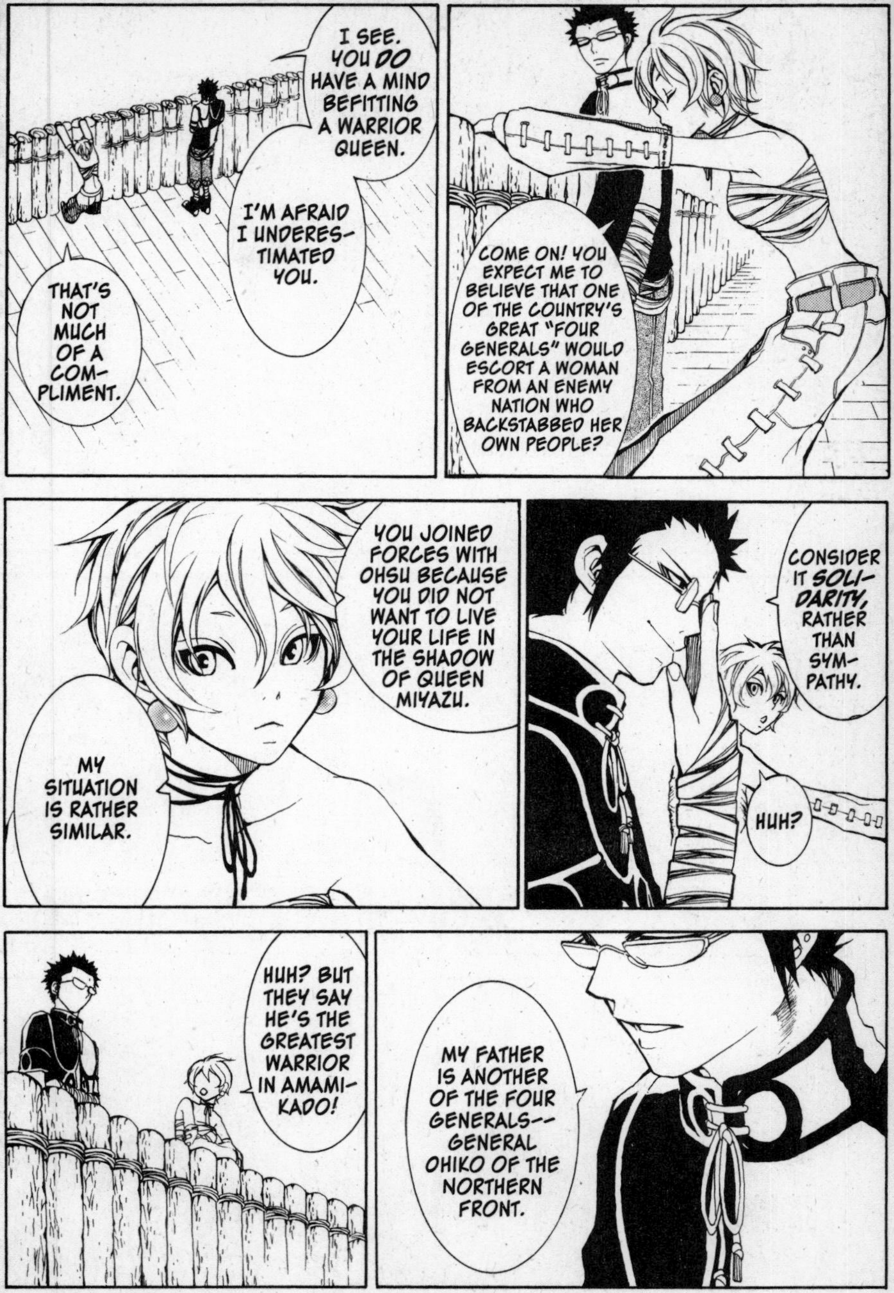
COME ON! YOU EXPECT ME TO BELIEVE THAT ONE OF THE COUNTRY'S GREAT "FOUR GENERALS" WOULD ESCORT A WOMAN FROM AN ENEMY NATION WHO BACKSTABBED HER OWN PEOPLE?
I SEE. YOU *DO* HAVE A MIND BEFITTING A WARRIOR QUEEN.
I'M AFRAID I UNDERESTIMATED YOU.
THAT'S NOT MUCH OF A COMPLIMENT.
CONSIDER IT *SOLIDARITY*, RATHER THAN SYMPATHY.
HUH?
YOU JOINED FORCES WITH OHSU BECAUSE YOU DID NOT WANT TO LIVE YOUR LIFE IN THE SHADOW OF QUEEN MIYAZU.
MY SITUATION IS RATHER SIMILAR.
MY FATHER IS ANOTHER OF THE FOUR GENERALS--GENERAL OHIKO OF THE NORTHERN FRONT.
HUH? BUT THEY SAY HE'S THE GREATEST WARRIOR IN AMAMIKADO!

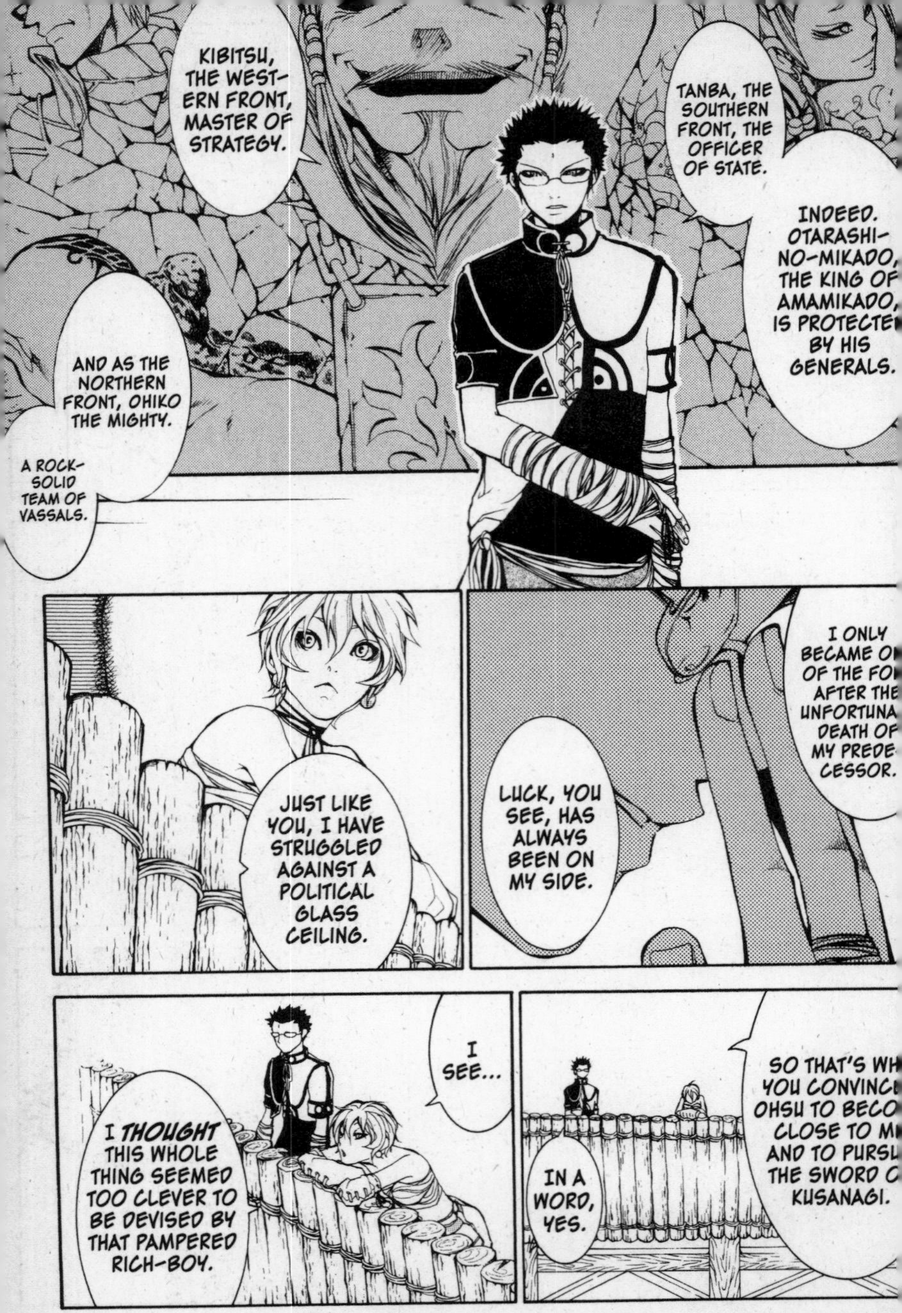
INDEED. OTARASHI-NO-MIKADO, THE KING OF AMAMIKADO, IS PROTECTE BY HIS GENERALS.
TANBA, THE SOUTHERN FRONT, THE OFFICER OF STATE.
KIBITSU, THE WESTERN FRONT, MASTER OF STRATEGY.
AND AS THE NORTHERN FRONT, OHIKO THE MIGHTY.
A ROCK-SOLID TEAM OF VASSALS.
I ONLY BECAME O OF THE FO AFTER THE UNFORTUNA DEATH OF MY PREDECESSOR.
LUCK, YOU SEE, HAS ALWAYS BEEN ON MY SIDE.
JUST LIKE YOU, I HAVE STRUGGLED AGAINST A POLITICAL GLASS CEILING.
SO THAT'S WH YOU CONVINCE OHSU TO BECO CLOSE TO M AND TO PURSU THE SWORD O KUSANAGI.
IN A WORD, YES.
I SEE...
I *THOUGHT* THIS WHOLE THING SEEMED TOO CLEVER TO BE DEVISED BY THAT PAMPERED RICH-BOY.

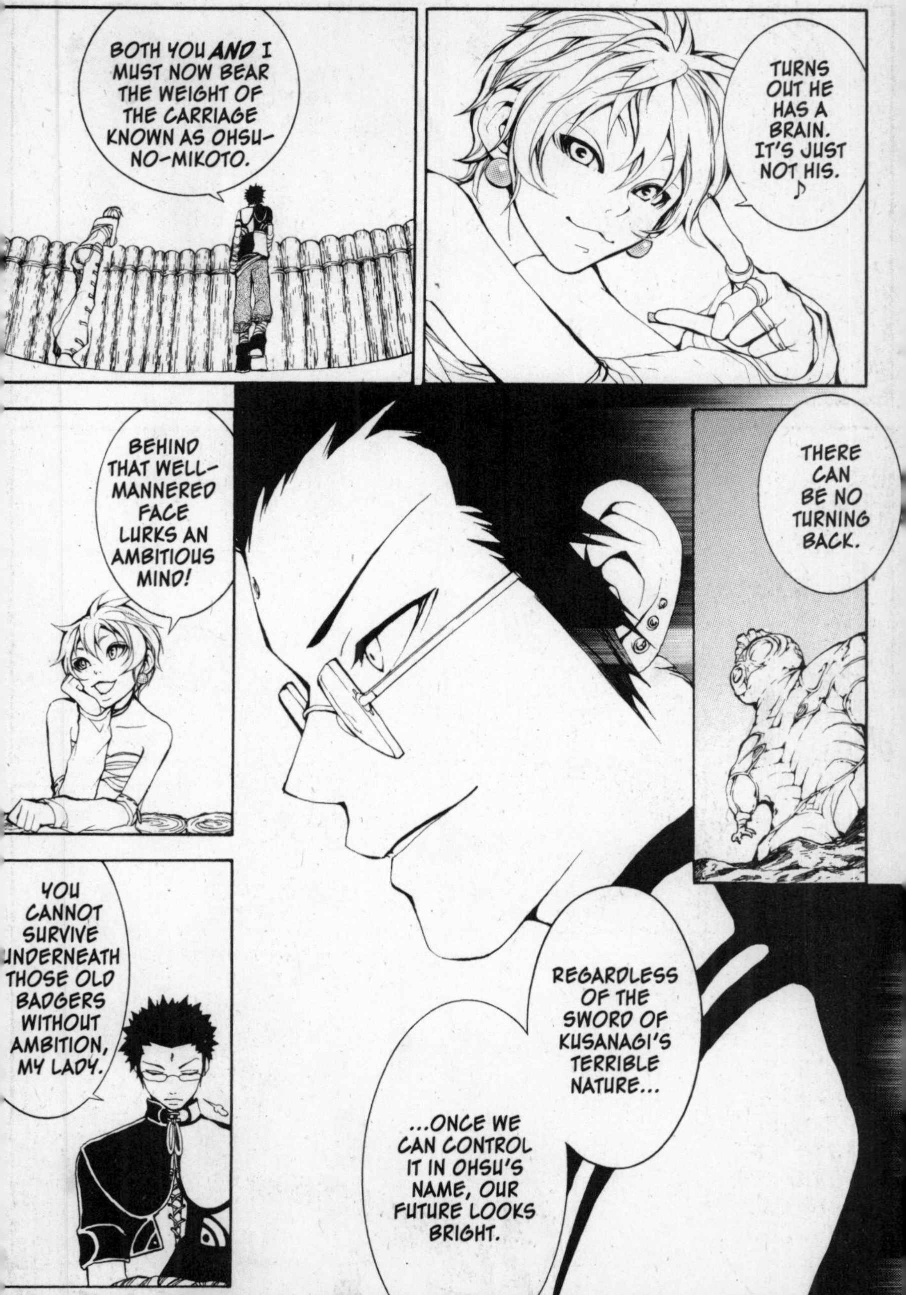

TURNS OUT HE HAS A BRAIN. IT'S JUST NOT HIS. ♪
BOTH YOU **AND** I MUST NOW BEAR THE WEIGHT OF THE CARRIAGE KNOWN AS OHSU-NO-MIKOTO.
THERE CAN BE NO TURNING BACK.
REGARDLESS OF THE SWORD OF KUSANAGI'S TERRIBLE NATURE...
...ONCE WE CAN CONTROL IT IN OHSU'S NAME, OUR FUTURE LOOKS BRIGHT.
BEHIND THAT WELL-MANNERED FACE LURKS AN AMBITIOUS MIND!
YOU CANNOT SURVIVE UNDERNEATH THOSE OLD BADGERS WITHOUT AMBITION, MY LADY.

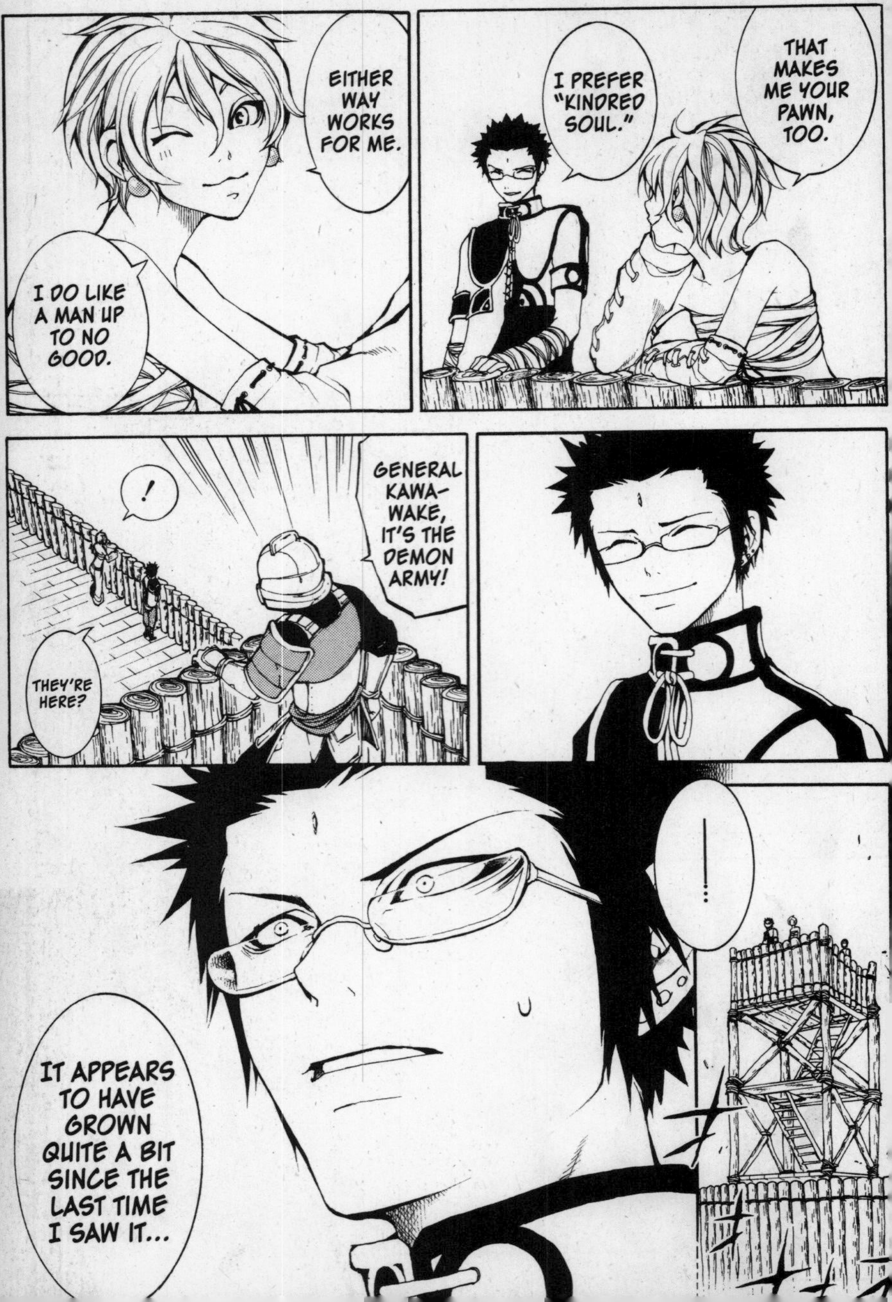
THAT MAKES ME YOUR PAWN, TOO.
I PREFER "KINDRED SOUL."
EITHER WAY WORKS FOR ME.
I DO LIKE A MAN UP TO NO GOOD.
GENERAL KAWA-WAKE, IT'S THE DEMON ARMY!
!
THEY'RE HERE?
...!
IT APPEARS TO HAVE GROWN QUITE A BIT SINCE THE LAST TIME I SAW IT...

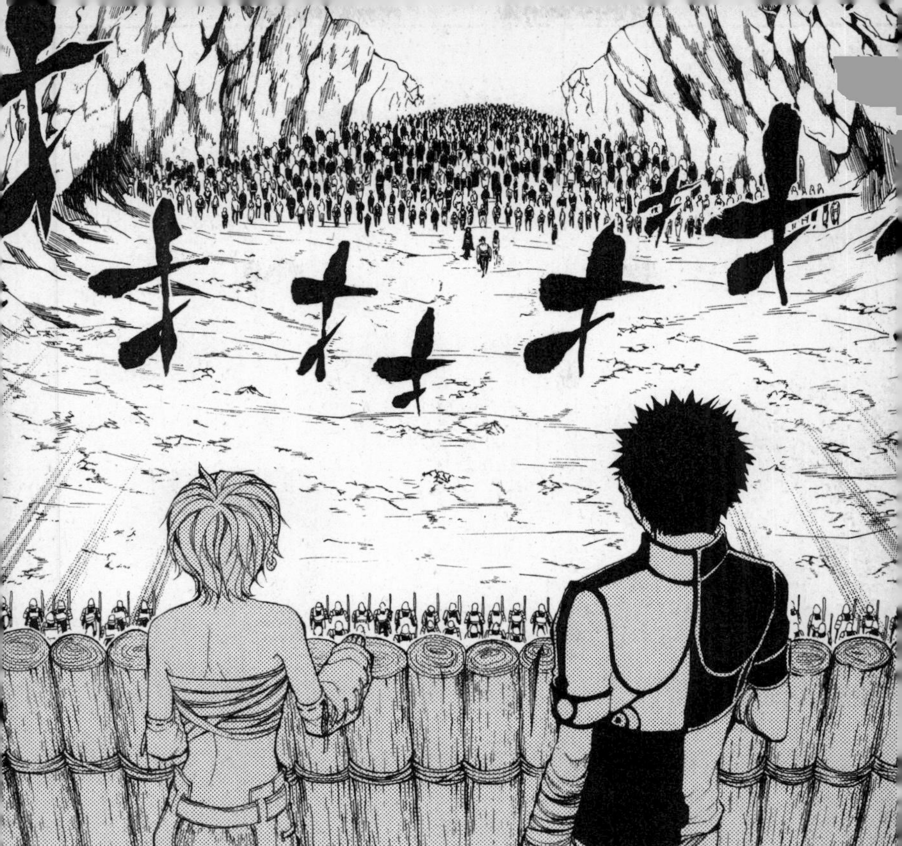

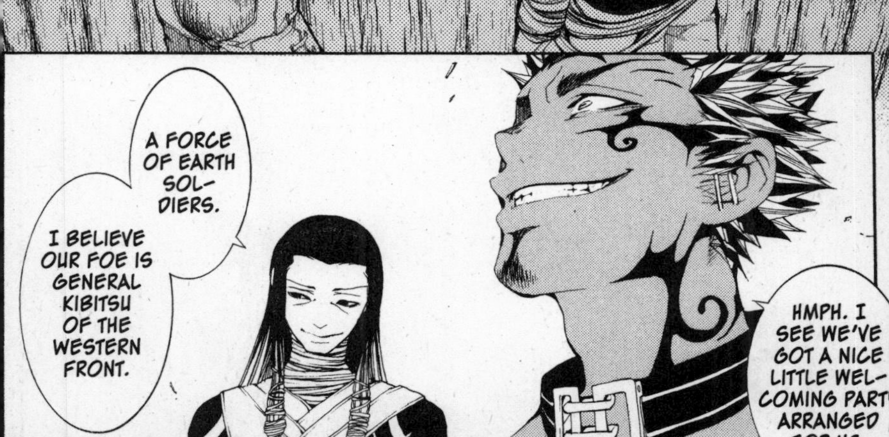
HMPH. I SEE WE'VE GOT A NICE LITTLE WEL-COMING PARTY ARRANGED FOR US.
A FORCE OF EARTH SOL-DIERS.
I BELIEVE OUR FOE IS GENERAL KIBITSU OF THE WESTERN FRONT.

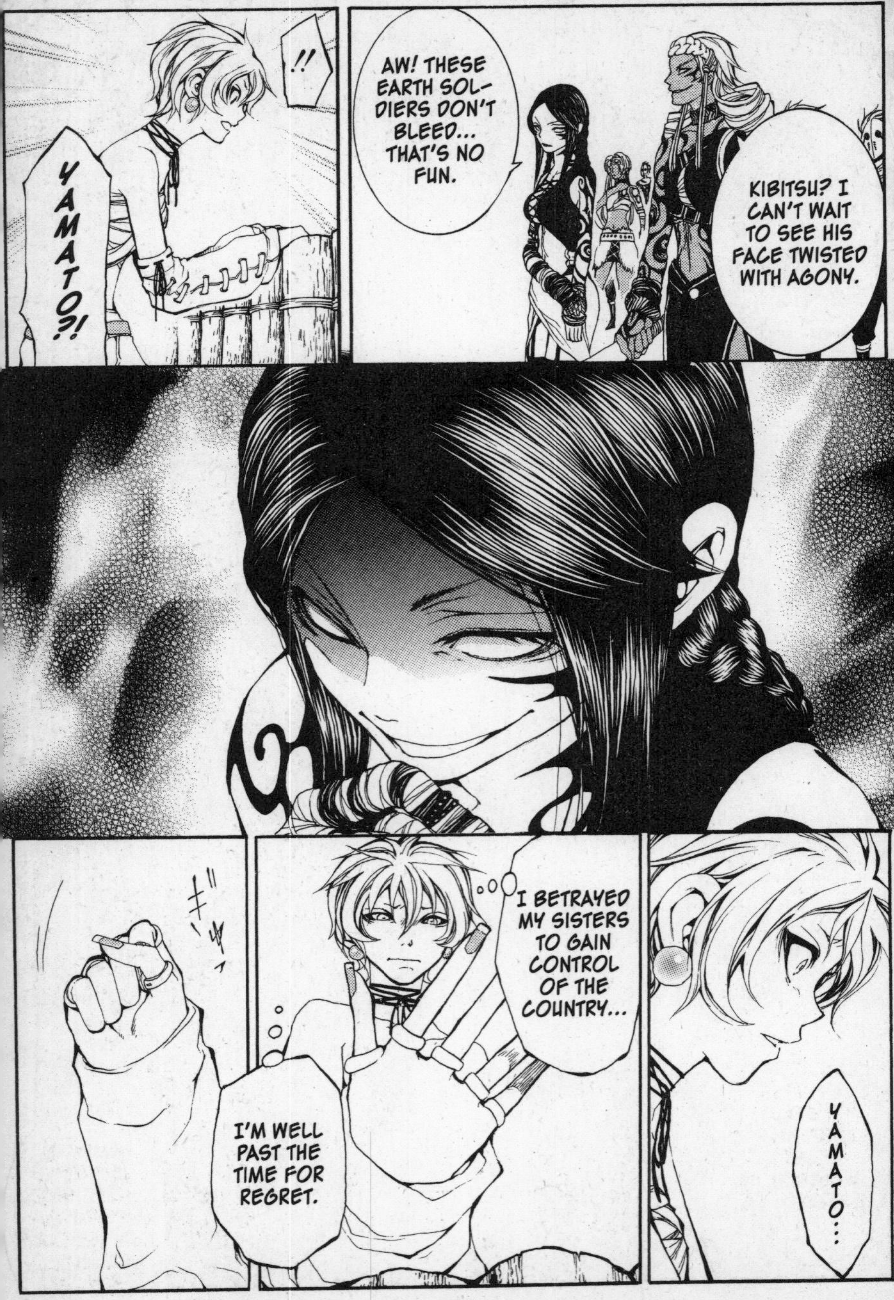
AW! THESE EARTH SOLDIERS DON'T BLEED... THAT'S NO FUN.
KIBITSU? I CAN'T WAIT TO SEE HIS FACE TWISTED WITH AGONY.
!!
YAMATO?!
YAMATO...
I BETRAYED MY SISTERS TO GAIN CONTROL OF THE COUNTRY...
I'M WELL PAST THE TIME FOR REGRET.

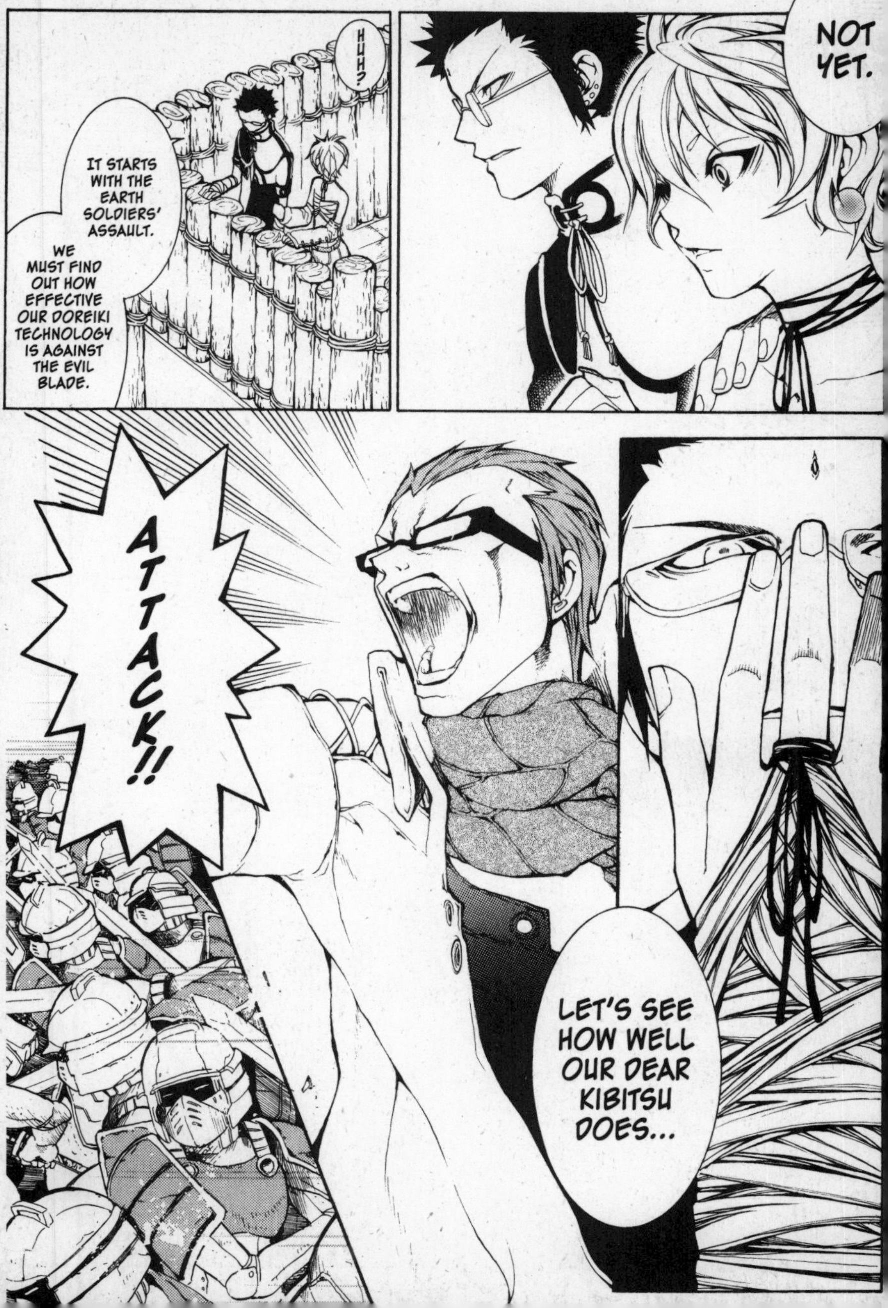
NOT YET.
HUH?
IT STARTS WITH THE EARTH SOLDIERS' ASSAULT.
WE MUST FIND OUT HOW EFFECTIVE OUR DOREIKI TECHNOLOGY IS AGAINST THE EVIL BLADE.
LET'S SEE HOW WELL OUR DEAR KIBITSU DOES...
ATTACK!!

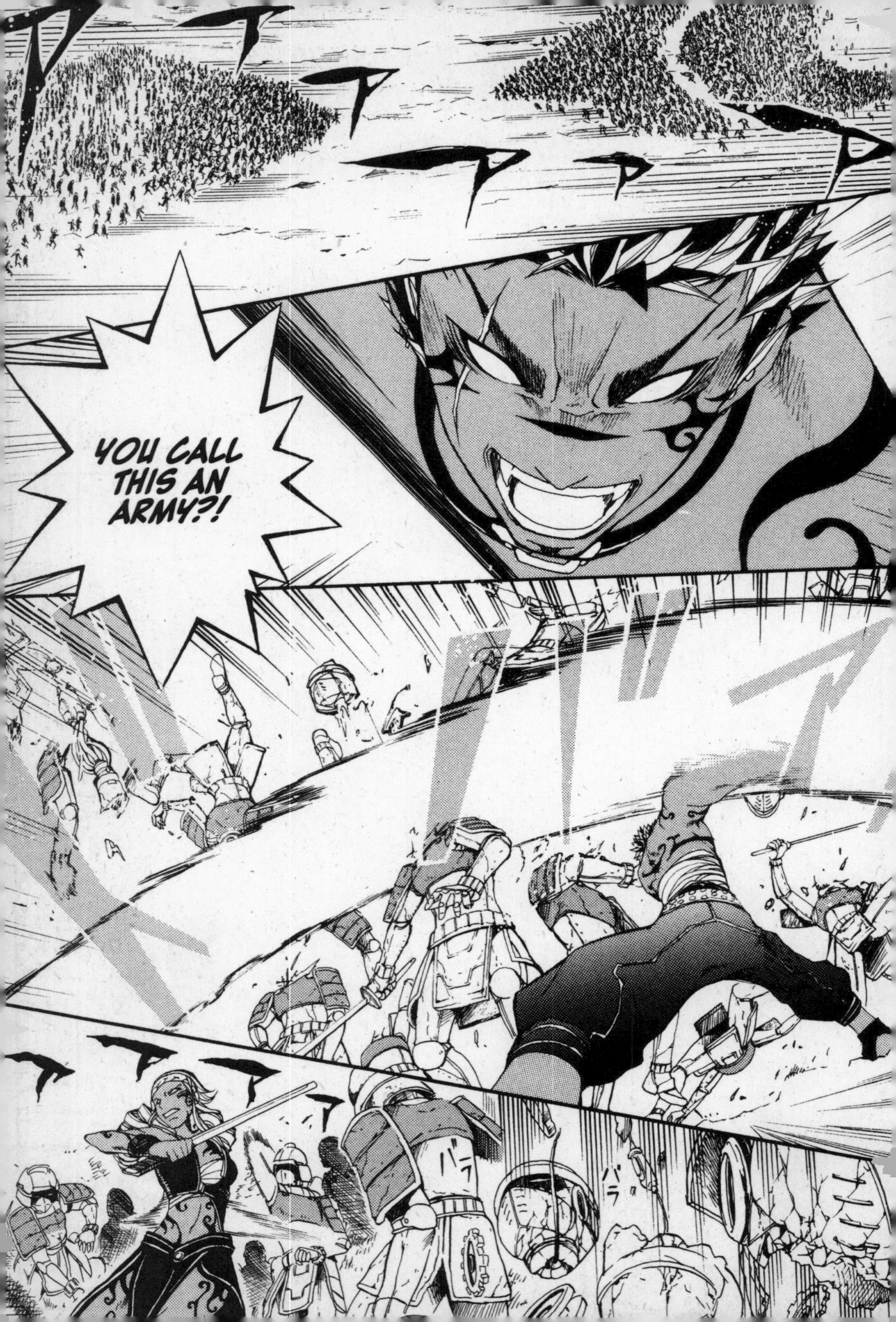
YOU CALL THIS AN ARMY?!

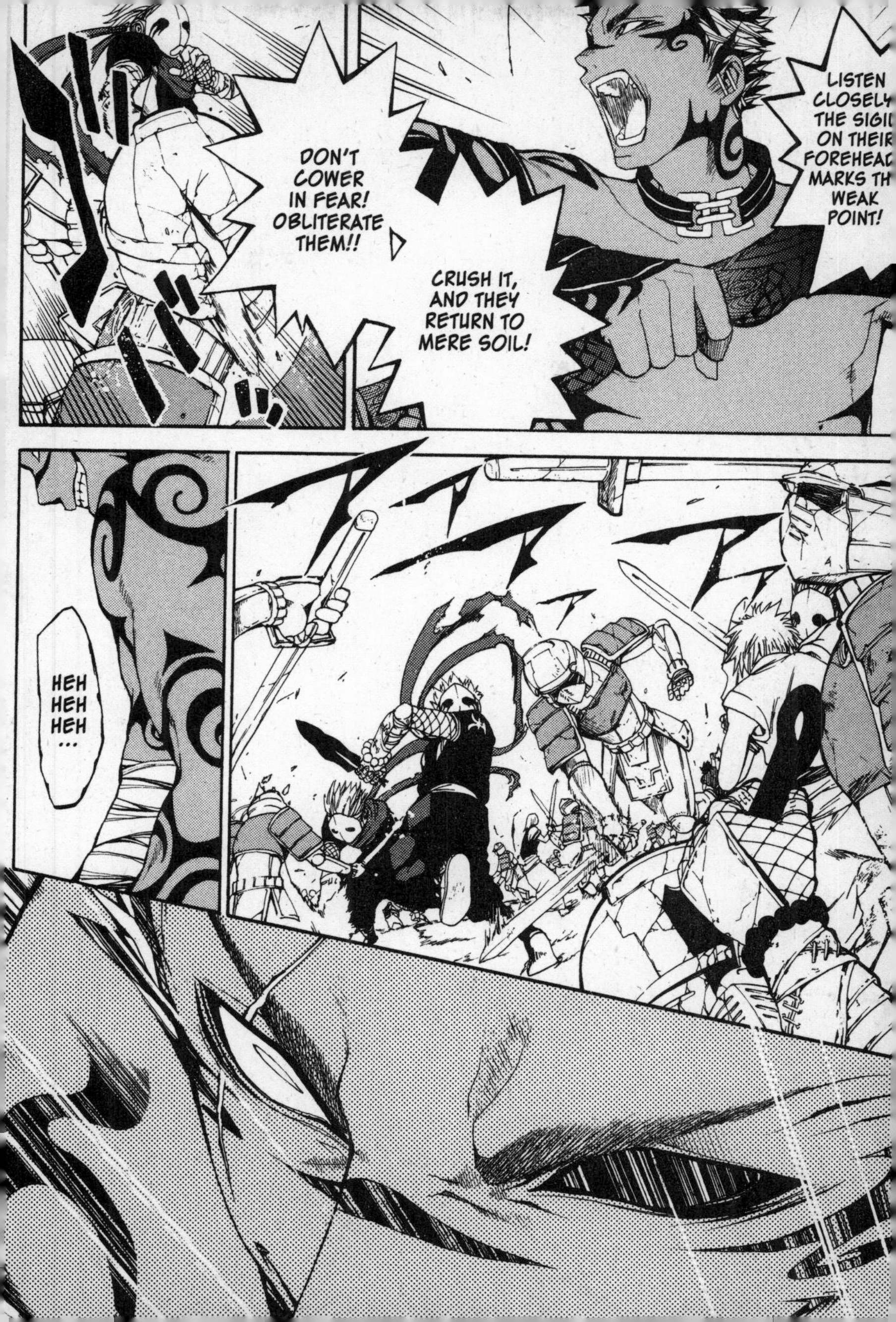

LISTEN CLOSELY THE SIGIL ON THEIR FOREHEAD MARKS TH WEAK POINT!
CRUSH IT, AND THEY RETURN TO MERE SOIL!
DON'T COWER IN FEAR! OBLITERATE THEM!!
HEH HEH HEH...

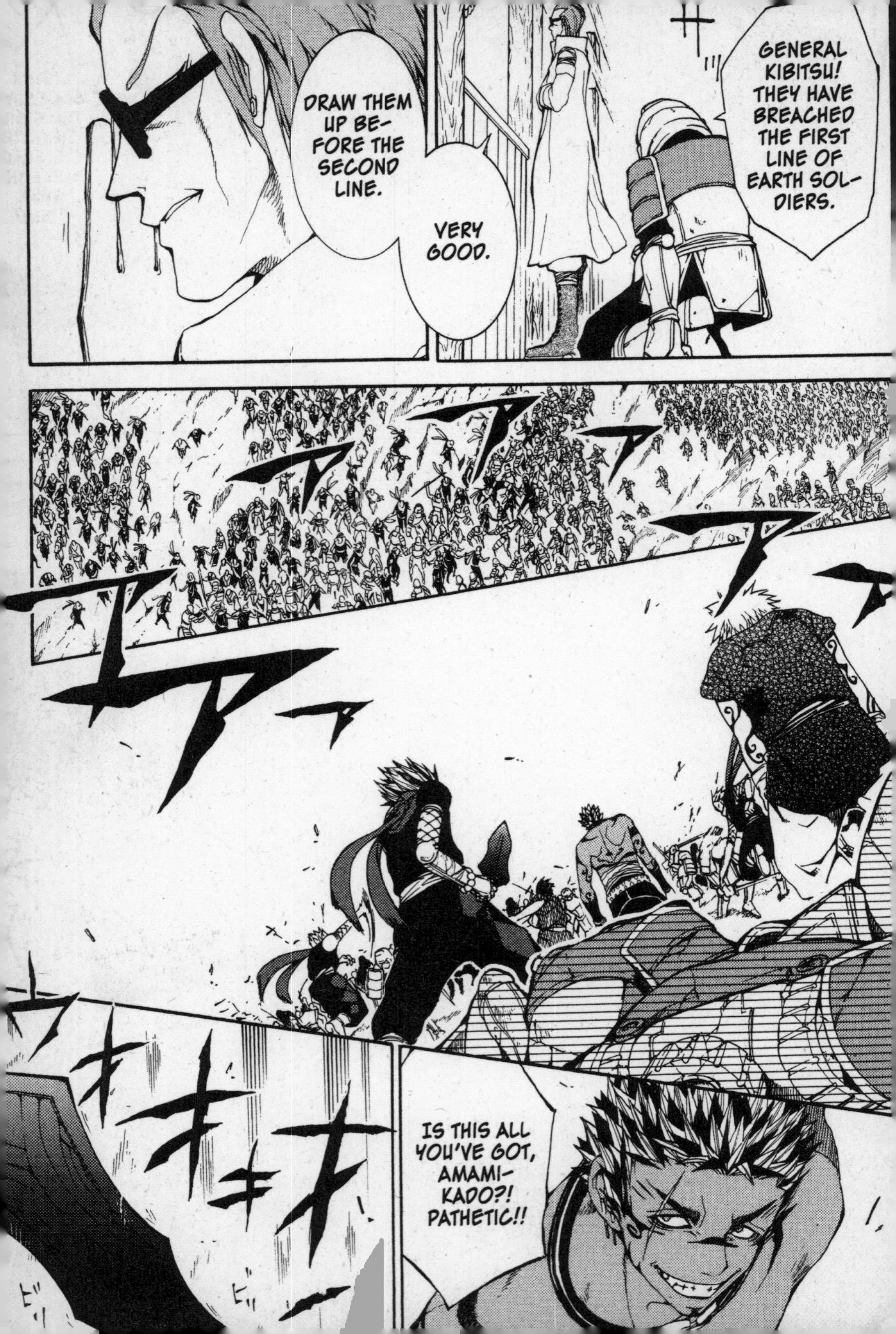
GENERAL KIBITSU! THEY HAVE BREACHED THE FIRST LINE OF EARTH SOL-DIERS.
VERY GOOD.
DRAW THEM UP BE-FORE THE SECOND LINE.
IS THIS ALL YOU'VE GOT, AMAMI-KADO?! PATHETIC!!

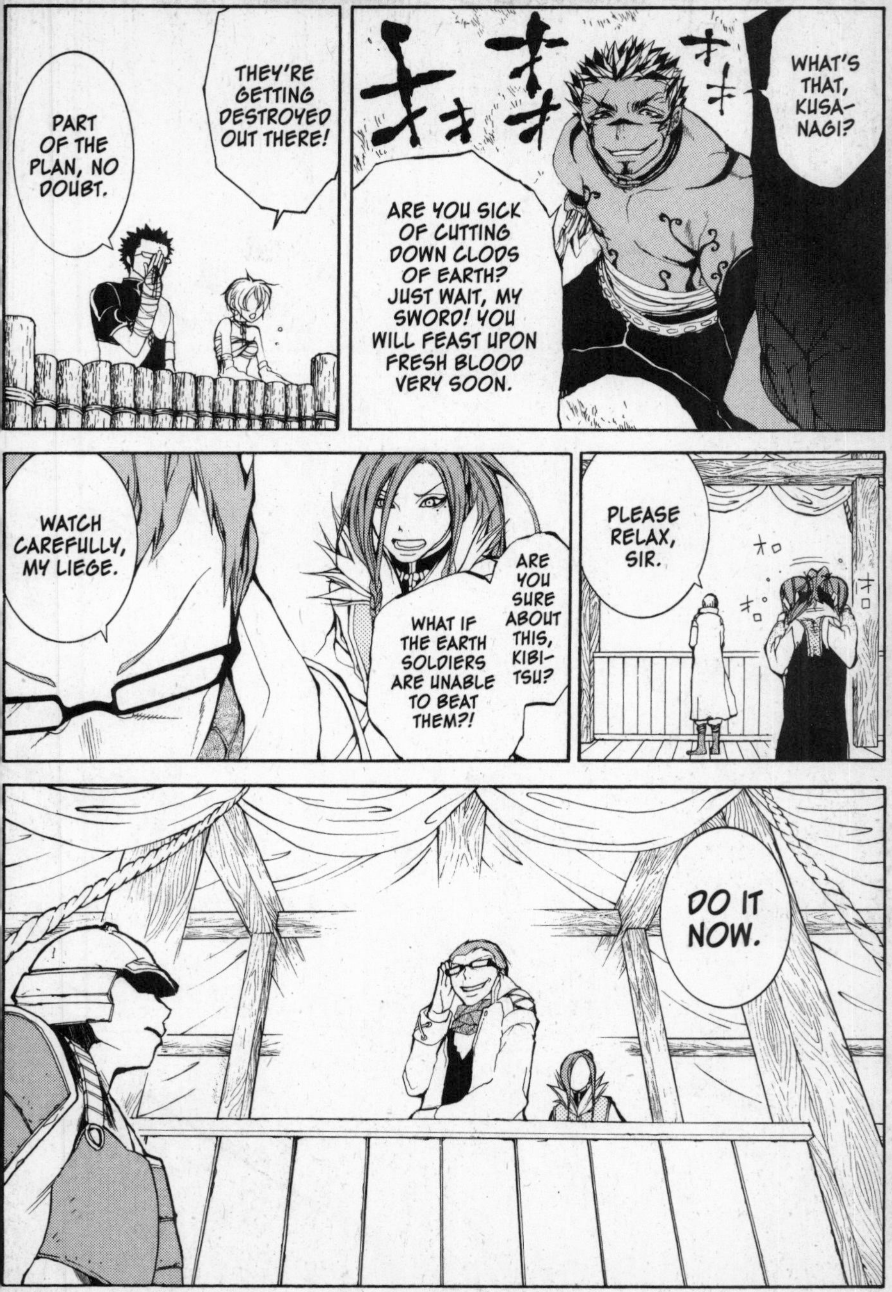
WHAT'S THAT, KUSANAGI?
ARE YOU SICK OF CUTTING DOWN CLODS OF EARTH? JUST WAIT, MY SWORD! YOU WILL FEAST UPON FRESH BLOOD VERY SOON.
THEY'RE GETTING DESTROYED OUT THERE!
PART OF THE PLAN, NO DOUBT.
PLEASE RELAX, SIR.
オロ
オロ
オロ
ARE YOU SURE ABOUT THIS, KIBITSU?
WHAT IF THE EARTH SOLDIERS ARE UNABLE TO BEAT THEM?!
WATCH CAREFULLY, MY LIEGE.
DO IT NOW.

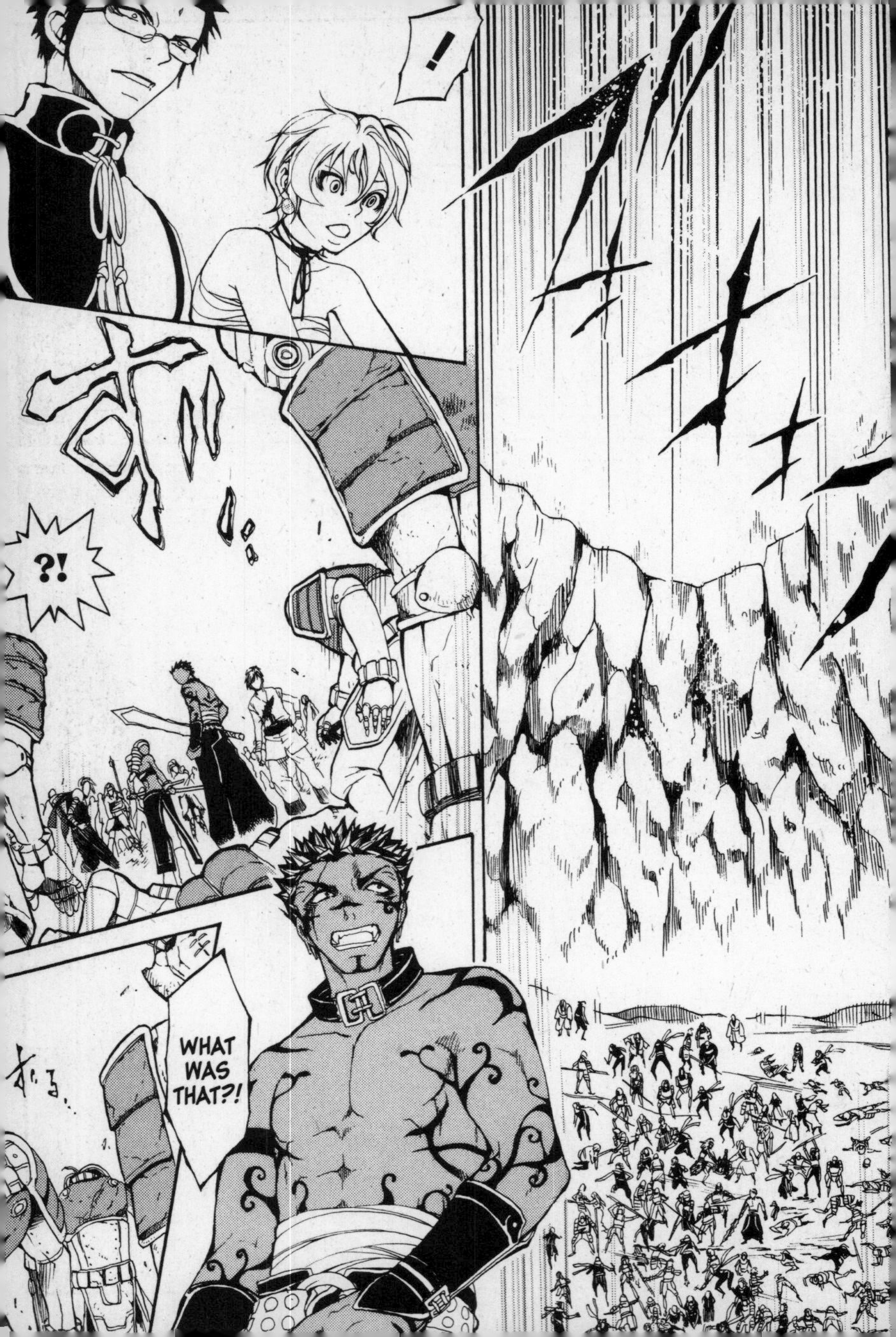
!
?!
WHAT WAS THAT?!

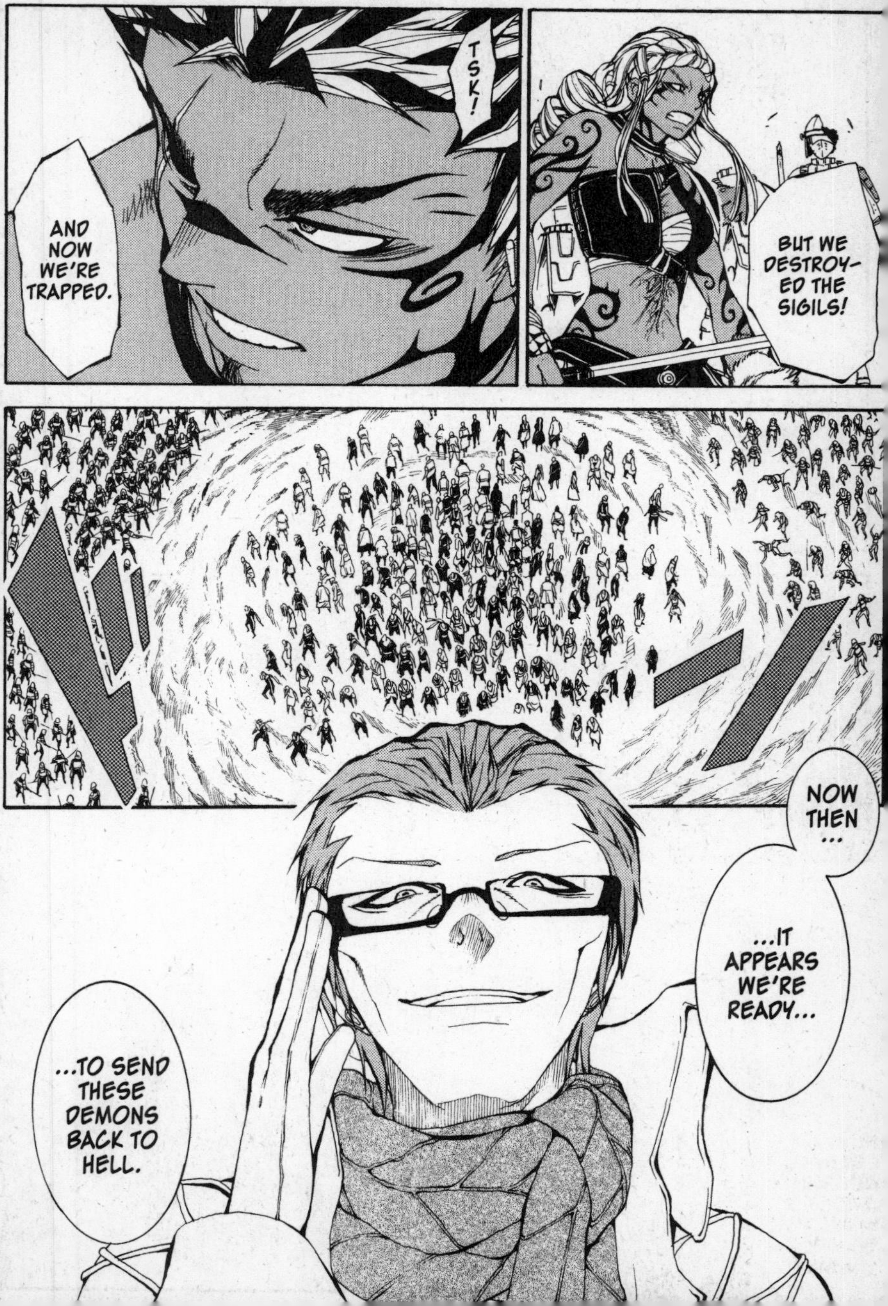
BUT WE DESTROY-ED THE SIGILS!
TSK!
AND NOW WE'RE TRAPPED.
NOW THEN ...
...IT APPEARS WE'RE READY...
...TO SEND THESE DEMONS BACK TO HELL.

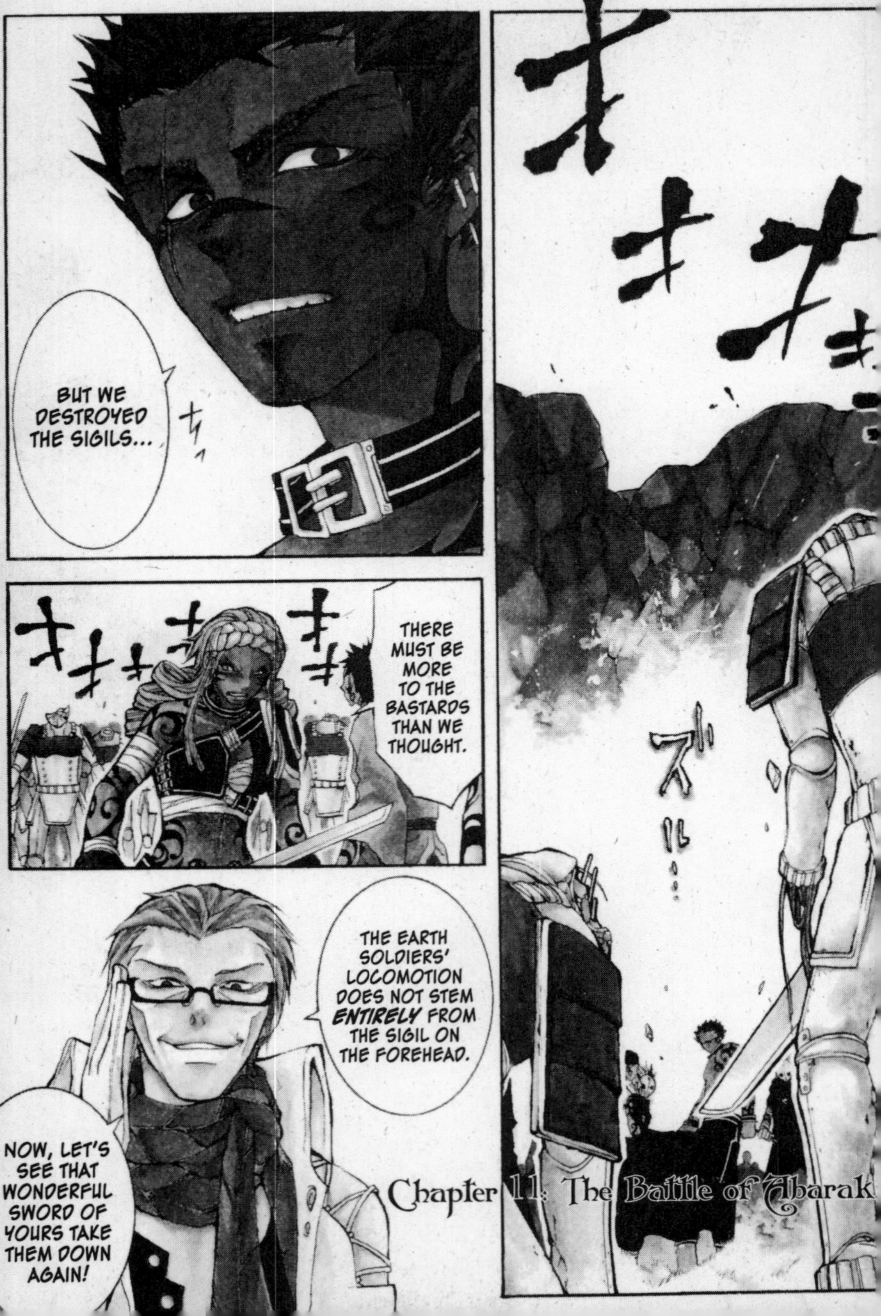
Chapter 11: The Battle of Abarak
BUT WE DESTROYED THE SIGILS...
THERE MUST BE MORE TO THE BASTARDS THAN WE THOUGHT.
THE EARTH SOLDIERS' LOCOMOTION DOES NOT STEM *ENTIRELY* FROM THE SIGIL ON THE FOREHEAD.
NOW, LET'S SEE THAT WONDERFUL SWORD OF YOURS TAKE THEM DOWN AGAIN!

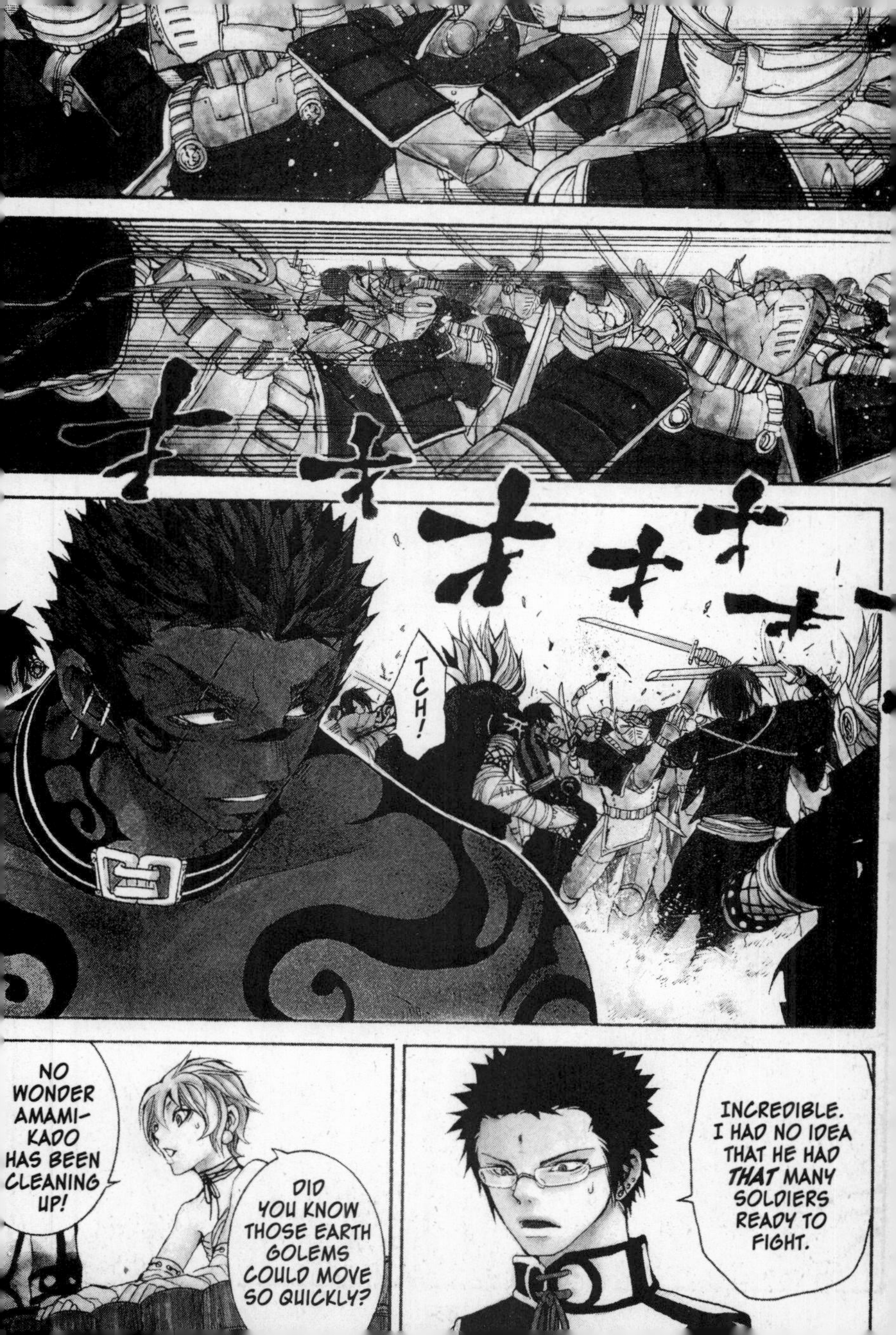
TCH!
INCREDIBLE. I HAD NO IDEA THAT HE HAD *THAT* MANY SOLDIERS READY TO FIGHT.
DID YOU KNOW THOSE EARTH GOLEMS COULD MOVE SO QUICKLY?
NO WONDER AMAMI-KADO HAS BEEN CLEANING UP!

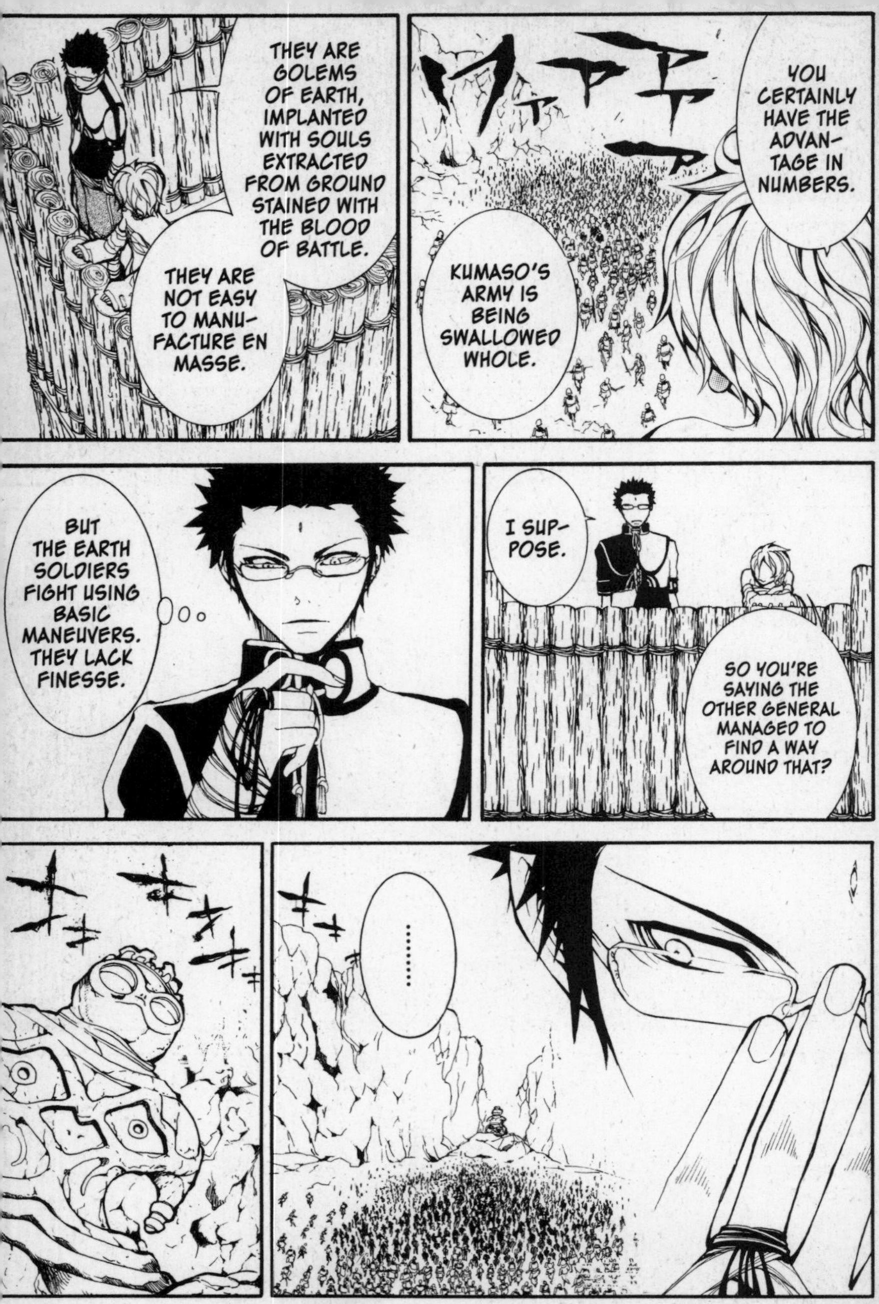
YOU CERTAINLY HAVE THE ADVAN-TAGE IN NUMBERS.
KUMASO'S ARMY IS BEING SWALLOWED WHOLE.
THEY ARE GOLEMS OF EARTH, IMPLANTED WITH SOULS EXTRACTED FROM GROUND STAINED WITH THE BLOOD OF BATTLE.
THEY ARE NOT EASY TO MANU-FACTURE EN MASSE.
I SUP-POSE.
SO YOU'RE SAYING THE OTHER GENERAL MANAGED TO FIND A WAY AROUND THAT?
BUT THE EARTH SOLDIERS FIGHT USING BASIC MANEUVERS. THEY LACK FINESSE.
......

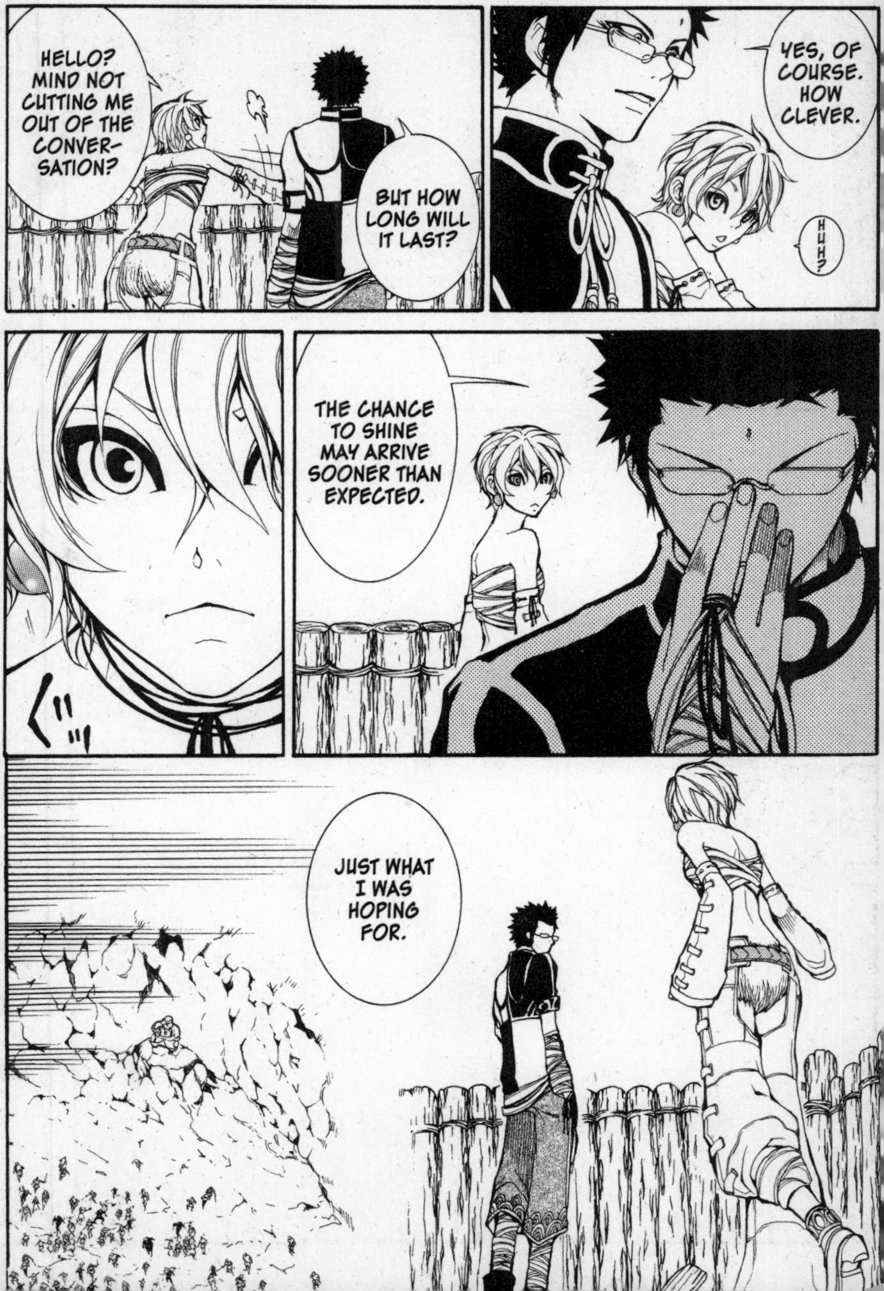
YES, OF COURSE. HOW CLEVER.
HUH?
BUT HOW LONG WILL IT LAST?
HELLO? MIND NOT CUTTING ME OUT OF THE CONVER-SATION?
THE CHANCE TO SHINE MAY ARRIVE SOONER THAN EXPECTED.
JUST WHAT I WAS HOPING FOR.

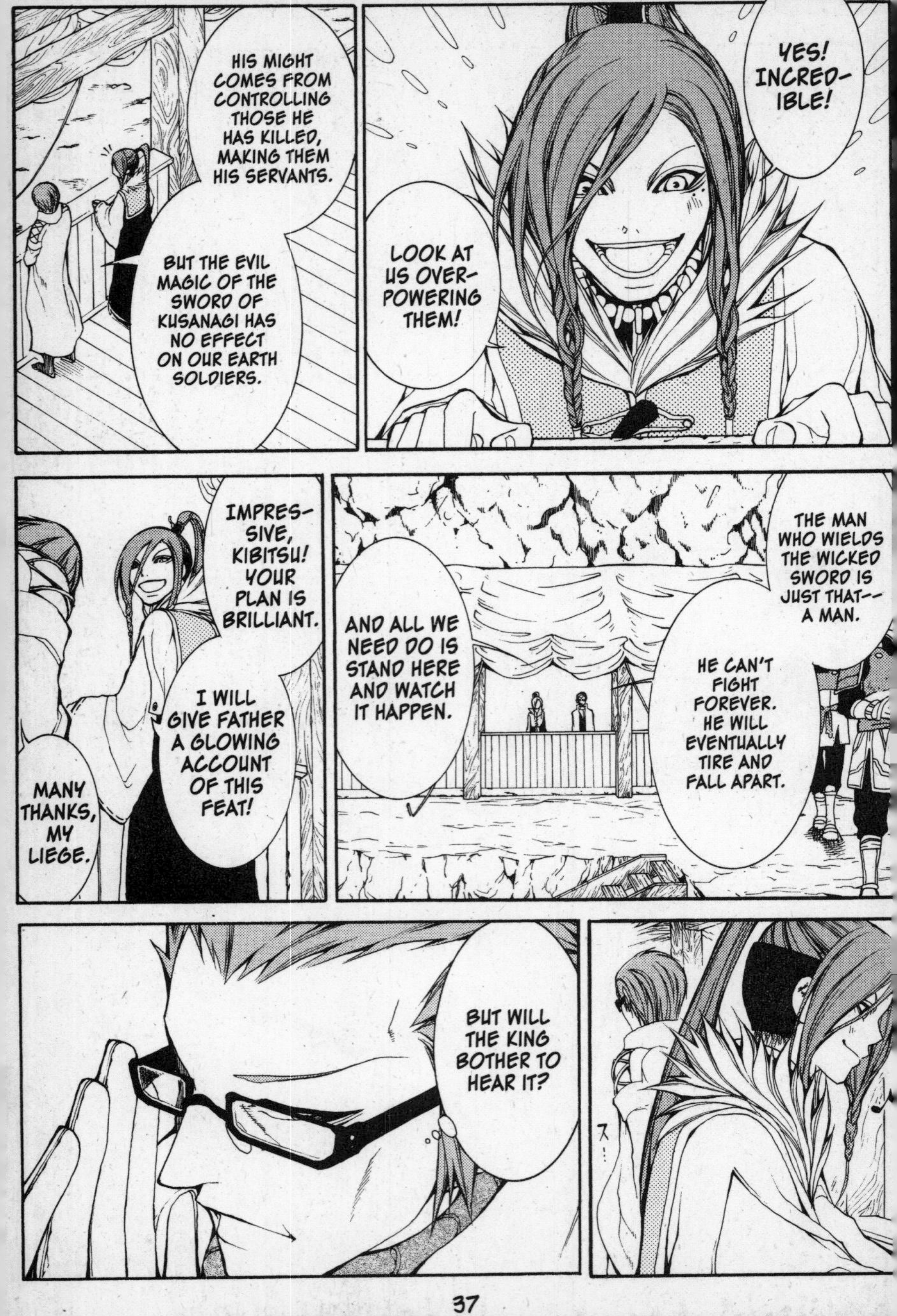
YES! INCREDIBLE!
LOOK AT US OVERPOWERING THEM!
HIS MIGHT COMES FROM CONTROLLING THOSE HE HAS KILLED, MAKING THEM HIS SERVANTS.
BUT THE EVIL MAGIC OF THE SWORD OF KUSANAGI HAS NO EFFECT ON OUR EARTH SOLDIERS.
THE MAN WHO WIELDS THE WICKED SWORD IS JUST THAT--A MAN.
HE CAN'T FIGHT FOREVER. HE WILL EVENTUALLY TIRE AND FALL APART.
AND ALL WE NEED DO IS STAND HERE AND WATCH IT HAPPEN.
IMPRESSIVE, KIBITSU! YOUR PLAN IS BRILLIANT.
I WILL GIVE FATHER A GLOWING ACCOUNT OF THIS FEAT!
MANY THANKS, MY LIEGE.
ス…
BUT WILL THE KING BOTHER TO HEAR IT?

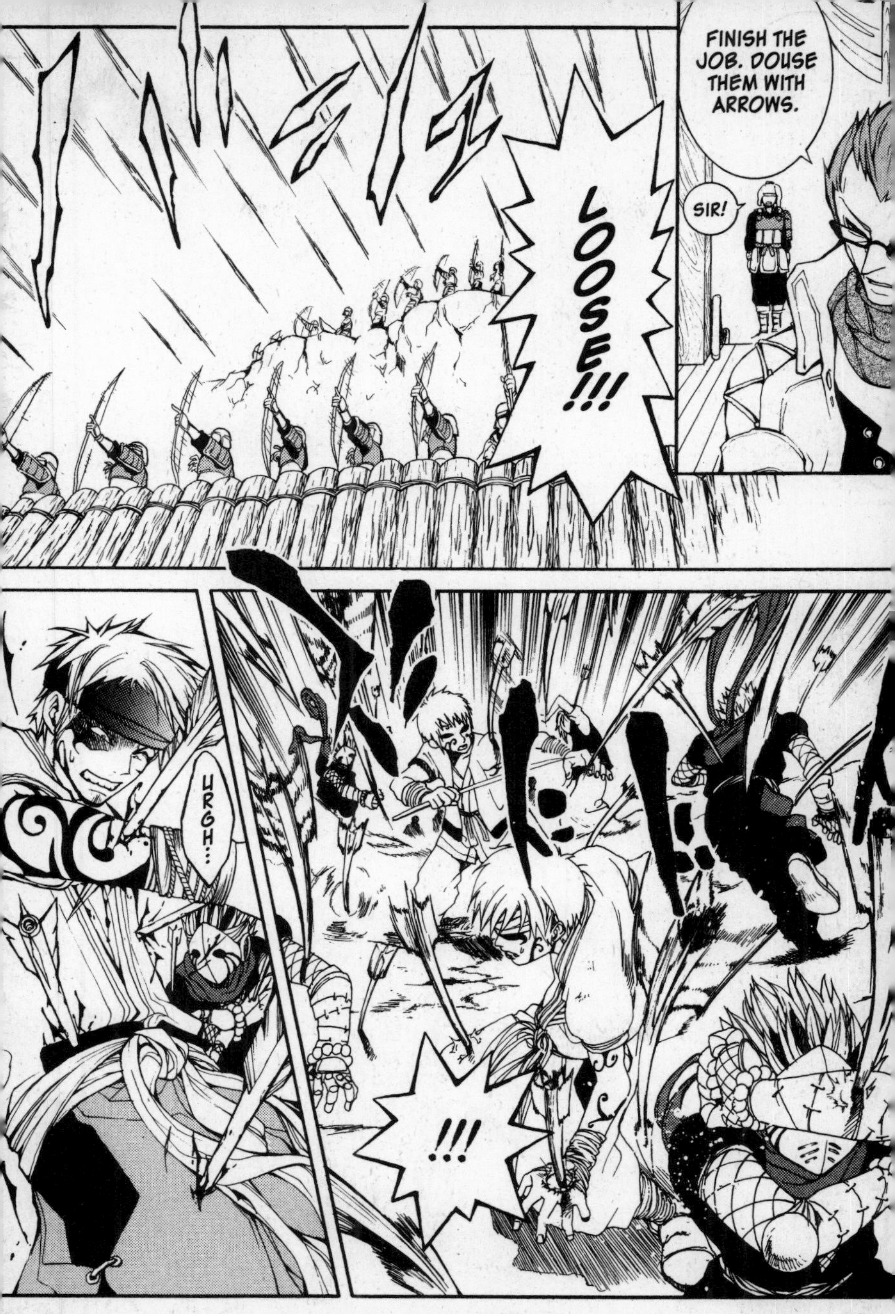
FINISH THE JOB. DOUSE THEM WITH ARROWS.
SIR!
LOOSE!!!
!!!
URGH...

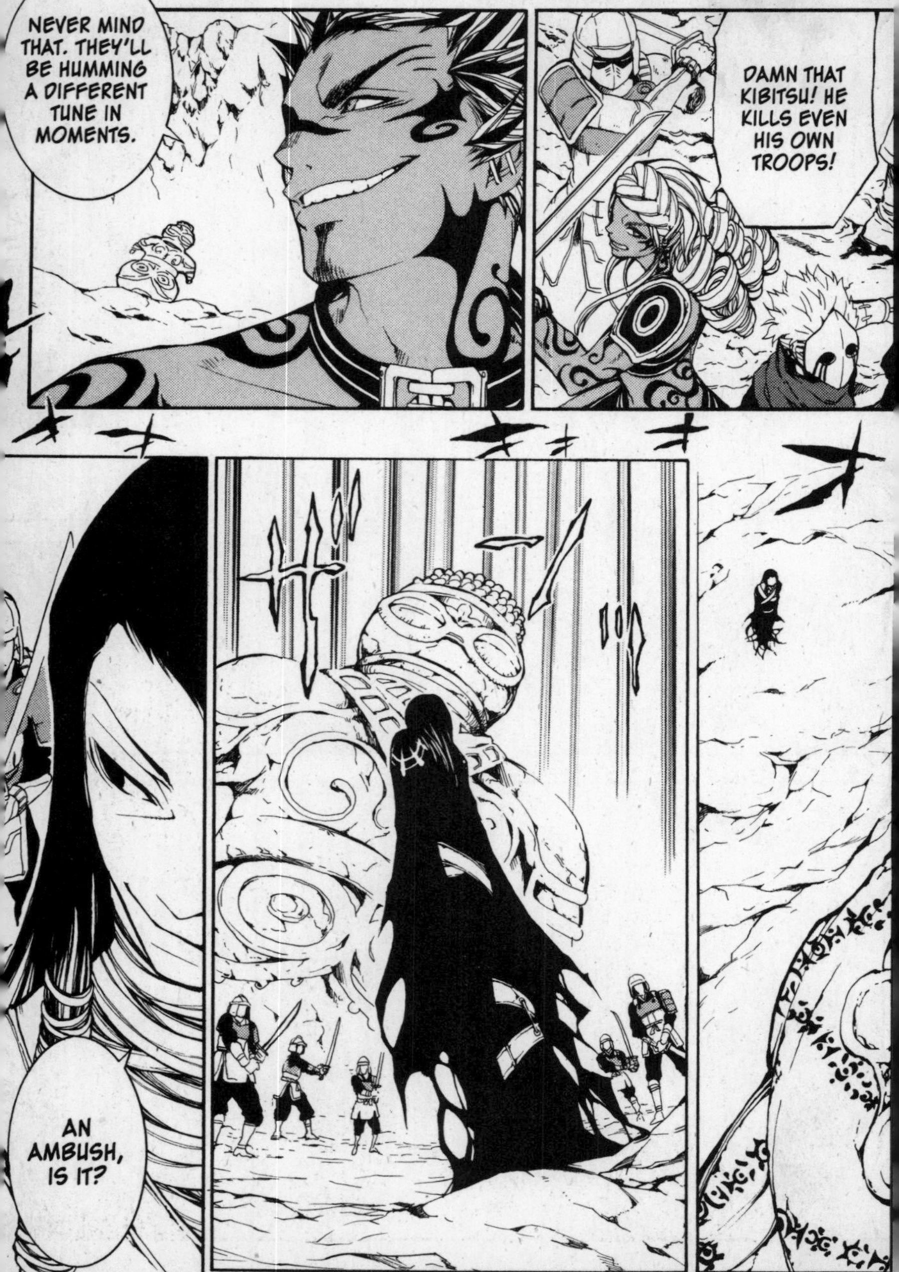
DAMN THAT KIBITSU! HE KILLS EVEN HIS OWN TROOPS!
NEVER MIND THAT. THEY'LL BE HUMMING A DIFFERENT TUNE IN MOMENTS.
AN AMBUSH, IS IT?

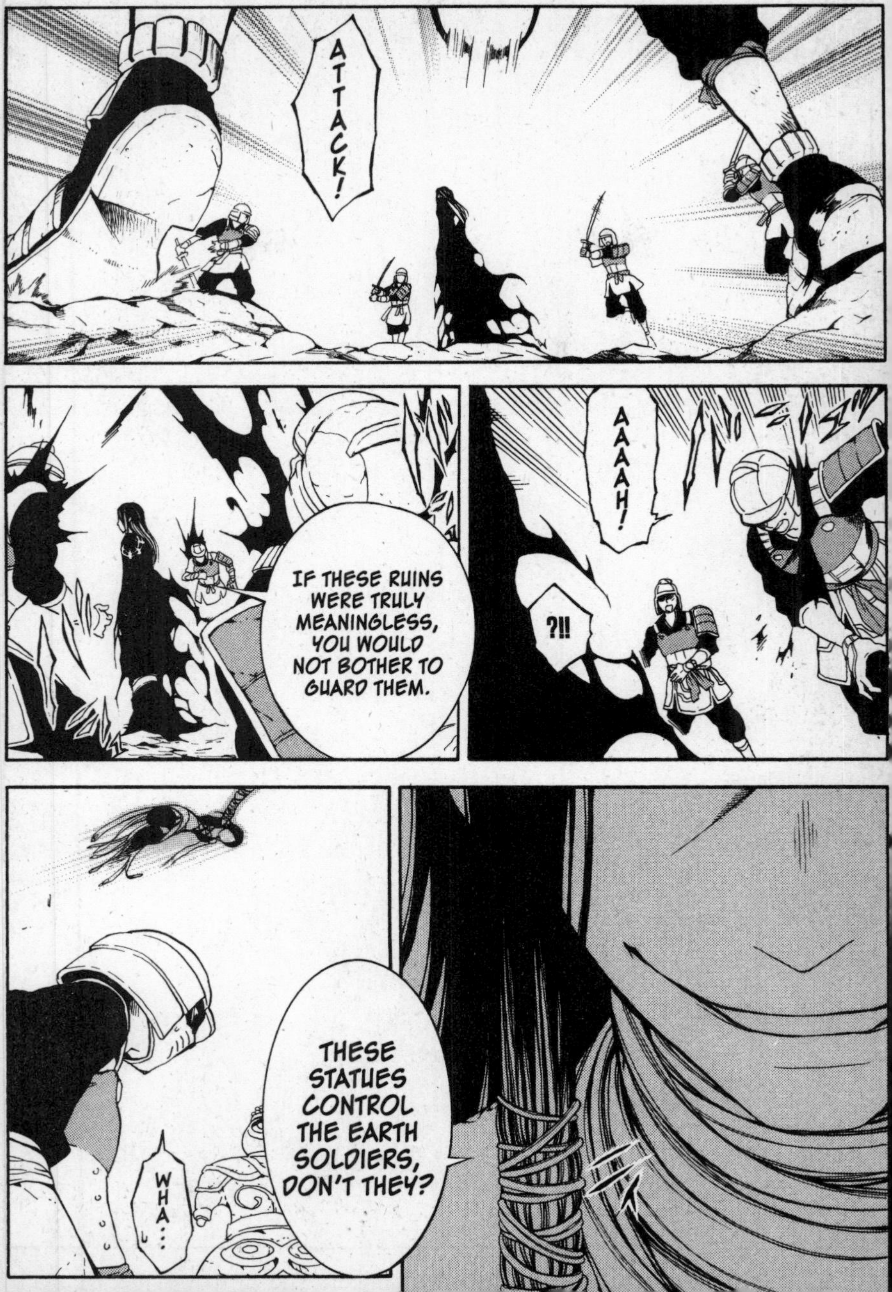
ATTACK!
AAAAH!
?!!
IF THESE RUINS WERE TRULY MEANINGLESS, YOU WOULD NOT BOTHER TO GUARD THEM.
THESE STATUES CONTROL THE EARTH SOLDIERS, DON'T THEY?
WHA...

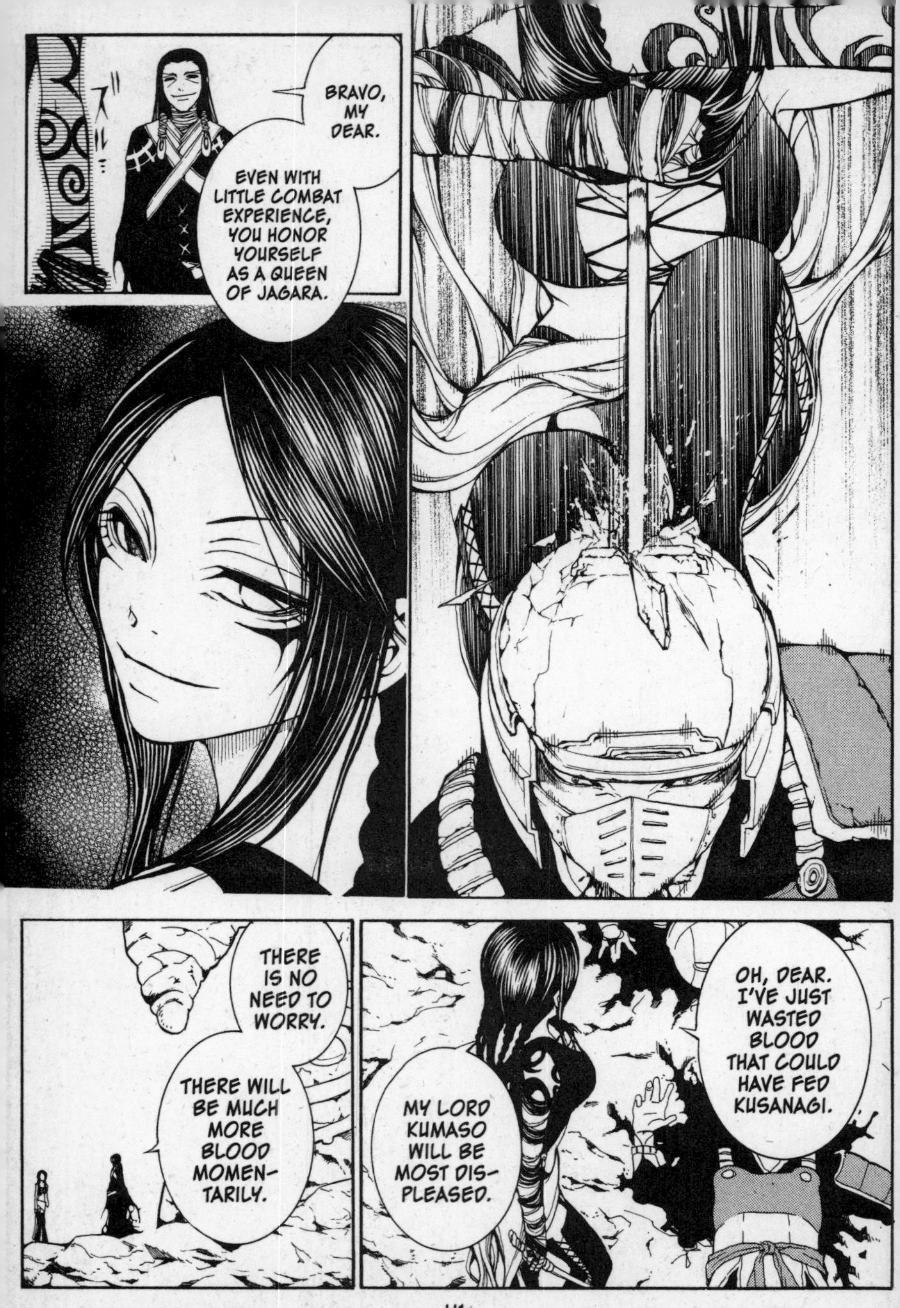
ズル
BRAVO, MY DEAR.
EVEN WITH LITTLE COMBAT EXPERIENCE, YOU HONOR YOURSELF AS A QUEEN OF JAGARA.
OH, DEAR. I'VE JUST WASTED BLOOD THAT COULD HAVE FED KUSANAGI.
MY LORD KUMASO WILL BE MOST DIS-PLEASED.
THERE IS NO NEED TO WORRY.
THERE WILL BE MUCH MORE BLOOD MOMEN-TARILY.

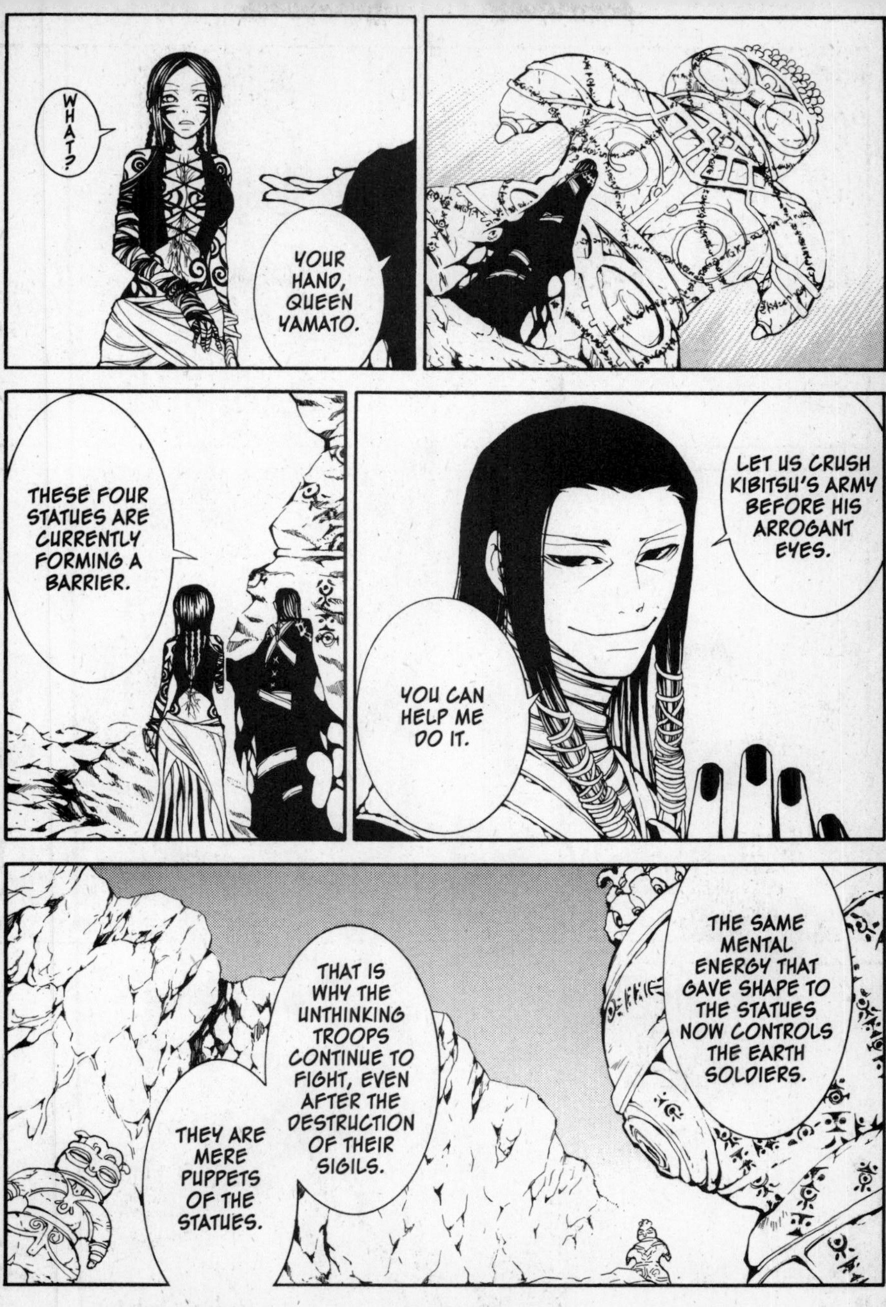
YOUR HAND, QUEEN YAMATO.
WHAT?
LET US CRUSH KIBITSU'S ARMY BEFORE HIS ARROGANT EYES.
YOU CAN HELP ME DO IT.
THESE FOUR STATUES ARE CURRENTLY FORMING A BARRIER.
THE SAME MENTAL ENERGY THAT GAVE SHAPE TO THE STATUES NOW CONTROLS THE EARTH SOLDIERS.
THAT IS WHY THE UNTHINKING TROOPS CONTINUE TO FIGHT, EVEN AFTER THE DESTRUCTION OF THEIR SIGILS.
THEY ARE MERE PUPPETS OF THE STATUES.

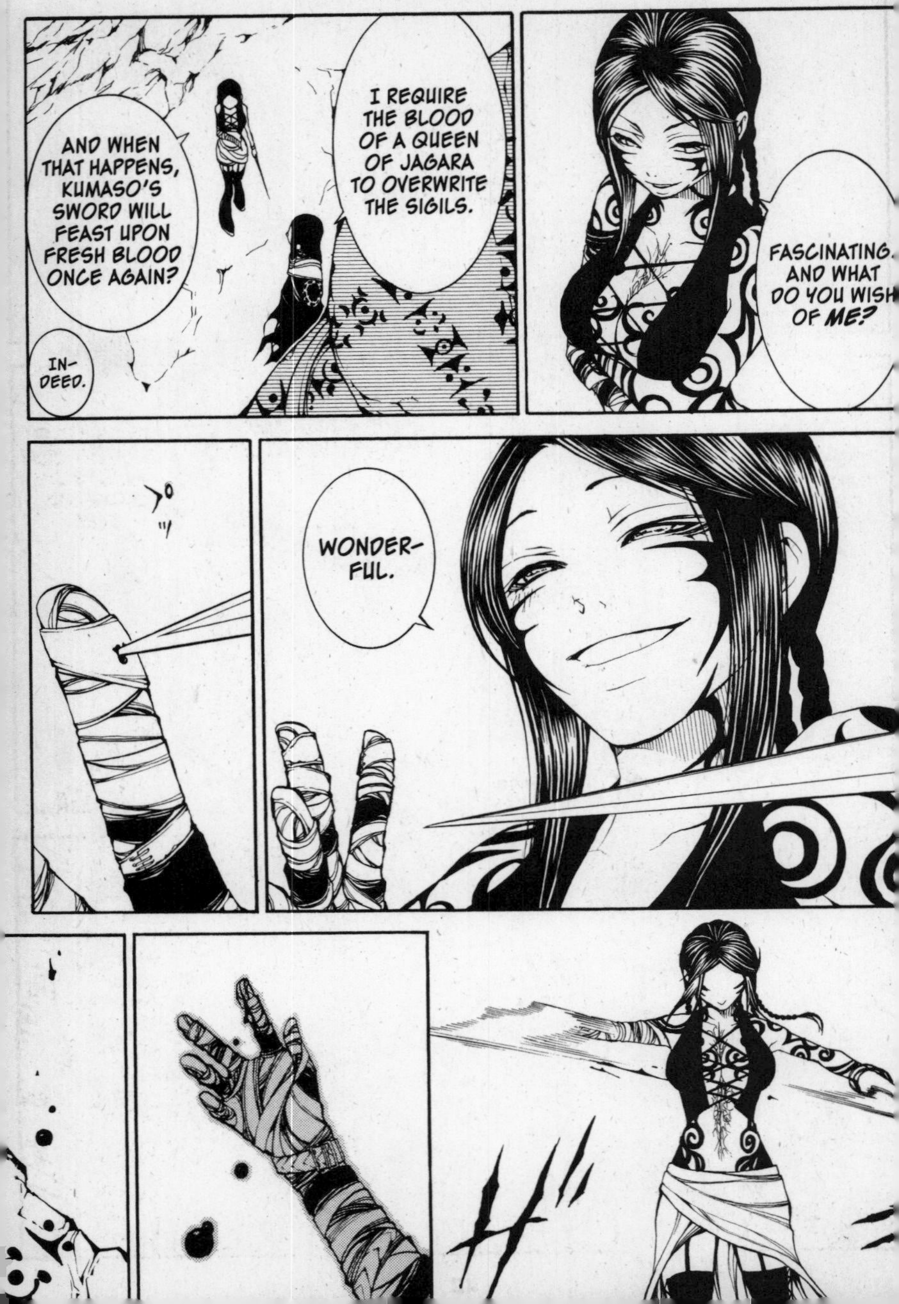
FASCINATING. AND WHAT DO YOU WISH OF ME?
I REQUIRE THE BLOOD OF A QUEEN OF JAGARA TO OVERWRITE THE SIGILS.
AND WHEN THAT HAPPENS, KUMASO'S SWORD WILL FEAST UPON FRESH BLOOD ONCE AGAIN?
IN-DEED.
WONDER-FUL.

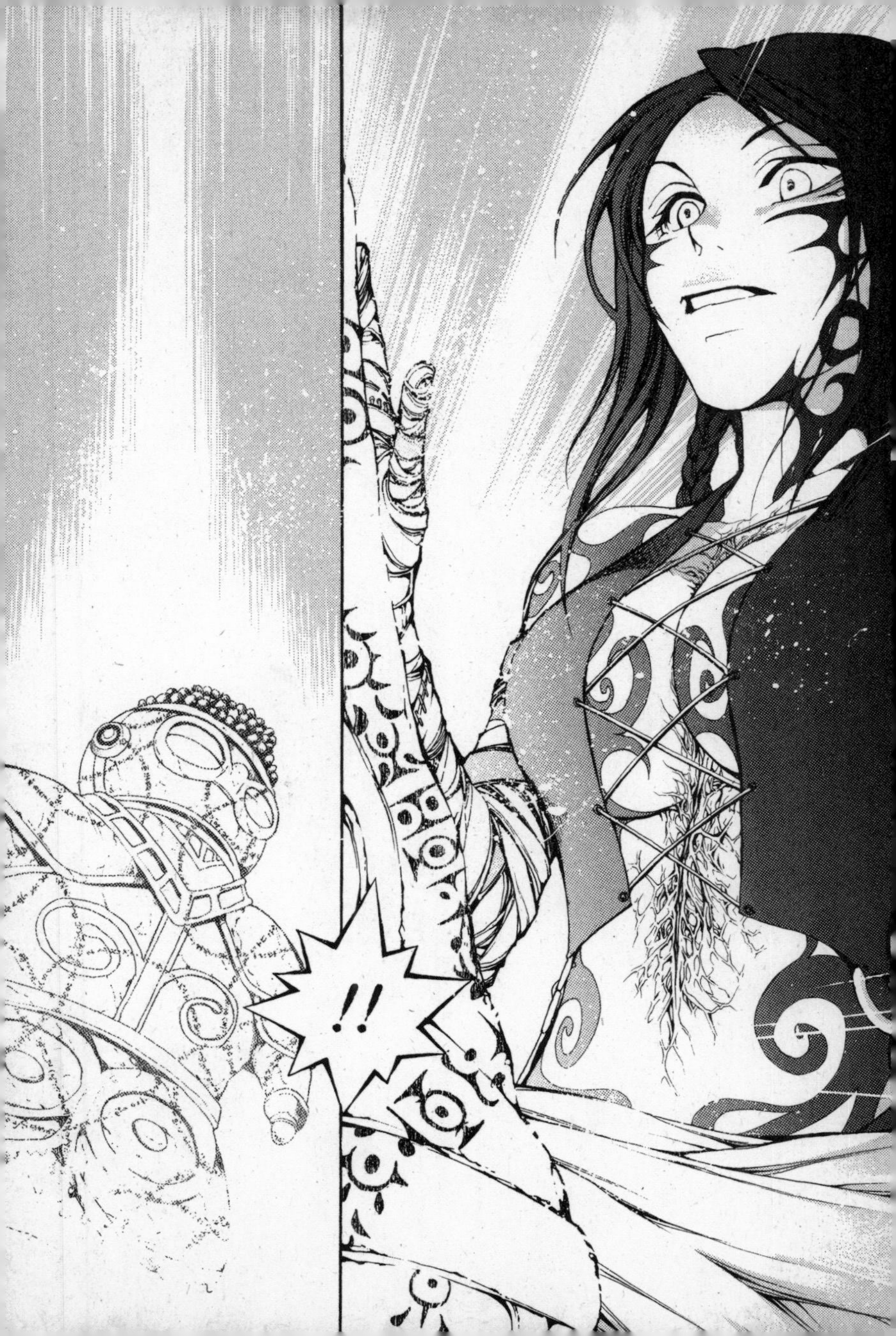
!!

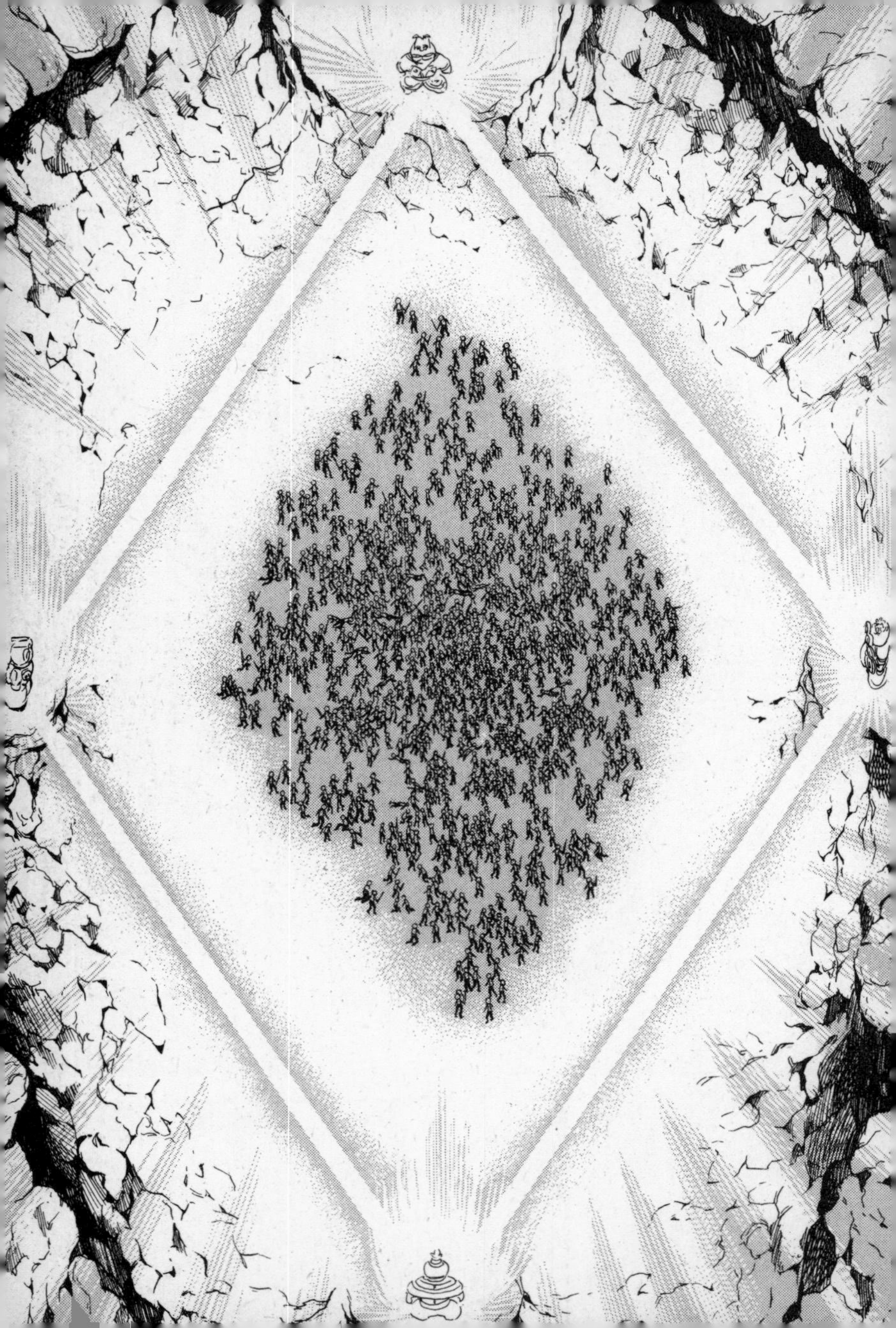

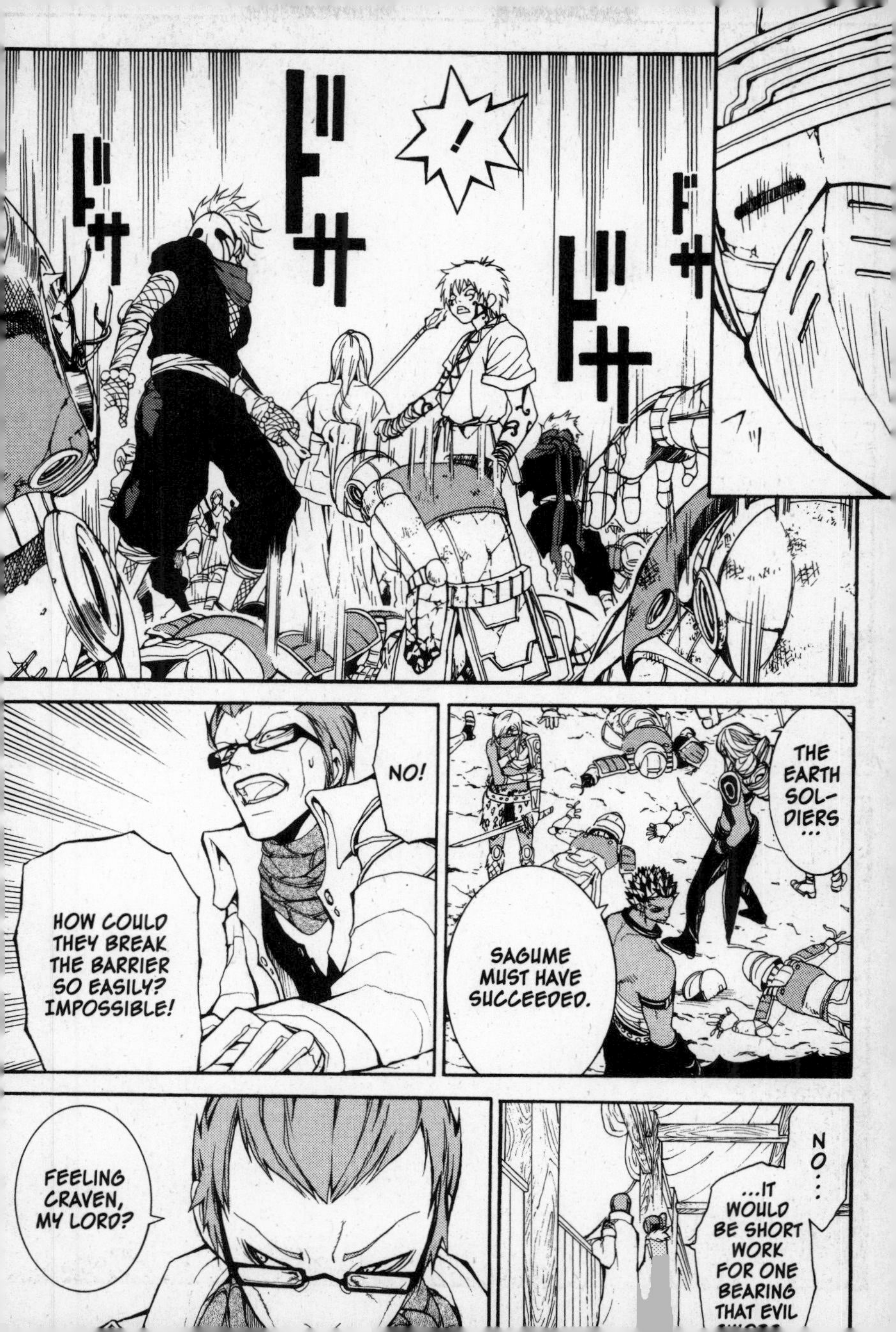

ドサ
ドサ
!
ドサ
ドサ
THE EARTH SOL-DIERS...
SAGUME MUST HAVE SUCCEEDED.
NO!
HOW COULD THEY BREAK THE BARRIER SO EASILY? IMPOSSIBLE!
NO...
...IT WOULD BE SHORT WORK FOR ONE BEARING THAT EVIL
FEELING CRAVEN, MY LORD?

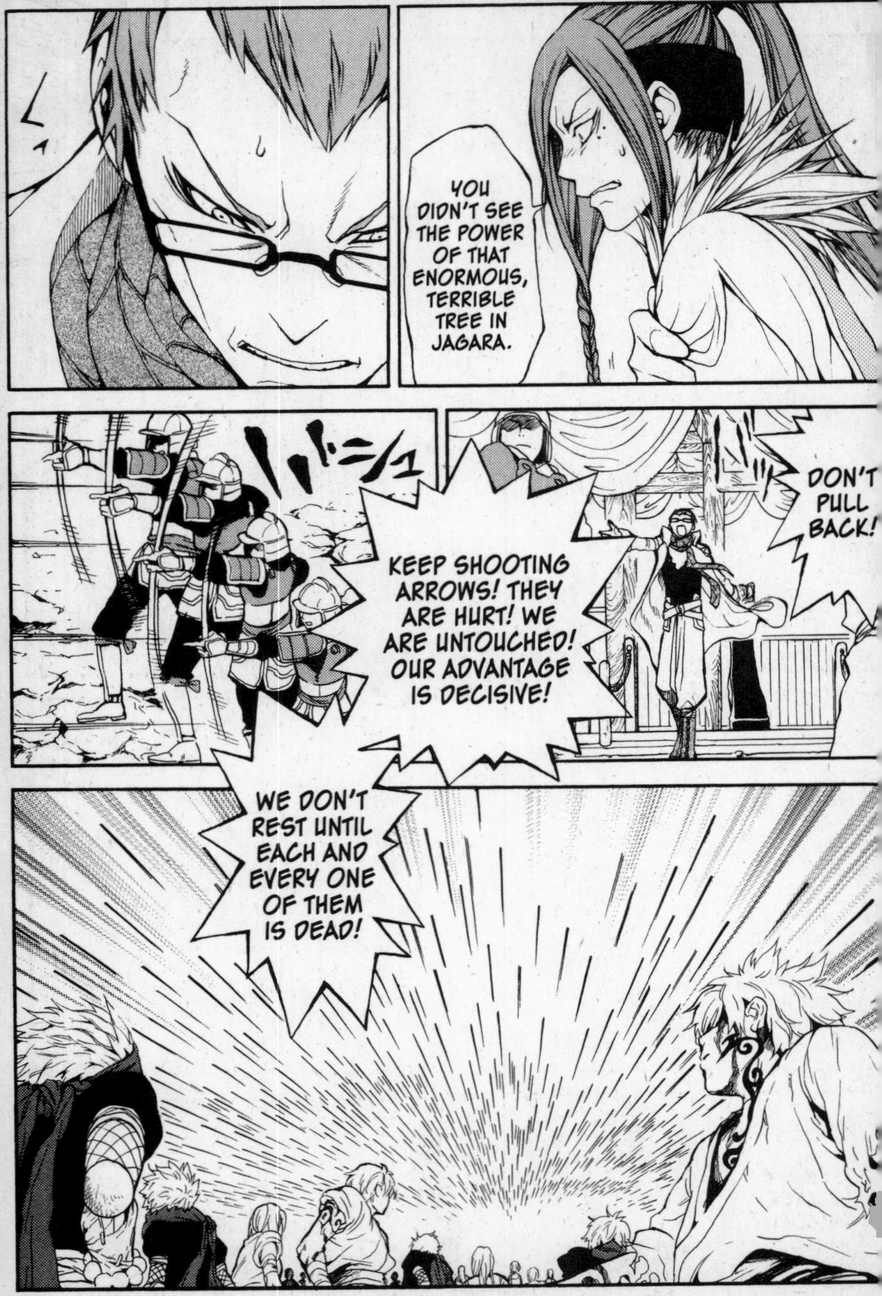
YOU DIDN'T SEE THE POWER OF THAT ENORMOUS, TERRIBLE TREE IN JAGARA.
DON'T PULL BACK!
KEEP SHOOTING ARROWS! THEY ARE HURT! WE ARE UNTOUCHED! OUR ADVANTAGE IS DECISIVE!
WE DON'T REST UNTIL EACH AND EVERY ONE OF THEM IS DEAD!

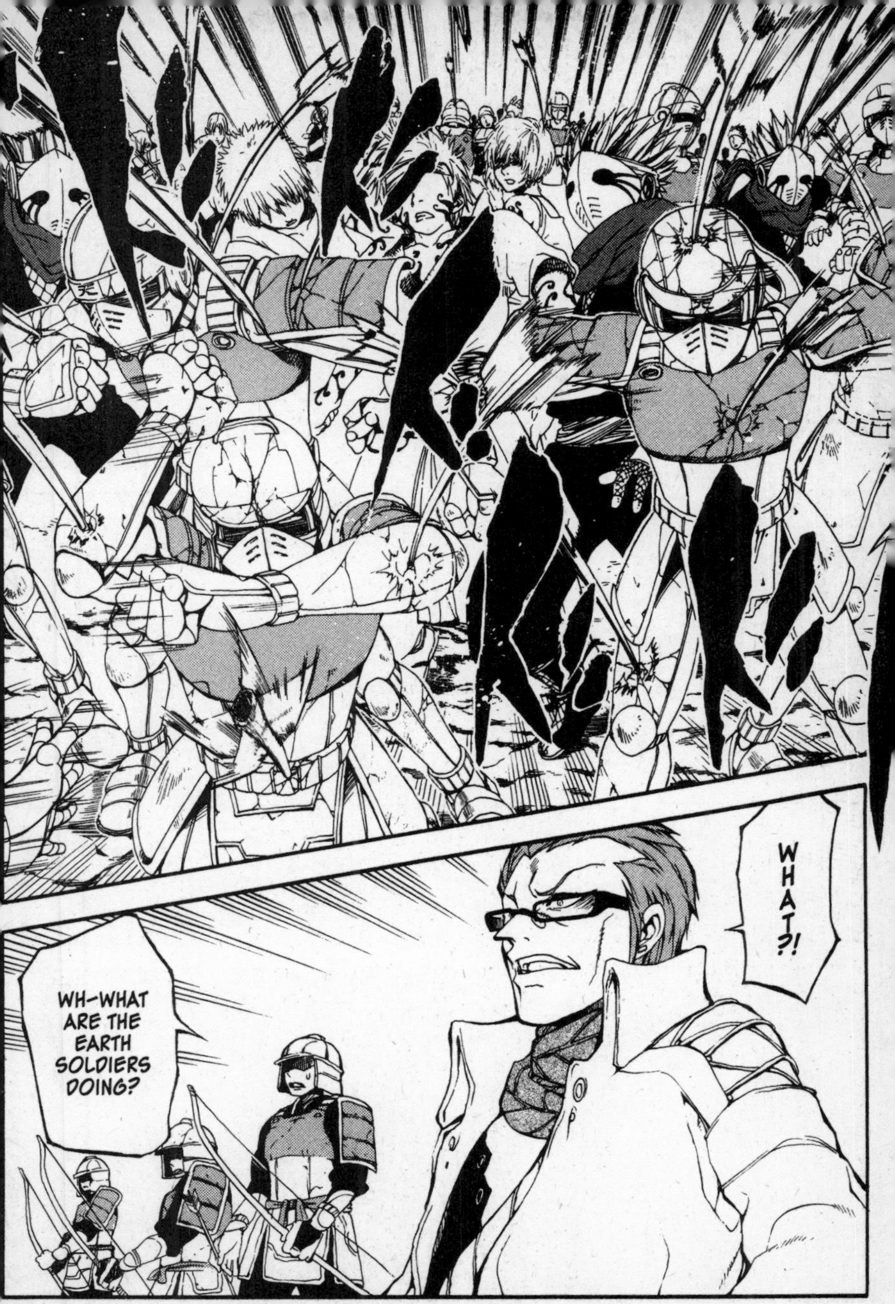
WHAT?!
WH-WHAT ARE THE EARTH SOLDIERS DOING?

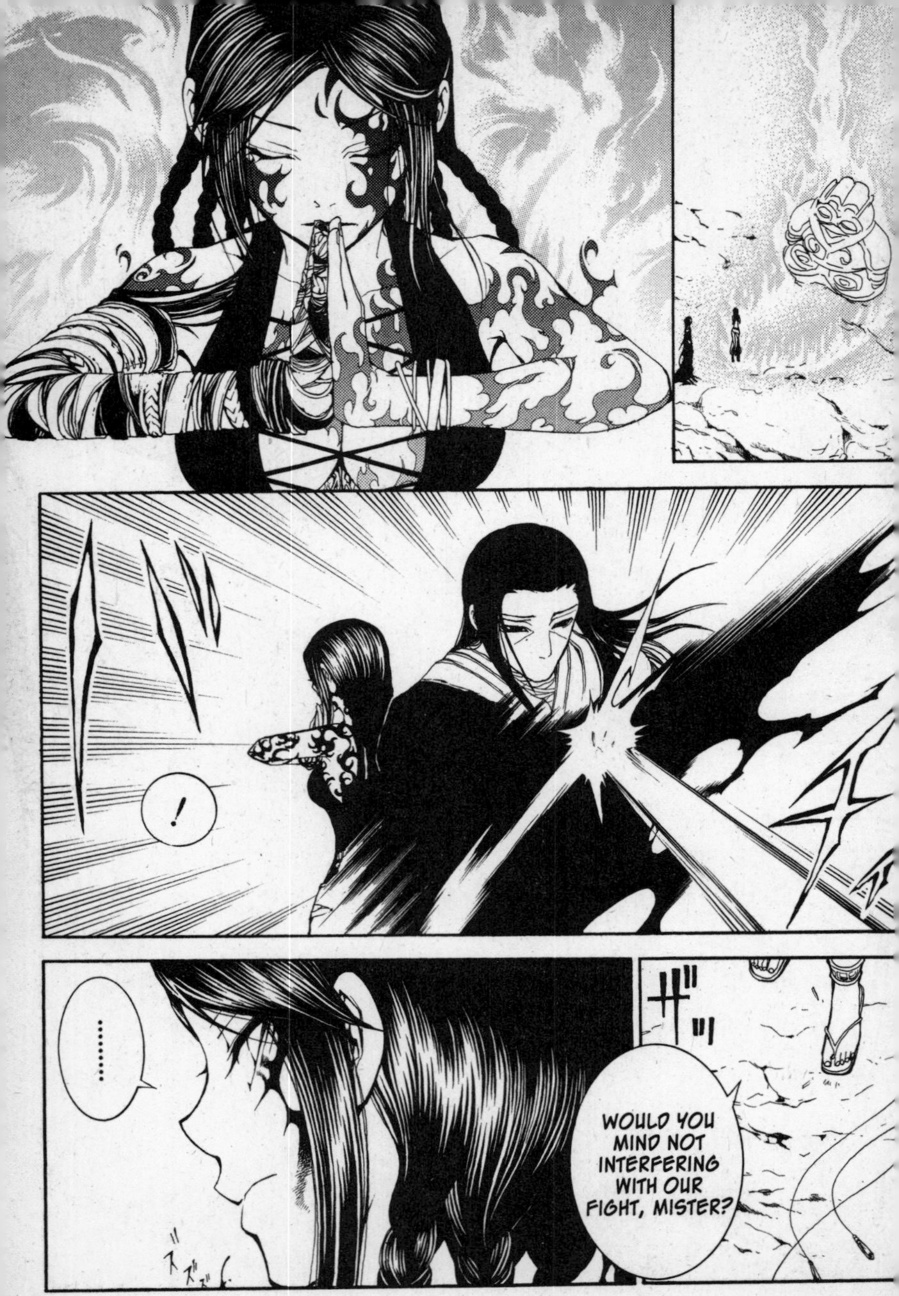
!
ザッ
WOULD YOU MIND NOT INTERFERING WITH OUR FIGHT, MISTER?
......

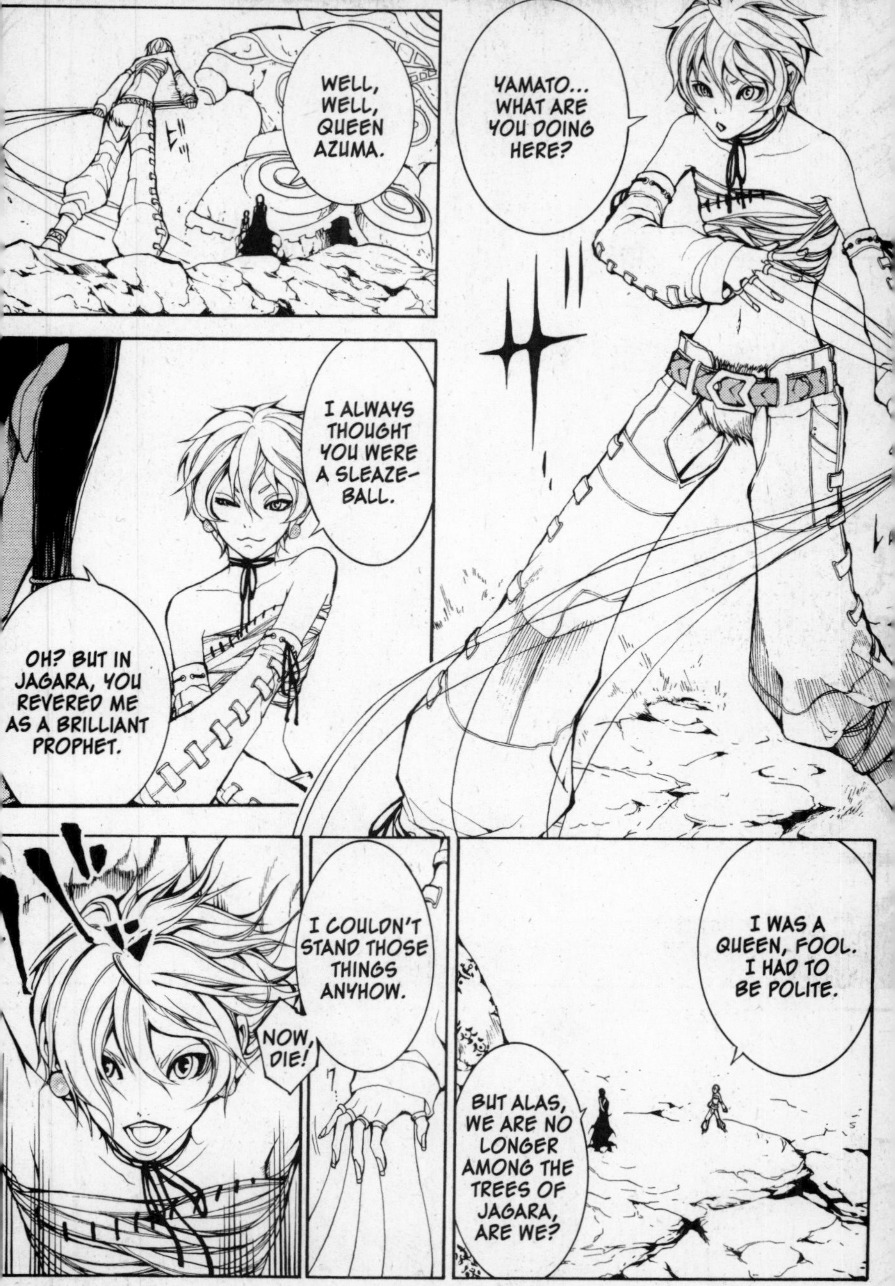
YAMATO... WHAT ARE YOU DOING HERE?
WELL, WELL, QUEEN AZUMA.
I ALWAYS THOUGHT YOU WERE A SLEAZE-BALL.
OH? BUT IN JAGARA, YOU REVERED ME AS A BRILLIANT PROPHET.
I WAS A QUEEN, FOOL. I HAD TO BE POLITE.
BUT ALAS, WE ARE NO LONGER AMONG THE TREES OF JAGARA, ARE WE?
I COULDN'T STAND THOSE THINGS ANYHOW.
NOW, DIE!

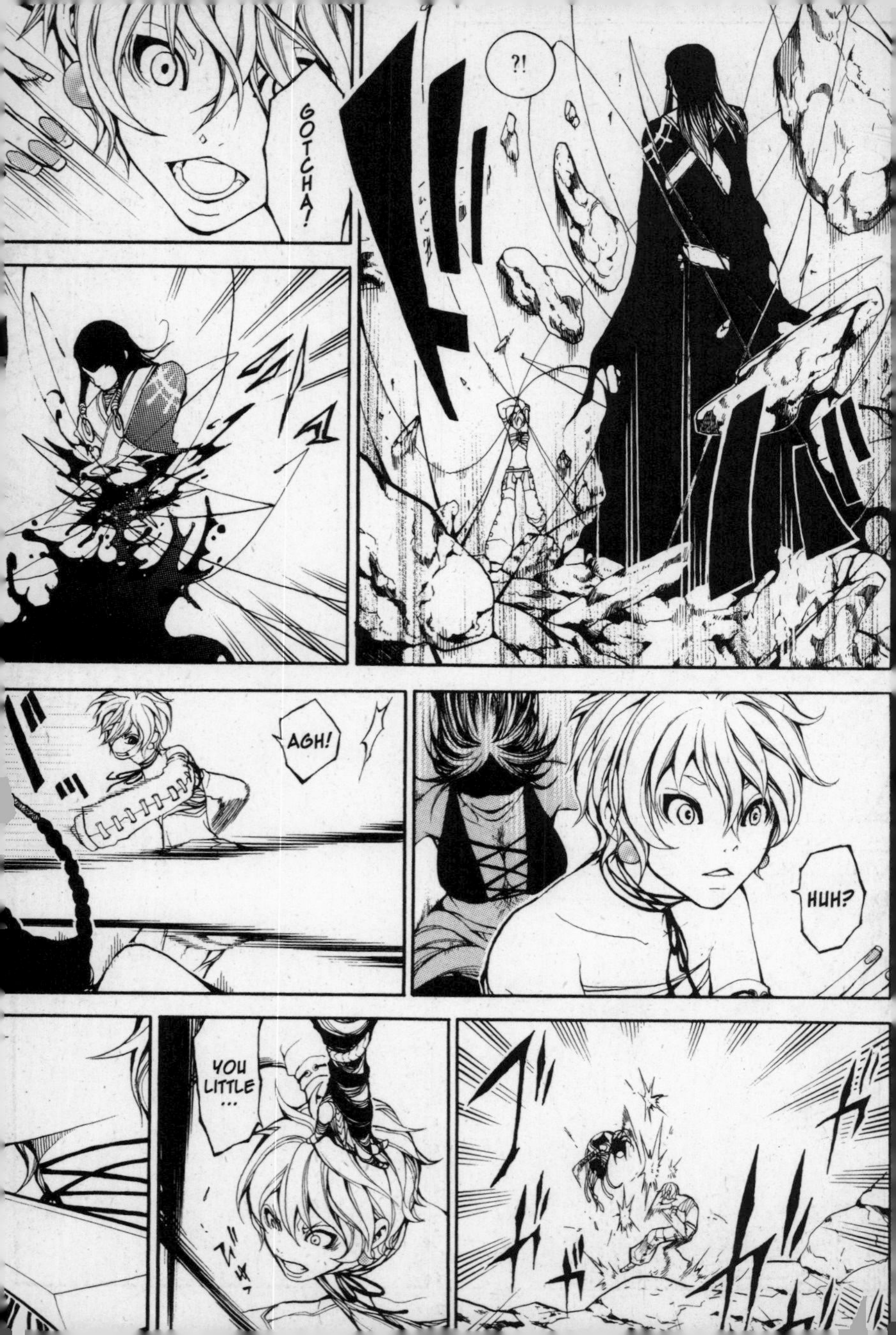
?!
GOTCHA!
HUH?
AGH!
YOU LITTLE ...

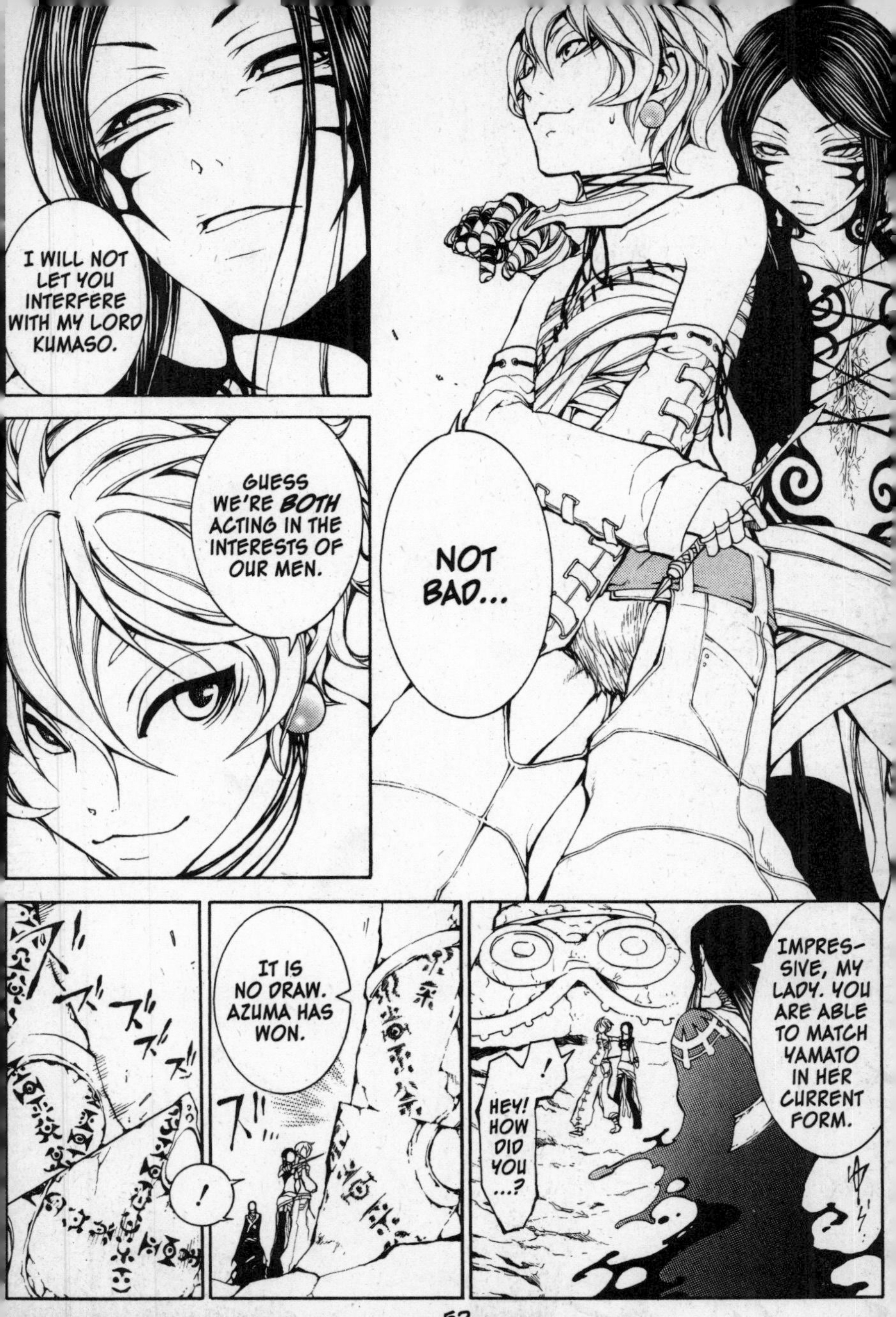
NOT BAD...
I WILL NOT LET YOU INTERFERE WITH MY LORD KUMASO.
GUESS WE'RE *BOTH* ACTING IN THE INTERESTS OF OUR MEN.
IMPRESSIVE, MY LADY. YOU ARE ABLE TO MATCH YAMATO IN HER CURRENT FORM.
HEY! HOW DID YOU ...?
IT IS NO DRAW. AZUMA HAS WON.
!

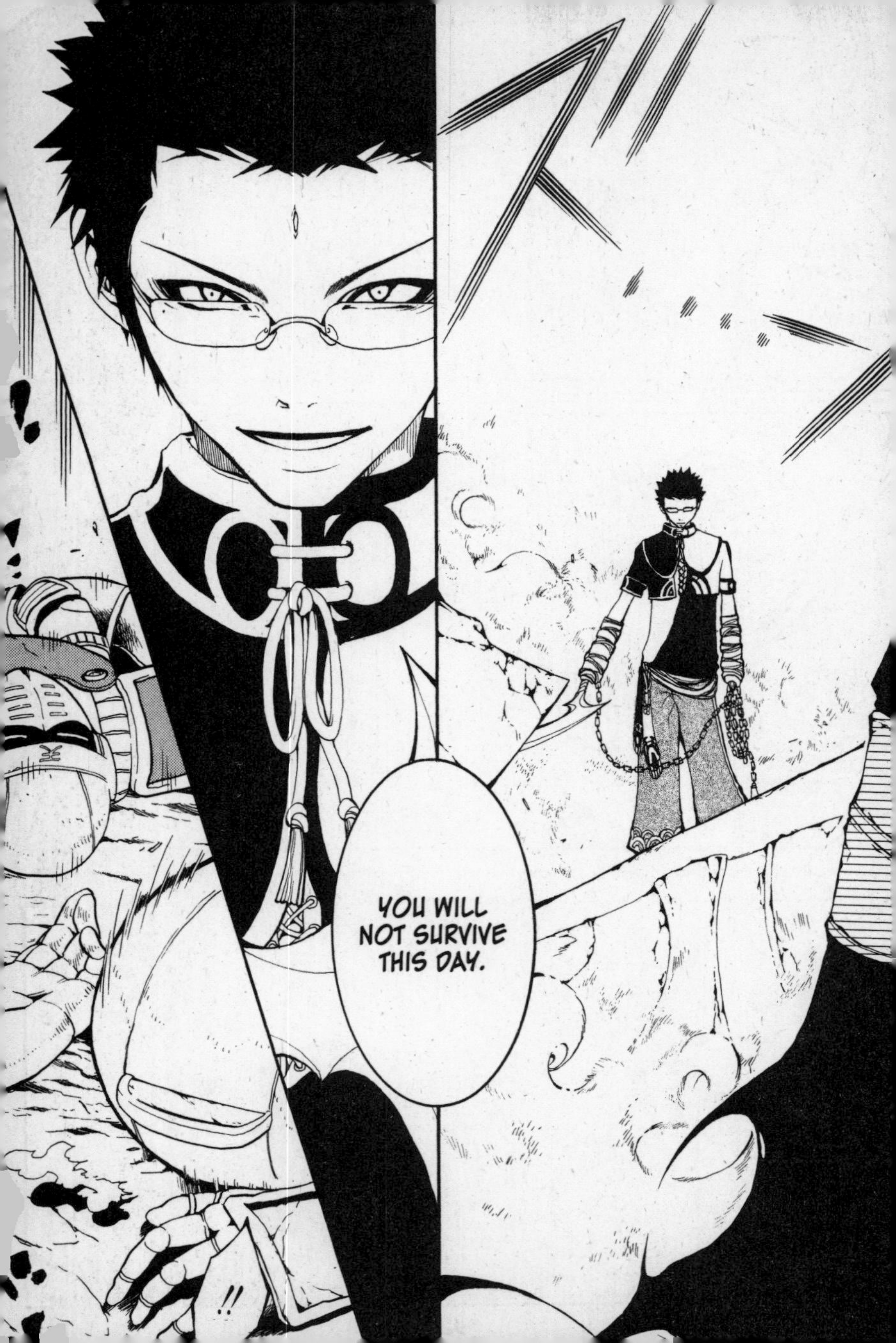
YOU WILL NOT SURVIVE THIS DAY.
!!

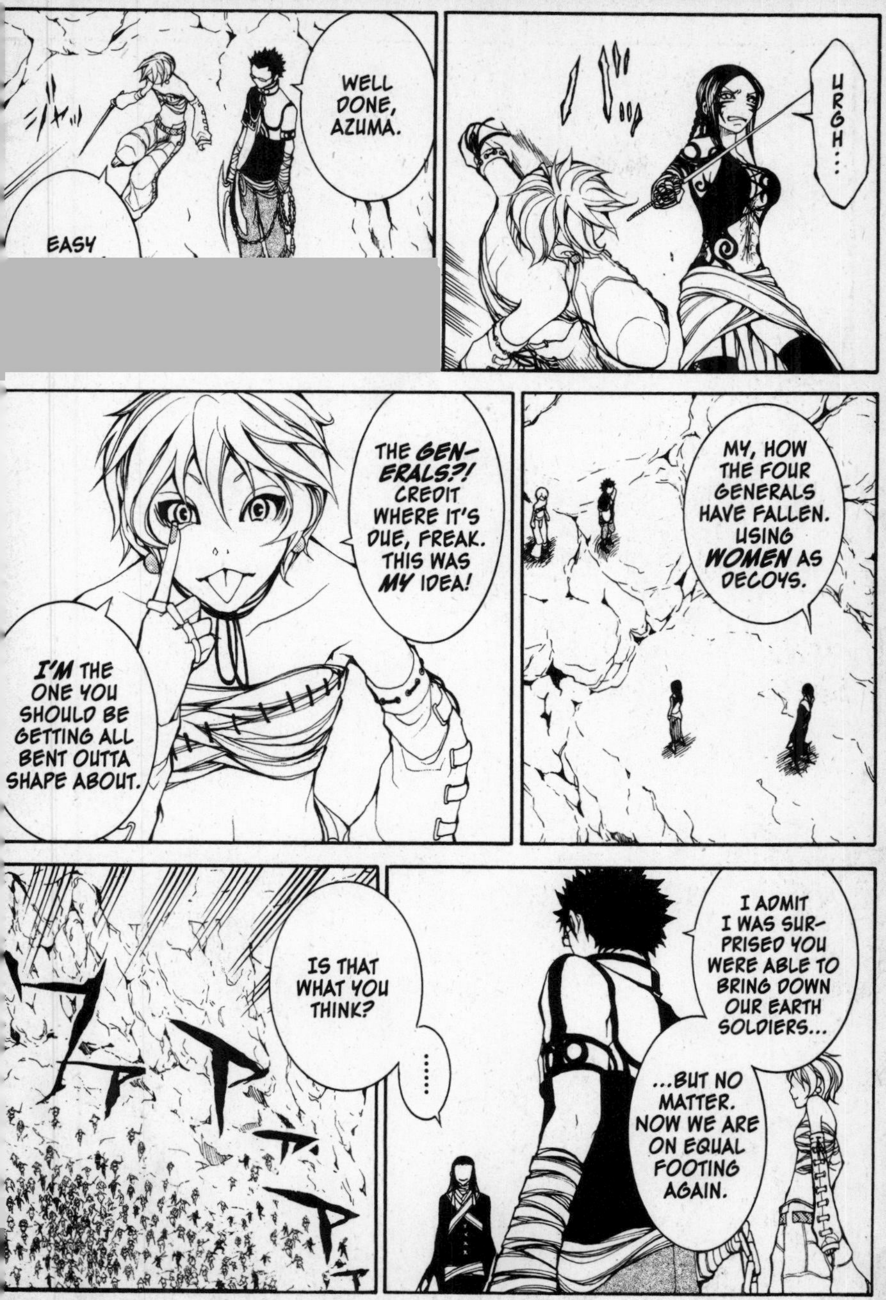
URGH...
WELL DONE, AZUMA.
EASY
MY, HOW THE FOUR GENERALS HAVE FALLEN. USING WOMEN AS DECOYS.
THE GENERALS?! CREDIT WHERE IT'S DUE, FREAK. THIS WAS MY IDEA!
I'M THE ONE YOU SHOULD BE GETTING ALL BENT OUTTA SHAPE ABOUT.
I ADMIT I WAS SURPRISED YOU WERE ABLE TO BRING DOWN OUR EARTH SOLDIERS...
...BUT NO MATTER. NOW WE ARE ON EQUAL FOOTING AGAIN.
IS THAT WHAT YOU THINK?
......

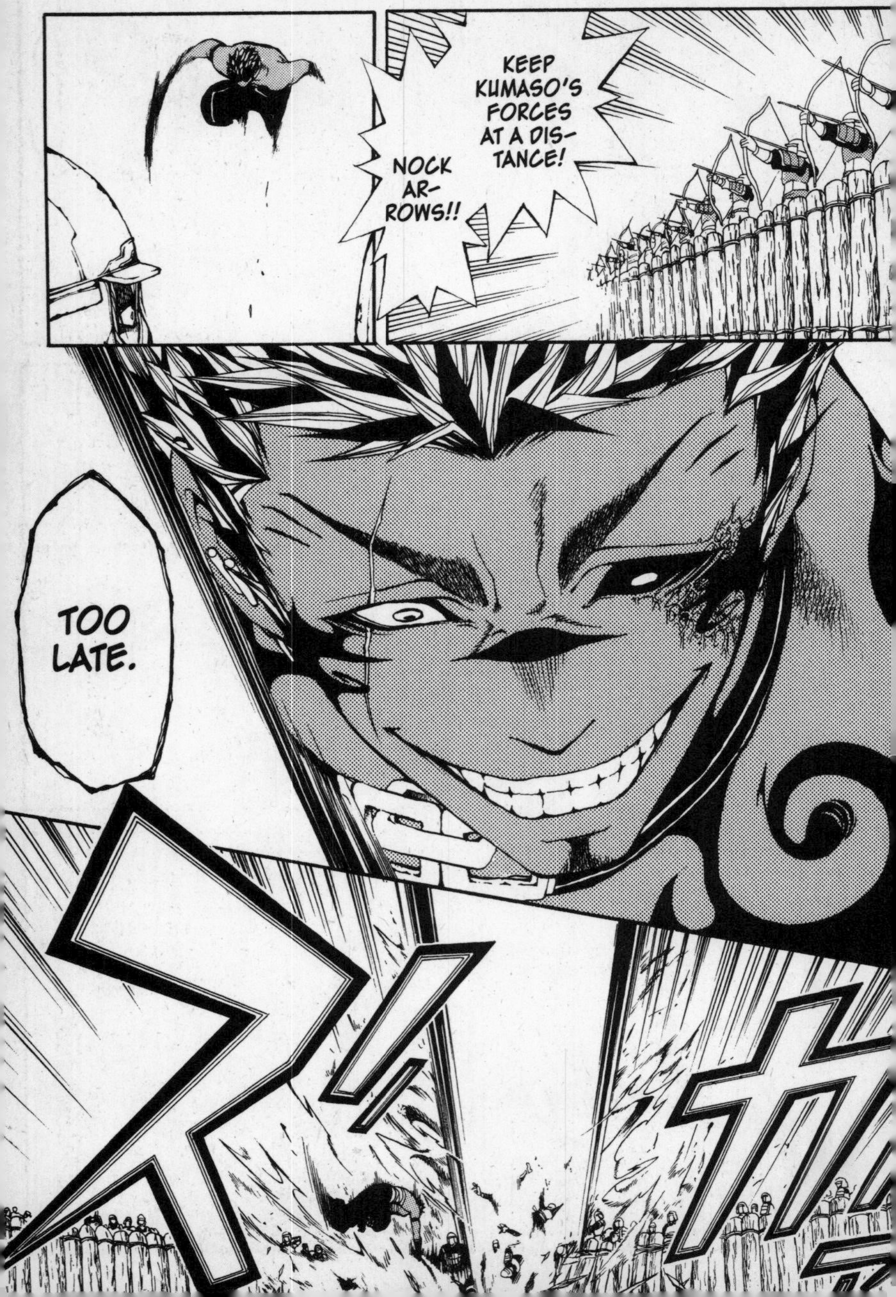
KEEP KUMASO'S FORCES AT A DISTANCE!
NOCK ARROWS!!
TOO LATE.

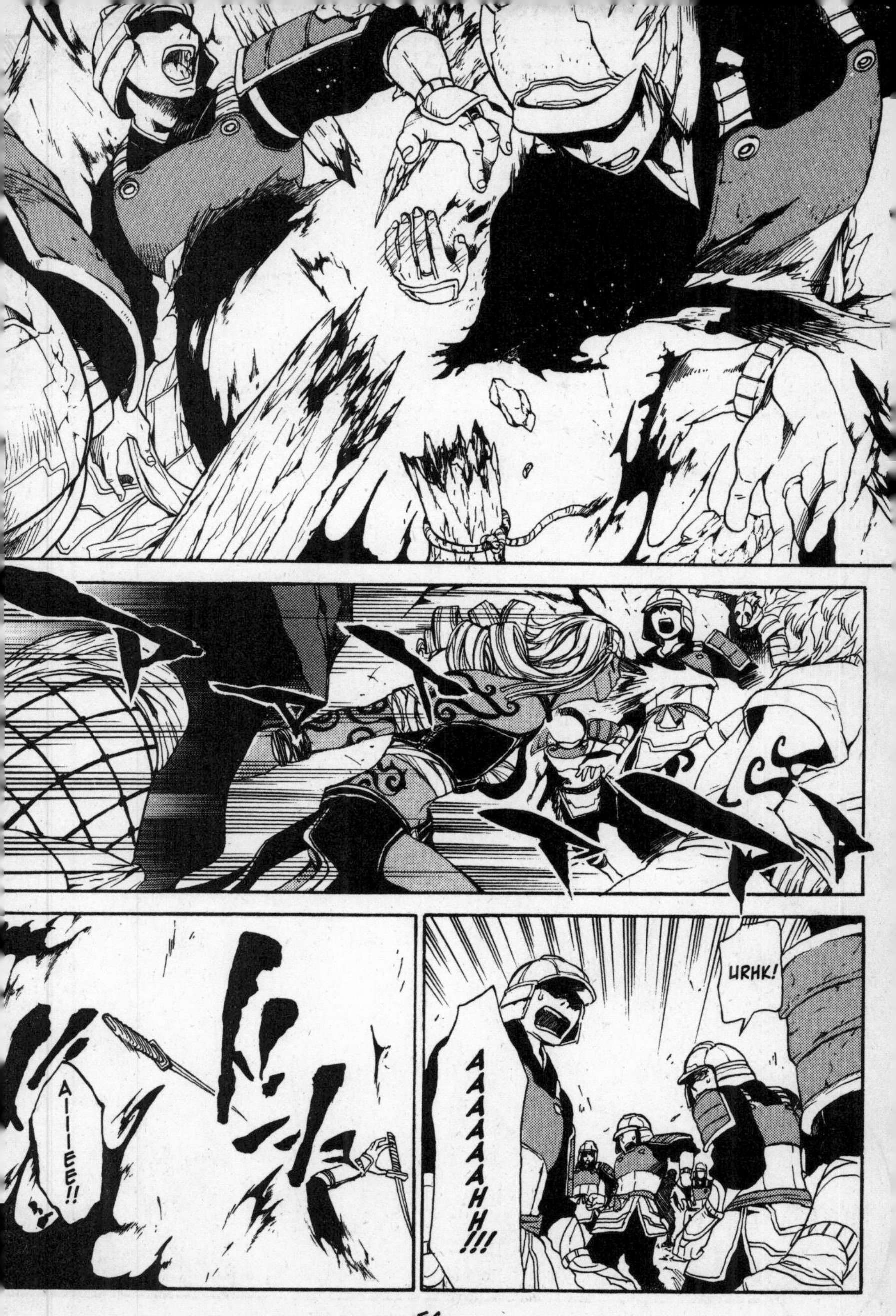
URHK!
AAAAAAHH!!!
AIIIEE!!

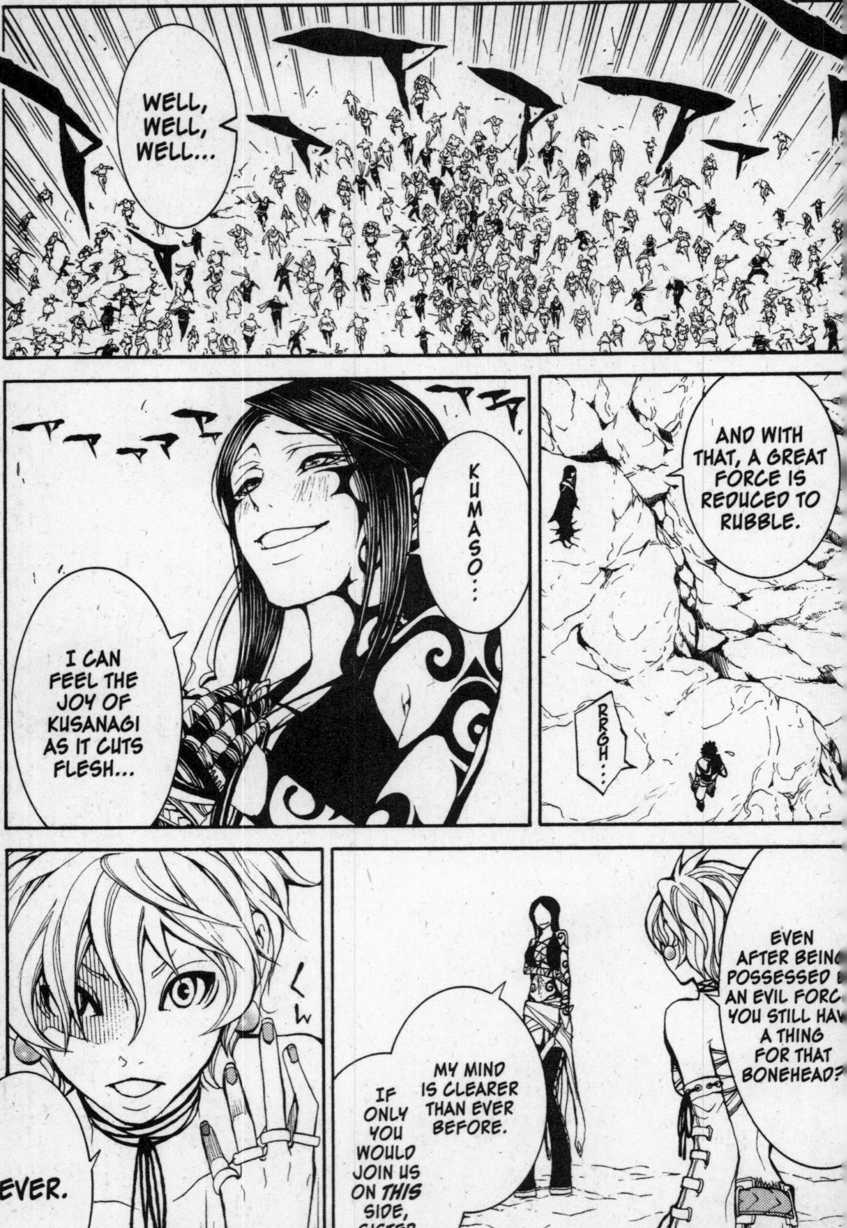
WELL, WELL, WELL...
AND WITH THAT, A GREAT FORCE IS REDUCED TO RUBBLE.
RRGH...
KUMASO...
I CAN FEEL THE JOY OF KUSANAGI AS IT CUTS FLESH...
EVEN AFTER BEING POSSESSED B AN EVIL FORC YOU STILL HAV A THING FOR THAT BONEHEAD?
MY MIND IS CLEARER THAN EVER BEFORE.
IF ONLY YOU WOULD JOIN US ON *THIS* SIDE, SISTER AZUMA.
NEVER.

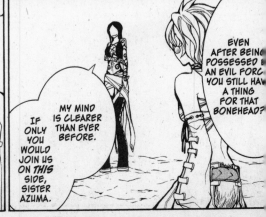

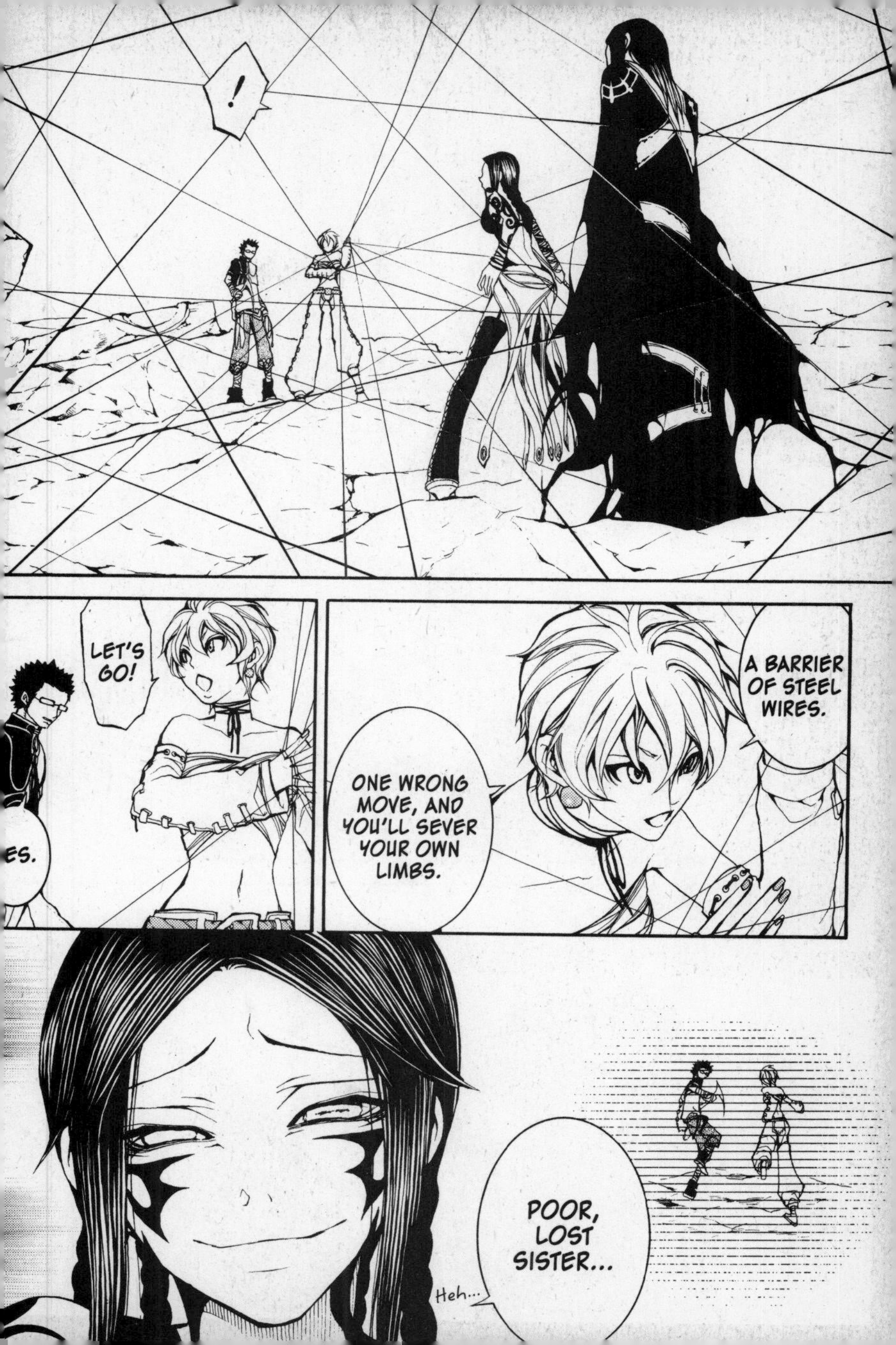
!
A BARRIER OF STEEL WIRES.
ONE WRONG MOVE, AND YOU'LL SEVER YOUR OWN LIMBS.
LET'S GO!
ES.
POOR, LOST SISTER...
Heh...

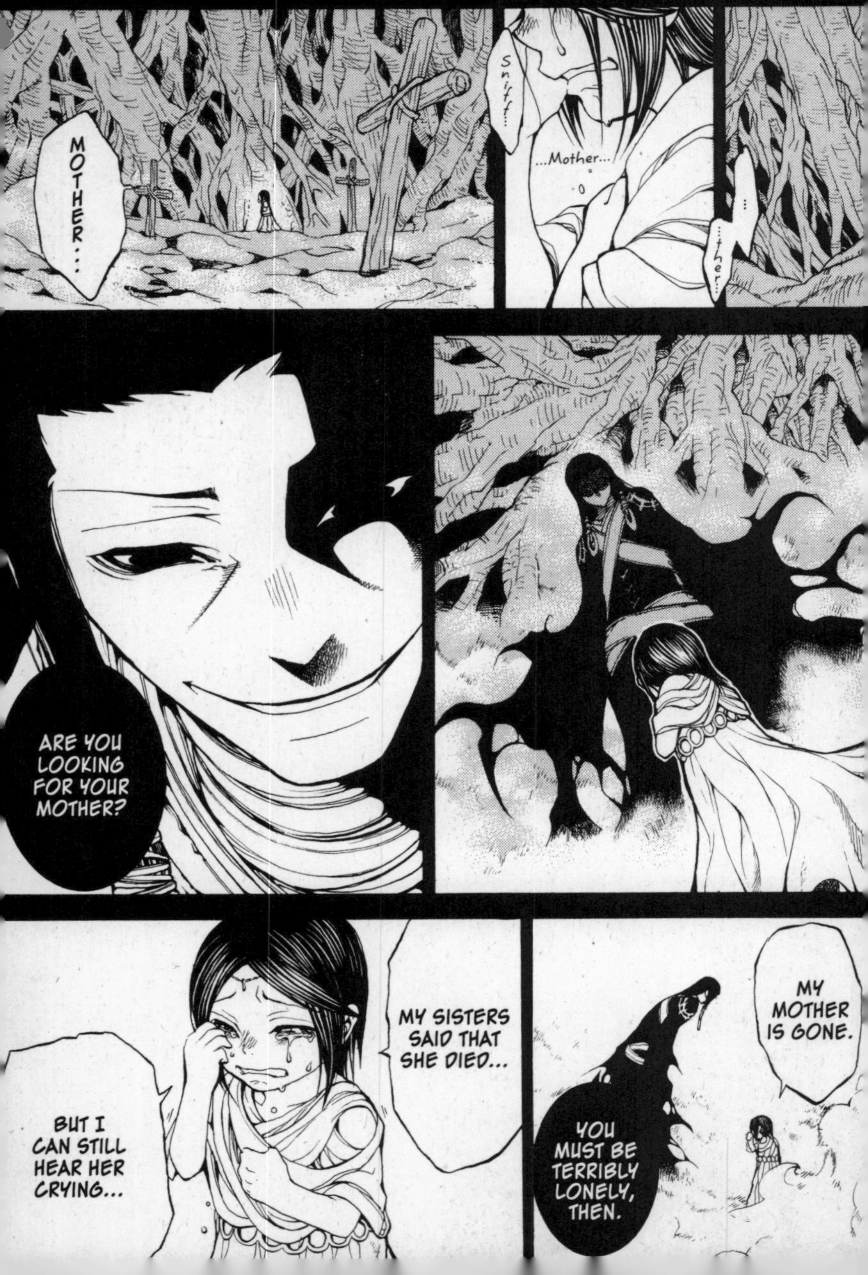
...ther...
Sniff...
...Mother...
MOTHER...
ARE YOU LOOKING FOR YOUR MOTHER?
MY MOTHER IS GONE.
YOU MUST BE TERRIBLY LONELY, THEN.
MY SISTERS SAID THAT SHE DIED...
BUT I CAN STILL HEAR HER CRYING...

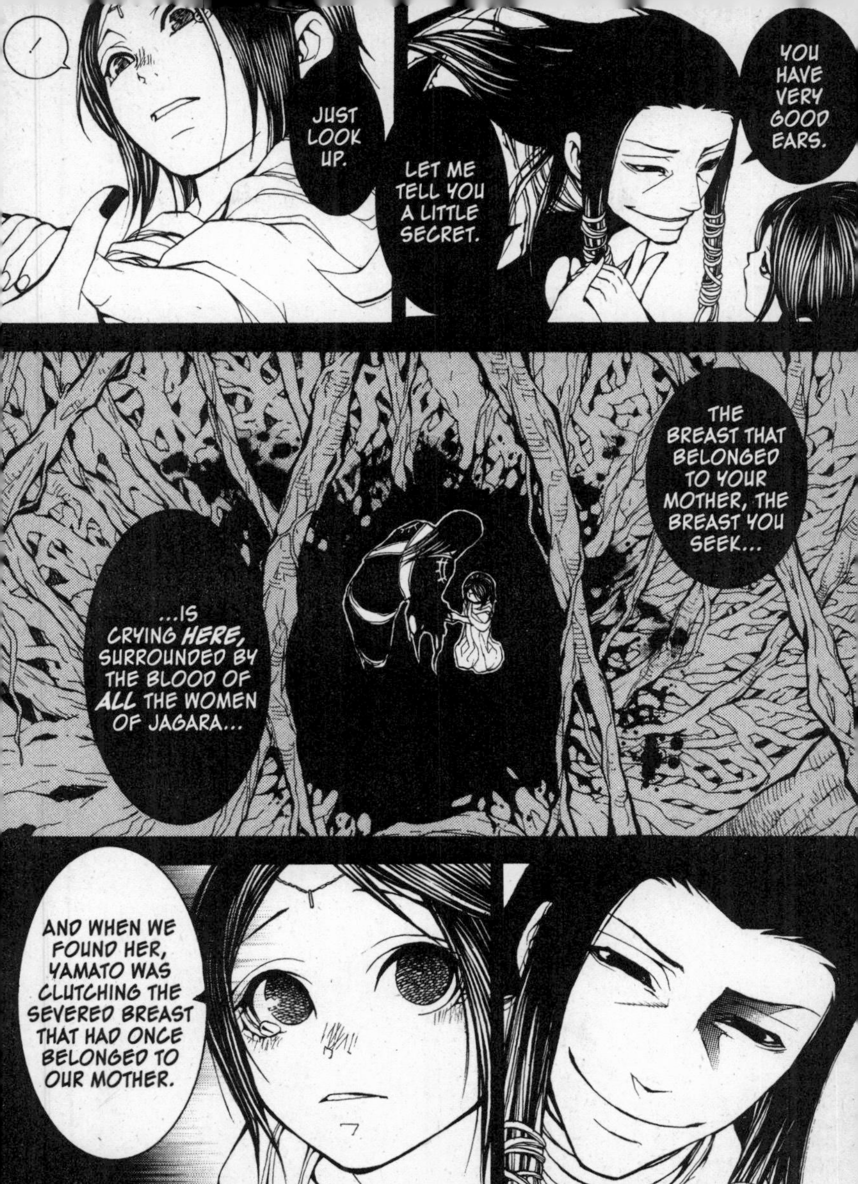
YOU HAVE VERY GOOD EARS.
LET ME TELL YOU A LITTLE SECRET.
JUST LOOK UP.
!
THE BREAST THAT BELONGED TO YOUR MOTHER, THE BREAST YOU SEEK...
...IS CRYING HERE, SURROUNDED BY THE BLOOD OF ALL THE WOMEN OF JAGARA...
AND WHEN WE FOUND HER, YAMATO WAS CLUTCHING THE SEVERED BREAST THAT HAD ONCE BELONGED TO OUR MOTHER.

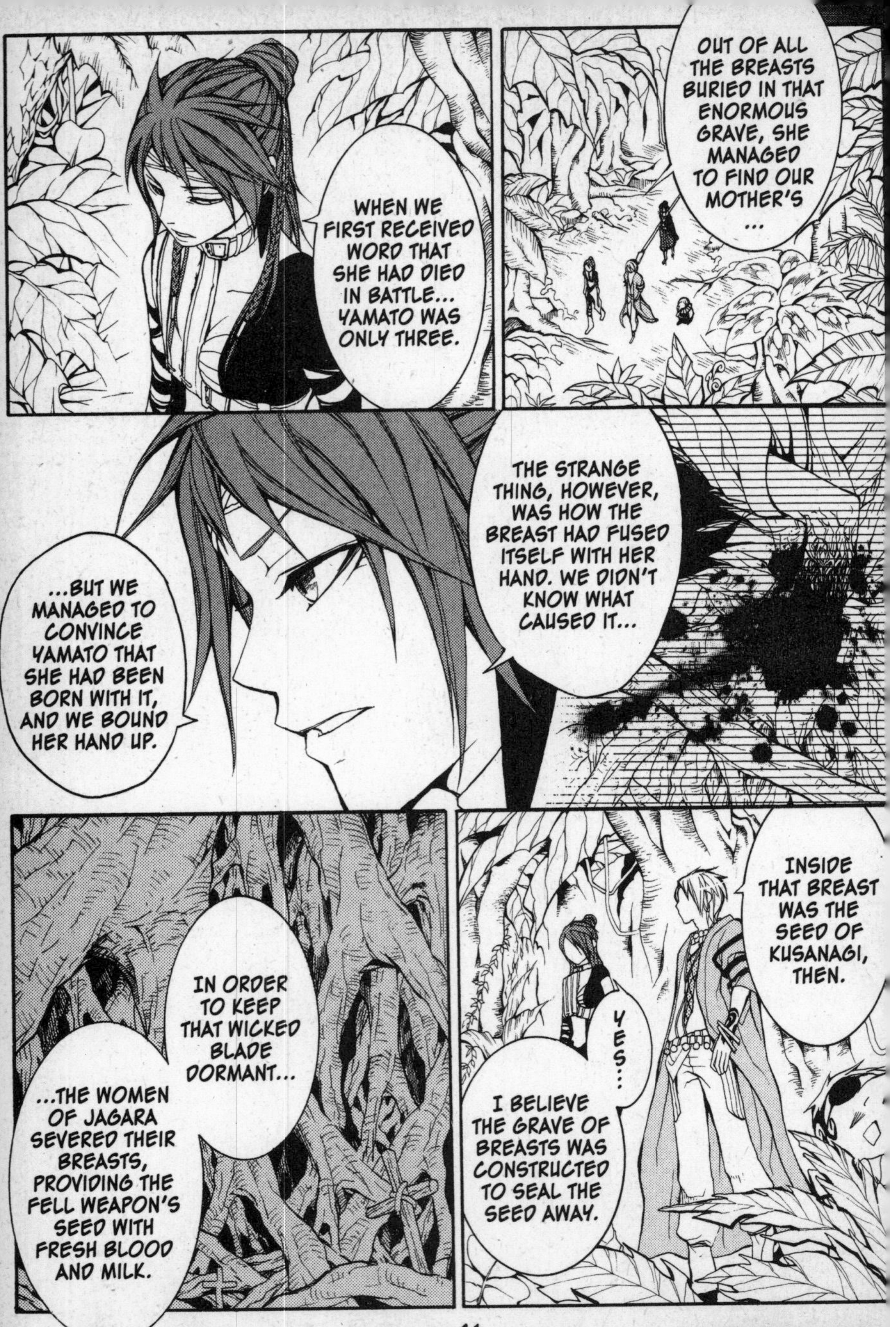
OUT OF ALL THE BREASTS BURIED IN THAT ENORMOUS GRAVE, SHE MANAGED TO FIND OUR MOTHER'S ...
WHEN WE FIRST RECEIVED WORD THAT SHE HAD DIED IN BATTLE... YAMATO WAS ONLY THREE.
THE STRANGE THING, HOWEVER, WAS HOW THE BREAST HAD FUSED ITSELF WITH HER HAND. WE DIDN'T KNOW WHAT CAUSED IT...
...BUT WE MANAGED TO CONVINCE YAMATO THAT SHE HAD BEEN BORN WITH IT, AND WE BOUND HER HAND UP.
INSIDE THAT BREAST WAS THE SEED OF KUSANAGI, THEN.
YES...
I BELIEVE THE GRAVE OF BREASTS WAS CONSTRUCTED TO SEAL THE SEED AWAY.
IN ORDER TO KEEP THAT WICKED BLADE DORMANT...
...THE WOMEN OF JAGARA SEVERED THEIR BREASTS, PROVIDING THE FELL WEAPON'S SEED WITH FRESH BLOOD AND MILK.

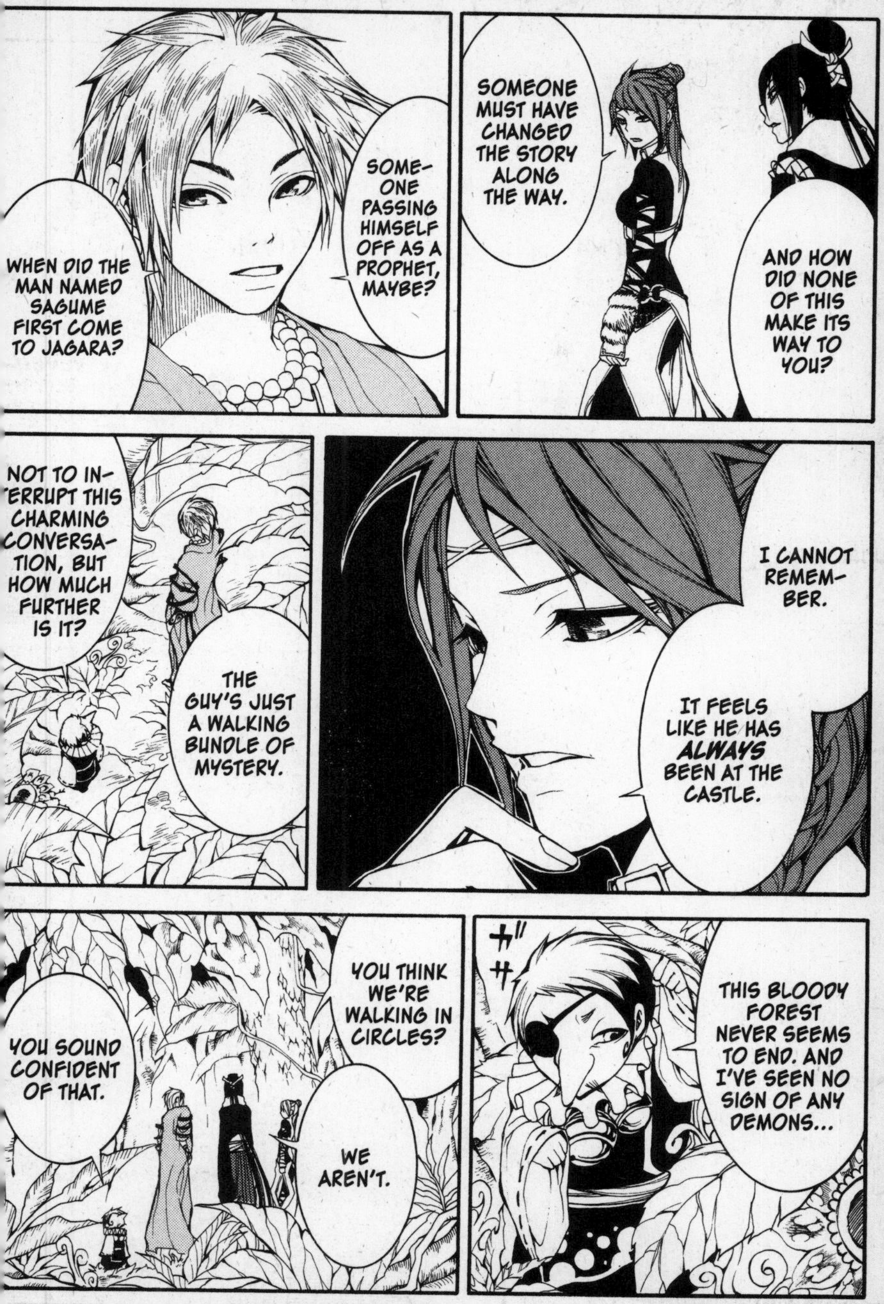
SOMEONE MUST HAVE CHANGED THE STORY ALONG THE WAY.
AND HOW DID NONE OF THIS MAKE ITS WAY TO YOU?
SOME-ONE PASSING HIMSELF OFF AS A PROPHET, MAYBE?
WHEN DID THE MAN NAMED SAGUME FIRST COME TO JAGARA?
I CANNOT REMEM-BER.
IT FEELS LIKE HE HAS ***ALWAYS*** BEEN AT THE CASTLE.
NOT TO IN-TERRUPT THIS CHARMING CONVERSA-TION, BUT HOW MUCH FURTHER IS IT?
THE GUY'S JUST A WALKING BUNDLE OF MYSTERY.
THIS BLOODY FOREST NEVER SEEMS TO END. AND I'VE SEEN NO SIGN OF ANY DEMONS...
YOU THINK WE'RE WALKING IN CIRCLES?
WE AREN'T.
YOU SOUND CONFIDENT OF THAT.

I REMEMBER THE SCENERY.

WE'RE NOT PASSING THE SAME LANDMARKS.

YOU COULD JUST BE SAYIN' THAT.

OGUNA NEVER SAYS ANYTHING JUST TO SAY IT. LET'S GO.

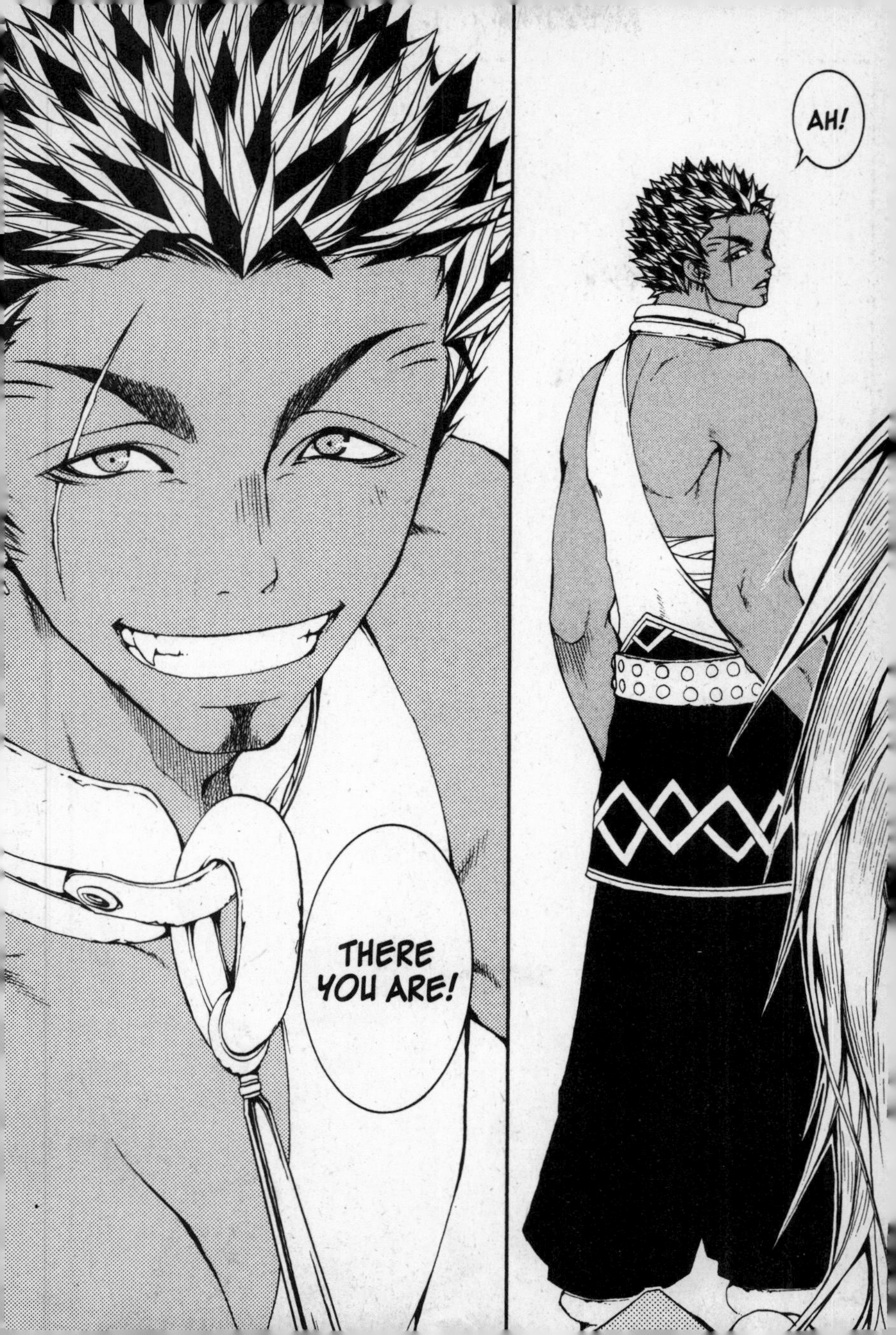
AH!
THERE YOU ARE!

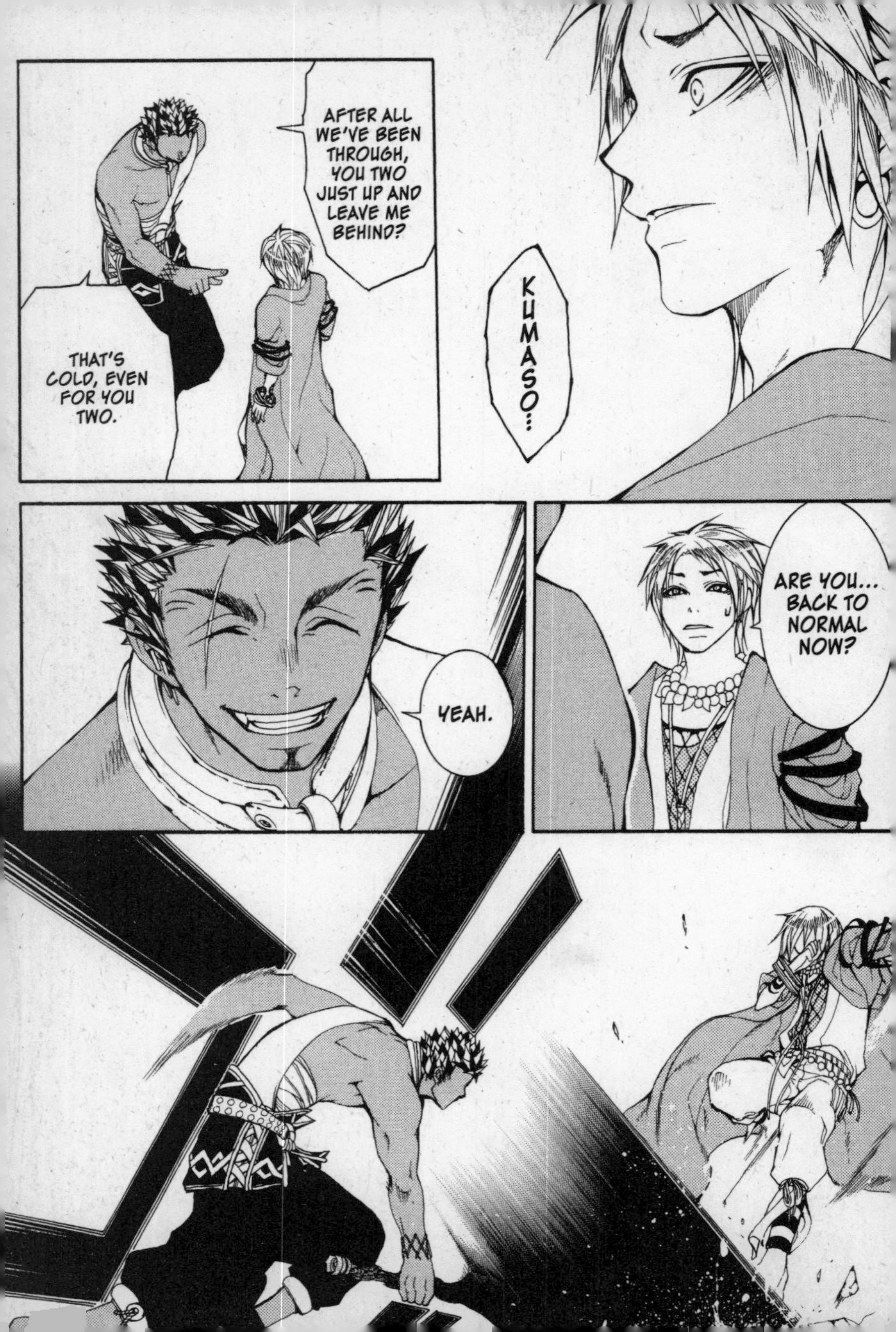
KUMASO...
AFTER ALL WE'VE BEEN THROUGH, YOU TWO JUST UP AND LEAVE ME BEHIND?
THAT'S COLD, EVEN FOR YOU TWO.
ARE YOU... BACK TO NORMAL NOW?
YEAH.

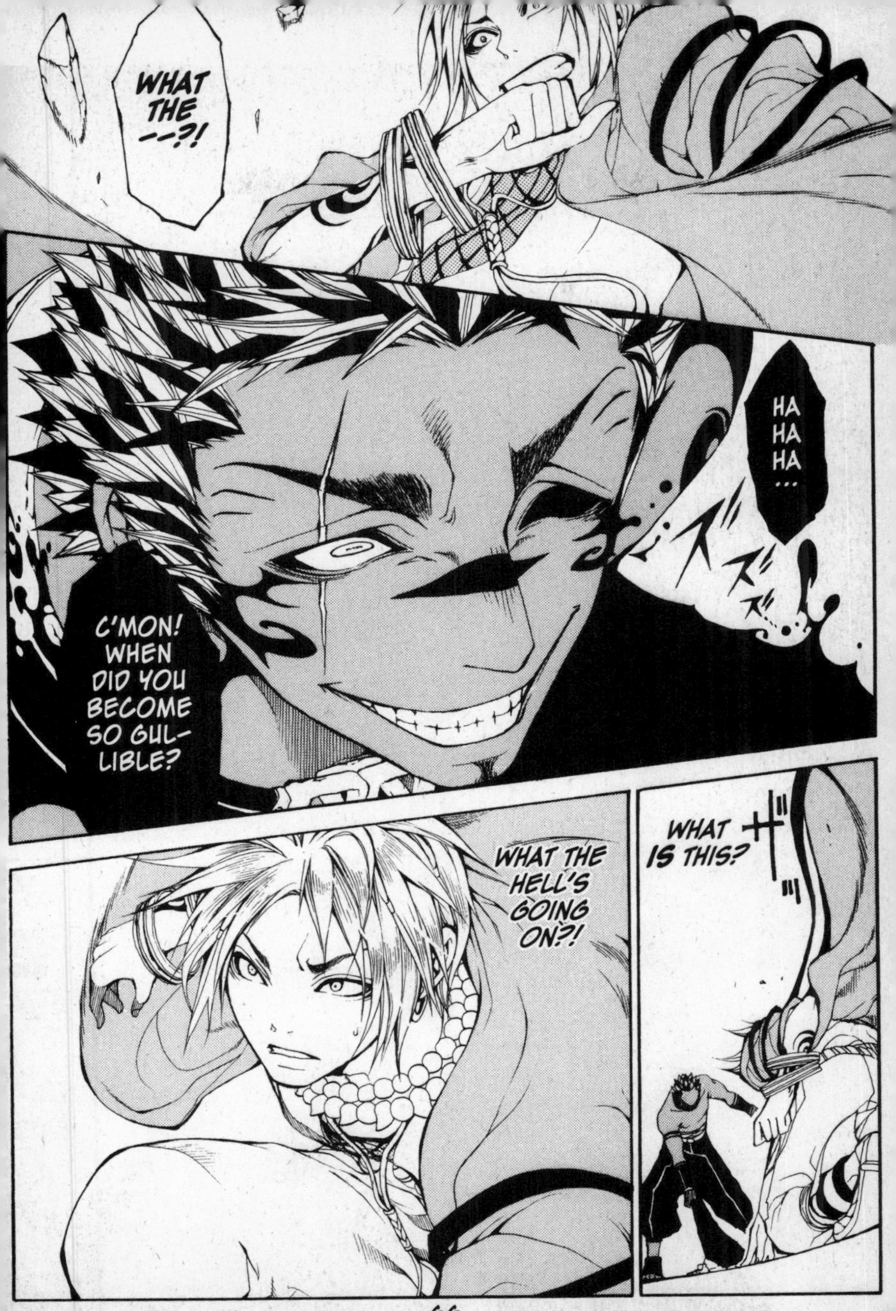
WHAT THE --?!
HA HA HA...
C'MON! WHEN DID YOU BECOME SO GUL-LIBLE?
WHAT IS THIS?
WHAT THE HELL'S GOING ON?!

Chapter 12: Forest of Demons

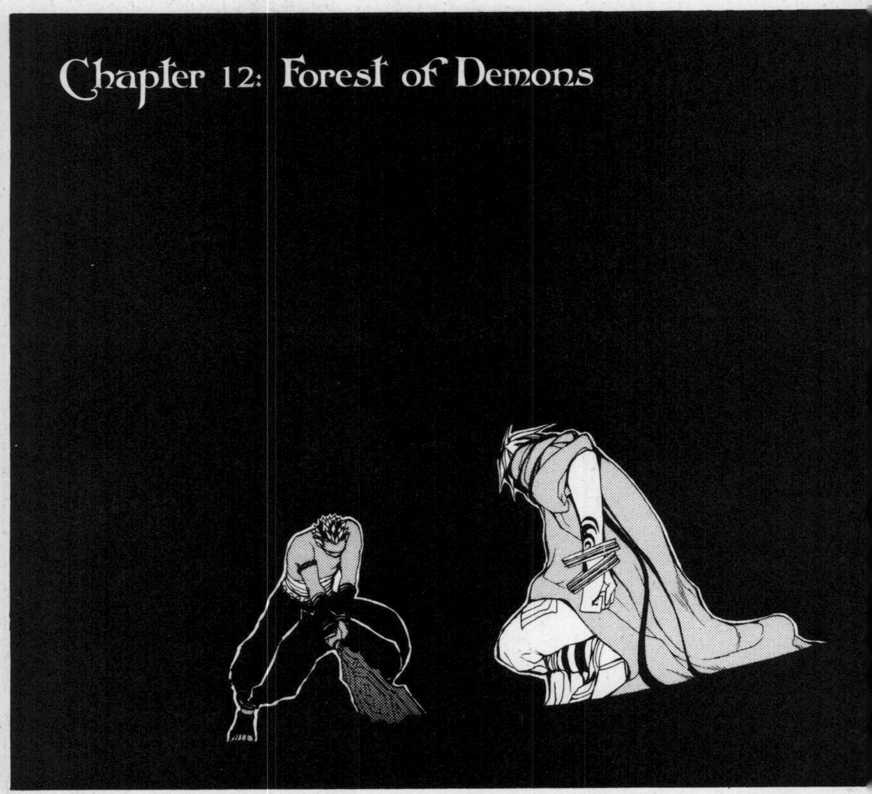

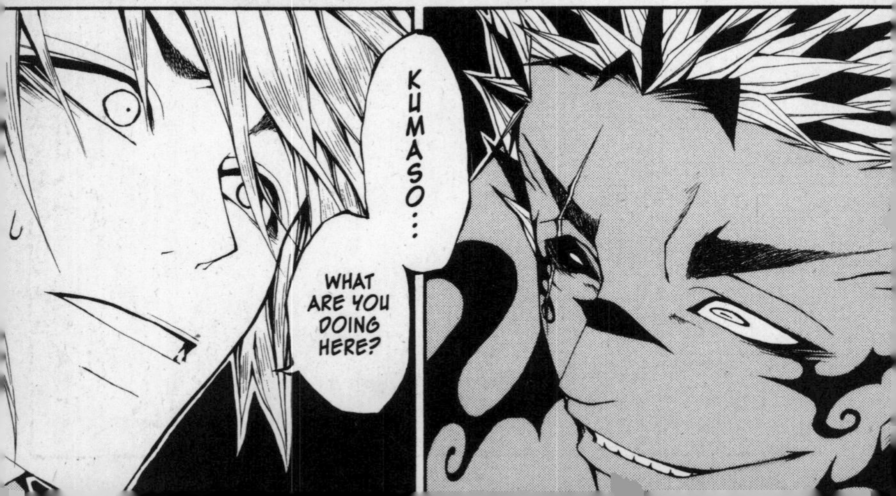
KUMASO...
WHAT ARE YOU DOING HERE?

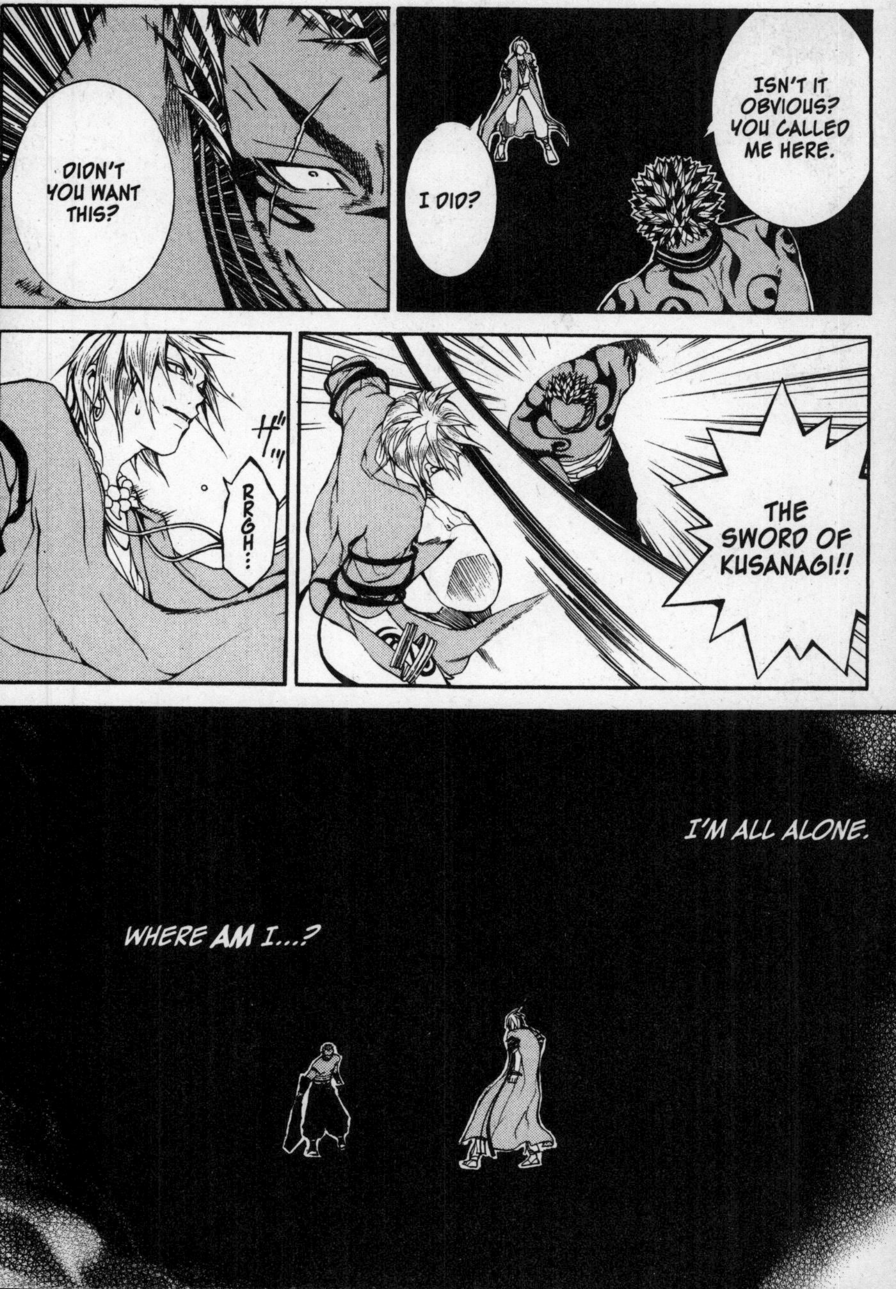
ISN'T IT OBVIOUS? YOU CALLED ME HERE.
I DID?
DIDN'T YOU WANT THIS?
THE SWORD OF KUSANAGI!!
ザッ
RRGH...
I'M ALL ALONE.
WHERE AM I...?

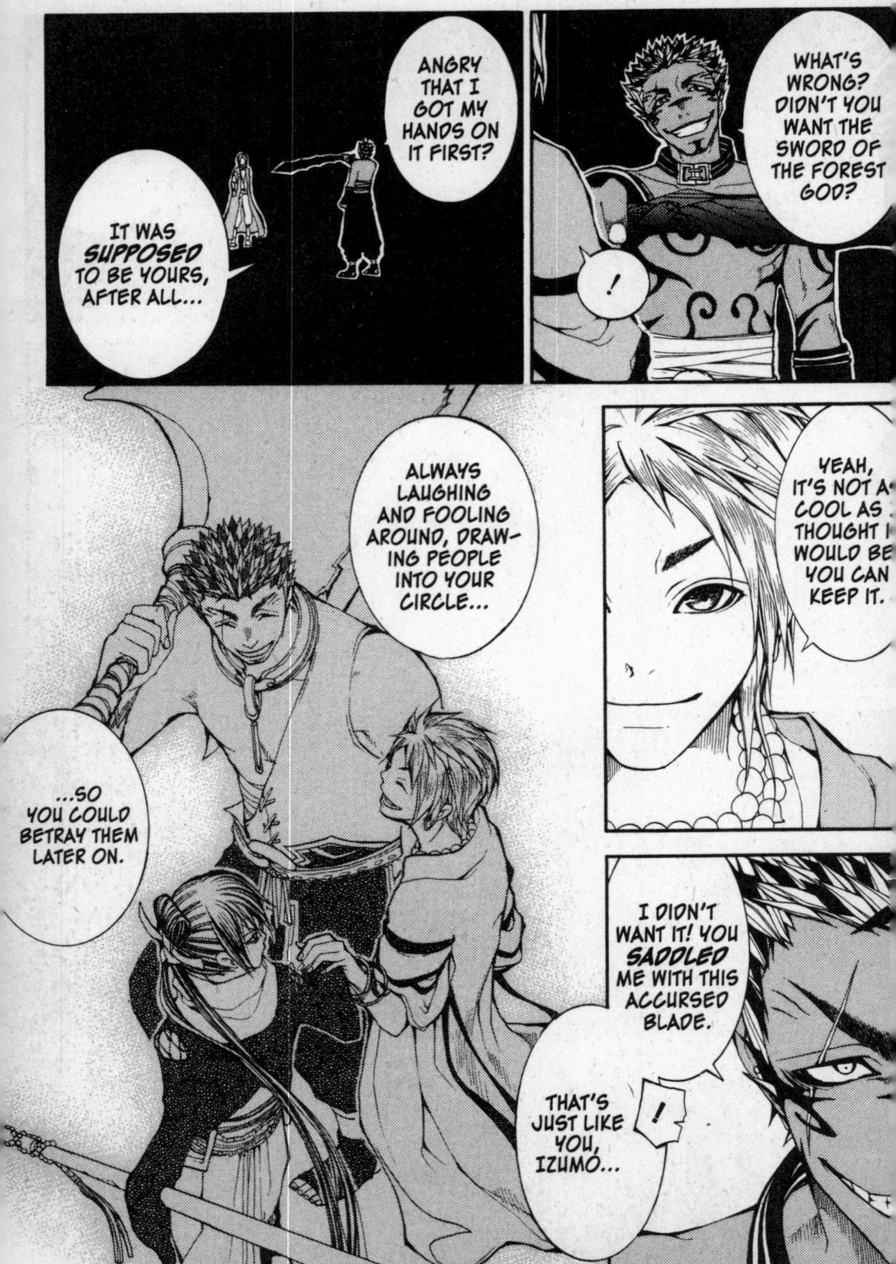
WHAT'S WRONG? DIDN'T YOU WANT THE SWORD OF THE FOREST GOD?
!
ANGRY THAT I GOT MY HANDS ON IT FIRST?
IT WAS *SUPPOSED* TO BE YOURS, AFTER ALL...
YEAH, IT'S NOT A COOL AS THOUGHT I WOULD BE YOU CAN KEEP IT.
I DIDN'T WANT IT! YOU *SADDLED* ME WITH THIS ACCURSED BLADE.
!
THAT'S JUST LIKE YOU, IZUMO...
ALWAYS LAUGHING AND FOOLING AROUND, DRAWING PEOPLE INTO YOUR CIRCLE...
...SO YOU COULD BETRAY THEM LATER ON.

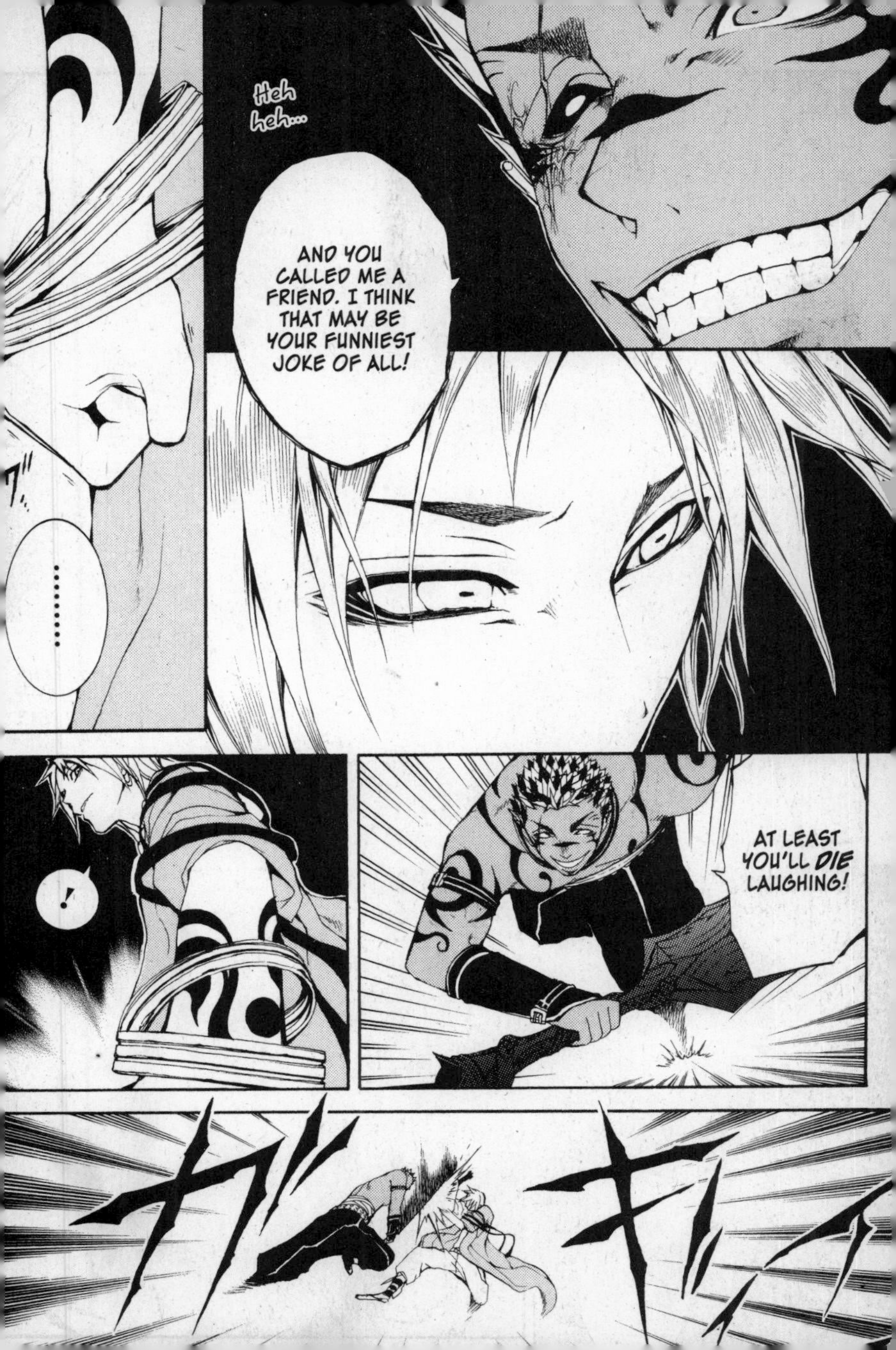
Heh heh...
AND YOU CALLED ME A FRIEND. I THINK THAT MAY BE YOUR FUNNIEST JOKE OF ALL!
....
AT LEAST YOU'LL *DIE* LAUGHING!
!

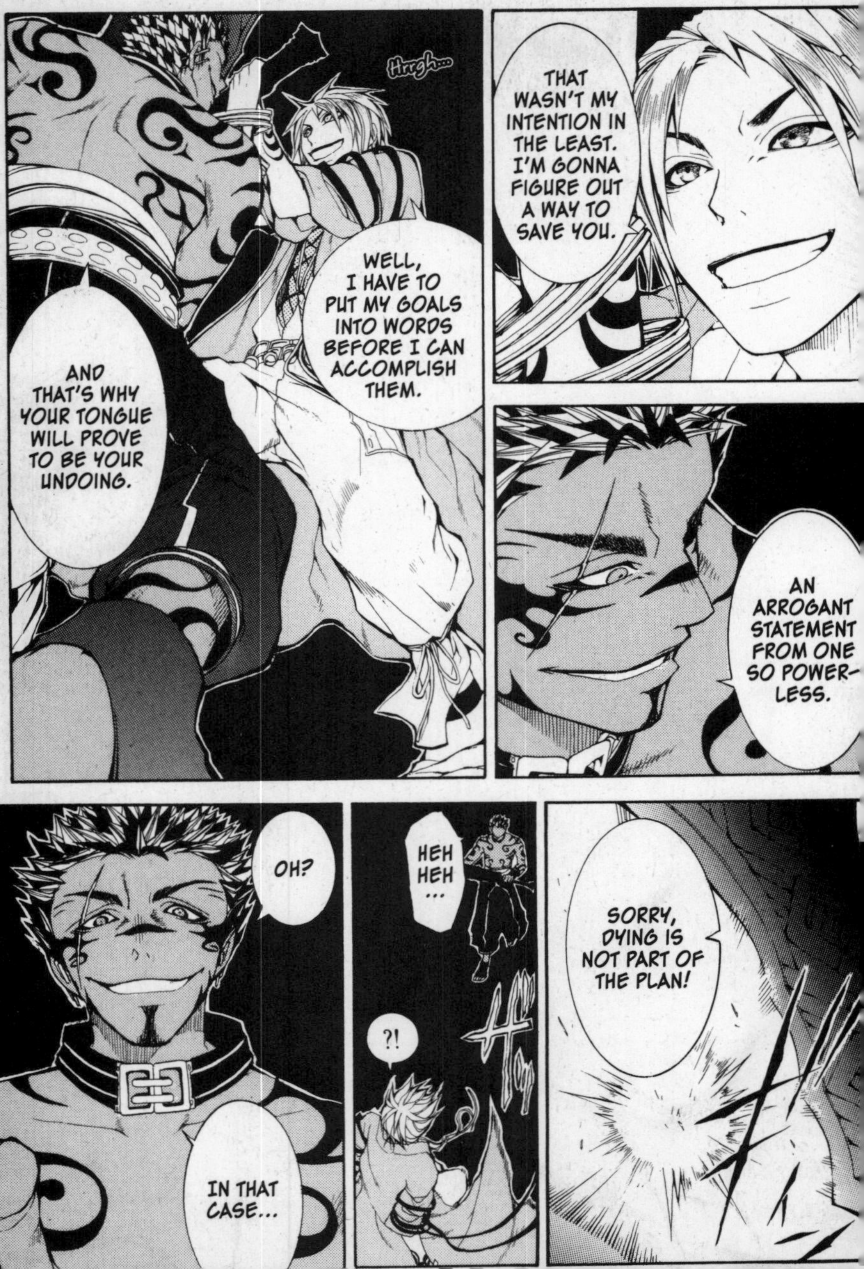
THAT WASN'T MY INTENTION IN THE LEAST. I'M GONNA FIGURE OUT A WAY TO SAVE YOU.
AN ARROGANT STATEMENT FROM ONE SO POWERLESS.
Hrrgh...
WELL, I HAVE TO PUT MY GOALS INTO WORDS BEFORE I CAN ACCOMPLISH THEM.
AND THAT'S WHY YOUR TONGUE WILL PROVE TO BE YOUR UNDOING.
SORRY, DYING IS NOT PART OF THE PLAN!
HEH HEH...
?!
OH?
IN THAT CASE...

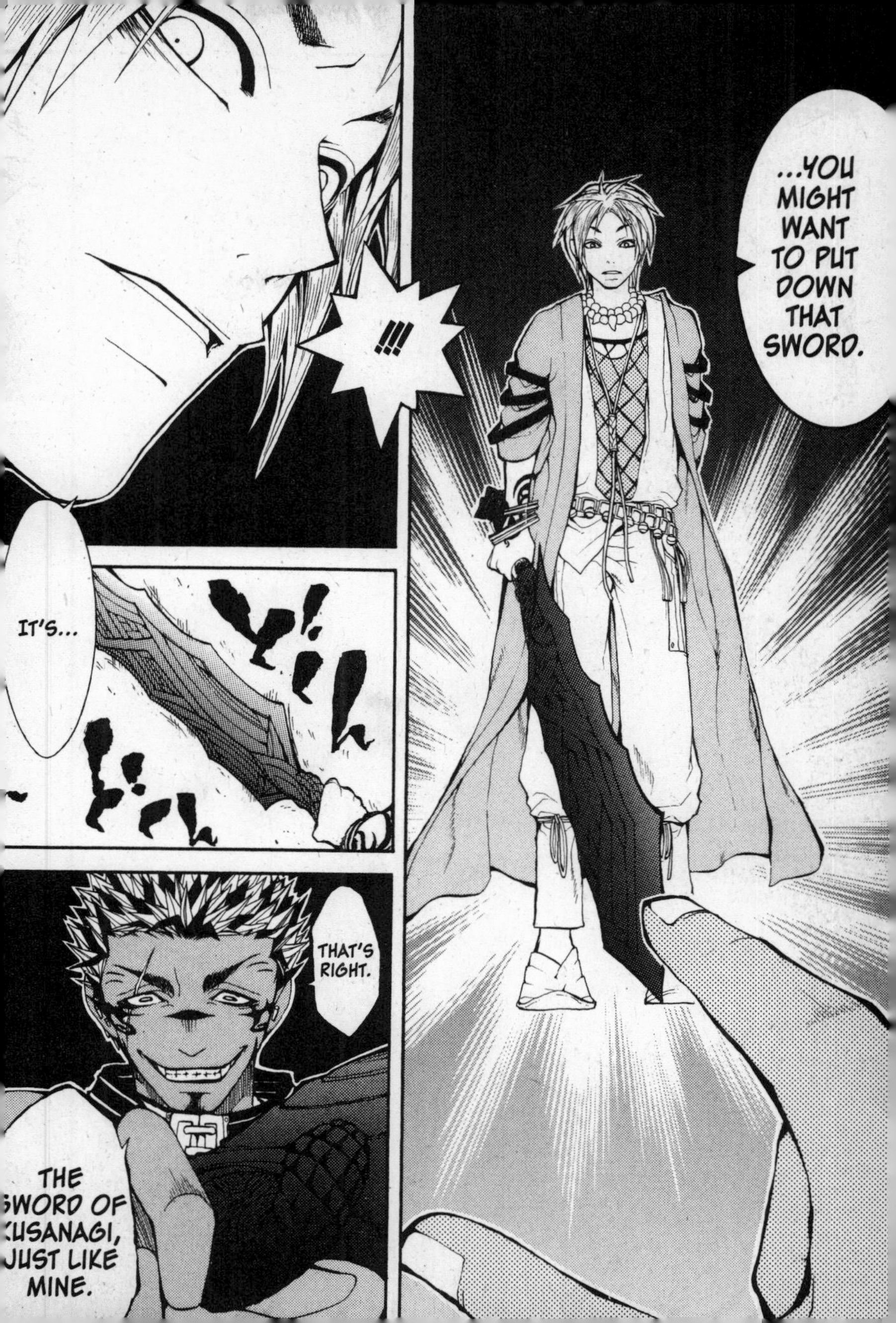
...YOU MIGHT WANT TO PUT DOWN THAT SWORD.
!!!
IT'S...
THAT'S RIGHT.
THE SWORD OF KUSANAGI, JUST LIKE MINE.

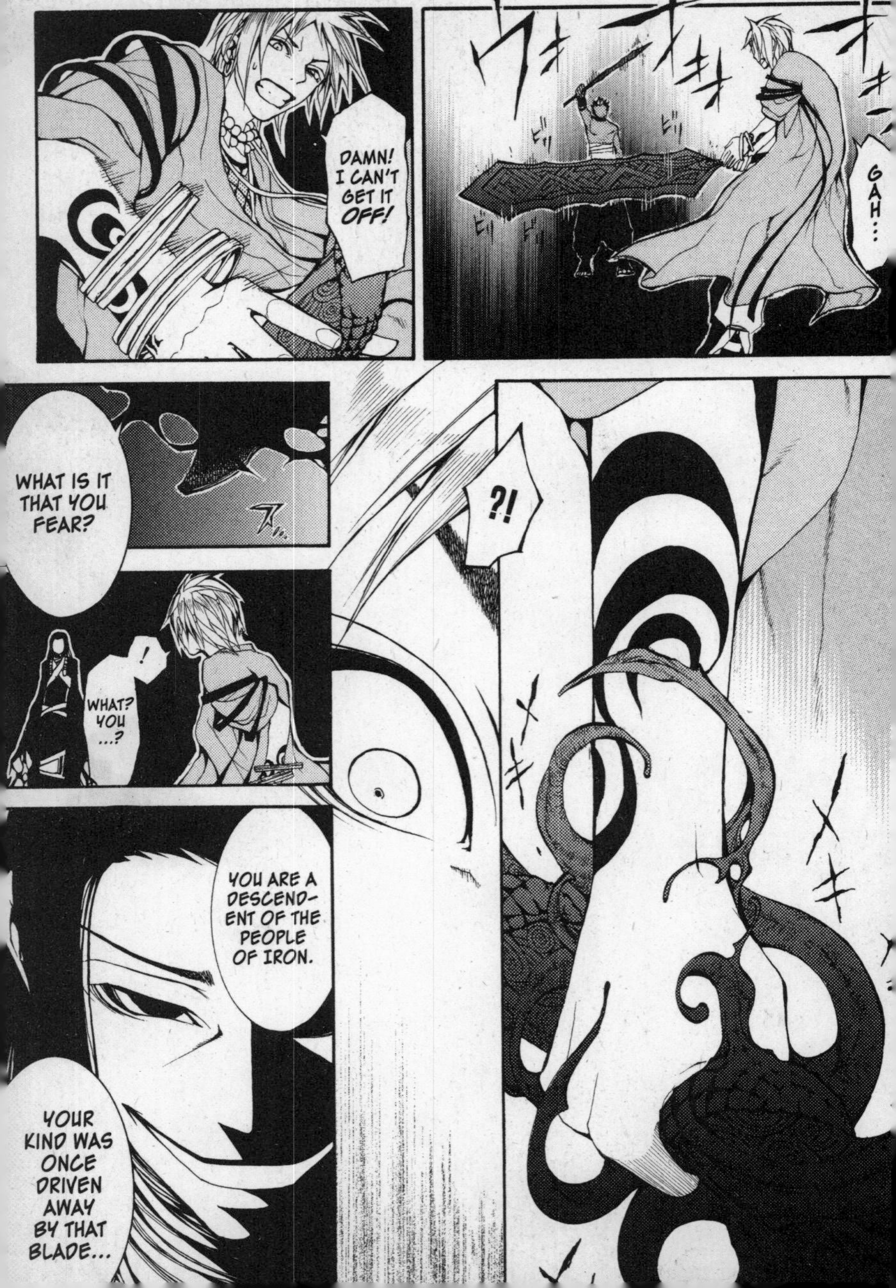
GAH...
DAMN! I CAN'T GET IT OFF!
?!
WHAT IS IT THAT YOU FEAR?
!
WHAT? YOU ...?
YOU ARE A DESCEND-ENT OF THE PEOPLE OF IRON.
YOUR KIND WAS ONCE DRIVEN AWAY BY THAT BLADE...

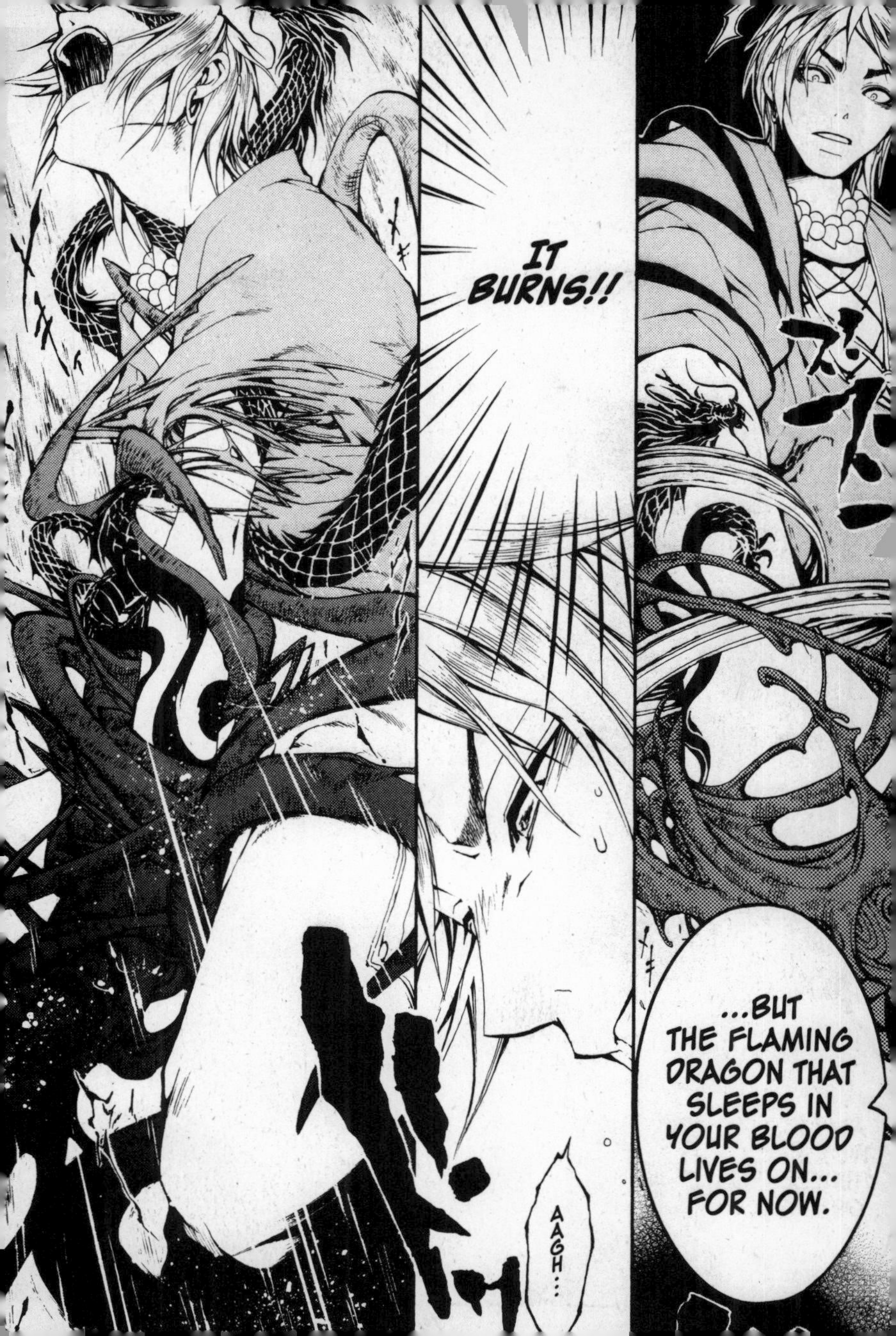
...BUT THE FLAMING DRAGON THAT SLEEPS IN YOUR BLOOD LIVES ON... FOR NOW.
IT BURNS!!
AAGH...

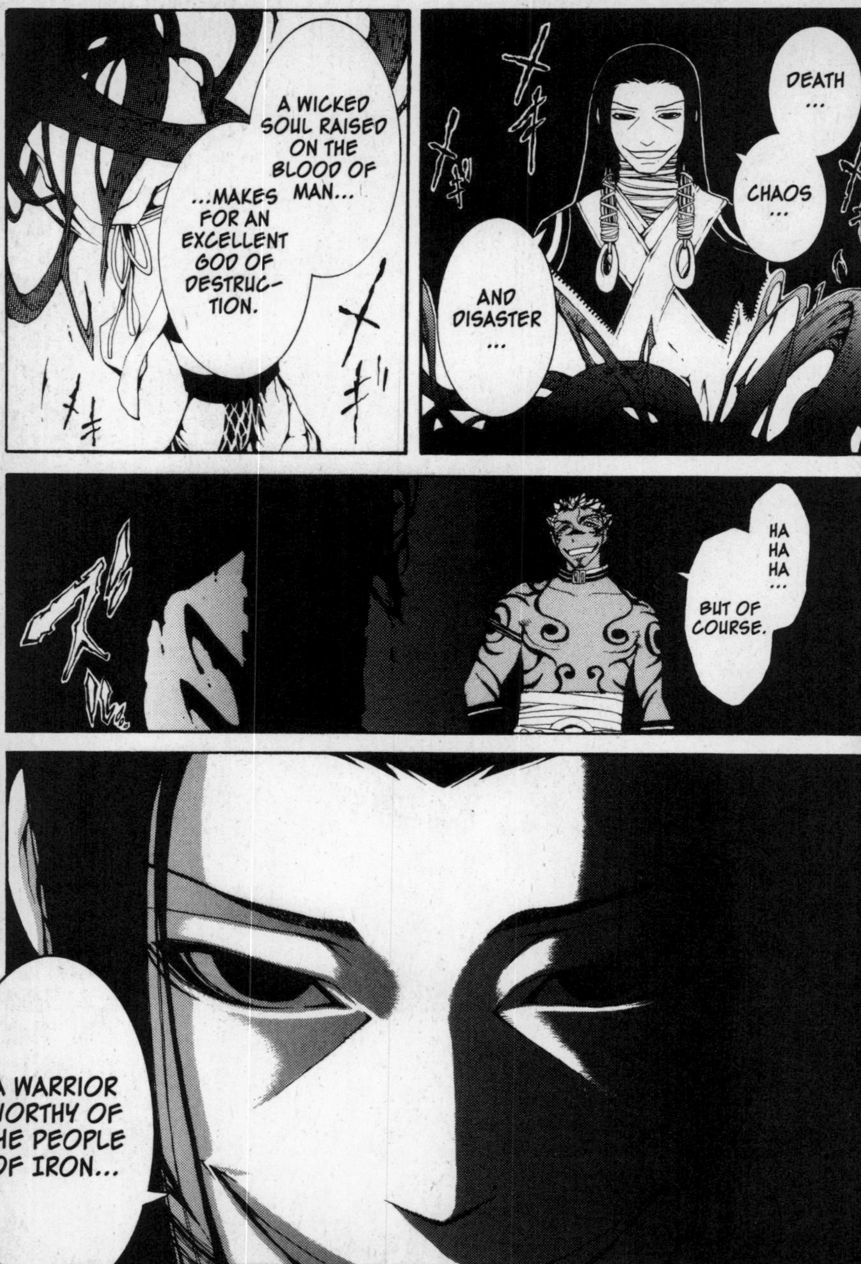
DEATH ...
CHAOS ...
AND DISASTER ...
A WICKED SOUL RAISED ON THE BLOOD OF MAN...
...MAKES FOR AN EXCELLENT GOD OF DESTRUCTION.
HA HA HA ... BUT OF COURSE.
A WARRIOR WORTHY OF THE PEOPLE OF IRON...

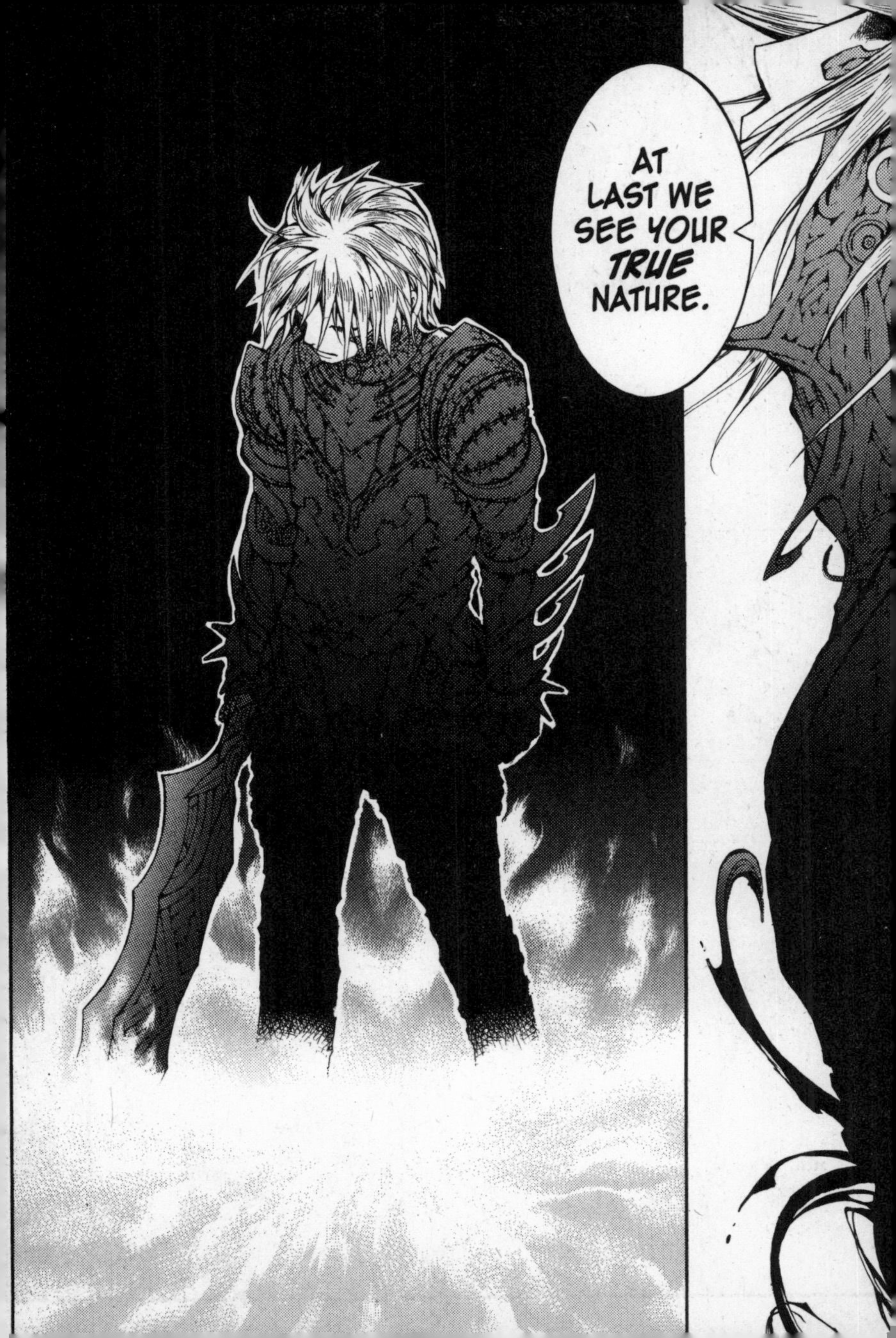
AT LAST WE SEE YOUR TRUE NATURE.

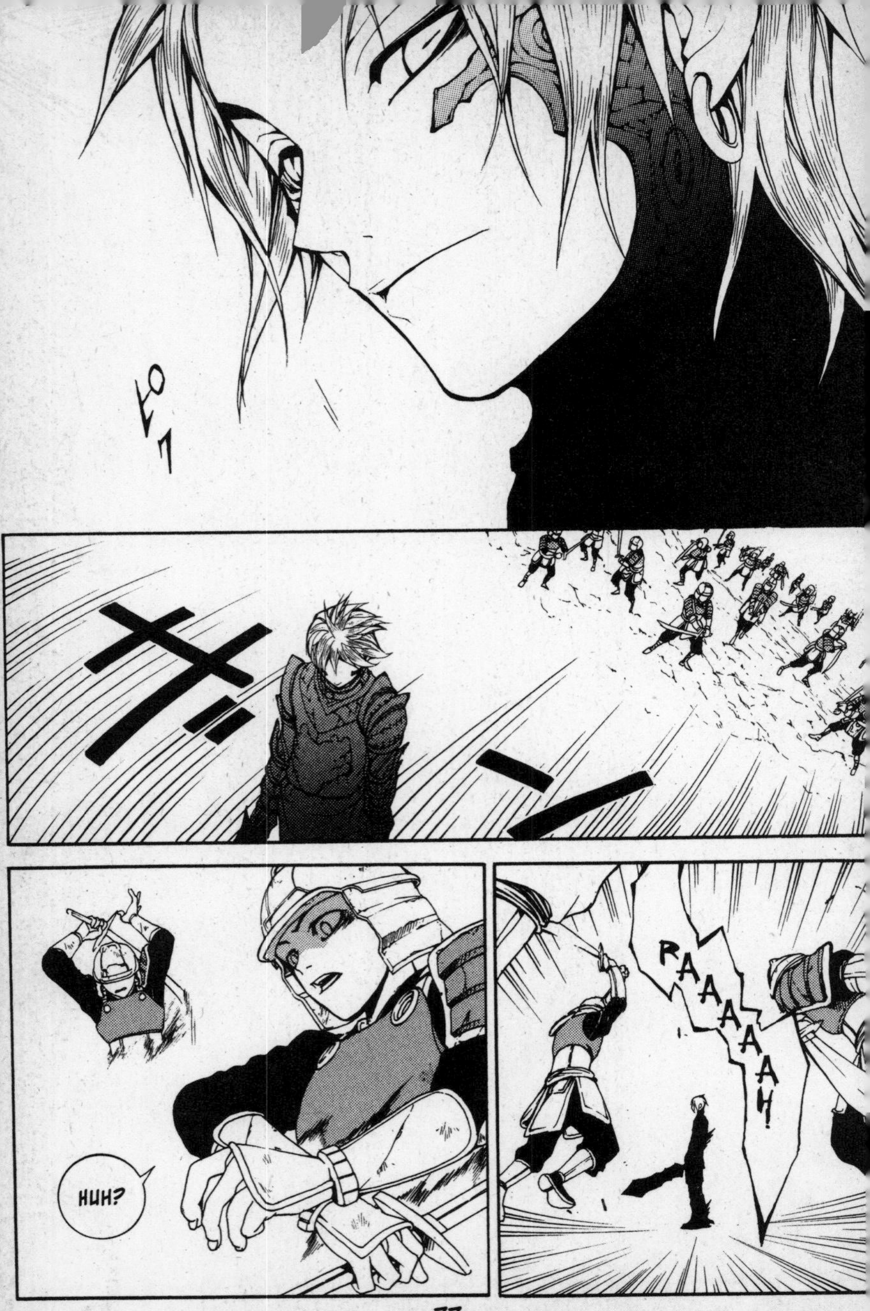
RAAAAAH!
HUH?

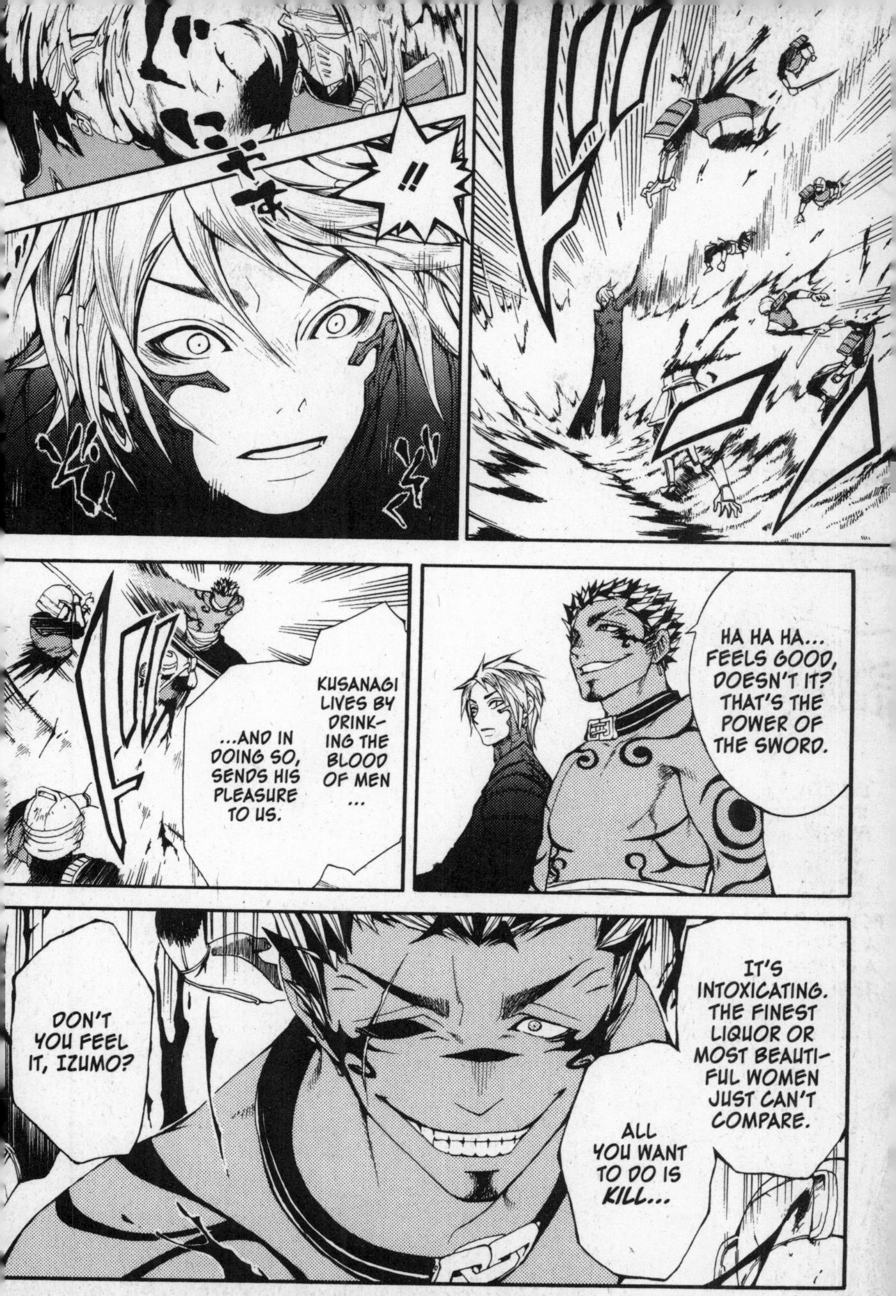
!!
HA HA HA... FEELS GOOD, DOESN'T IT? THAT'S THE POWER OF THE SWORD.
KUSANAGI LIVES BY DRINKING THE BLOOD OF MEN...
...AND IN DOING SO, SENDS HIS PLEASURE TO US.
IT'S INTOXICATING. THE FINEST LIQUOR OR MOST BEAUTIFUL WOMEN JUST CAN'T COMPARE.
ALL YOU WANT TO DO IS *KILL*...
DON'T YOU FEEL IT, IZUMO?

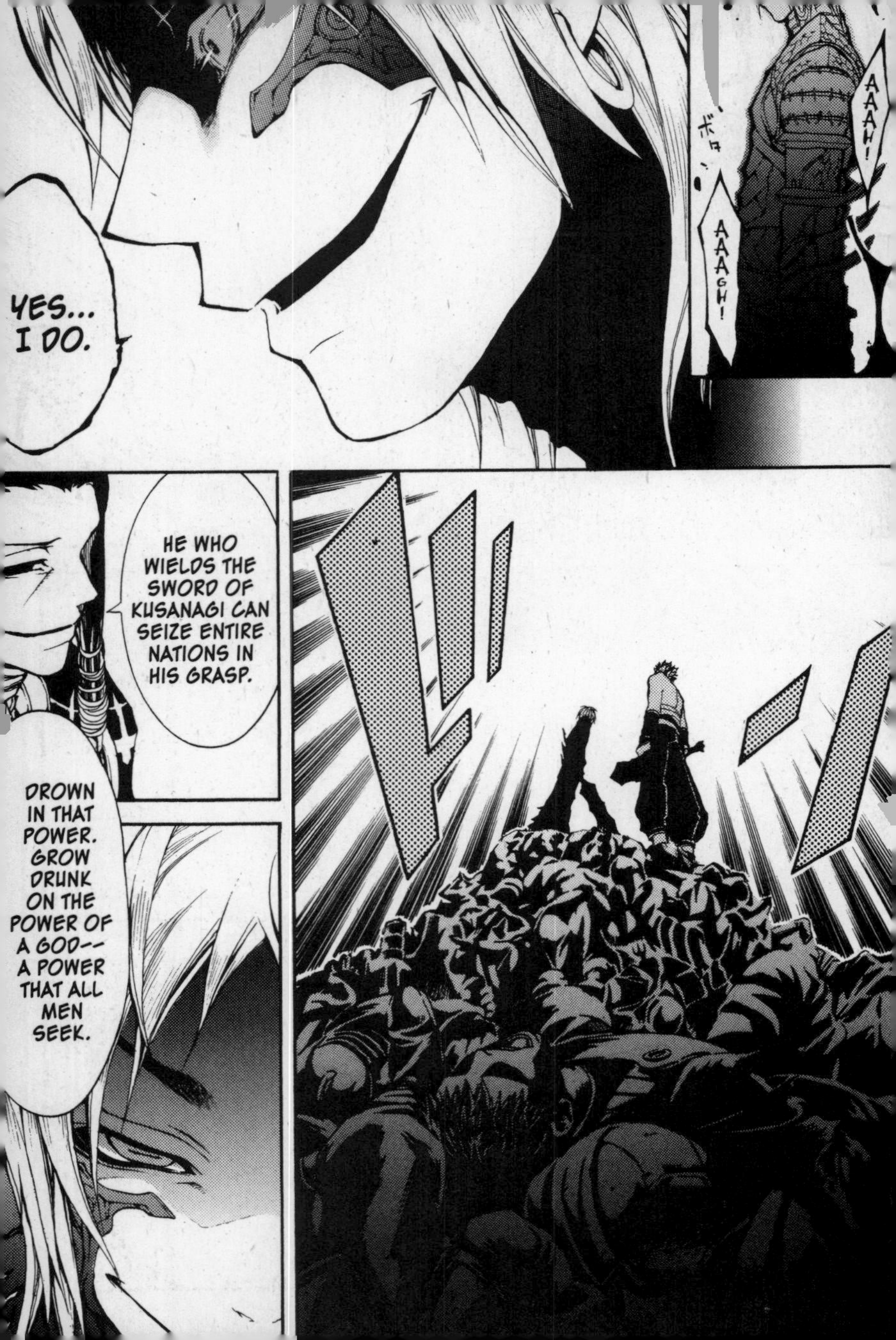
AAAH!
AAAAGH!
YES... I DO.
HE WHO WIELDS THE SWORD OF KUSANAGI CAN SEIZE ENTIRE NATIONS IN HIS GRASP.
DROWN IN THAT POWER. GROW DRUNK ON THE POWER OF A GOD-- A POWER THAT ALL MEN SEEK.

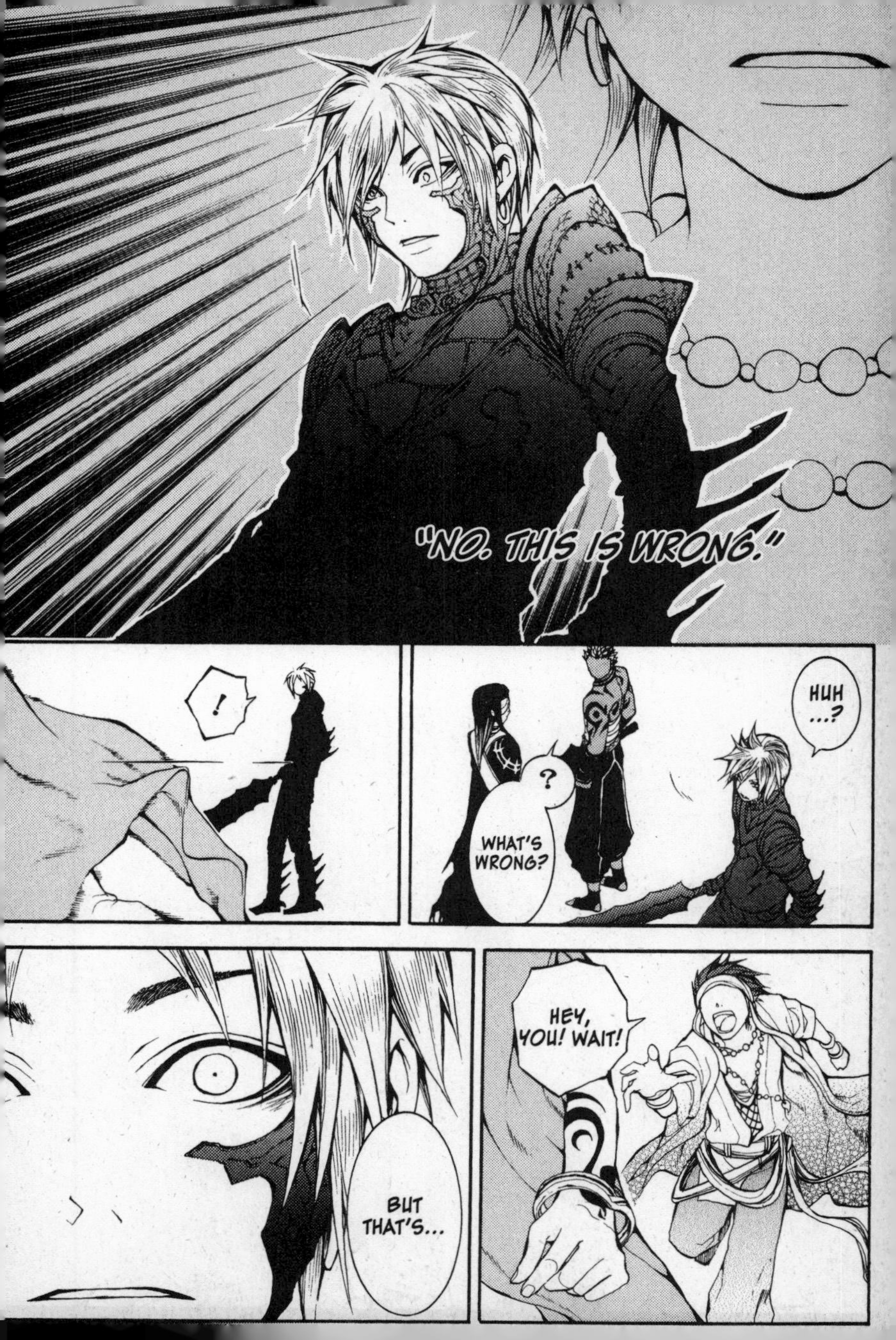
"NO. THIS IS WRONG."
HUH ...?
?
WHAT'S WRONG?
!
HEY, YOU! WAIT!
BUT THAT'S...

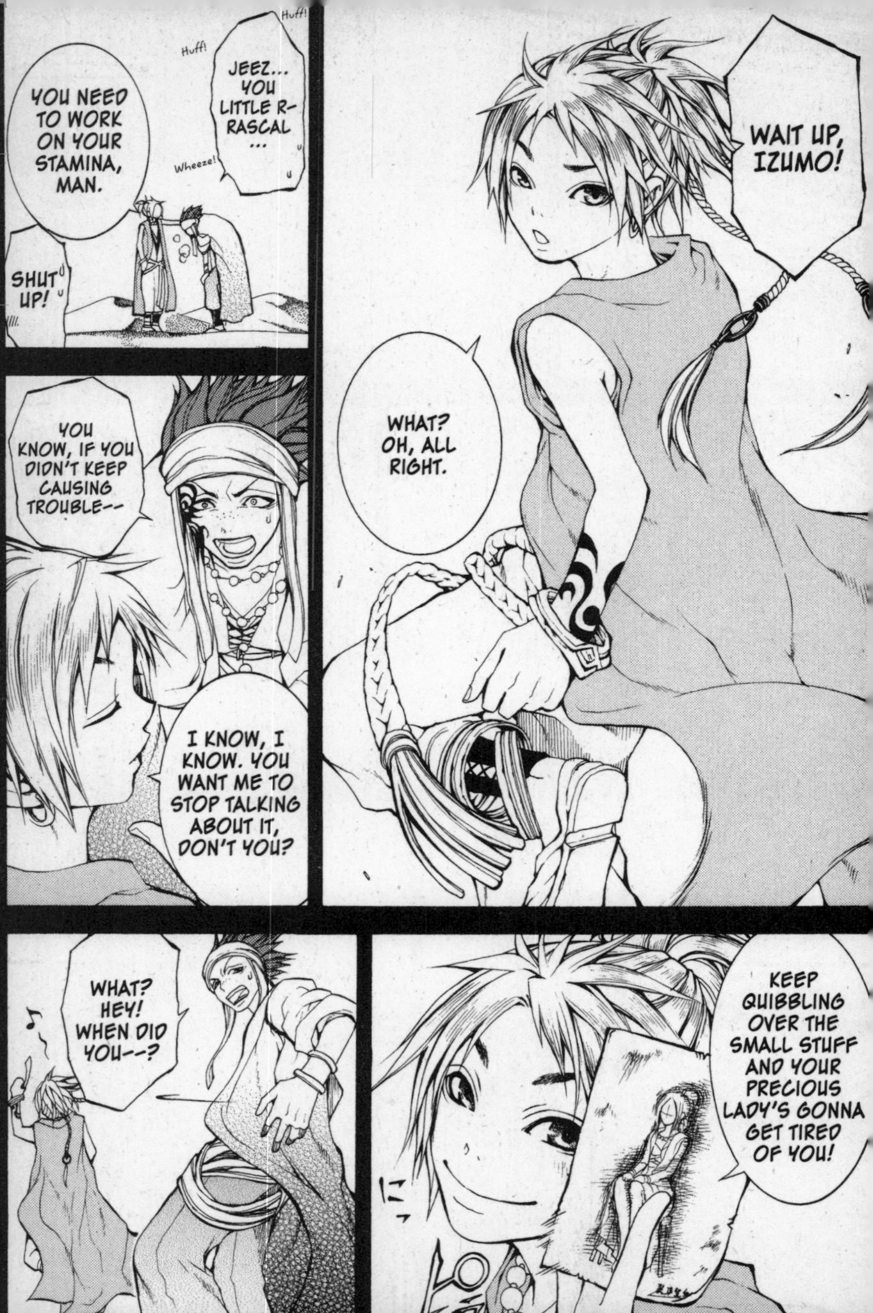
WAIT UP, IZUMO!
WHAT? OH, ALL RIGHT.
Huff!
JEEZ... YOU LITTLE R-RASCAL ...
Huff!
Wheeze!
YOU NEED TO WORK ON YOUR STAMINA, MAN.
SHUT UP!
YOU KNOW, IF YOU DIDN'T KEEP CAUSING TROUBLE--
I KNOW, I KNOW. YOU WANT ME TO STOP TALKING ABOUT IT, DON'T YOU?
KEEP QUIBBLING OVER THE SMALL STUFF AND YOUR PRECIOUS LADY'S GONNA GET TIRED OF YOU!
WHAT? HEY! WHEN DID YOU--?

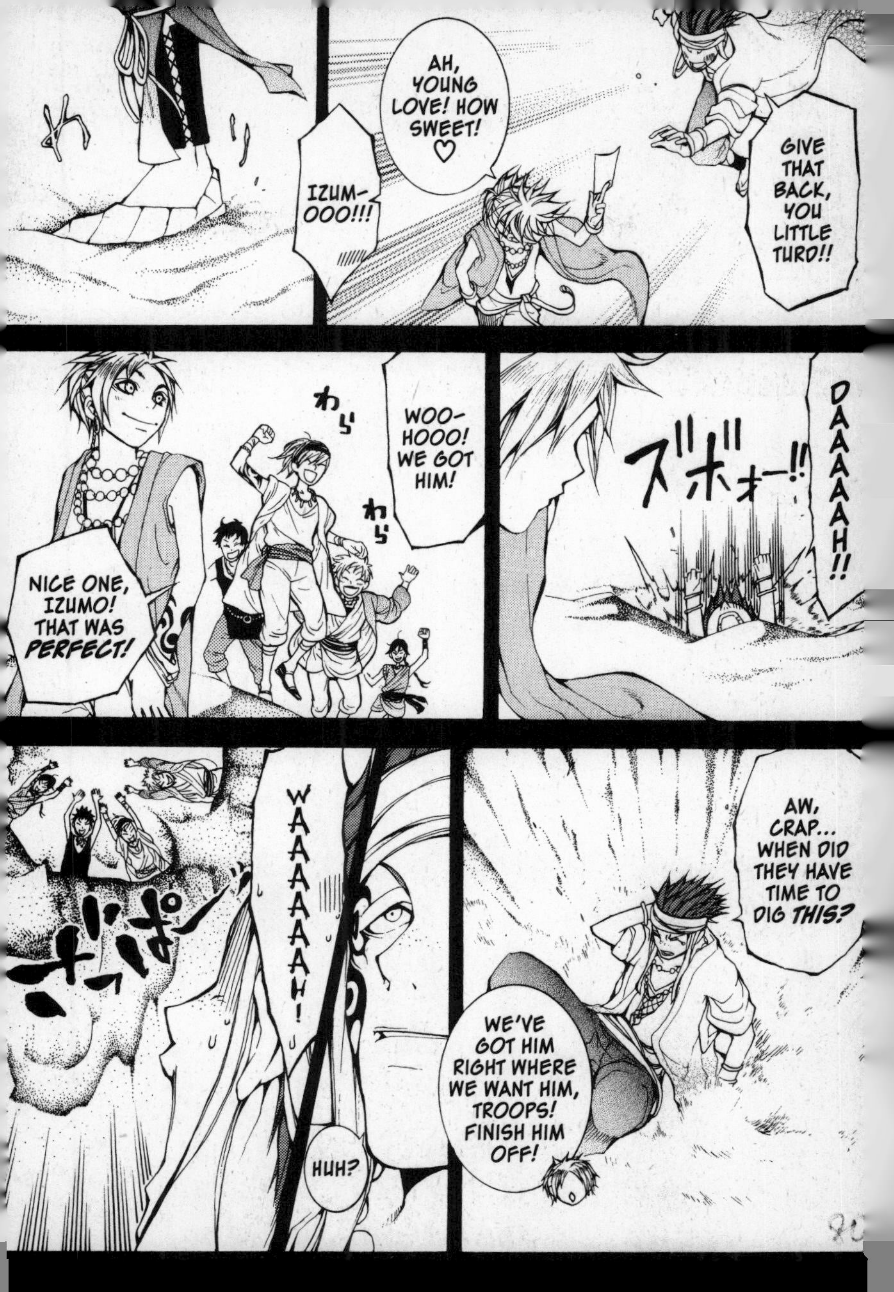
GIVE THAT BACK, YOU LITTLE TURD!!
AH, YOUNG LOVE! HOW SWEET! ♡
IZUM-OOO!!!
DAAAAAAH!!
ズボォー!!
WOO-HOOO! WE GOT HIM!
わら
わら
NICE ONE, IZUMO! THAT WAS *PERFECT!*
AW, CRAP... WHEN DID THEY HAVE TIME TO DIG *THIS?*
WE'VE GOT HIM RIGHT WHERE WE WANT HIM, TROOPS! FINISH HIM OFF!
WAAAAAAAH!
HUH?

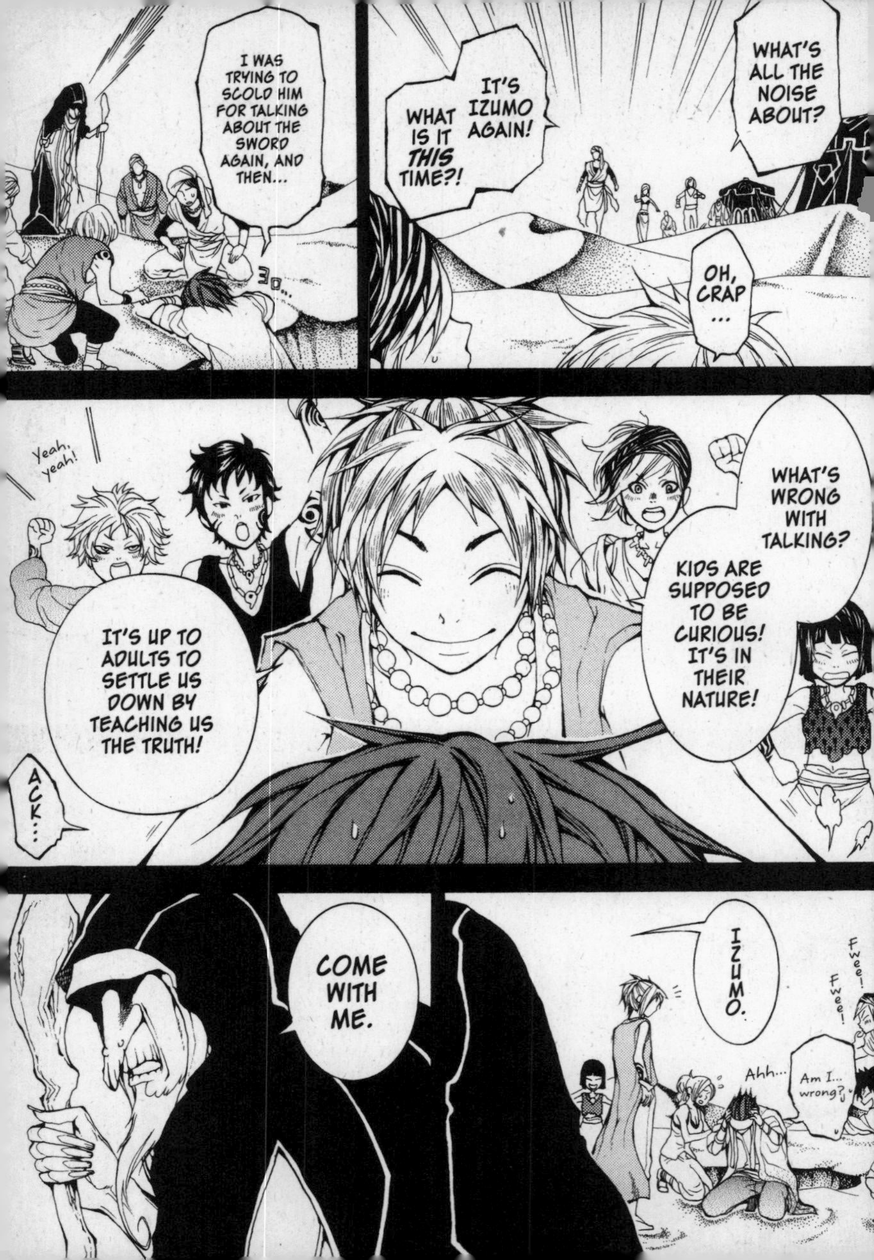
WHAT'S ALL THE NOISE ABOUT?
IT'S IZUMO AGAIN!
WHAT IS IT THIS TIME?!
OH, CRAP ...
I WAS TRYING TO SCOLD HIM FOR TALKING ABOUT THE SWORD AGAIN, AND THEN...
WHAT'S WRONG WITH TALKING?
KIDS ARE SUPPOSED TO BE CURIOUS! IT'S IN THEIR NATURE!
Yeah, yeah!
IT'S UP TO ADULTS TO SETTLE US DOWN BY TEACHING US THE TRUTH!
ACK...
IZUMO.
Fwee! Fwee!
Am I... wrong?
Ahh...
COME WITH ME.

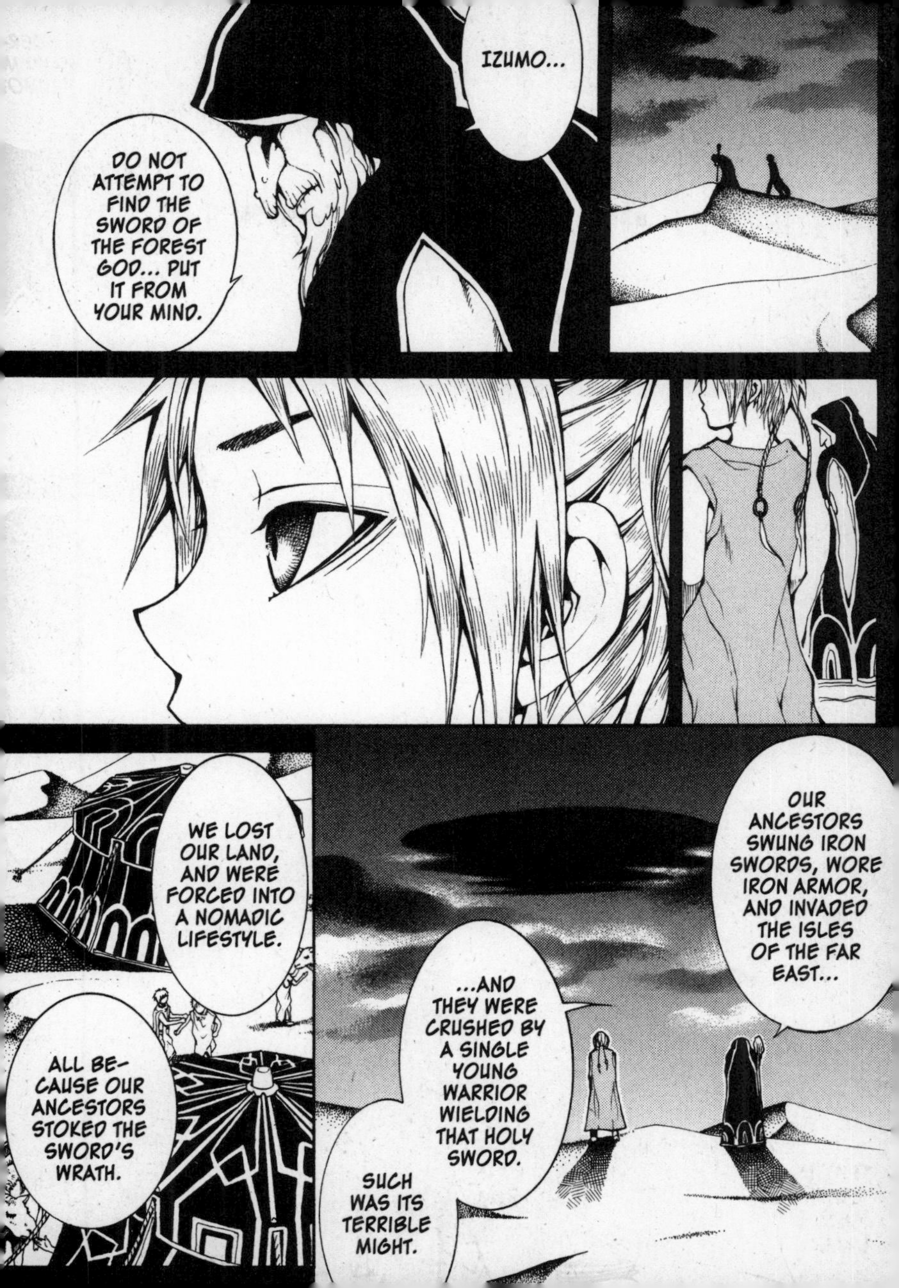
IZUMO...
DO NOT ATTEMPT TO FIND THE SWORD OF THE FOREST GOD... PUT IT FROM YOUR MIND.
OUR ANCESTORS SWUNG IRON SWORDS, WORE IRON ARMOR, AND INVADED THE ISLES OF THE FAR EAST...
...AND THEY WERE CRUSHED BY A SINGLE YOUNG WARRIOR WIELDING THAT HOLY SWORD.
SUCH WAS ITS TERRIBLE MIGHT.
WE LOST OUR LAND, AND WERE FORCED INTO A NOMADIC LIFESTYLE.
ALL BE-CAUSE OUR ANCESTORS STOKED THE SWORD'S WRATH.

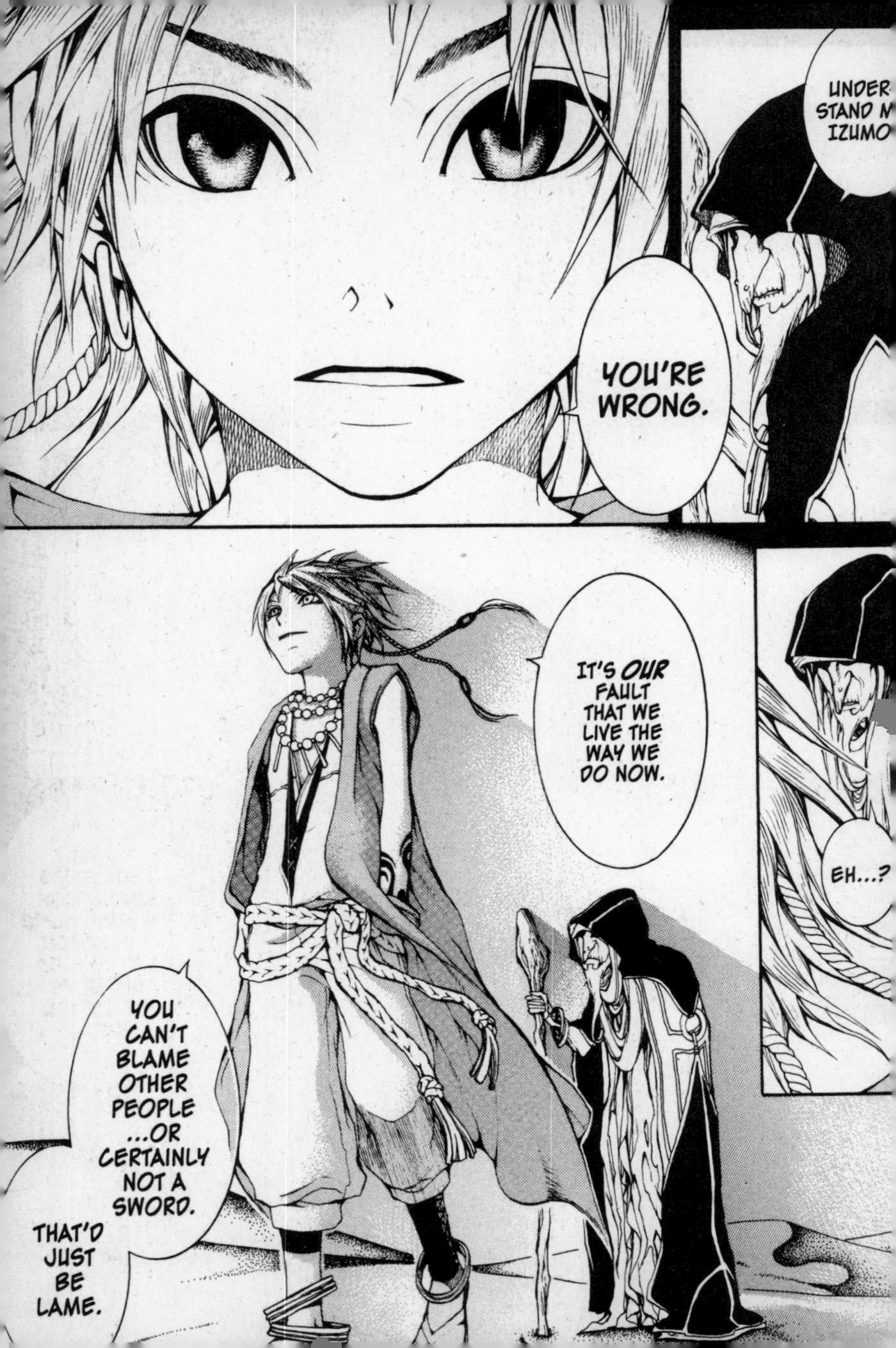
UNDER-STAND M IZUMO
YOU'RE WRONG.
EH...?
IT'S *OUR* FAULT THAT WE LIVE THE WAY WE DO NOW.
YOU CAN'T BLAME OTHER PEOPLE ...OR CERTAINLY NOT A SWORD.
THAT'D JUST BE LAME.

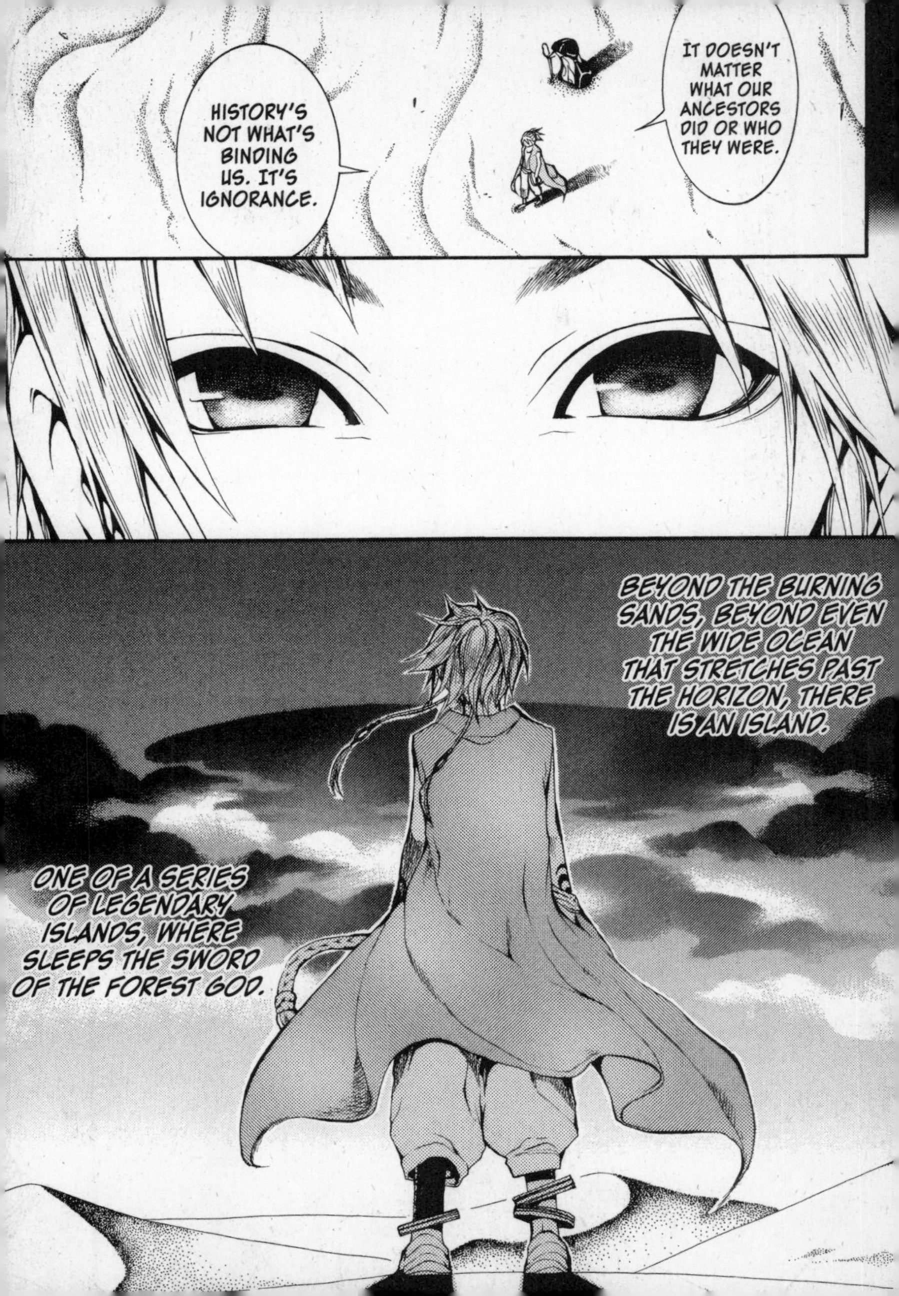
IT DOESN'T MATTER WHAT OUR ANCESTORS DID OR WHO THEY WERE.
HISTORY'S NOT WHAT'S BINDING US. IT'S IGNORANCE.
BEYOND THE BURNING SANDS, BEYOND EVEN THE WIDE OCEAN THAT STRETCHES PAST THE HORIZON, THERE IS AN ISLAND.
ONE OF A SERIES OF LEGENDARY ISLANDS, WHERE SLEEPS THE SWORD OF THE FOREST GOD.

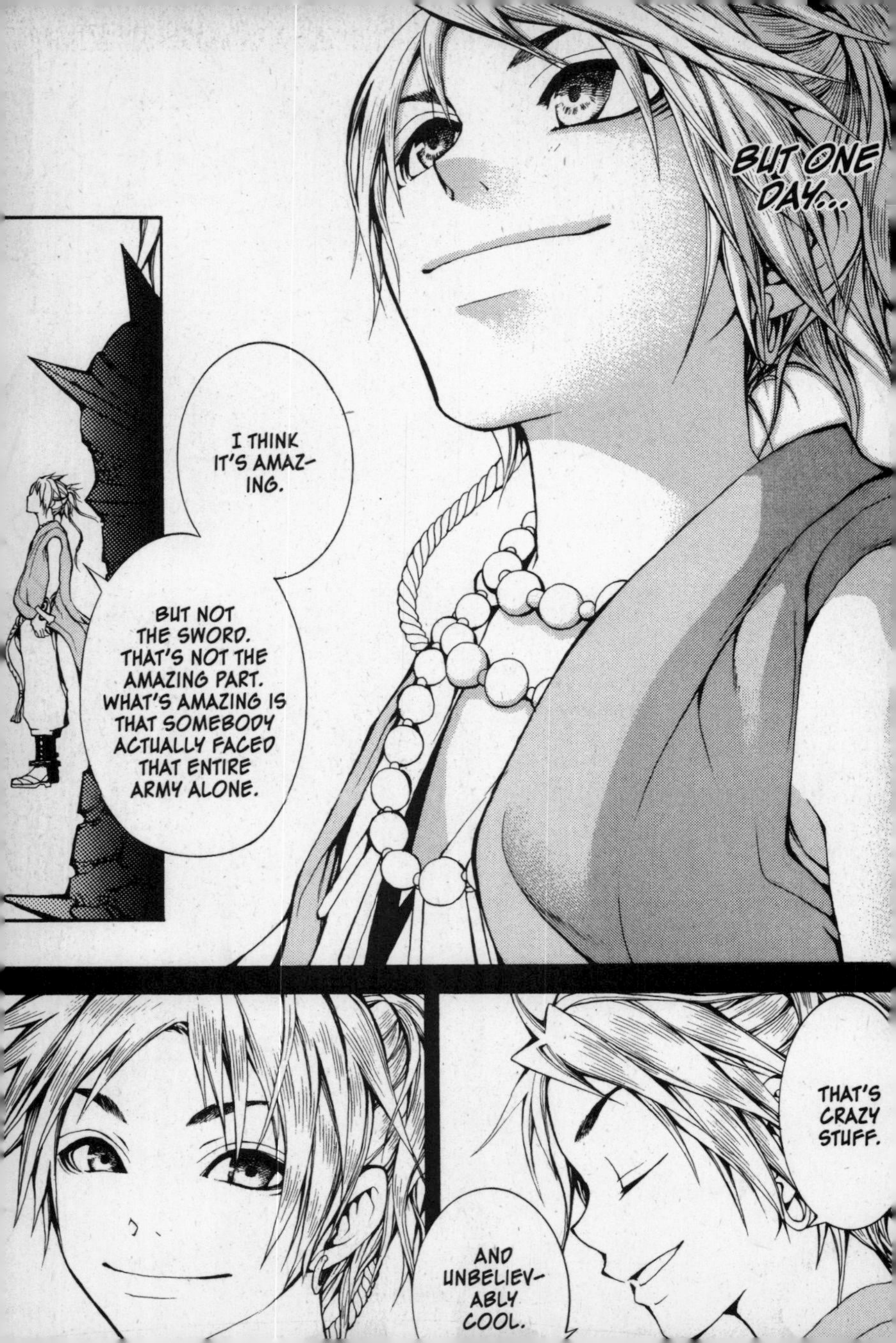
BUT ONE DAY...
I THINK IT'S AMAZ-ING.
BUT NOT THE SWORD. THAT'S NOT THE AMAZING PART. WHAT'S AMAZING IS THAT SOMEBODY ACTUALLY FACED THAT ENTIRE ARMY ALONE.
THAT'S CRAZY STUFF.
AND UNBELIEV-ABLY COOL.

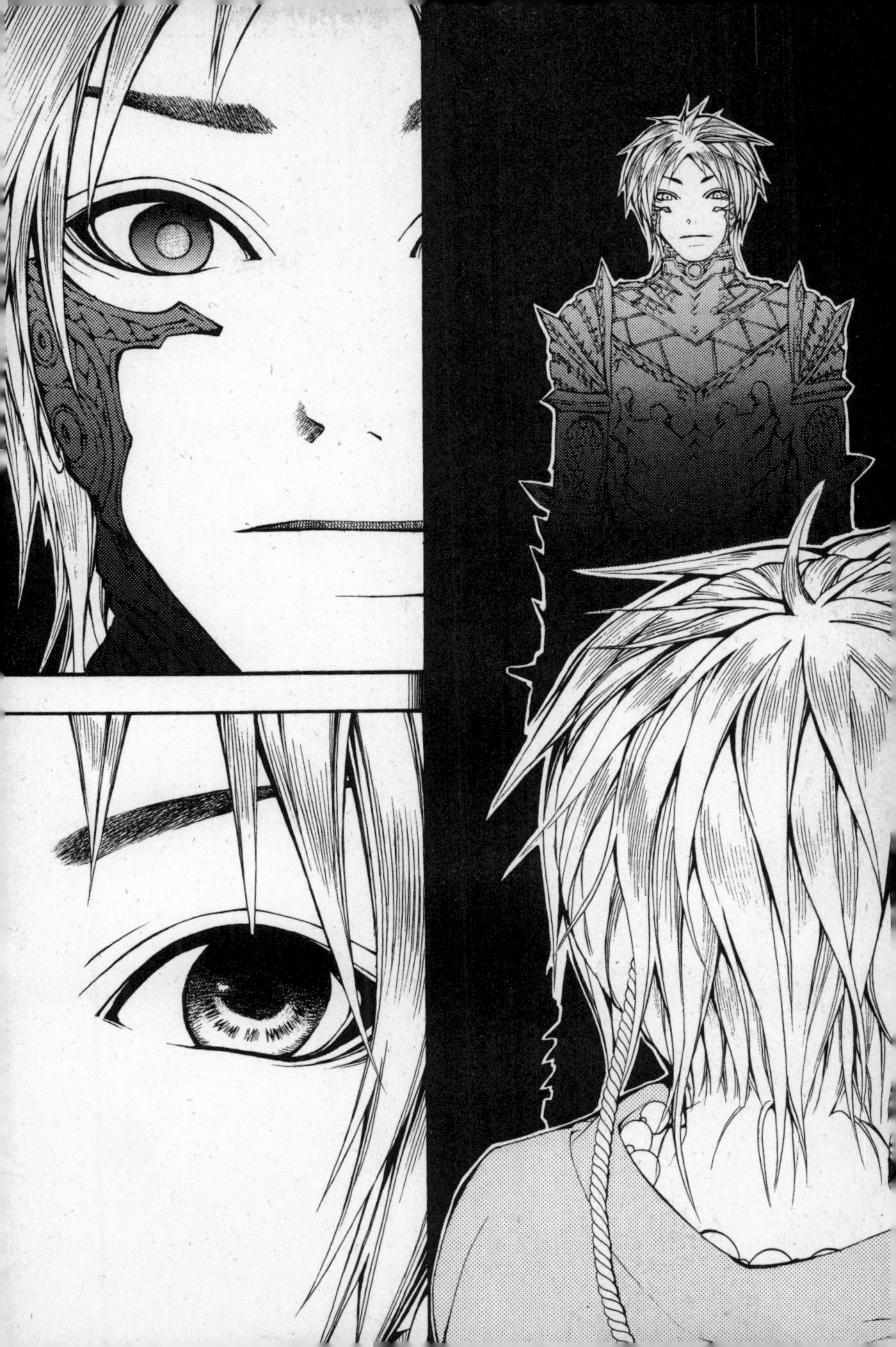

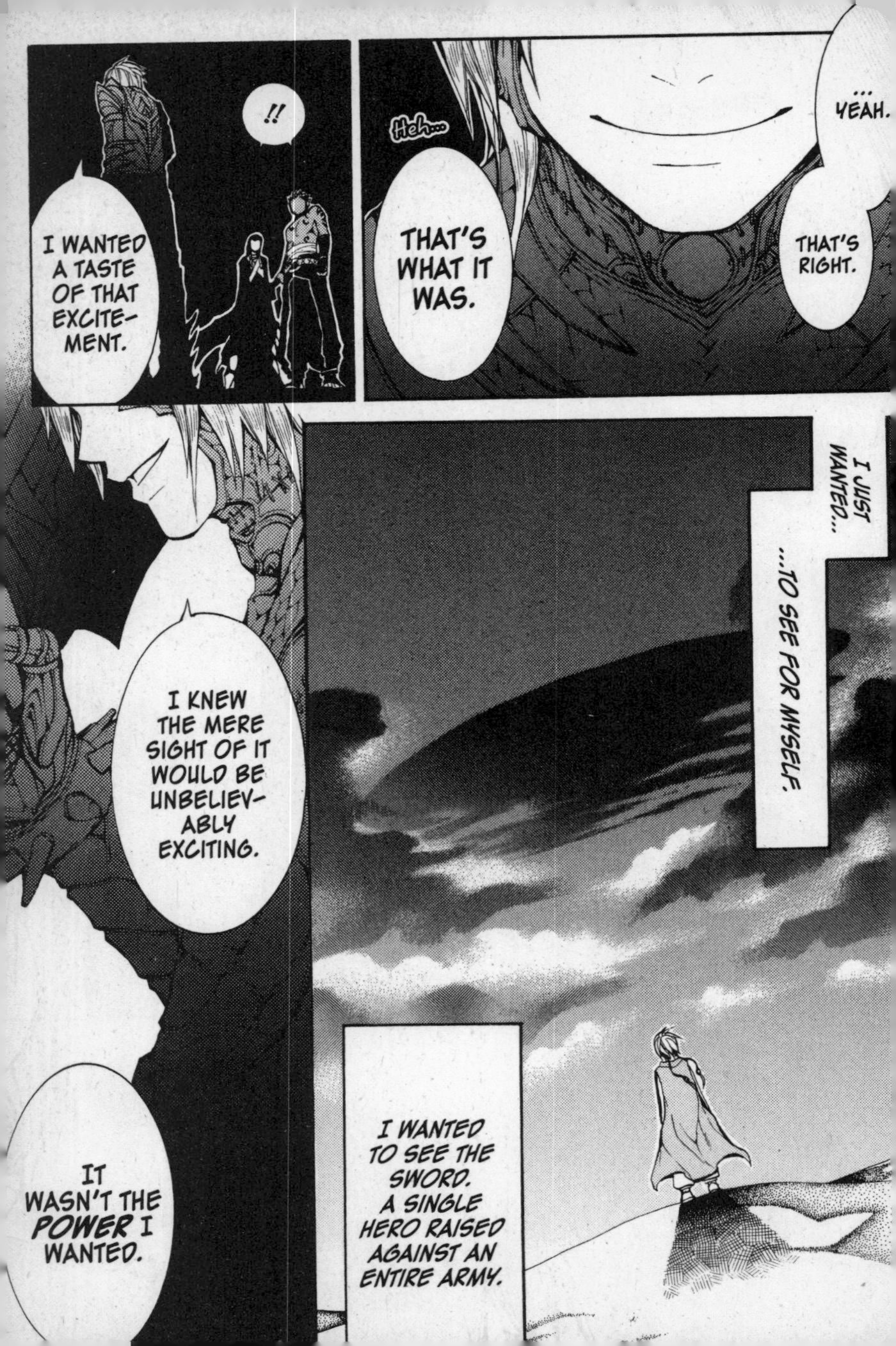
...YEAH.
THAT'S RIGHT.
Heh...
THAT'S WHAT IT WAS.
!!
I WANTED A TASTE OF THAT EXCITEMENT.
I JUST WANTED...
...TO SEE FOR MYSELF.
I WANTED TO SEE THE SWORD. A SINGLE HERO RAISED AGAINST AN ENTIRE ARMY.
I KNEW THE MERE SIGHT OF IT WOULD BE UNBELIEVABLY EXCITING.
IT WASN'T THE *POWER* I WANTED.

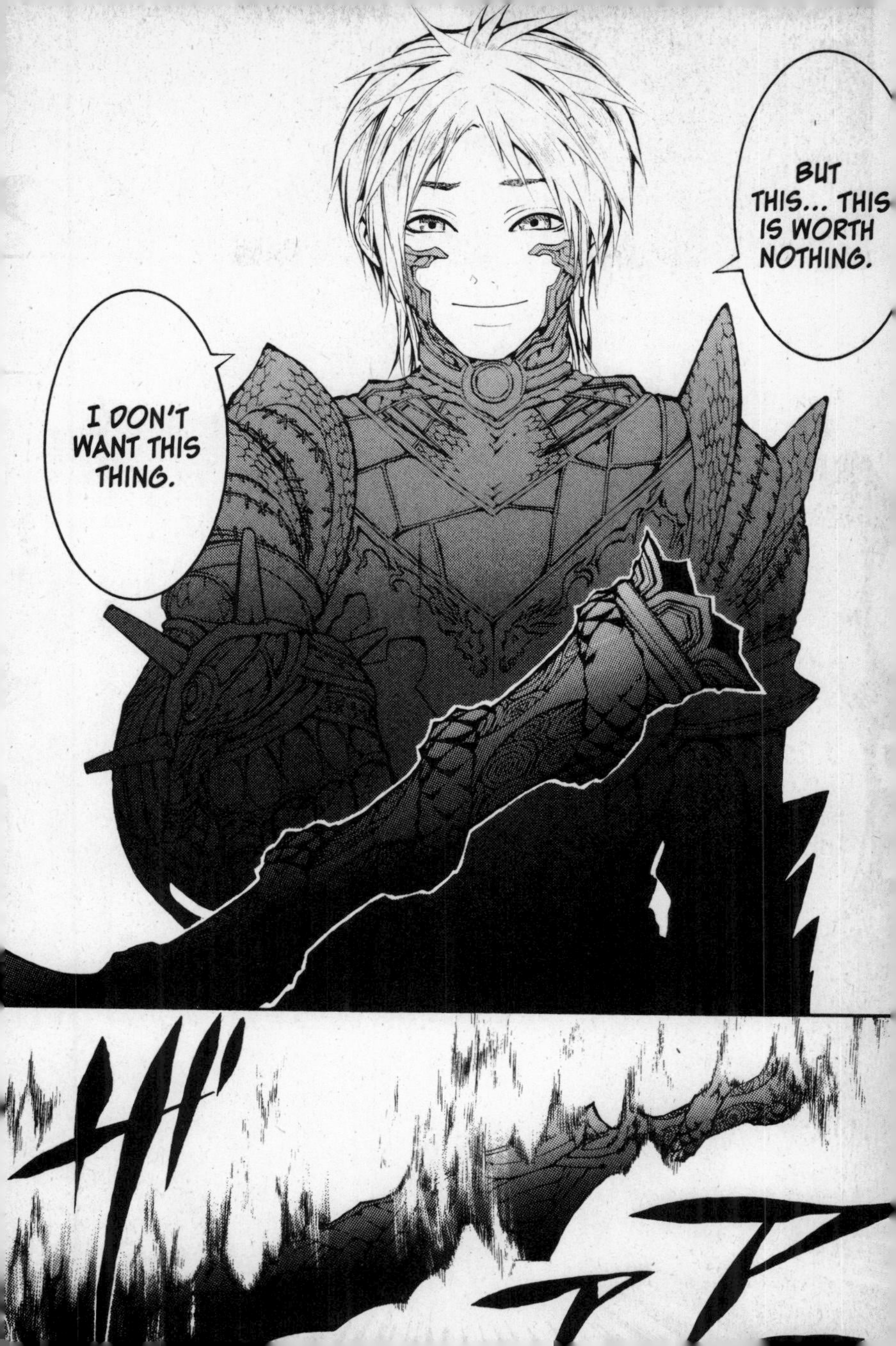
BUT THIS... THIS IS WORTH NOTHING.
I DON'T WANT THIS THING.

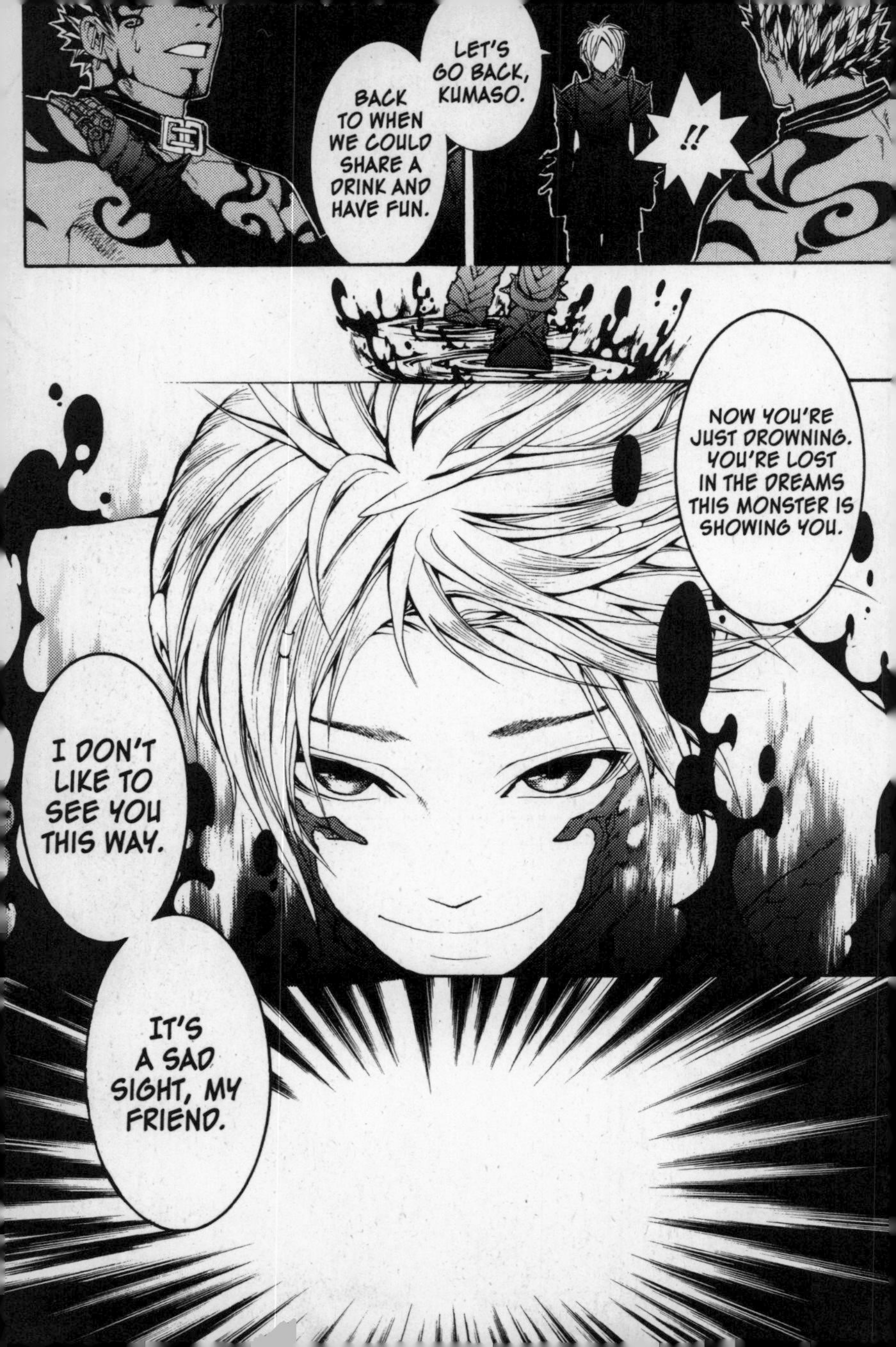
!!
LET'S GO BACK, KUMASO.
BACK TO WHEN WE COULD SHARE A DRINK AND HAVE FUN.
NOW YOU'RE JUST DROWNING. YOU'RE LOST IN THE DREAMS THIS MONSTER IS SHOWING YOU.
I DON'T LIKE TO SEE YOU THIS WAY.
IT'S A SAD SIGHT, MY FRIEND.

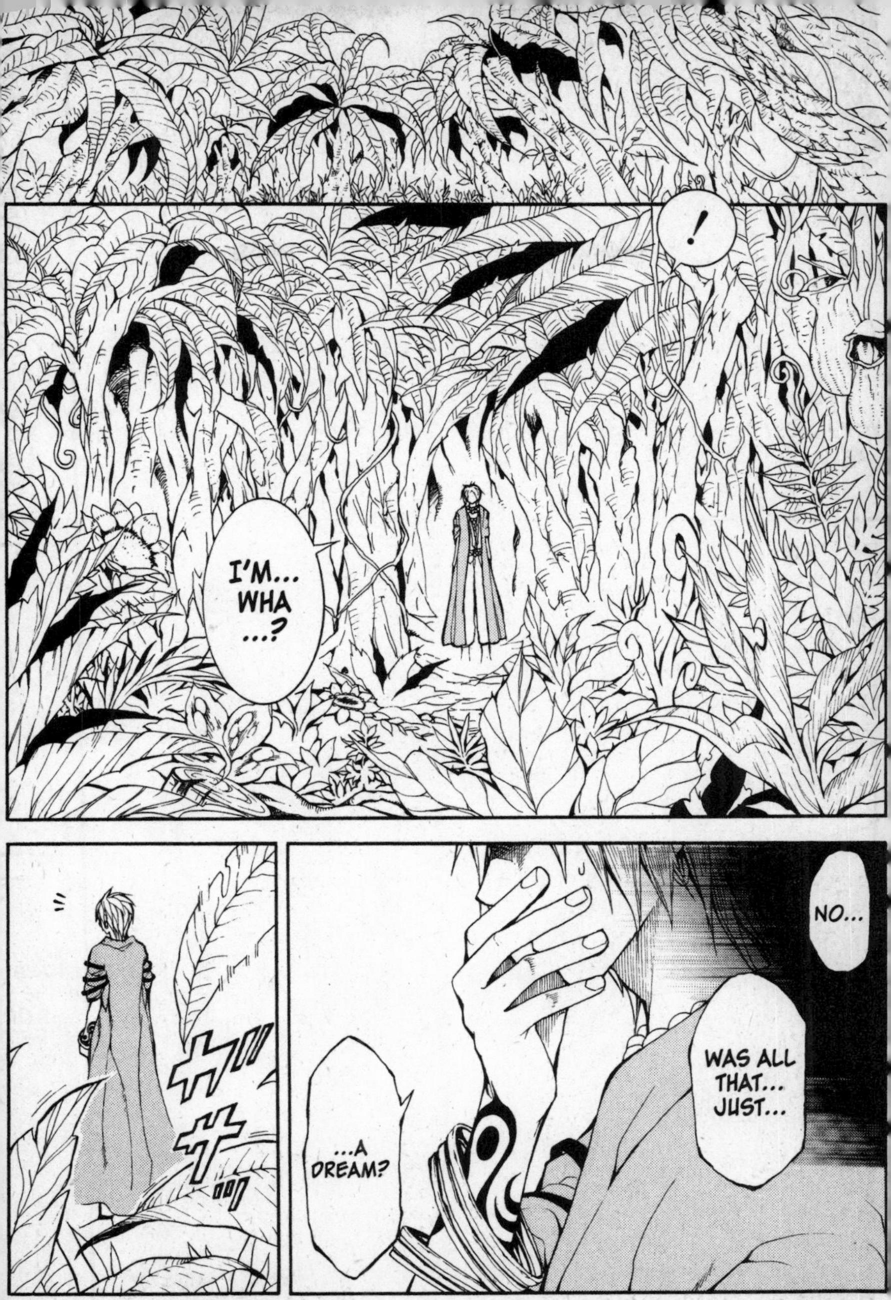
!
I'M... WHA ...?
NO...
WAS ALL THAT... JUST...
...A DREAM?

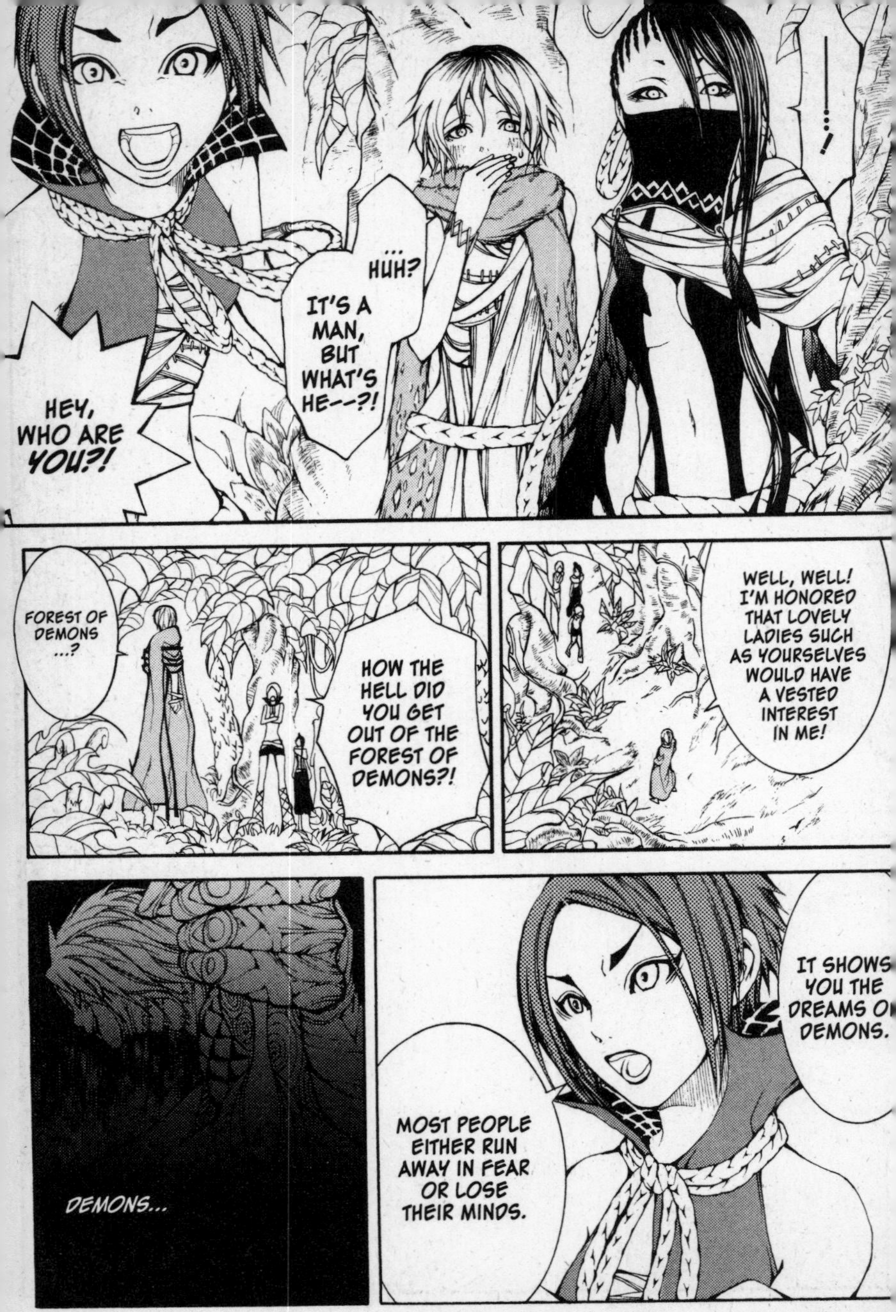
...!
... HUH?
IT'S A MAN, BUT WHAT'S HE--?!
HEY, WHO ARE YOU?!
WELL, WELL! I'M HONORED THAT LOVELY LADIES SUCH AS YOURSELVES WOULD HAVE A VESTED INTEREST IN ME!
HOW THE HELL DID YOU GET OUT OF THE FOREST OF DEMONS?!
FOREST OF DEMONS ...?
IT SHOWS YOU THE DREAMS O DEMONS.
MOST PEOPLE EITHER RUN AWAY IN FEAR OR LOSE THEIR MINDS.
DEMONS...

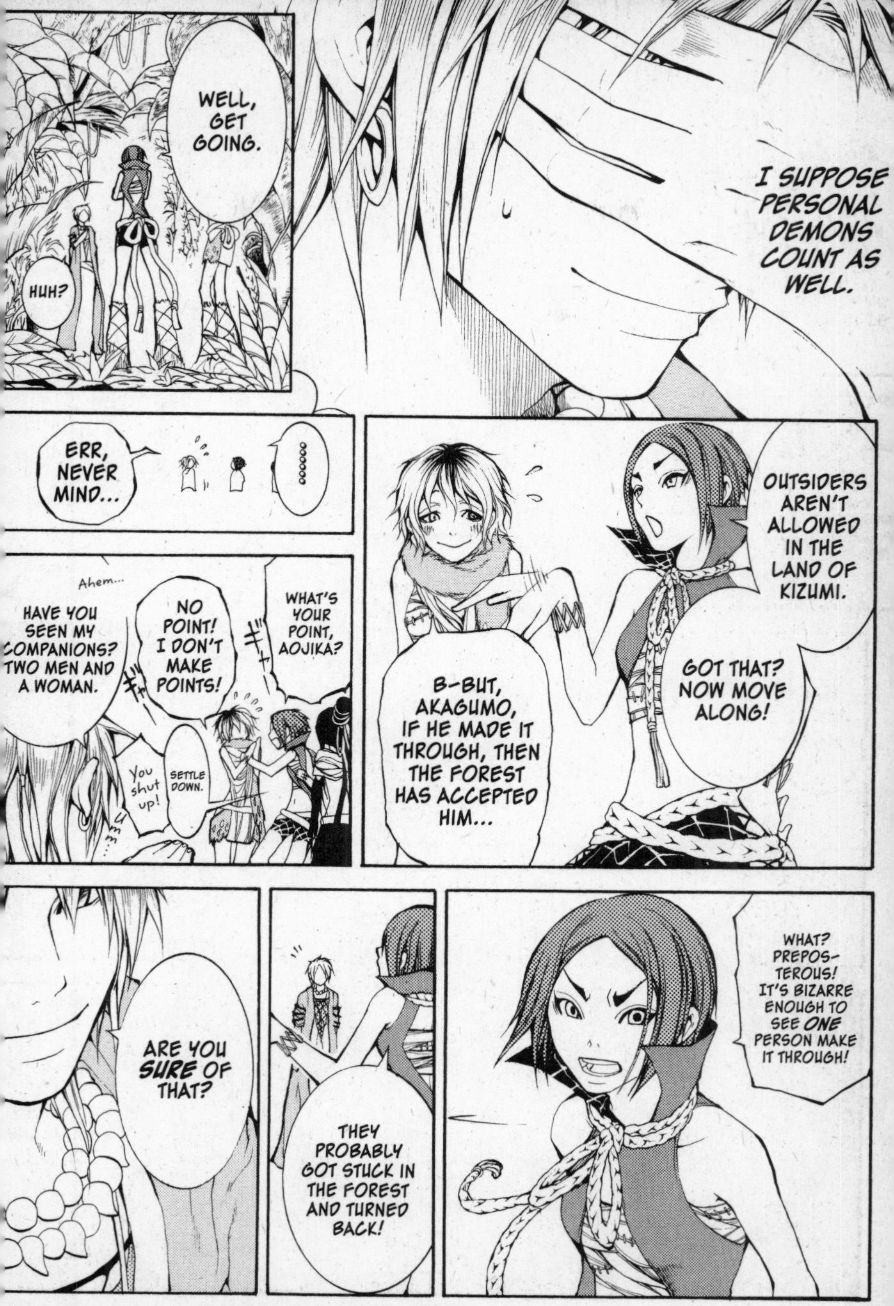
I SUPPOSE PERSONAL DEMONS COUNT AS WELL.
WELL, GET GOING.
HUH?
OUTSIDERS AREN'T ALLOWED IN THE LAND OF KIZUMI.
GOT THAT? NOW MOVE ALONG!
B-BUT, AKAGUMO, IF HE MADE IT THROUGH, THEN THE FOREST HAS ACCEPTED HIM...
......
ERR, NEVER MIND...
WHAT'S YOUR POINT, AOJIKA?
NO POINT! I DON'T MAKE POINTS!
Ahem...
HAVE YOU SEEN MY COMPANIONS? TWO MEN AND A WOMAN.
SETTLE DOWN.
You shut up!
Umm...
WHAT? PREPOSTEROUS! IT'S BIZARRE ENOUGH TO SEE *ONE* PERSON MAKE IT THROUGH!
THEY PROBABLY GOT STUCK IN THE FOREST AND TURNED BACK!
ARE YOU *SURE* OF THAT?

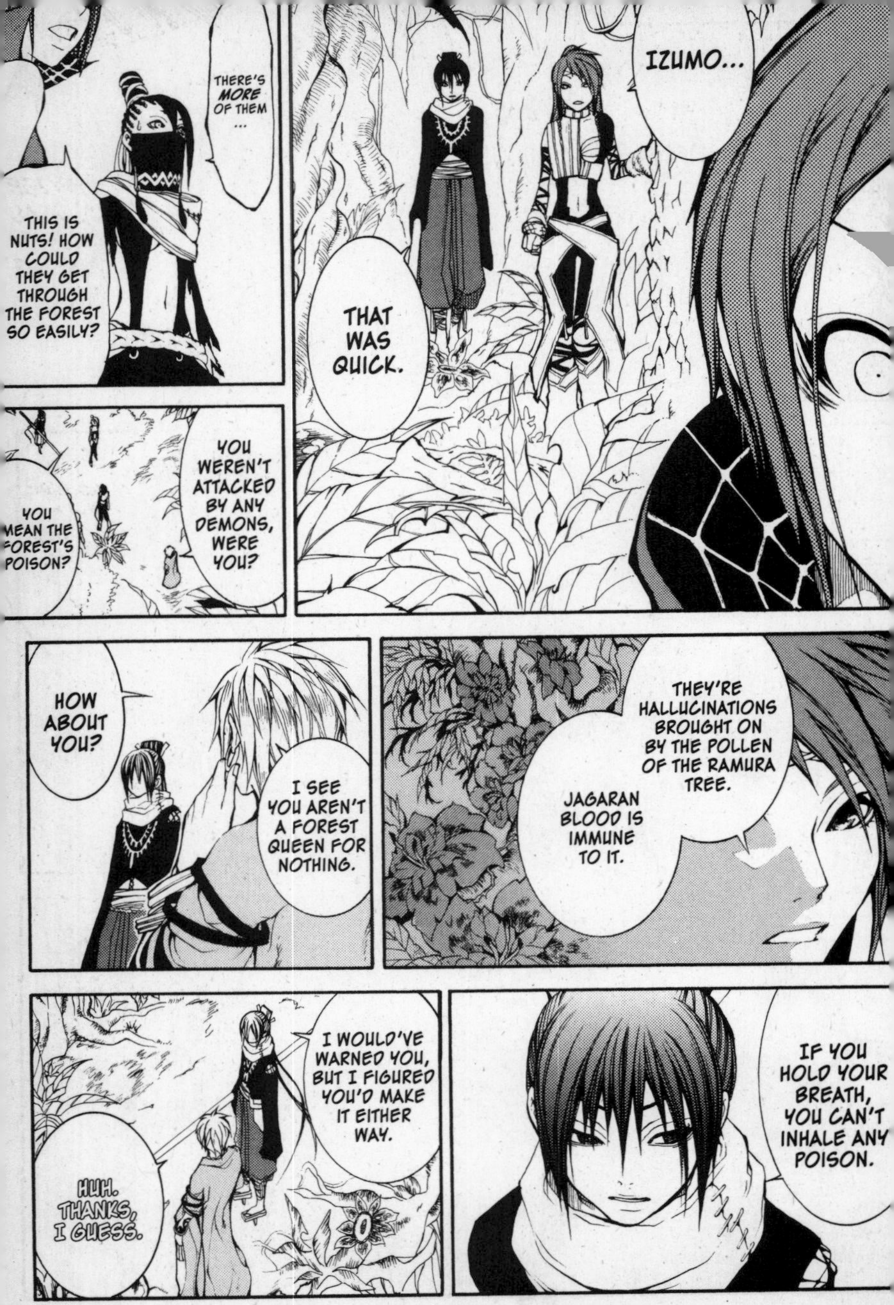
IZUMO...
THAT WAS QUICK.
THERE'S MORE OF THEM ...
THIS IS NUTS! HOW COULD THEY GET THROUGH THE FOREST SO EASILY?
YOU WEREN'T ATTACKED BY ANY DEMONS, WERE YOU?
YOU MEAN THE FOREST'S POISON?
THEY'RE HALLUCINATIONS BROUGHT ON BY THE POLLEN OF THE RAMURA TREE.
JAGARAN BLOOD IS IMMUNE TO IT.
HOW ABOUT YOU?
I SEE YOU AREN'T A FOREST QUEEN FOR NOTHING.
IF YOU HOLD YOUR BREATH, YOU CAN'T INHALE ANY POISON.
I WOULD'VE WARNED YOU, BUT I FIGURED YOU'D MAKE IT EITHER WAY.
HUH. THANKS, I GUESS.

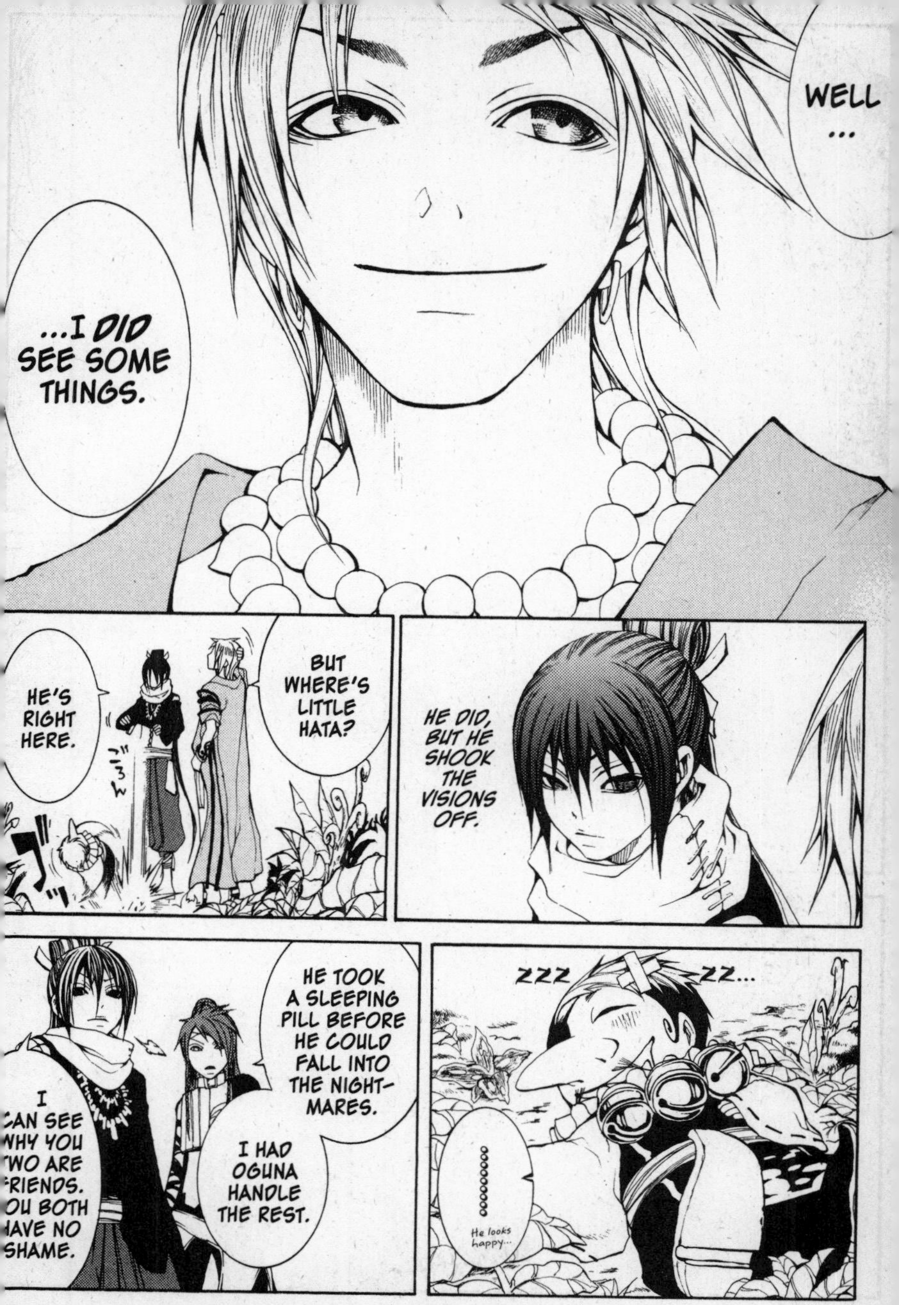
WELL ...
...I DID SEE SOME THINGS.
HE DID, BUT HE SHOOK THE VISIONS OFF.
BUT WHERE'S LITTLE HATA?
HE'S RIGHT HERE.
ZZZ ZZ...
......
He looks happy...
HE TOOK A SLEEPING PILL BEFORE HE COULD FALL INTO THE NIGHT-MARES.
I HAD OGUNA HANDLE THE REST.
I CAN SEE WHY YOU TWO ARE FRIENDS. OU BOTH HAVE NO SHAME.

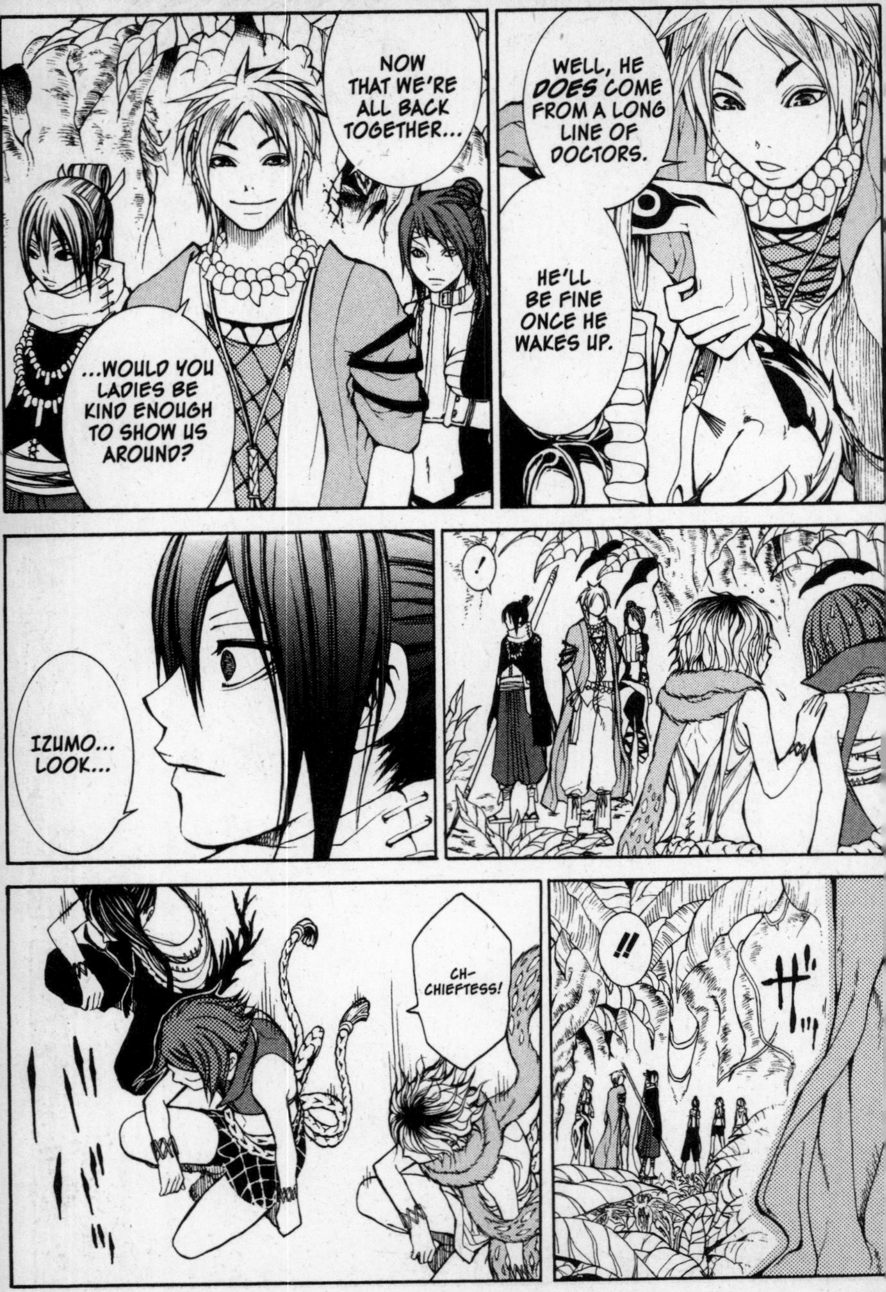
WELL, HE *DOES* COME FROM A LONG LINE OF DOCTORS.
HE'LL BE FINE ONCE HE WAKES UP.
NOW THAT WE'RE ALL BACK TOGETHER...
...WOULD YOU LADIES BE KIND ENOUGH TO SHOW US AROUND?
!
IZUMO... LOOK...
!!
CH-CHIEFTESS!

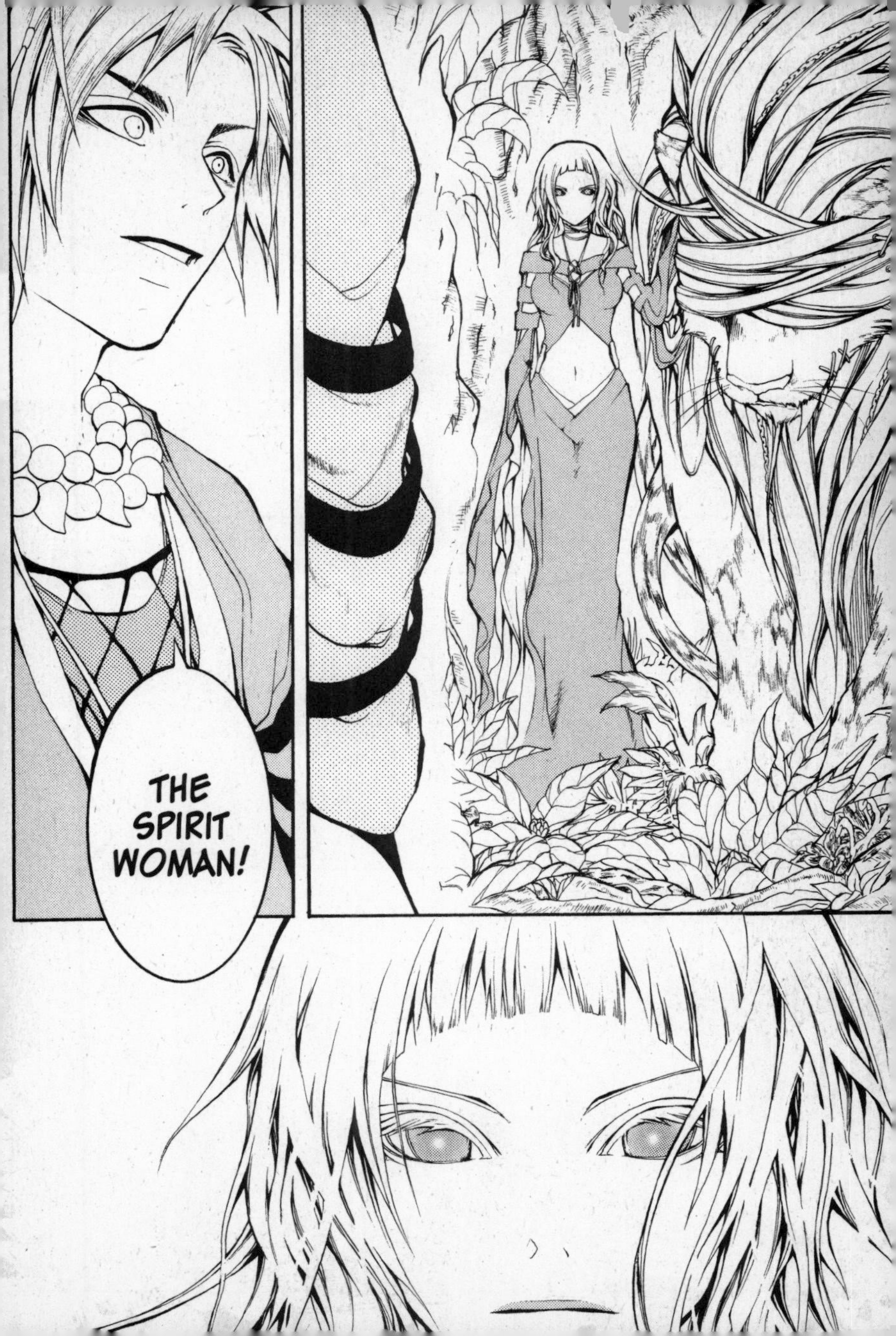
THE SPIRIT WOMAN!

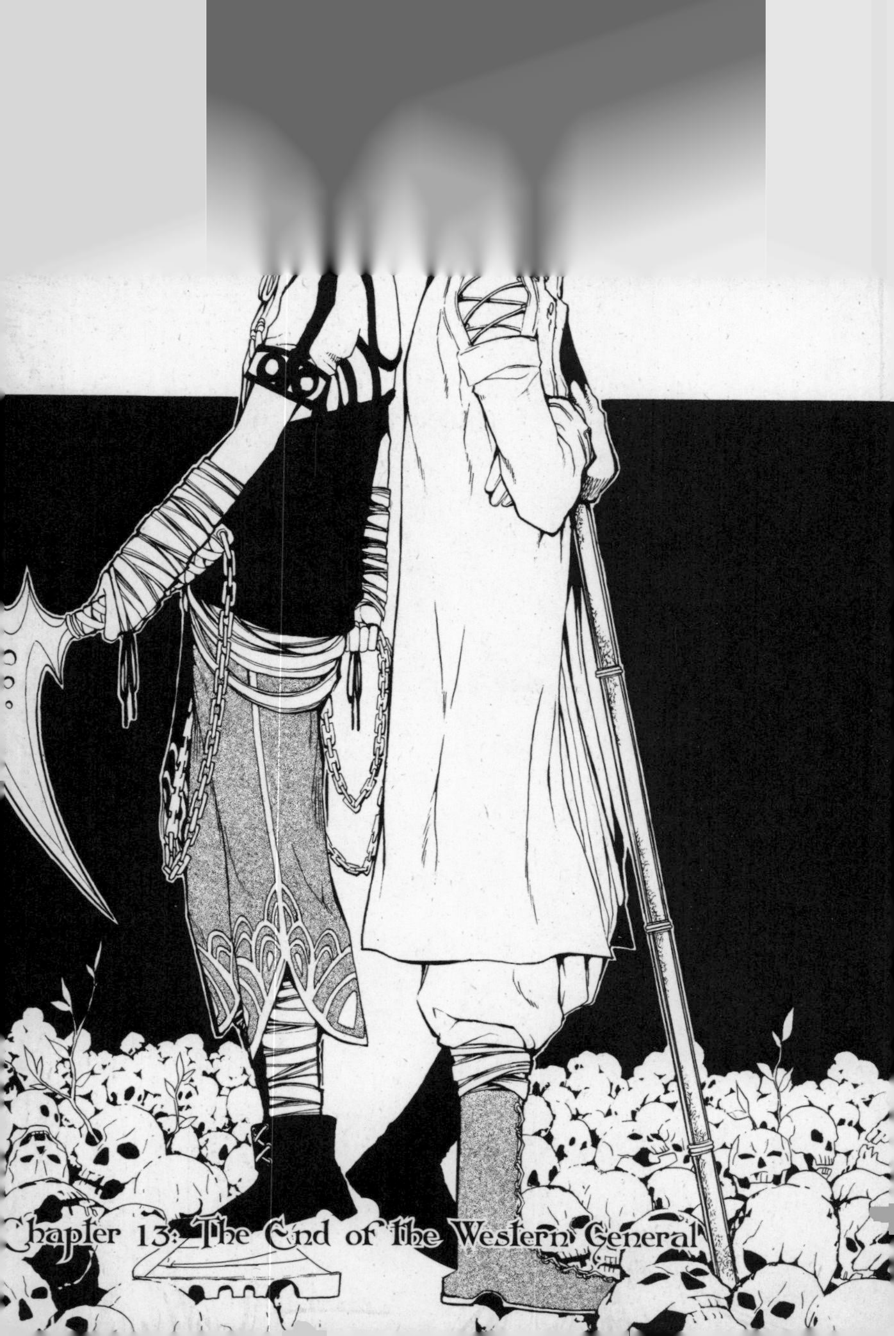
Chapter 13: The End of the Western General

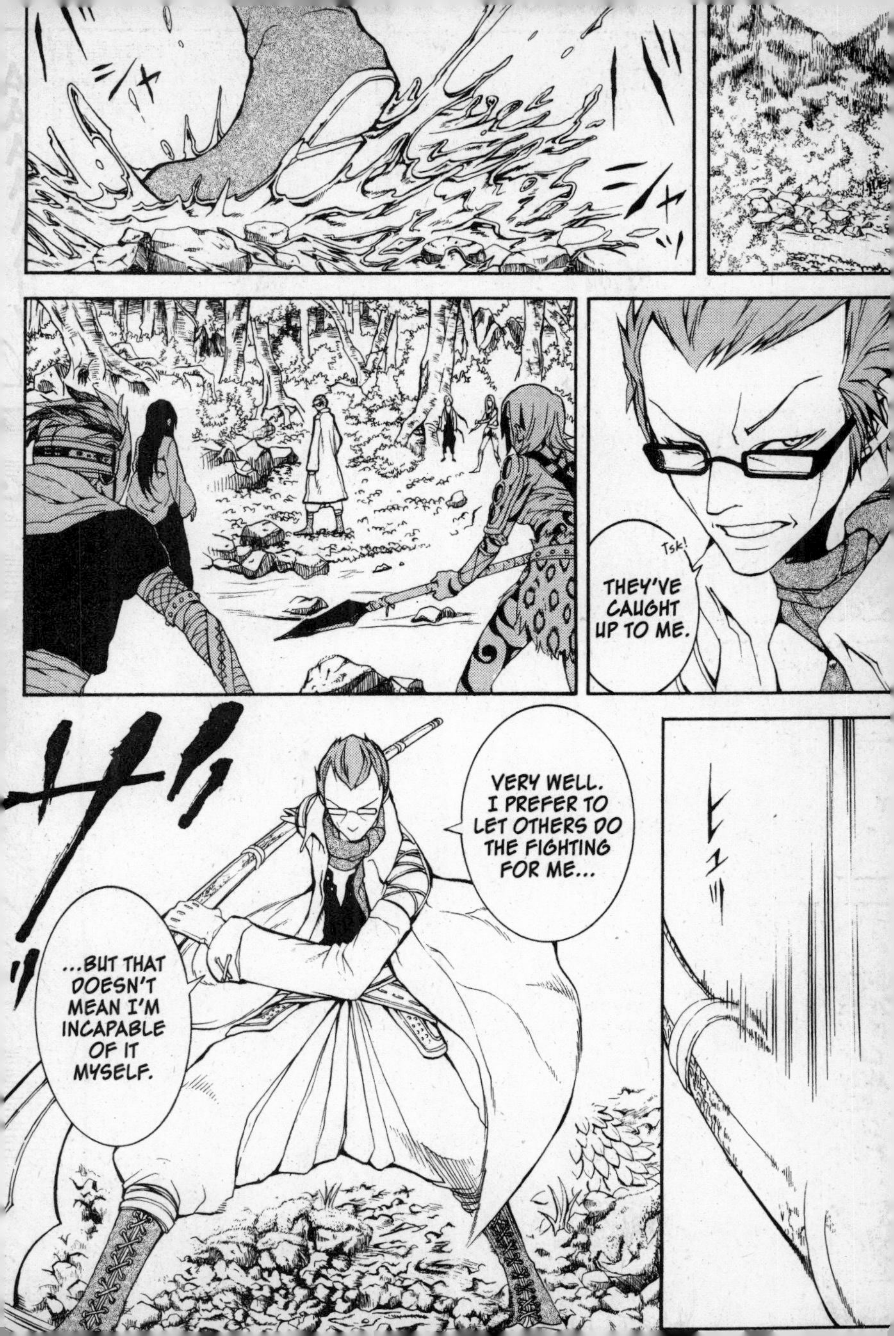
Tsk!
THEY'VE CAUGHT UP TO ME.
VERY WELL. I PREFER TO LET OTHERS DO THE FIGHTING FOR ME...
...BUT THAT DOESN'T MEAN I'M INCAPABLE OF IT MYSELF.

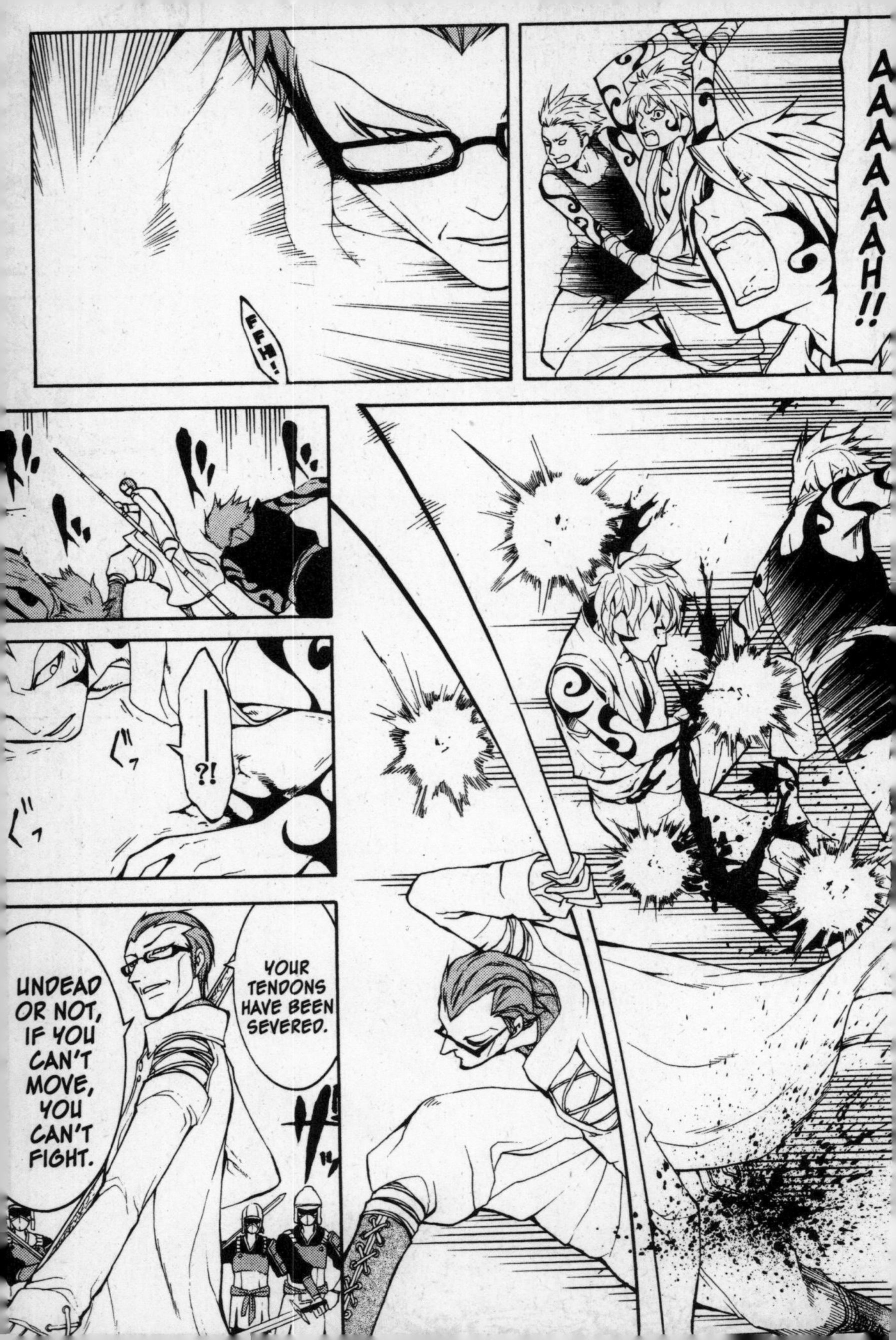
AAAAAAAH!!
FFH!
—?!
YOUR TENDONS HAVE BEEN SEVERED.
UNDEAD OR NOT, IF YOU CAN'T MOVE, YOU CAN'T FIGHT.

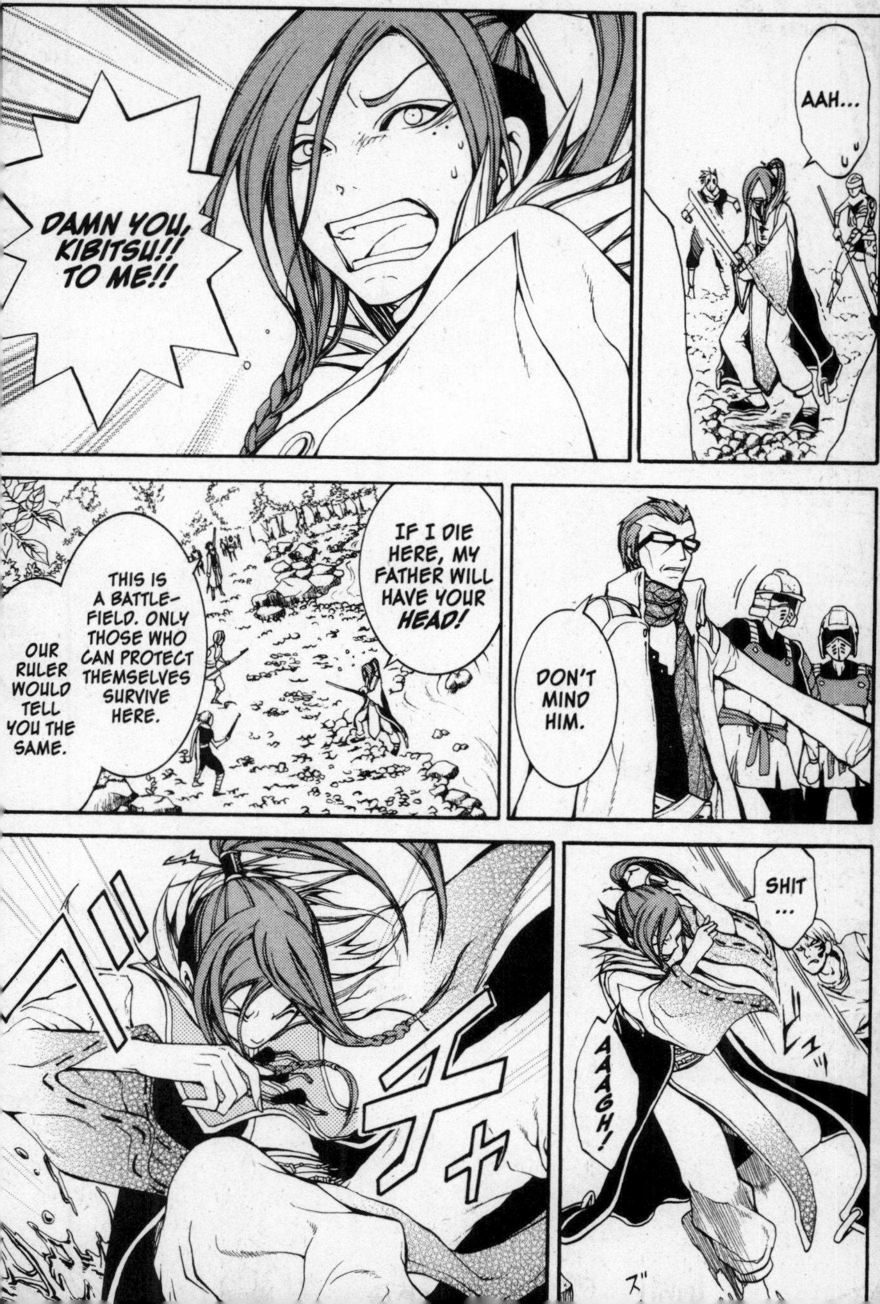
AAH...
DAMN YOU, KIBITSU!! TO ME!!
DON'T MIND HIM.
IF I DIE HERE, MY FATHER WILL HAVE YOUR HEAD!
THIS IS A BATTLE-FIELD. ONLY THOSE WHO CAN PROTECT THEMSELVES SURVIVE HERE.
OUR RULER WOULD TELL YOU THE SAME.
SHIT ...
AAAGH!

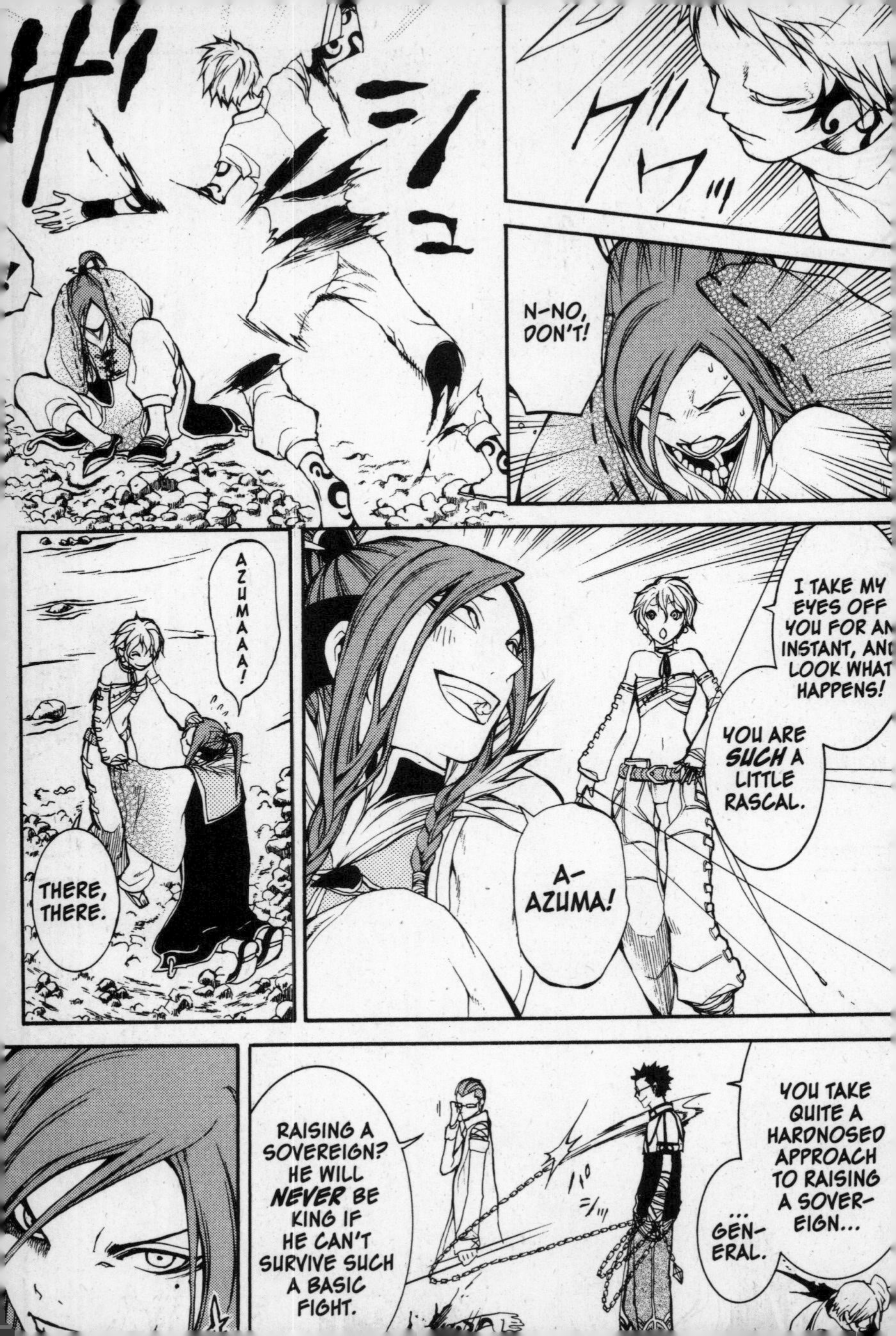
N-NO, DON'T!
I TAKE MY EYES OFF YOU FOR AN INSTANT, AND LOOK WHAT HAPPENS!
YOU ARE SUCH A LITTLE RASCAL.
A-AZUMA!
AZUMAAAA!
THERE, THERE.
YOU TAKE QUITE A HARDNOSED APPROACH TO RAISING A SOVER-EIGN...
...GEN-ERAL.
RAISING A SOVEREIGN? HE WILL NEVER BE KING IF HE CAN'T SURVIVE SUCH A BASIC FIGHT.

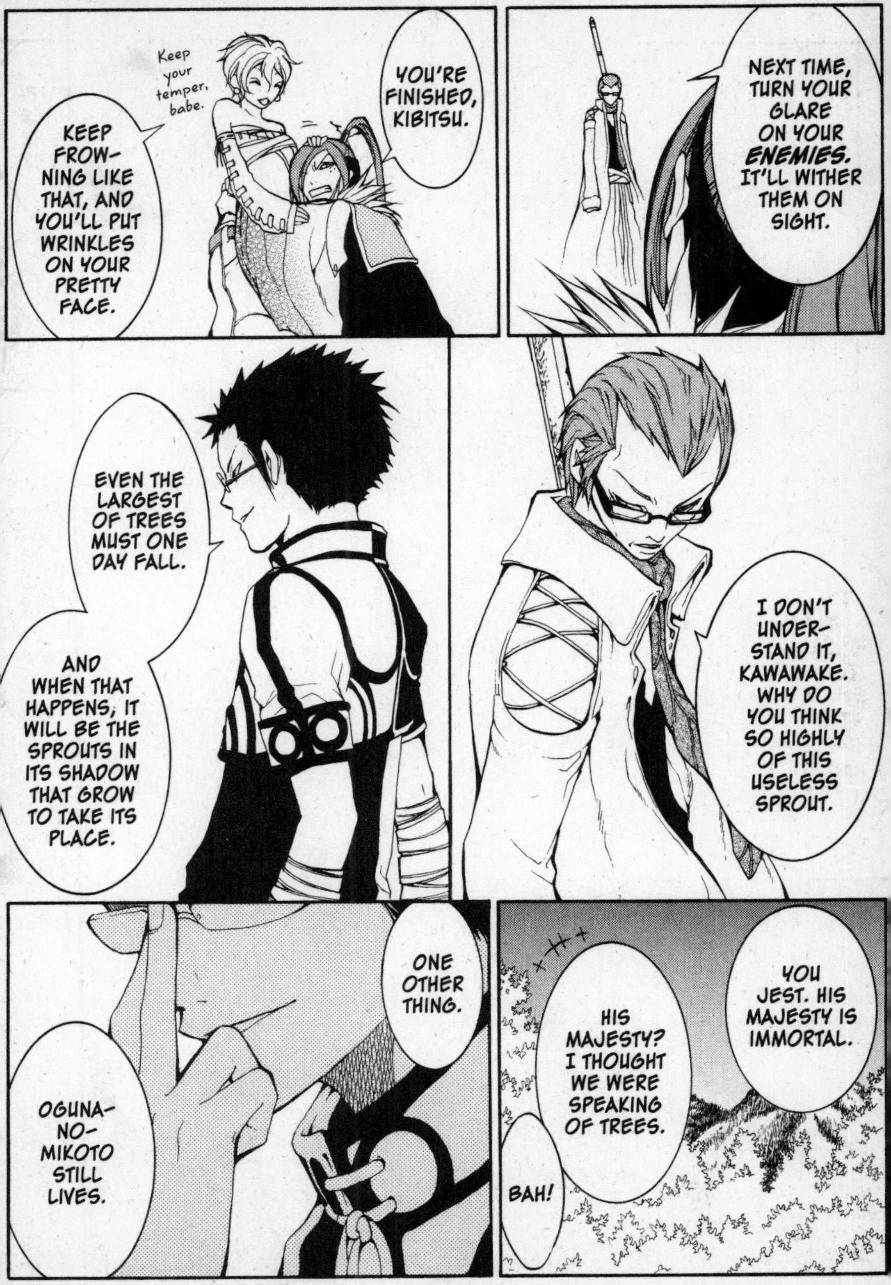
NEXT TIME, TURN YOUR GLARE ON YOUR *ENEMIES.* IT'LL WITHER THEM ON SIGHT.
YOU'RE FINISHED, KIBITSU.
Keep your temper, babe.
KEEP FROWNING LIKE THAT, AND YOU'LL PUT WRINKLES ON YOUR PRETTY FACE.
I DON'T UNDERSTAND IT, KAWAWAKE. WHY DO YOU THINK SO HIGHLY OF THIS USELESS SPROUT.
EVEN THE LARGEST OF TREES MUST ONE DAY FALL.
AND WHEN THAT HAPPENS, IT WILL BE THE SPROUTS IN ITS SHADOW THAT GROW TO TAKE ITS PLACE.
YOU JEST. HIS MAJESTY IS IMMORTAL.
HIS MAJESTY? I THOUGHT WE WERE SPEAKING OF TREES.
BAH!
ONE OTHER THING.
OGUNA-NO-MIKOTO STILL LIVES.

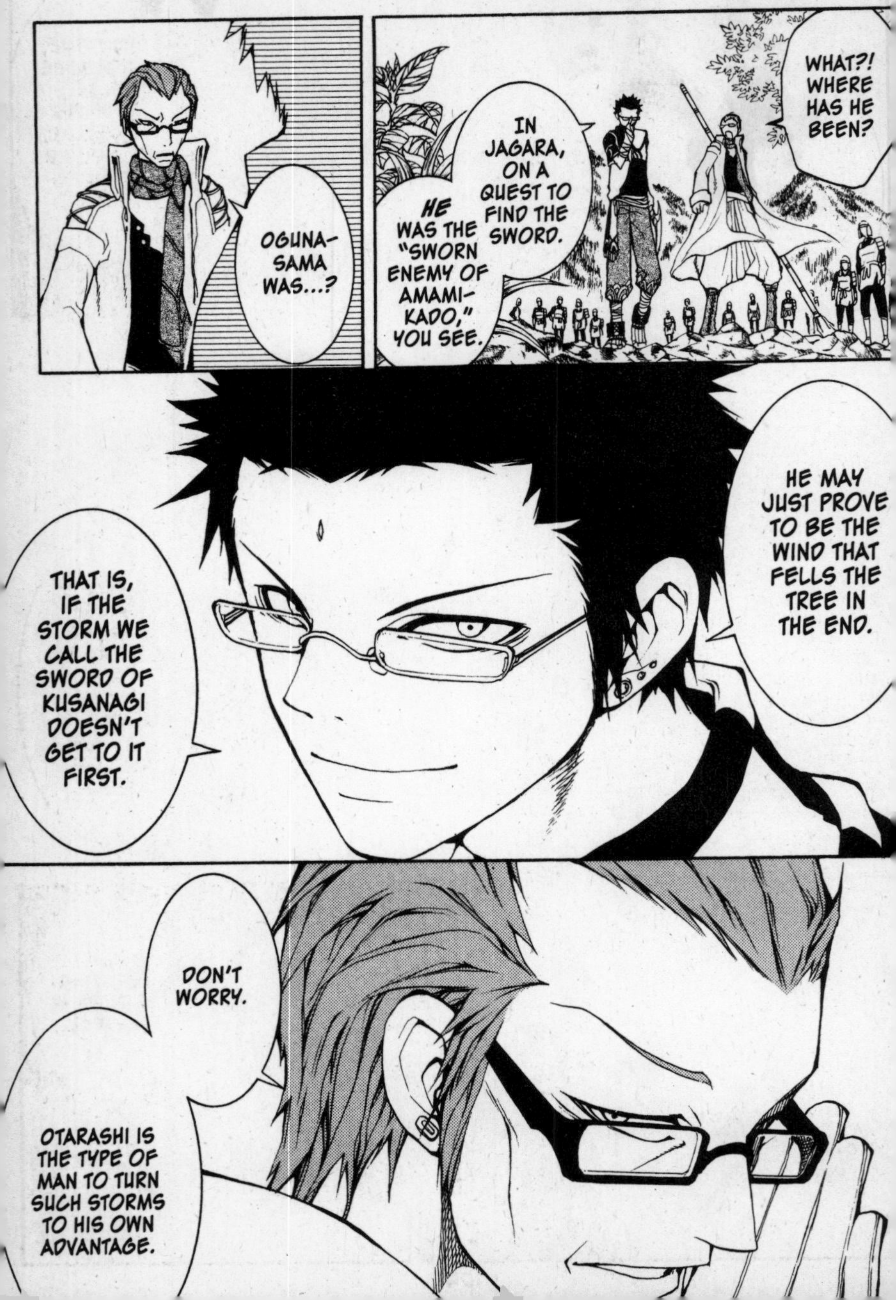
WHAT?! WHERE HAS HE BEEN?
IN JAGARA, ON A QUEST TO FIND THE SWORD.
HE WAS THE "SWORN ENEMY OF AMAMI-KADO," YOU SEE.
OGUNA-SAMA WAS...?
HE MAY JUST PROVE TO BE THE WIND THAT FELLS THE TREE IN THE END.
THAT IS, IF THE STORM WE CALL THE SWORD OF KUSANAGI DOESN'T GET TO IT FIRST.
DON'T WORRY.
OTARASHI IS THE TYPE OF MAN TO TURN SUCH STORMS TO HIS OWN ADVANTAGE.

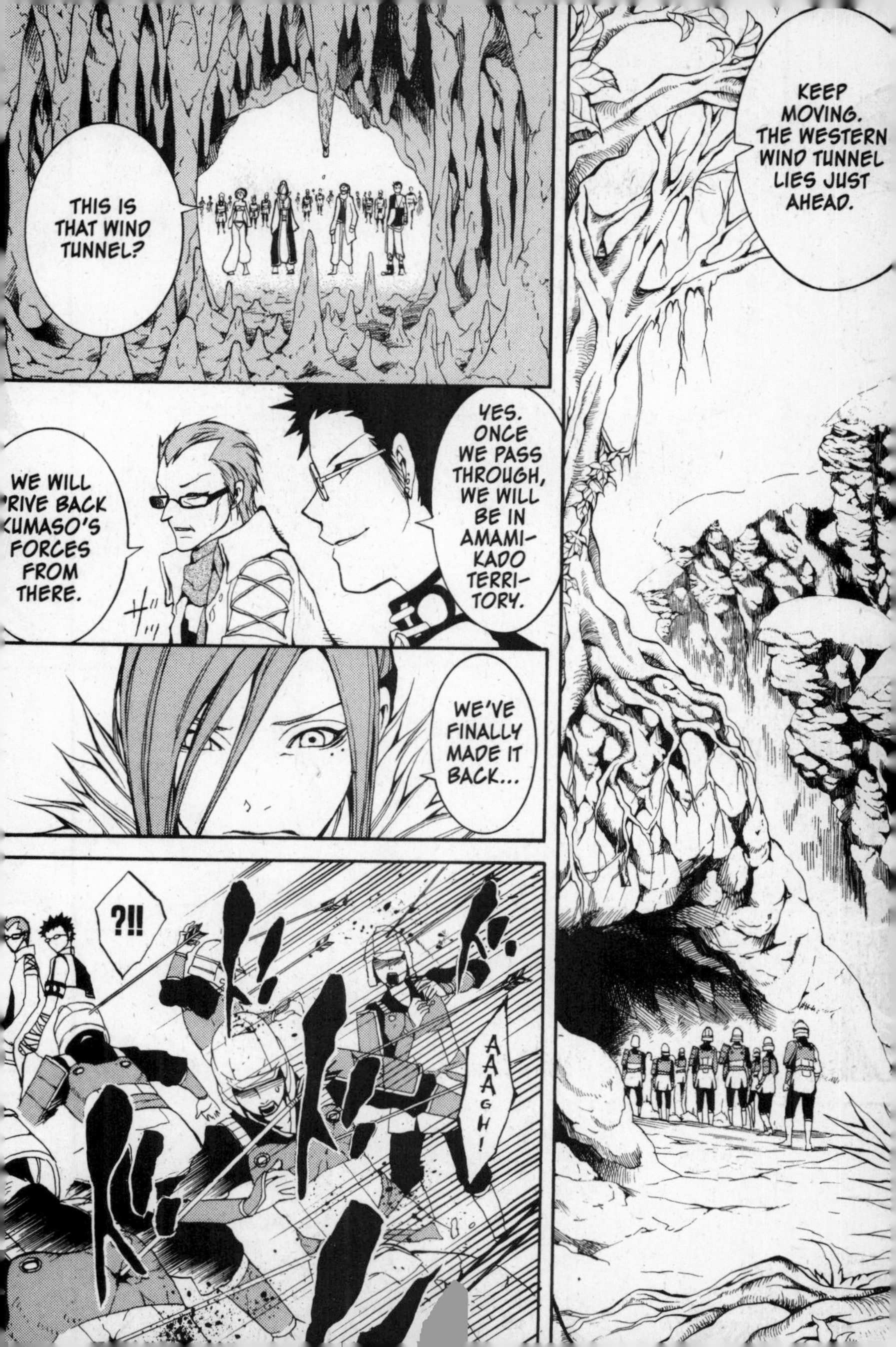
KEEP MOVING. THE WESTERN WIND TUNNEL LIES JUST AHEAD.
THIS IS THAT WIND TUNNEL?
YES. ONCE WE PASS THROUGH, WE WILL BE IN AMAMI-KADO TERRI-TORY.
WE WILL DRIVE BACK KUMASO'S FORCES FROM THERE.
WE'VE FINALLY MADE IT BACK...
?!!
AAAGH!

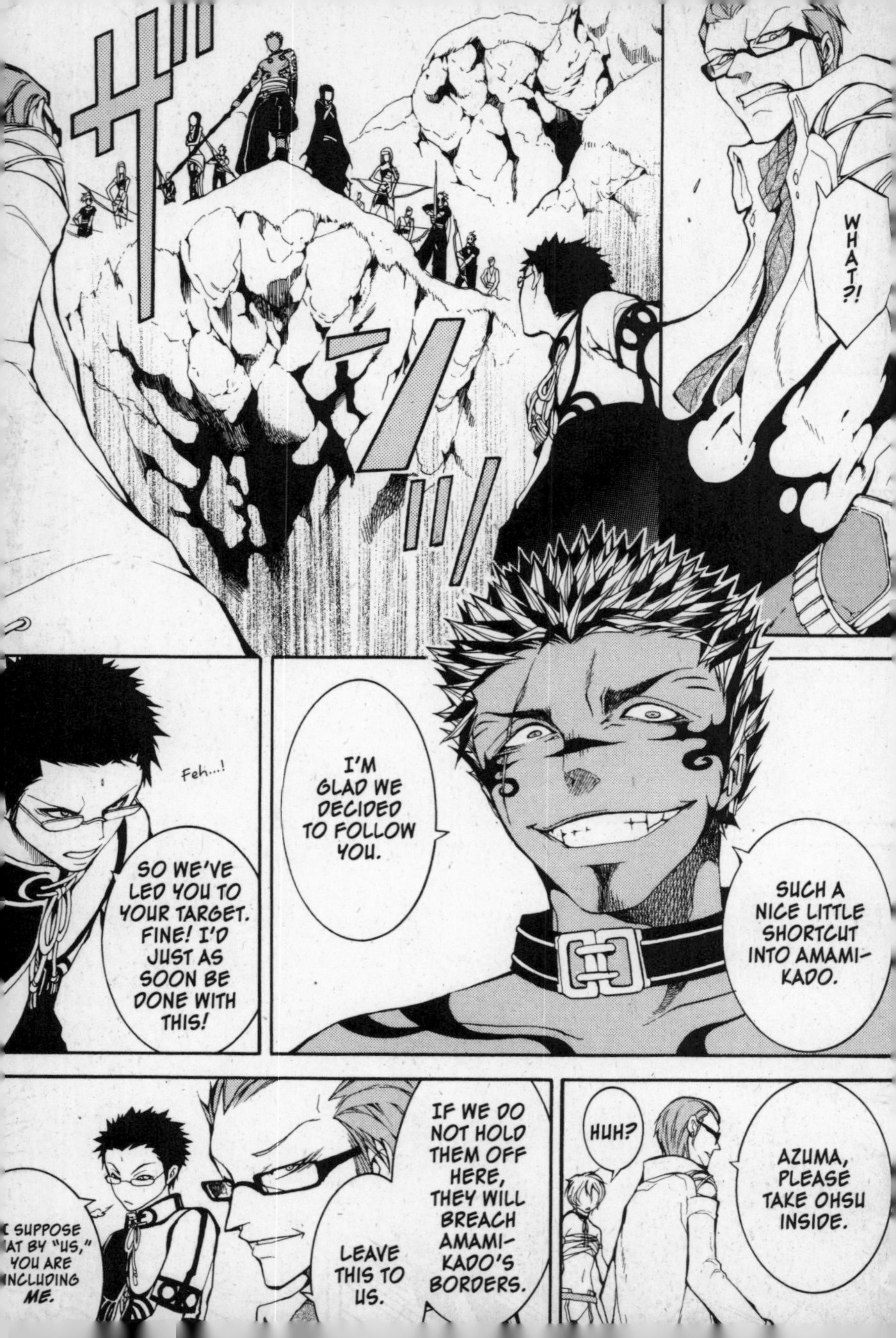
WHAT?!
SUCH A NICE LITTLE SHORTCUT INTO AMAMI-KADO.
I'M GLAD WE DECIDED TO FOLLOW YOU.
Feh...!
SO WE'VE LED YOU TO YOUR TARGET. FINE! I'D JUST AS SOON BE DONE WITH THIS!
AZUMA, PLEASE TAKE OHSU INSIDE.
HUH?
IF WE DO NOT HOLD THEM OFF HERE, THEY WILL BREACH AMAMI-KADO'S BORDERS.
LEAVE THIS TO US.
SUPPOSE AT BY "US," YOU ARE NCLUDING ME.

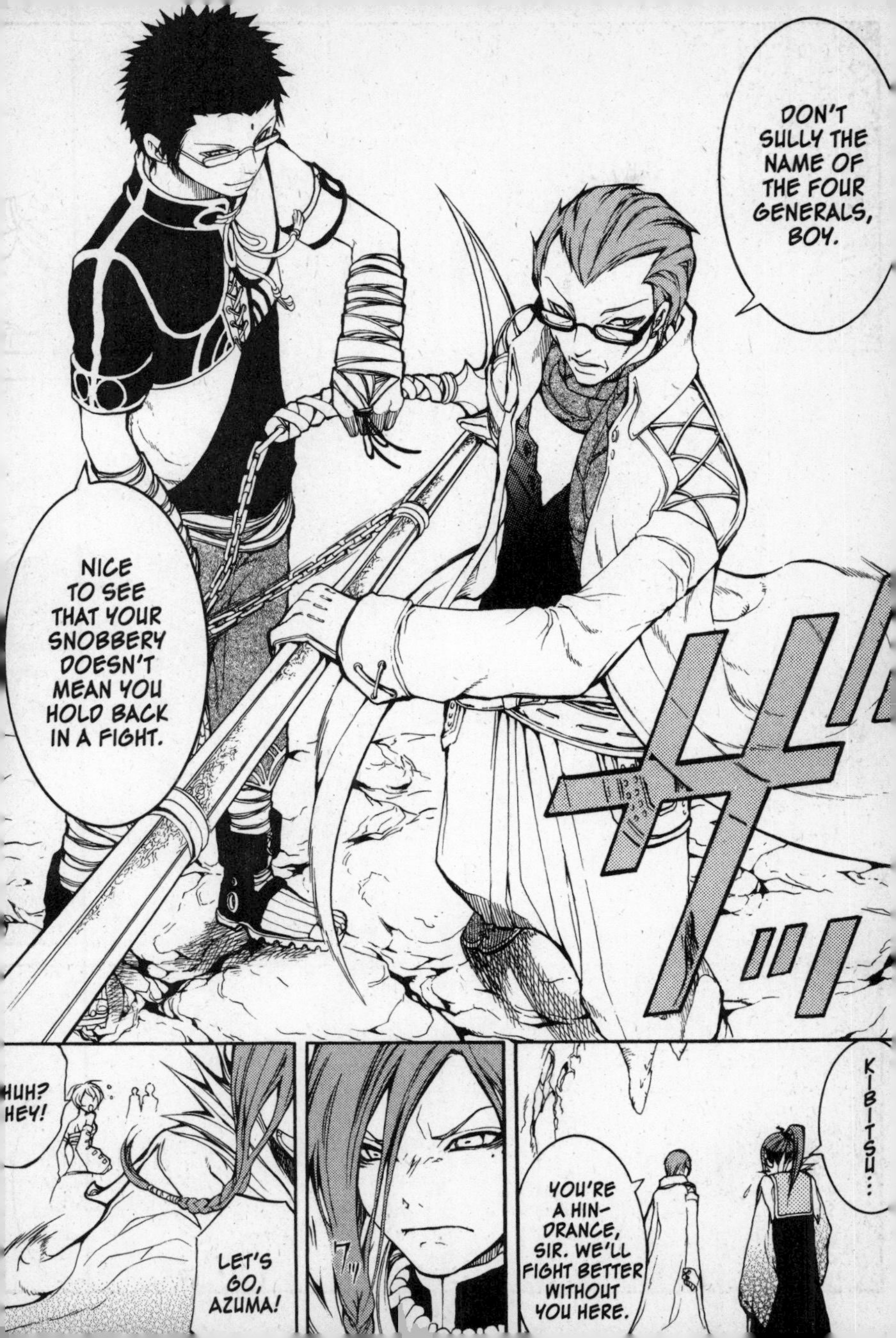
DON'T SULLY THE NAME OF THE FOUR GENERALS, BOY.
NICE TO SEE THAT YOUR SNOBBERY DOESN'T MEAN YOU HOLD BACK IN A FIGHT.
KIBITSU...
YOU'RE A HIN-DRANCE, SIR. WE'LL FIGHT BETTER WITHOUT YOU HERE.
HUH? HEY!
LET'S GO, AZUMA!

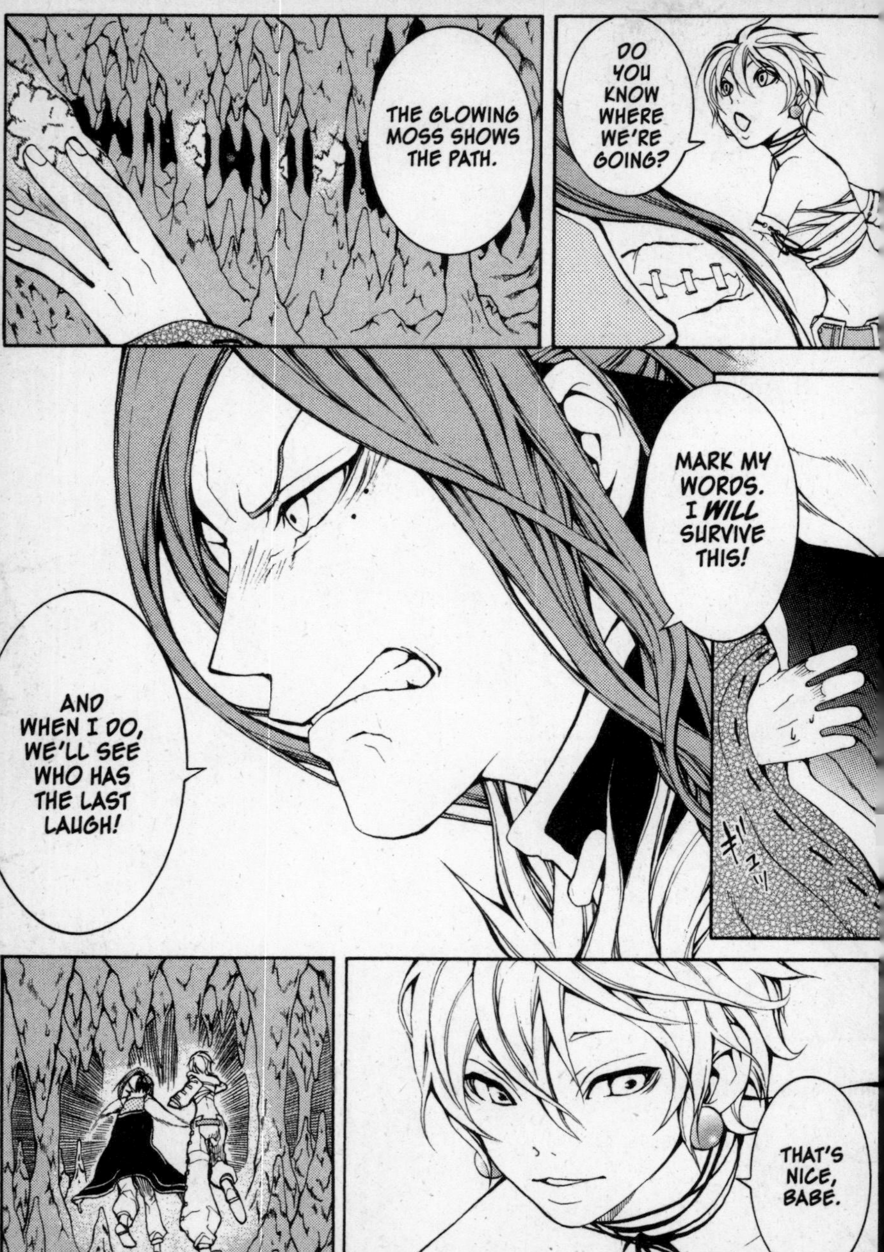
DO YOU KNOW WHERE WE'RE GOING?
THE GLOWING MOSS SHOWS THE PATH.
MARK MY WORDS. I *WILL* SURVIVE THIS!
ギュッ
AND WHEN I DO, WE'LL SEE WHO HAS THE LAST LAUGH!
THAT'S NICE, BABE.

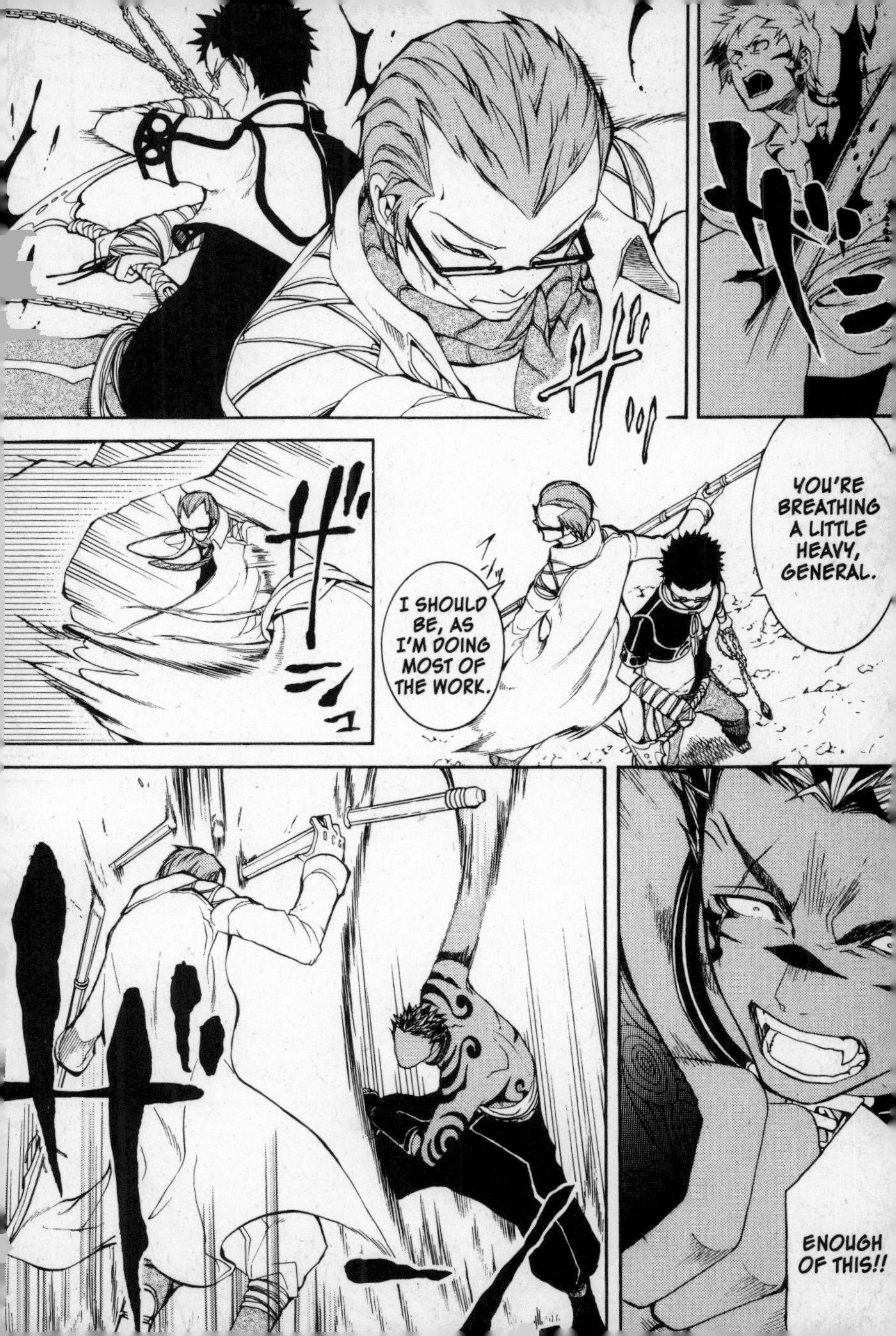

YOU'RE BREATHING A LITTLE HEAVY, GENERAL.
I SHOULD BE, AS I'M DOING MOST OF THE WORK.
ENOUGH OF THIS!!

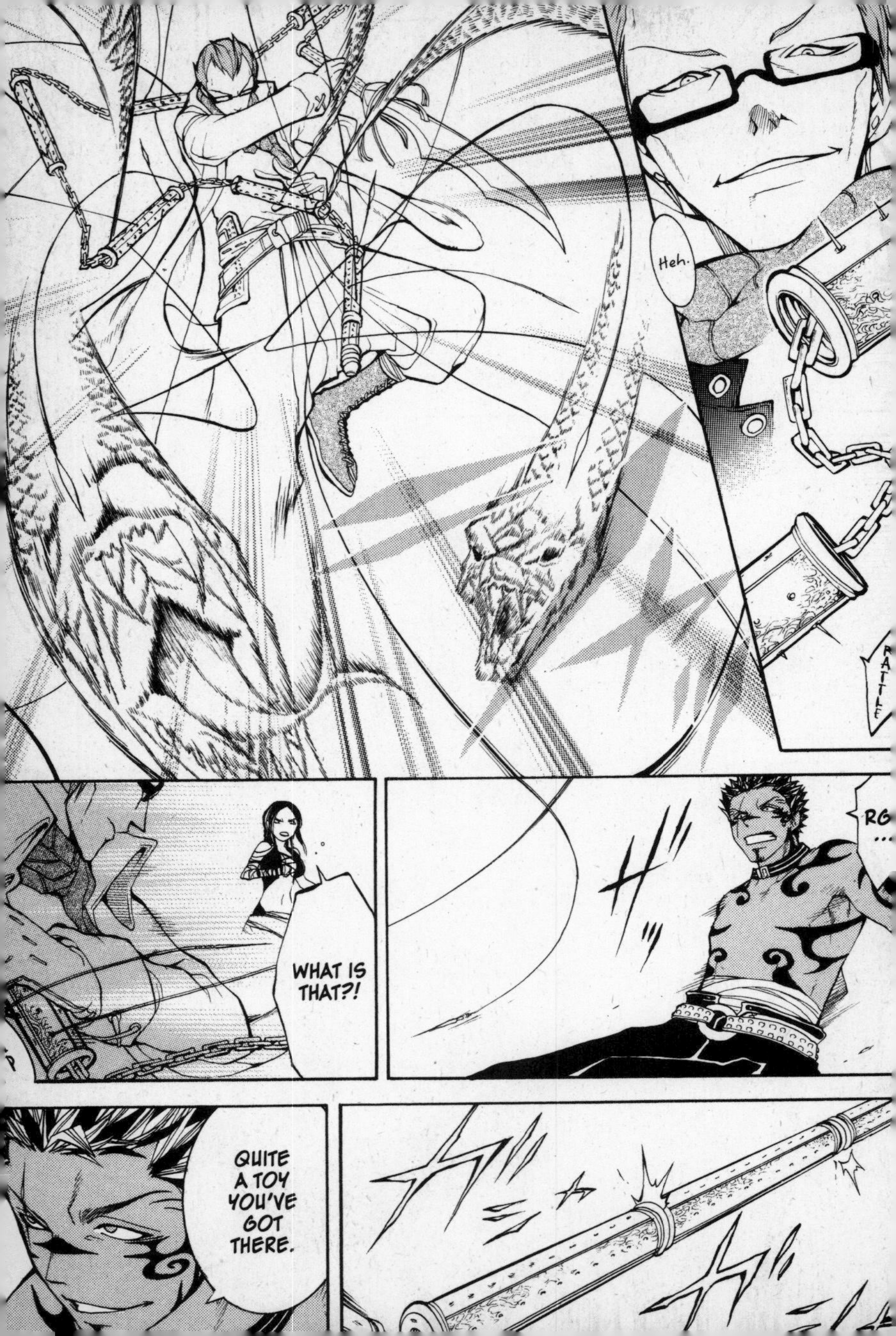
Heh.
RATTLE
RG...
WHAT IS THAT?!
QUITE A TOY YOU'VE GOT THERE.

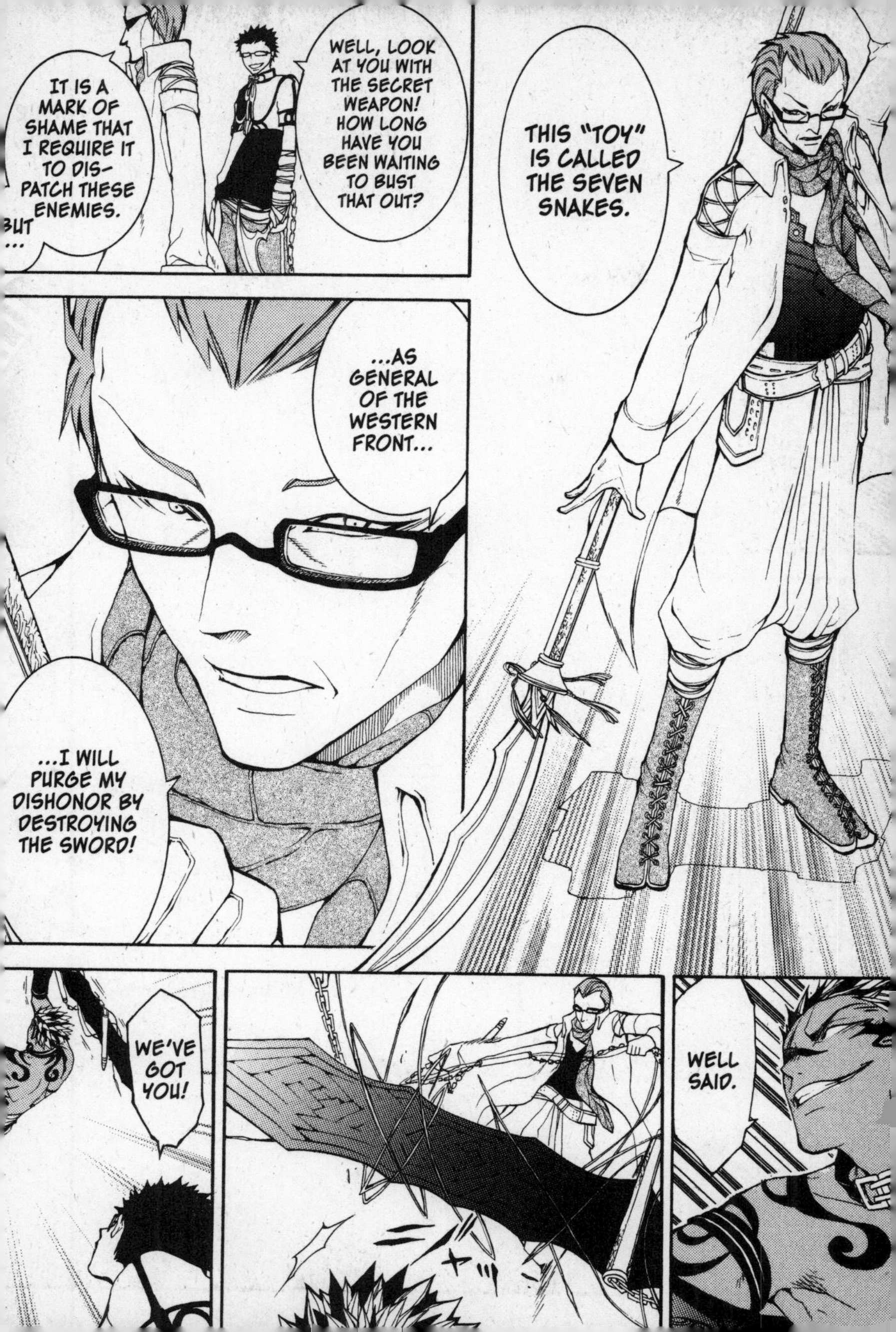
THIS "TOY" IS CALLED THE SEVEN SNAKES.
WELL, LOOK AT YOU WITH THE SECRET WEAPON! HOW LONG HAVE YOU BEEN WAITING TO BUST THAT OUT?
IT IS A MARK OF SHAME THAT I REQUIRE IT TO DIS-PATCH THESE ENEMIES. BUT ...
...AS GENERAL OF THE WESTERN FRONT...
...I WILL PURGE MY DISHONOR BY DESTROYING THE SWORD!
WELL SAID.
WE'VE GOT YOU!

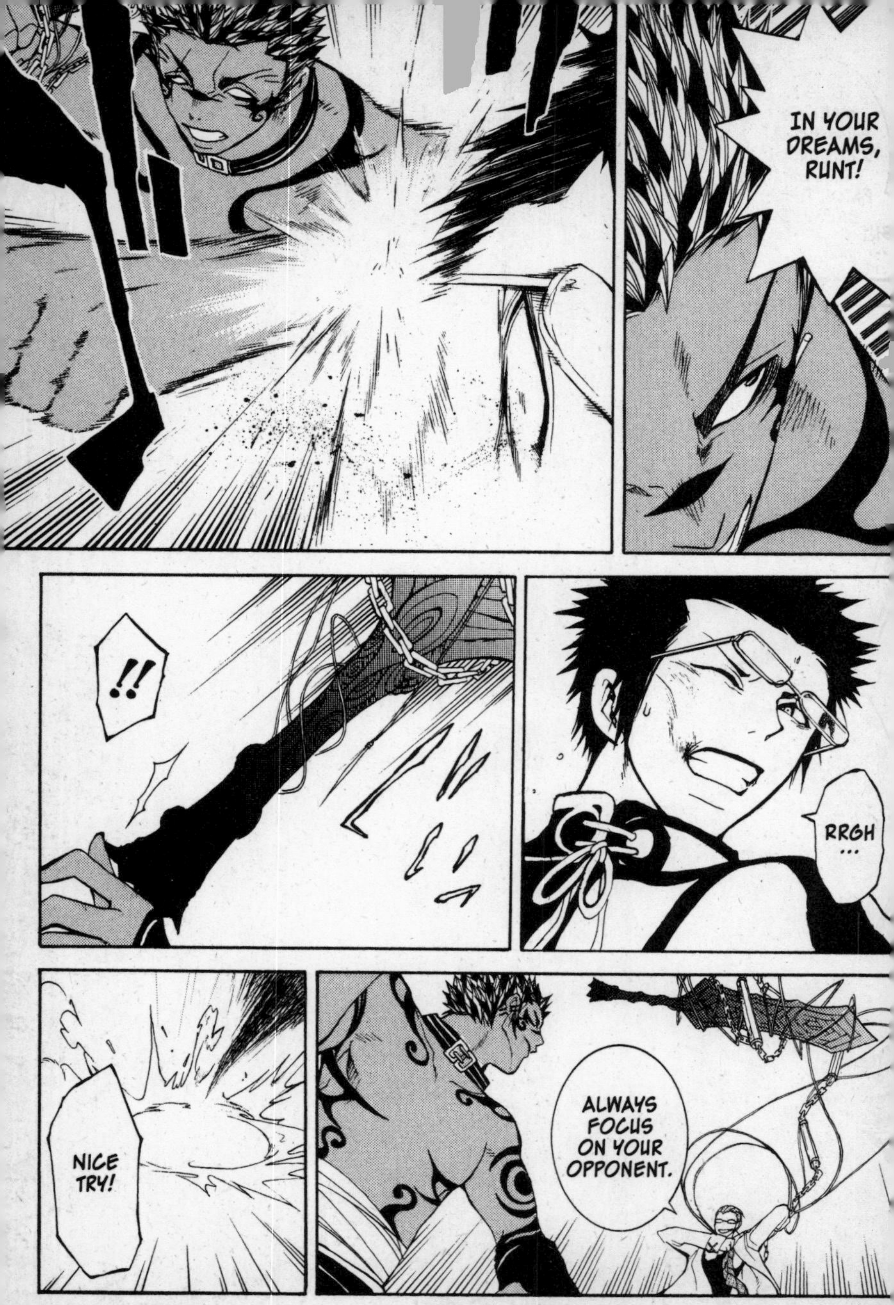
IN YOUR DREAMS, RUNT!
RRGH...
!!
ALWAYS FOCUS ON YOUR OPPONENT.
NICE TRY!

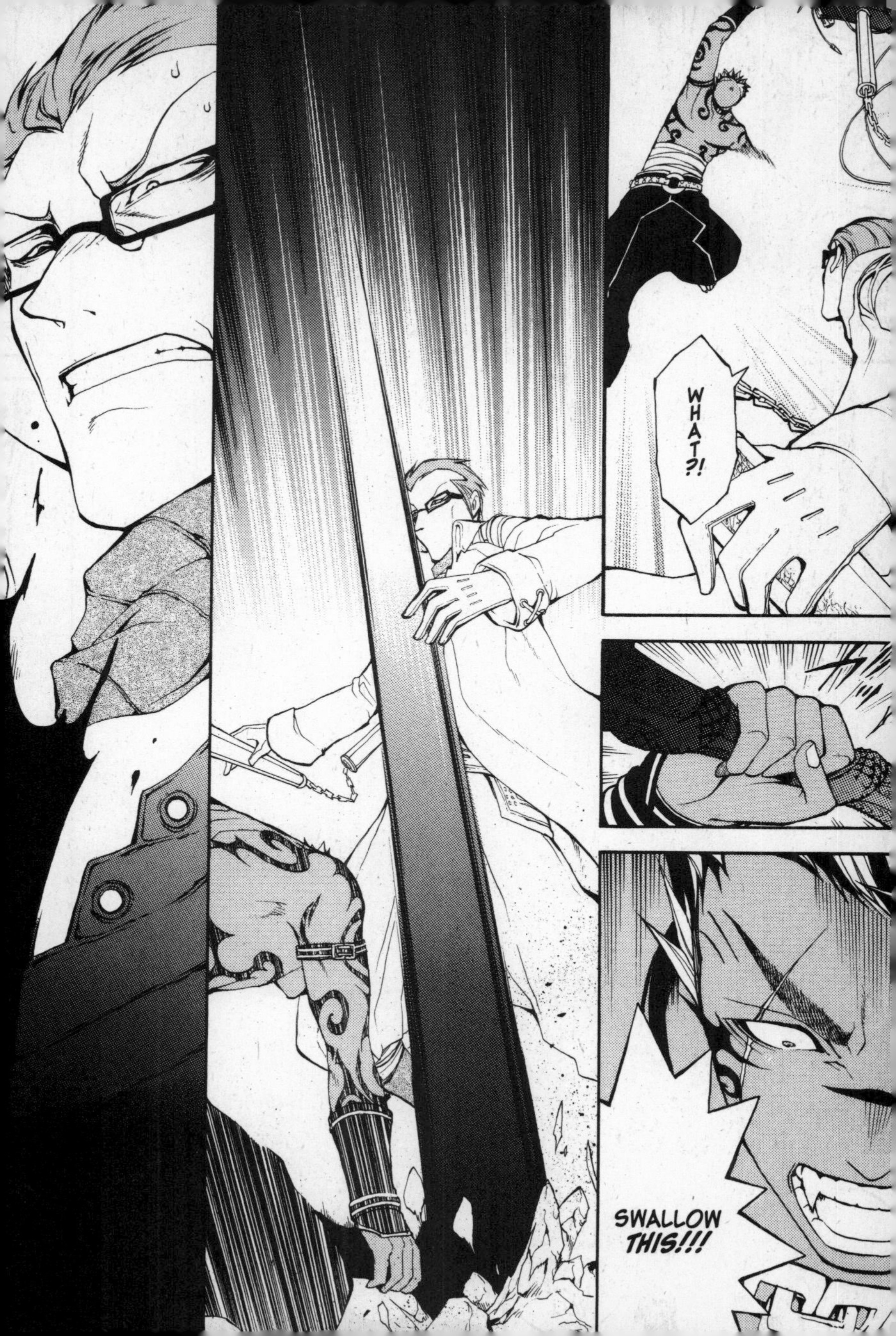
WHAT?!
SWALLOW THIS!!!

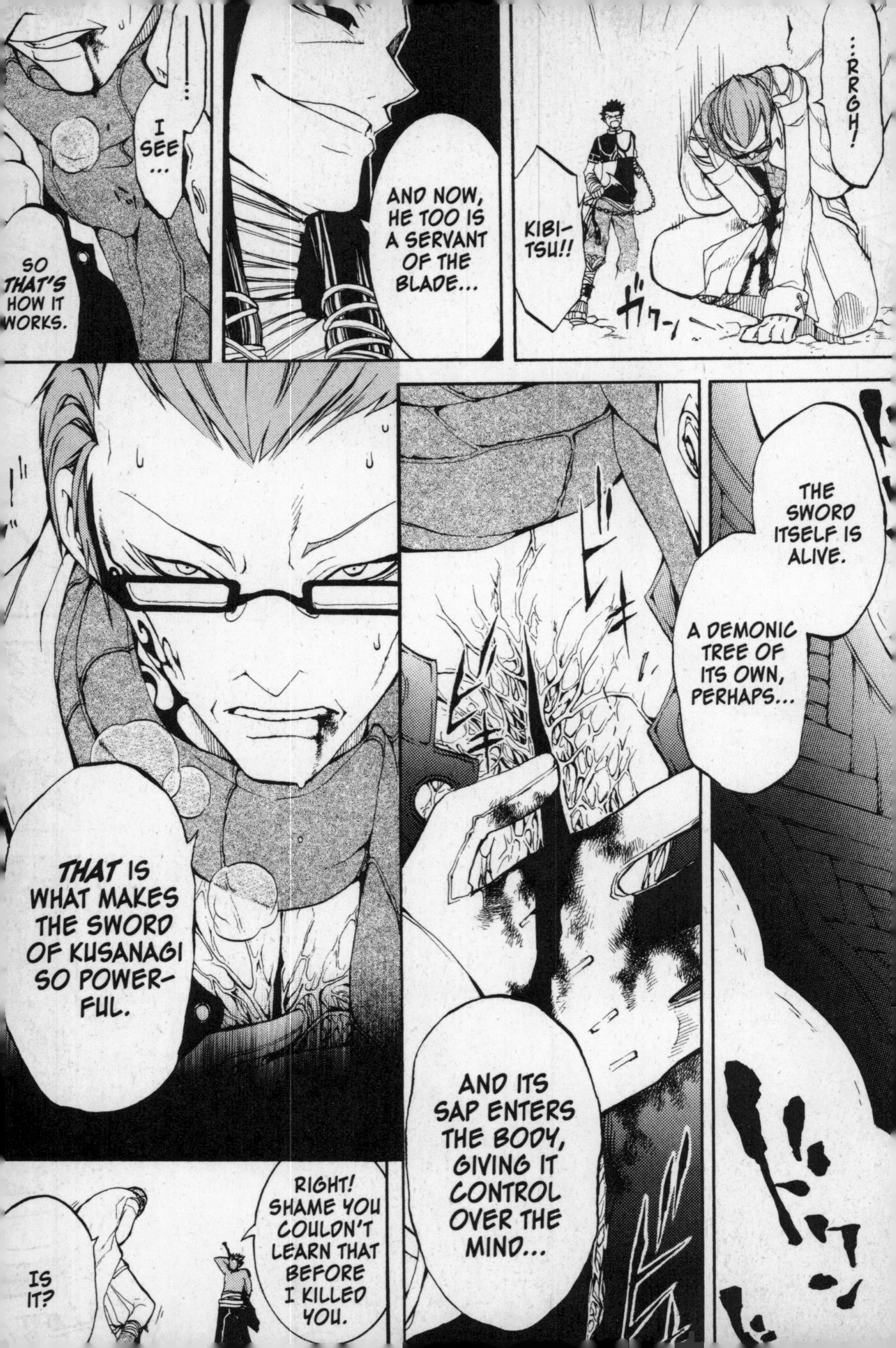
...RRGH!
KIBI-TSU!!
AND NOW, HE TOO IS A SERVANT OF THE BLADE...
...!
I SEE...
SO *THAT'S* HOW IT WORKS.
THE SWORD ITSELF IS ALIVE.
A DEMONIC TREE OF ITS OWN, PERHAPS...
AND ITS SAP ENTERS THE BODY, GIVING IT CONTROL OVER THE MIND...
THAT IS WHAT MAKES THE SWORD OF KUSANAGI SO POWER-FUL.
RIGHT! SHAME YOU COULDN'T LEARN THAT BEFORE I KILLED YOU.
IS IT?

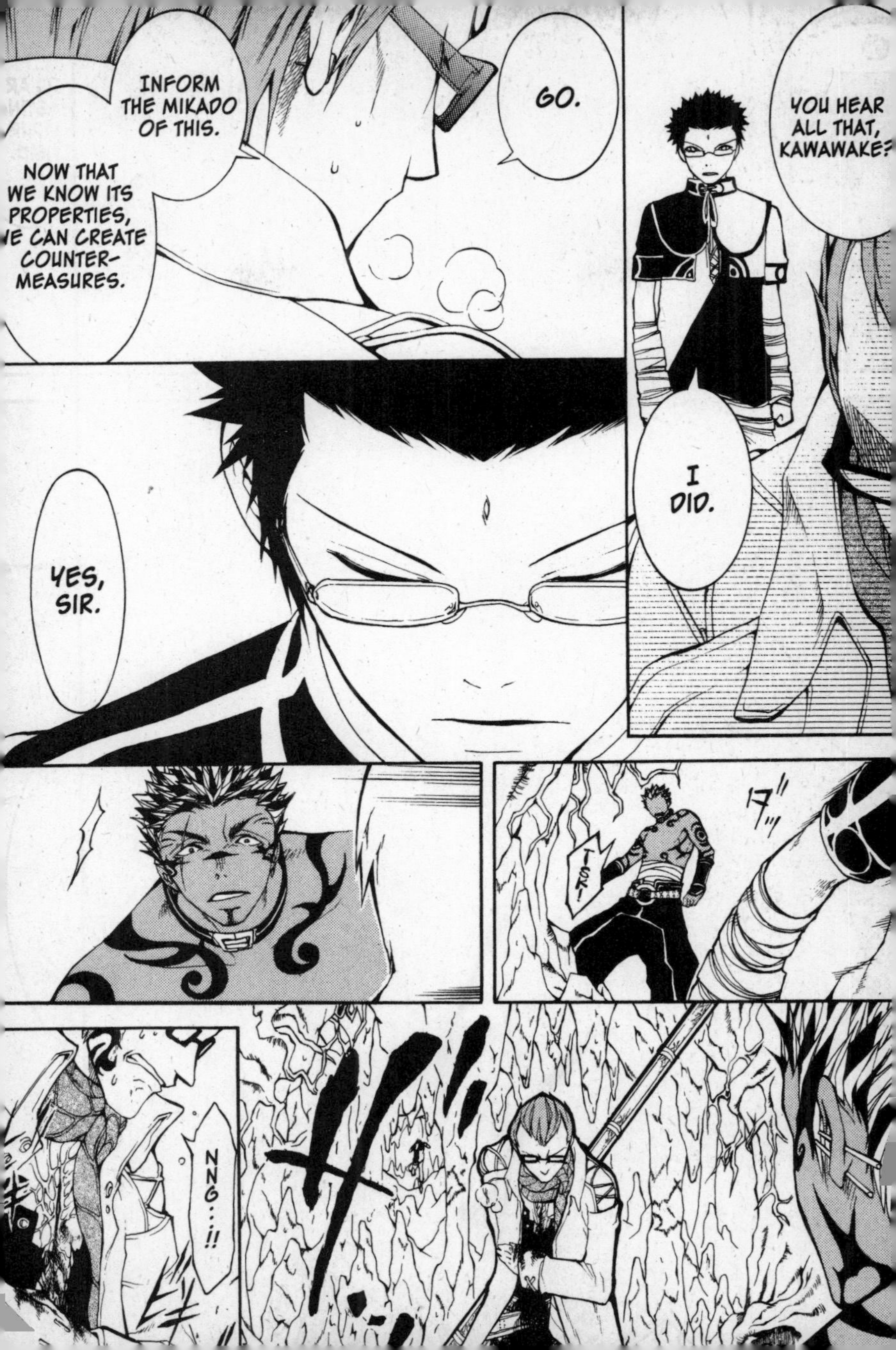
YOU HEAR ALL THAT, KAWAWAKE?
I DID.
GO.
INFORM THE MIKADO OF THIS.
NOW THAT WE KNOW ITS PROPERTIES, E CAN CREATE COUNTER-MEASURES.
YES, SIR.
TSK!
NNG...!!

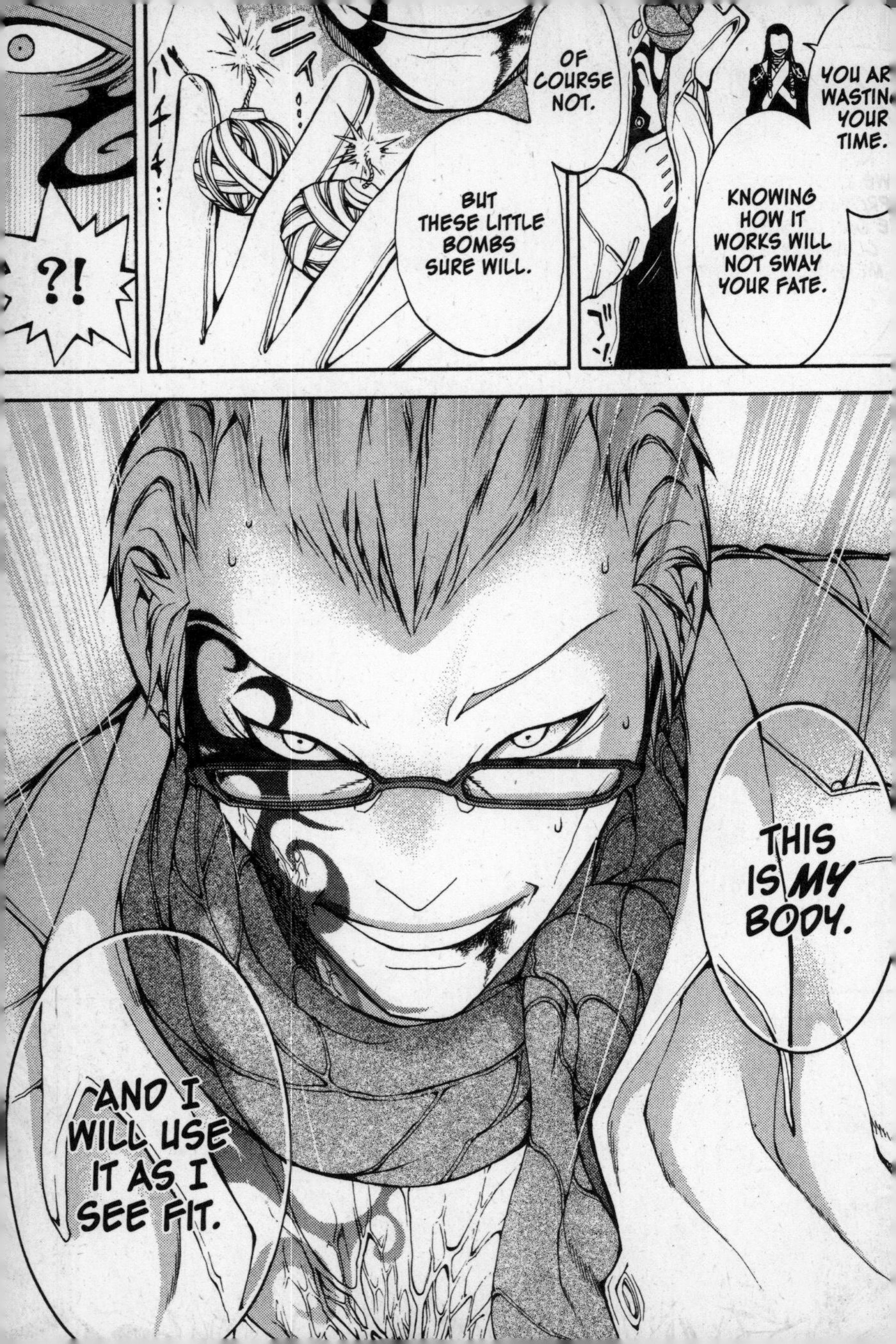
YOU AR WASTIN YOUR TIME.
KNOWING HOW IT WORKS WILL NOT SWAY YOUR FATE.
OF COURSE NOT.
BUT THESE LITTLE BOMBS SURE WILL.
?!
THIS IS MY BODY.
AND I WILL USE IT AS I SEE FIT.

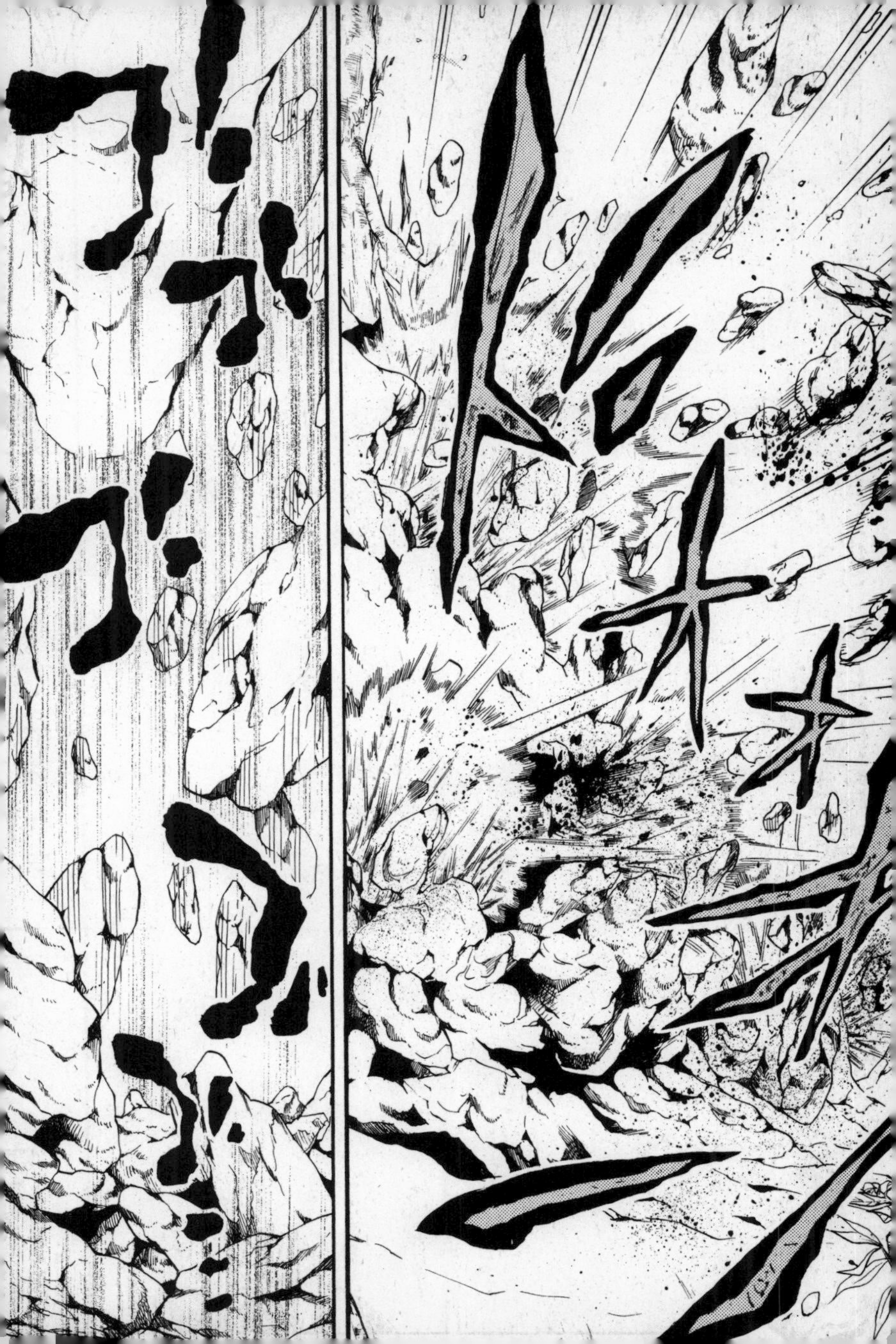

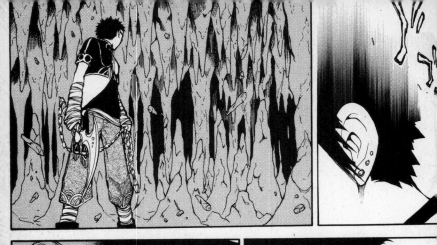

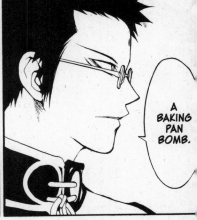

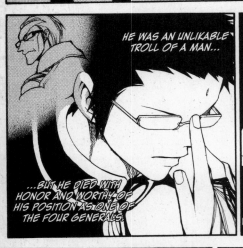

A BAKING PAN BOMB.
HE WAS AN UNLIKABLE TROLL OF A MAN...
...BUT HE DIED WITH HONOR AND WORTHY OF HIS POSITION AS ONE OF THE FOUR GENERALS.

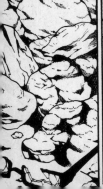

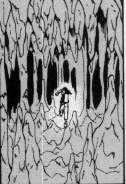

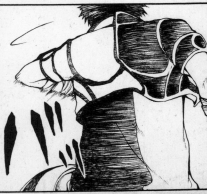

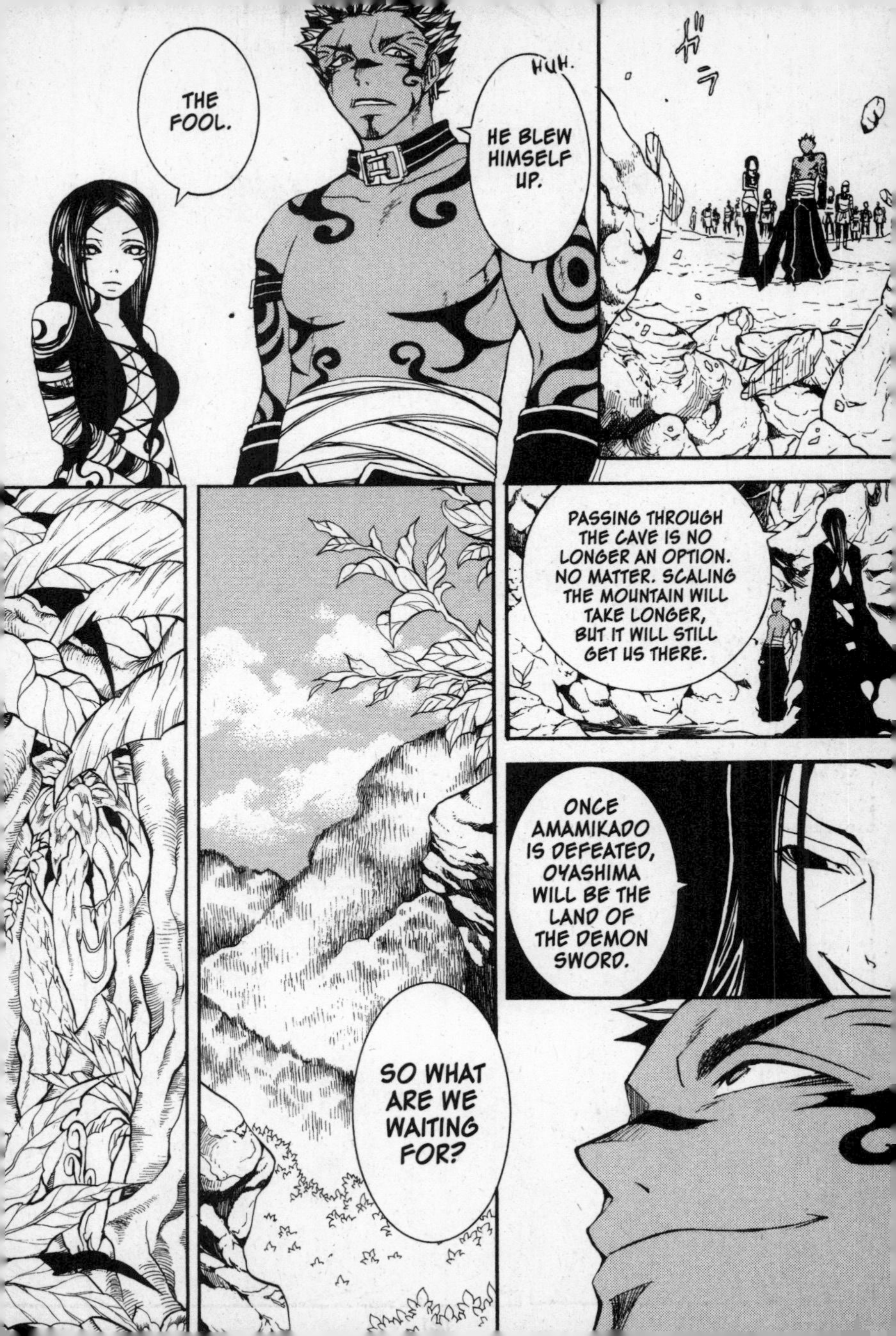
ガラ
HUH.
HE BLEW HIMSELF UP.
THE FOOL.
PASSING THROUGH THE CAVE IS NO LONGER AN OPTION. NO MATTER. SCALING THE MOUNTAIN WILL TAKE LONGER, BUT IT WILL STILL GET US THERE.
ONCE AMAMIKADO IS DEFEATED, OYASHIMA WILL BE THE LAND OF THE DEMON SWORD.
SO WHAT ARE WE WAITING FOR?

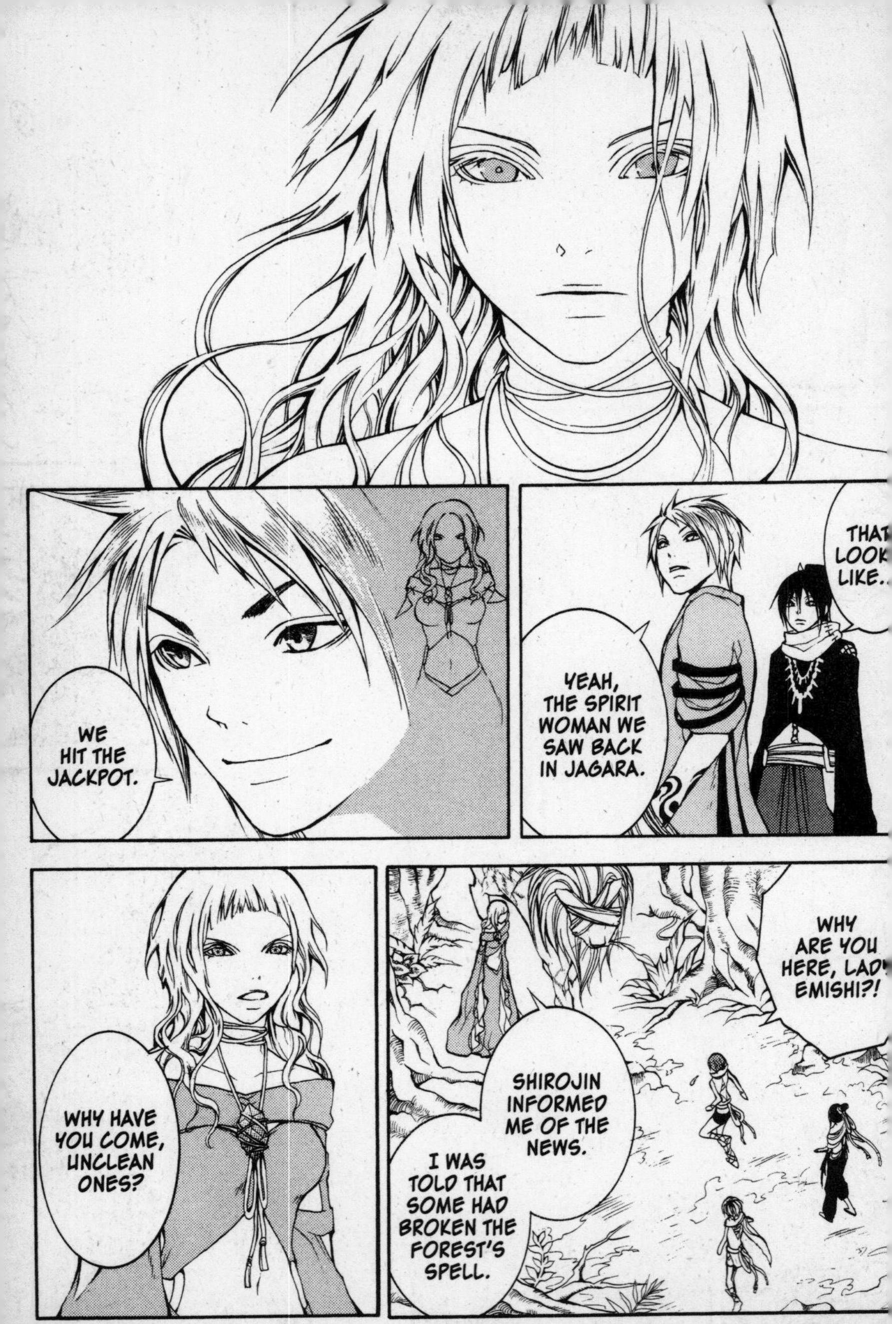

THAT LOOK LIKE...
YEAH, THE SPIRIT WOMAN WE SAW BACK IN JAGARA.
WE HIT THE JACKPOT.
WHY ARE YOU HERE, LAD EMISHI?!
SHIROJIN INFORMED ME OF THE NEWS.
I WAS TOLD THAT SOME HAD BROKEN THE FOREST'S SPELL.
WHY HAVE YOU COME, UNCLEAN ONES?

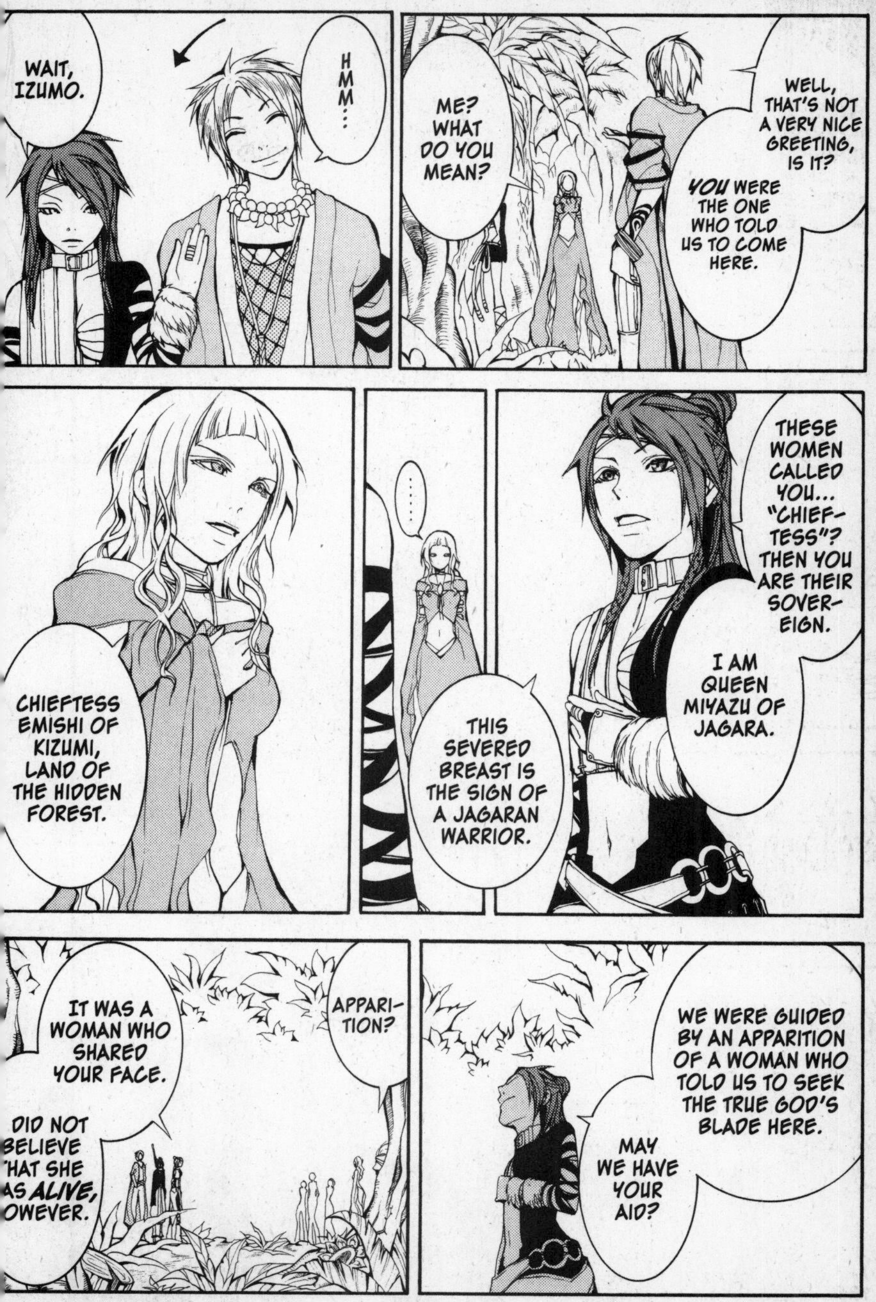
WELL, THAT'S NOT A VERY NICE GREETING, IS IT?
YOU WERE THE ONE WHO TOLD US TO COME HERE.
ME? WHAT DO YOU MEAN?
HMM...
WAIT, IZUMO.
THESE WOMEN CALLED YOU... "CHIEF-TESS"? THEN YOU ARE THEIR SOVER-EIGN.
I AM QUEEN MIYAZU OF JAGARA.
THIS SEVERED BREAST IS THE SIGN OF A JAGARAN WARRIOR.
......
CHIEFTESS EMISHI OF KIZUMI, LAND OF THE HIDDEN FOREST.
WE WERE GUIDED BY AN APPARITION OF A WOMAN WHO TOLD US TO SEEK THE TRUE GOD'S BLADE HERE.
MAY WE HAVE YOUR AID?
APPARI-TION?
IT WAS A WOMAN WHO SHARED YOUR FACE.
DID NOT BELIEVE THAT SHE AS *ALIVE*, OWEVER.

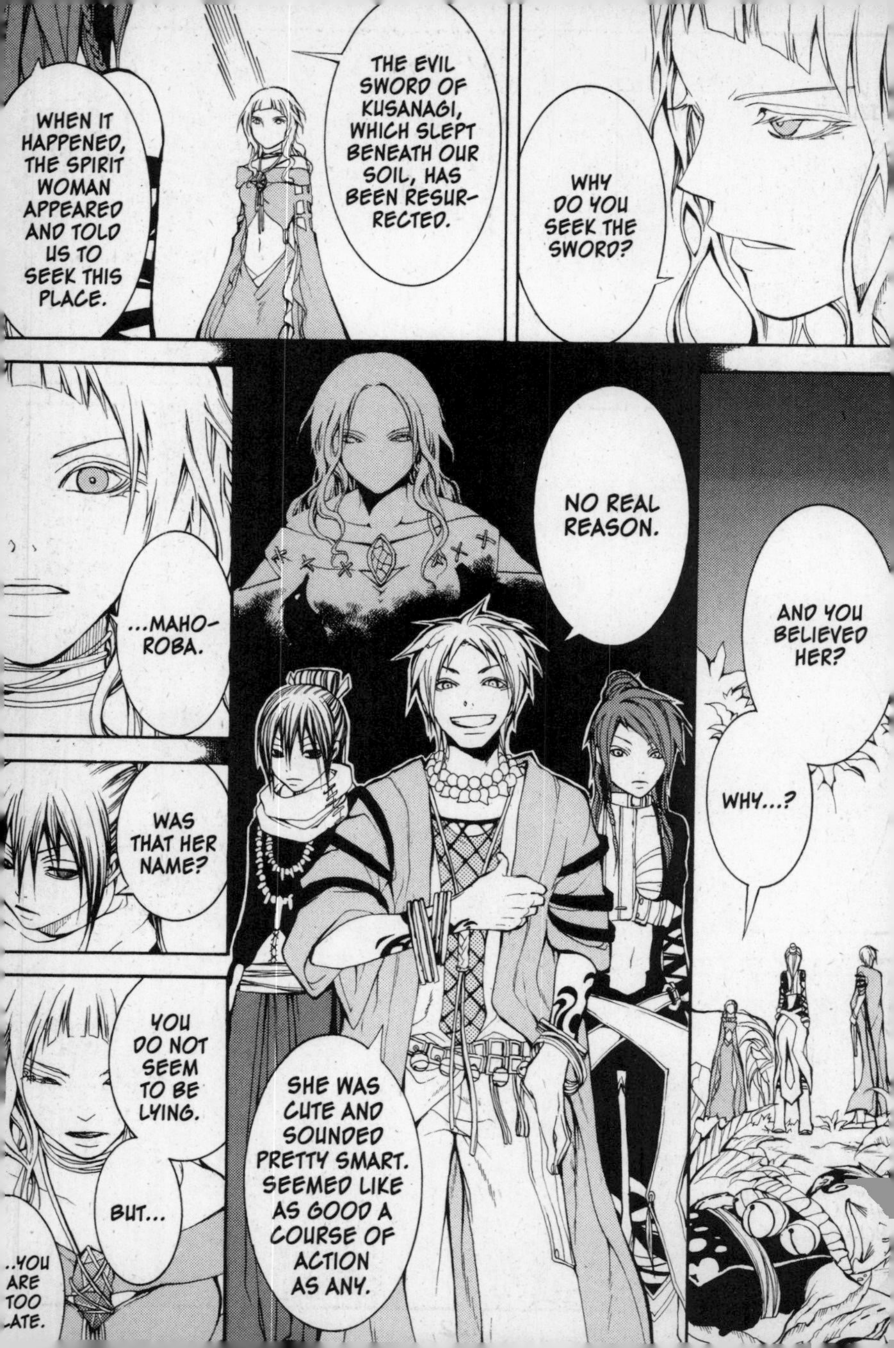
WHY DO YOU SEEK THE SWORD?
THE EVIL SWORD OF KUSANAGI, WHICH SLEPT BENEATH OUR SOIL, HAS BEEN RESUR-RECTED.
WHEN IT HAPPENED, THE SPIRIT WOMAN APPEARED AND TOLD US TO SEEK THIS PLACE.
AND YOU BELIEVED HER?
WHY...?
NO REAL REASON.
SHE WAS CUTE AND SOUNDED PRETTY SMART. SEEMED LIKE AS GOOD A COURSE OF ACTION AS ANY.
...MAHO-ROBA.
WAS THAT HER NAME?
YOU DO NOT SEEM TO BE LYING.
BUT...
..YOU ARE TOO LATE.

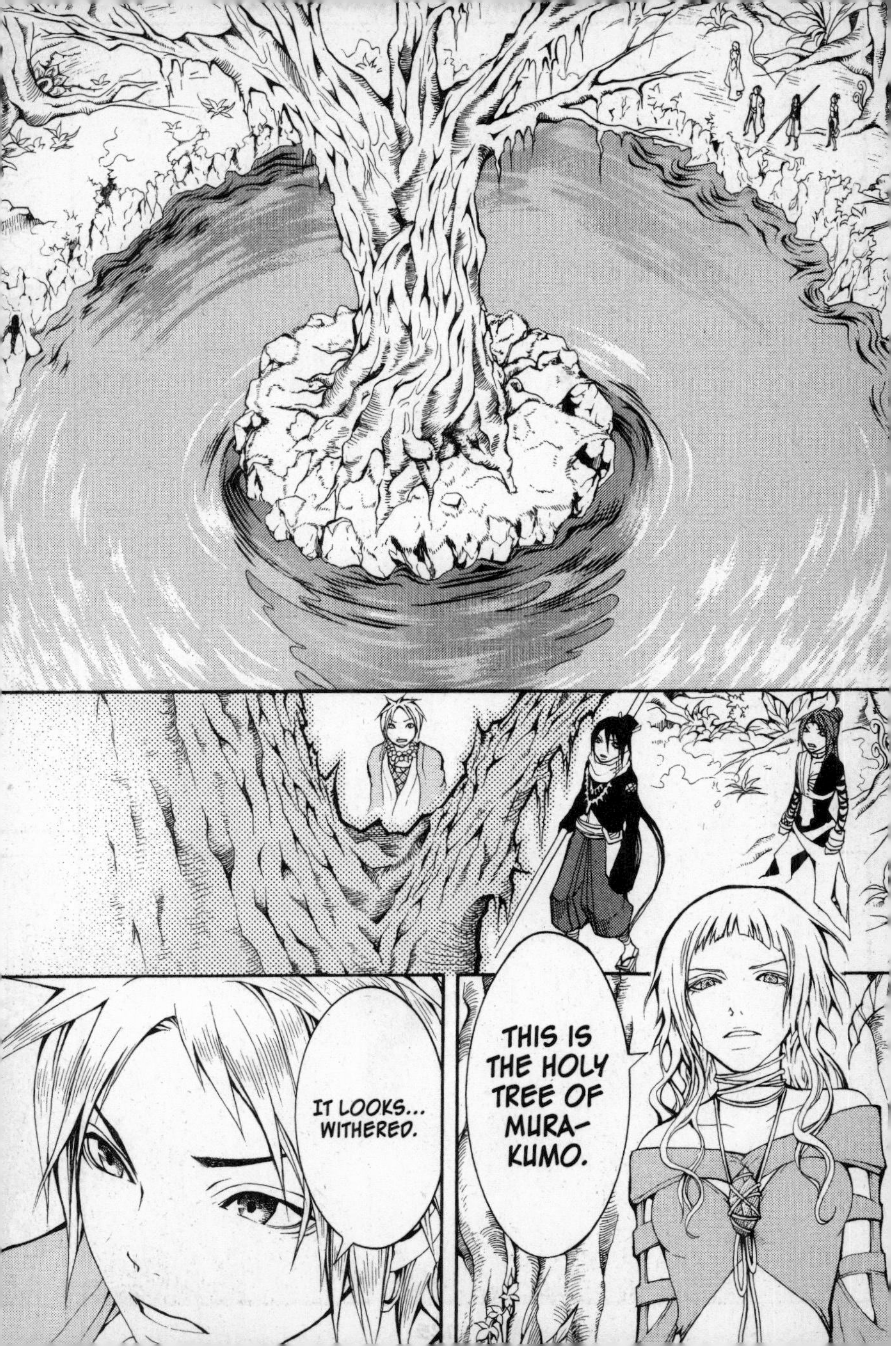
THIS IS THE HOLY TREE OF MURA-KUMO.
IT LOOKS... WITHERED.

Chapter 14: The Dying Holy Tree

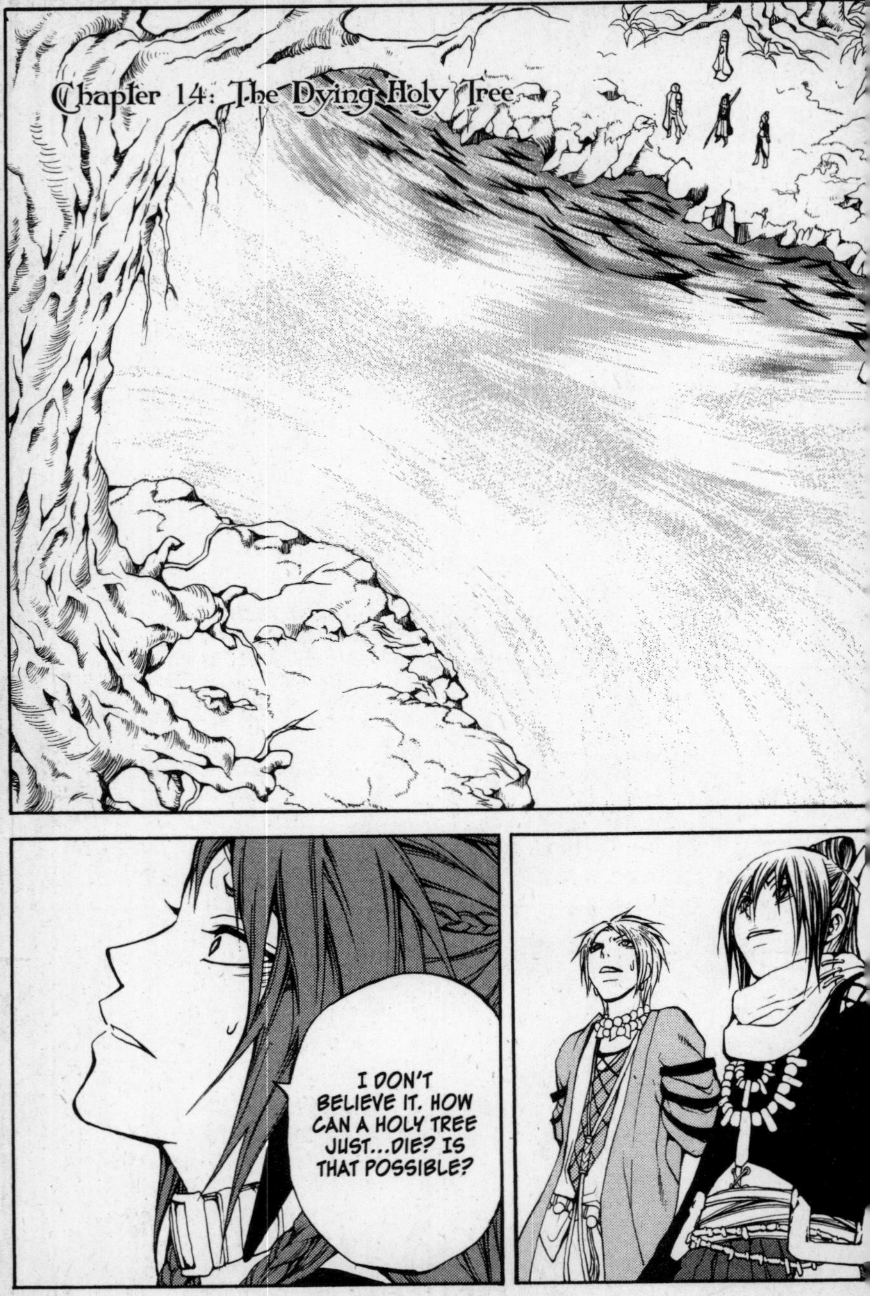
I DON'T BELIEVE IT. HOW CAN A HOLY TREE JUST...DIE? IS THAT POSSIBLE?

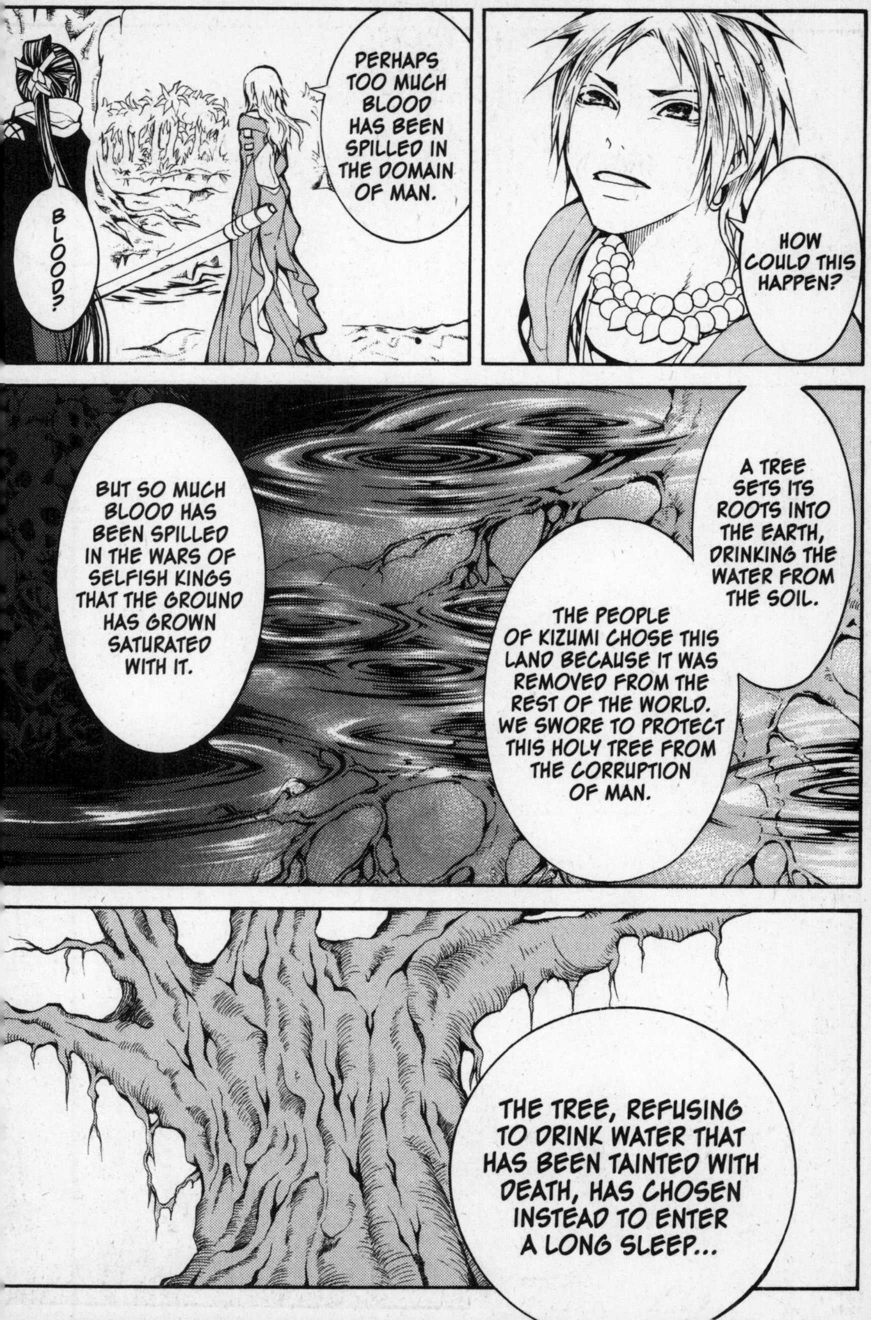
HOW COULD THIS HAPPEN?
PERHAPS TOO MUCH BLOOD HAS BEEN SPILLED IN THE DOMAIN OF MAN.
BLOOD?
A TREE SETS ITS ROOTS INTO THE EARTH, DRINKING THE WATER FROM THE SOIL.
THE PEOPLE OF KIZUMI CHOSE THIS LAND BECAUSE IT WAS REMOVED FROM THE REST OF THE WORLD. WE SWORE TO PROTECT THIS HOLY TREE FROM THE CORRUPTION OF MAN.
BUT SO MUCH BLOOD HAS BEEN SPILLED IN THE WARS OF SELFISH KINGS THAT THE GROUND HAS GROWN SATURATED WITH IT.
THE TREE, REFUSING TO DRINK WATER THAT HAS BEEN TAINTED WITH DEATH, HAS CHOSEN INSTEAD TO ENTER A LONG SLEEP...

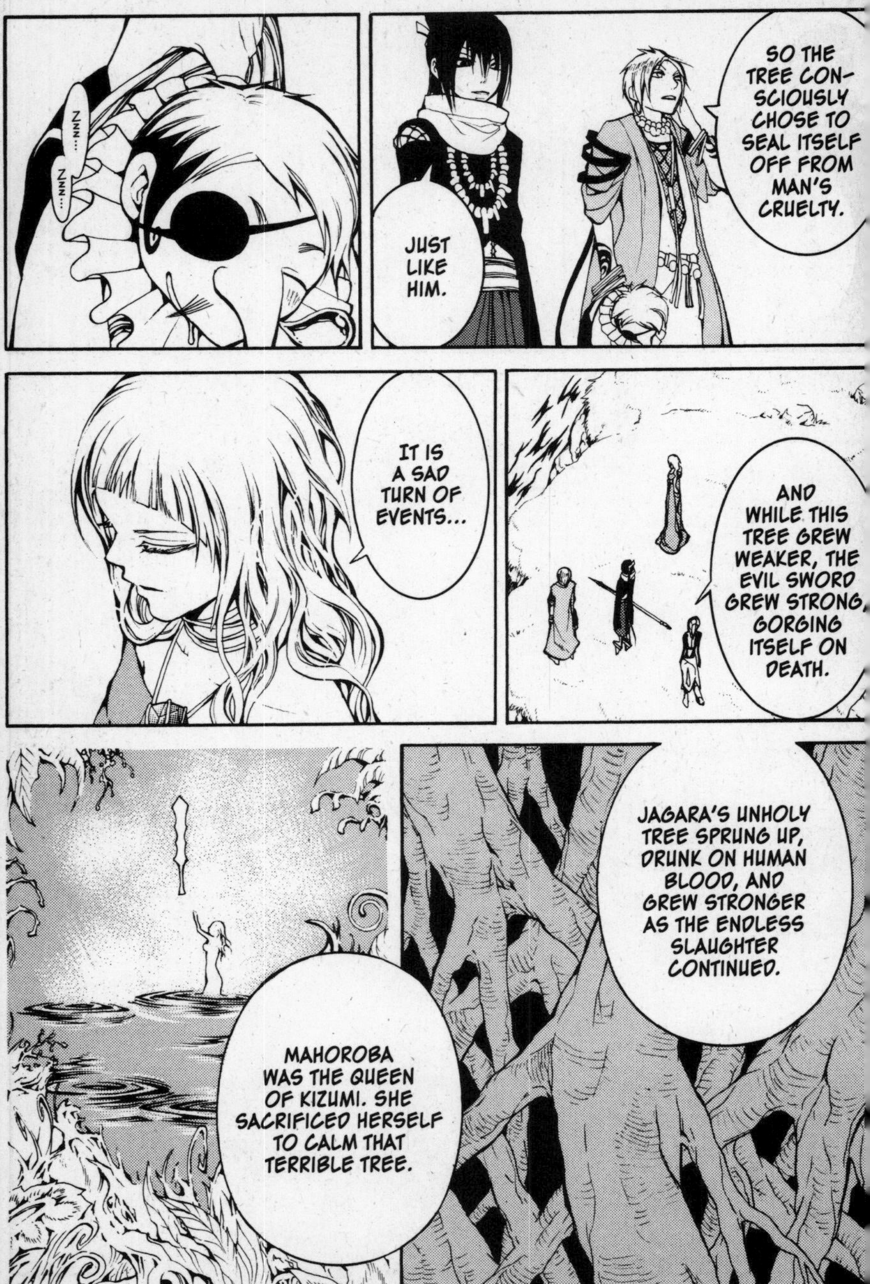
SO THE TREE CONSCIOUSLY CHOSE TO SEAL ITSELF OFF FROM MAN'S CRUELTY.
JUST LIKE HIM.
Zzz...
Zzz...
AND WHILE THIS TREE GREW WEAKER, THE EVIL SWORD GREW STRONG, GORGING ITSELF ON DEATH.
IT IS A SAD TURN OF EVENTS...
JAGARA'S UNHOLY TREE SPRUNG UP, DRUNK ON HUMAN BLOOD, AND GREW STRONGER AS THE ENDLESS SLAUGHTER CONTINUED.
MAHOROBA WAS THE QUEEN OF KIZUMI. SHE SACRIFICED HERSELF TO CALM THAT TERRIBLE TREE.

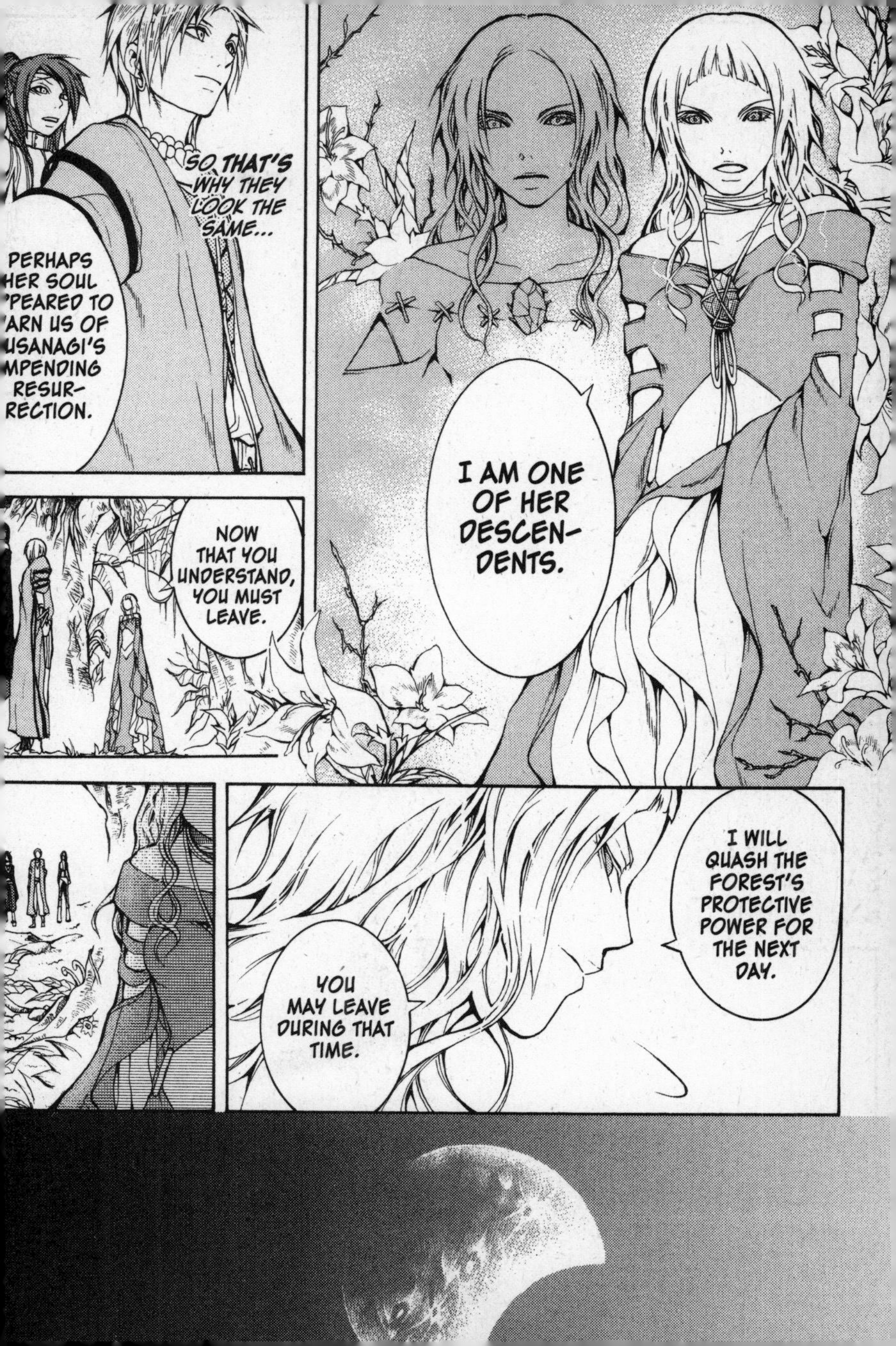
I AM ONE OF HER DESCENDENTS.
SO THAT'S WHY THEY LOOK THE SAME...
PERHAPS HER SOUL 'PEARED TO 'ARN US OF USANAGI'S MPENDING RESURRECTION.
NOW THAT YOU UNDERSTAND, YOU MUST LEAVE.
I WILL QUASH THE FOREST'S PROTECTIVE POWER FOR THE NEXT DAY.
YOU MAY LEAVE DURING THAT TIME.

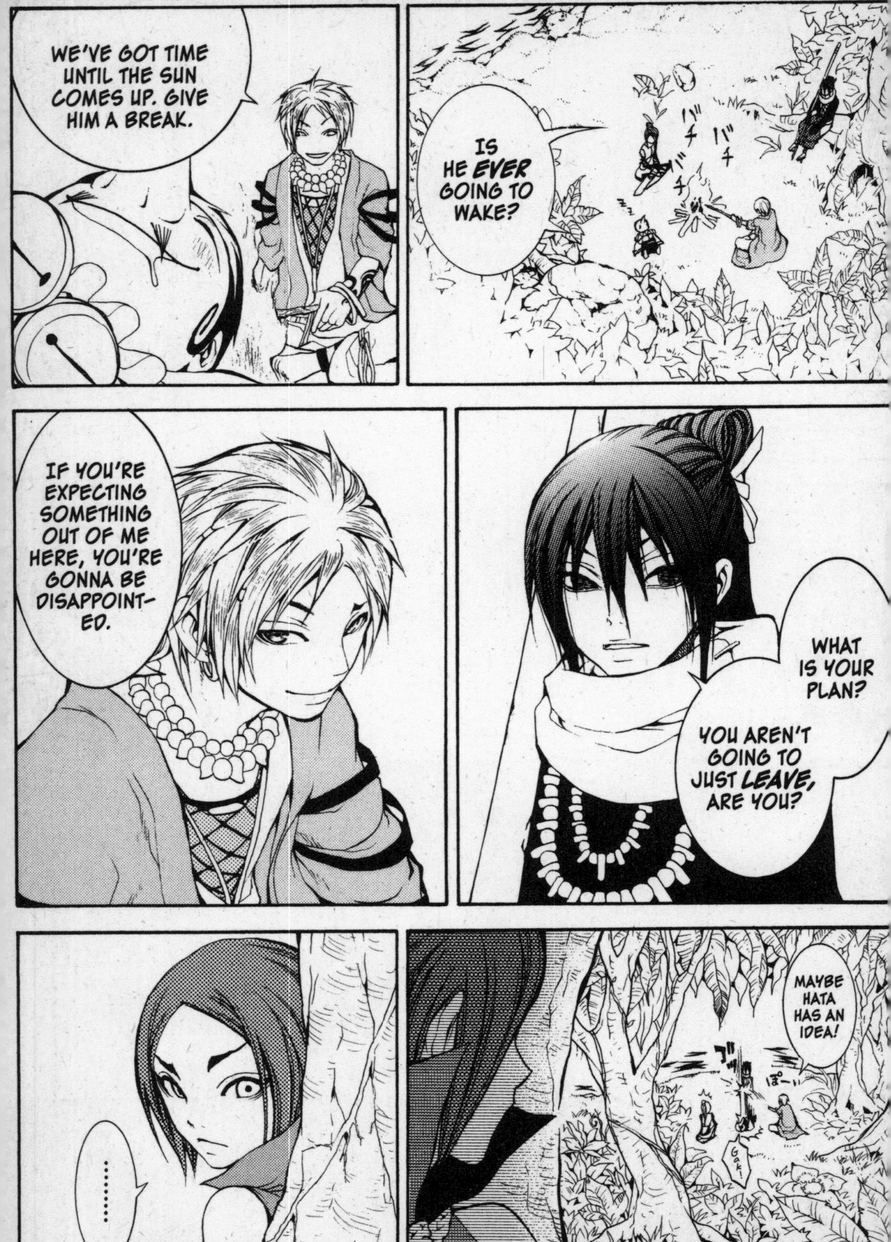
IS HE EVER GOING TO WAKE?
WE'VE GOT TIME UNTIL THE SUN COMES UP. GIVE HIM A BREAK.
WHAT IS YOUR PLAN?
YOU AREN'T GOING TO JUST LEAVE, ARE YOU?
IF YOU'RE EXPECTING SOMETHING OUT OF ME HERE, YOU'RE GONNA BE DISAPPOINT-ED.
MAYBE HATA HAS AN IDEA!
Gak!
......

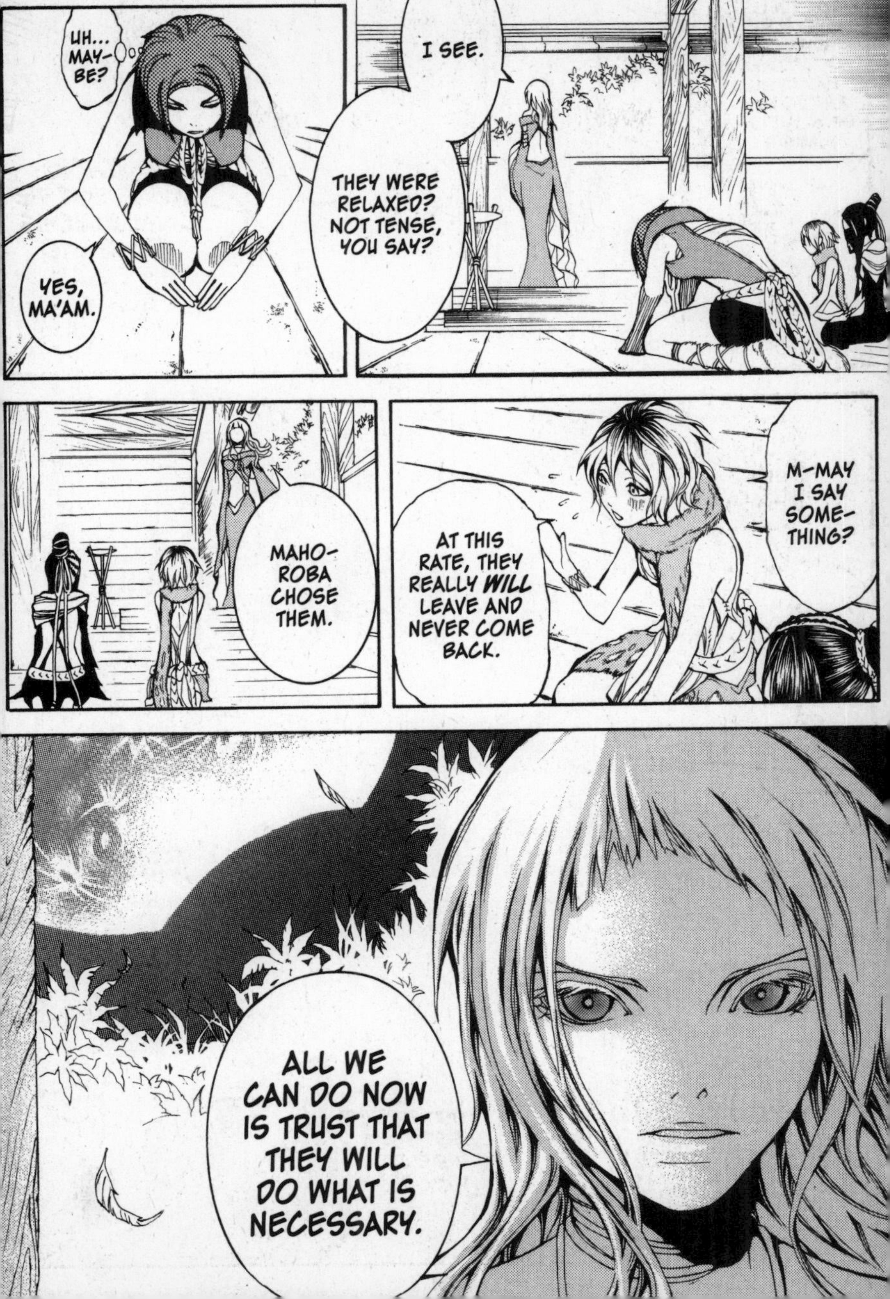

I SEE.
THEY WERE RELAXED? NOT TENSE, YOU SAY?
UH... MAY-BE?
YES, MA'AM.
M-MAY I SAY SOME-THING?
AT THIS RATE, THEY REALLY ***WILL*** LEAVE AND NEVER COME BACK.
MAHO-ROBA CHOSE THEM.
ALL WE CAN DO NOW IS TRUST THAT THEY WILL DO WHAT IS NECESSARY.

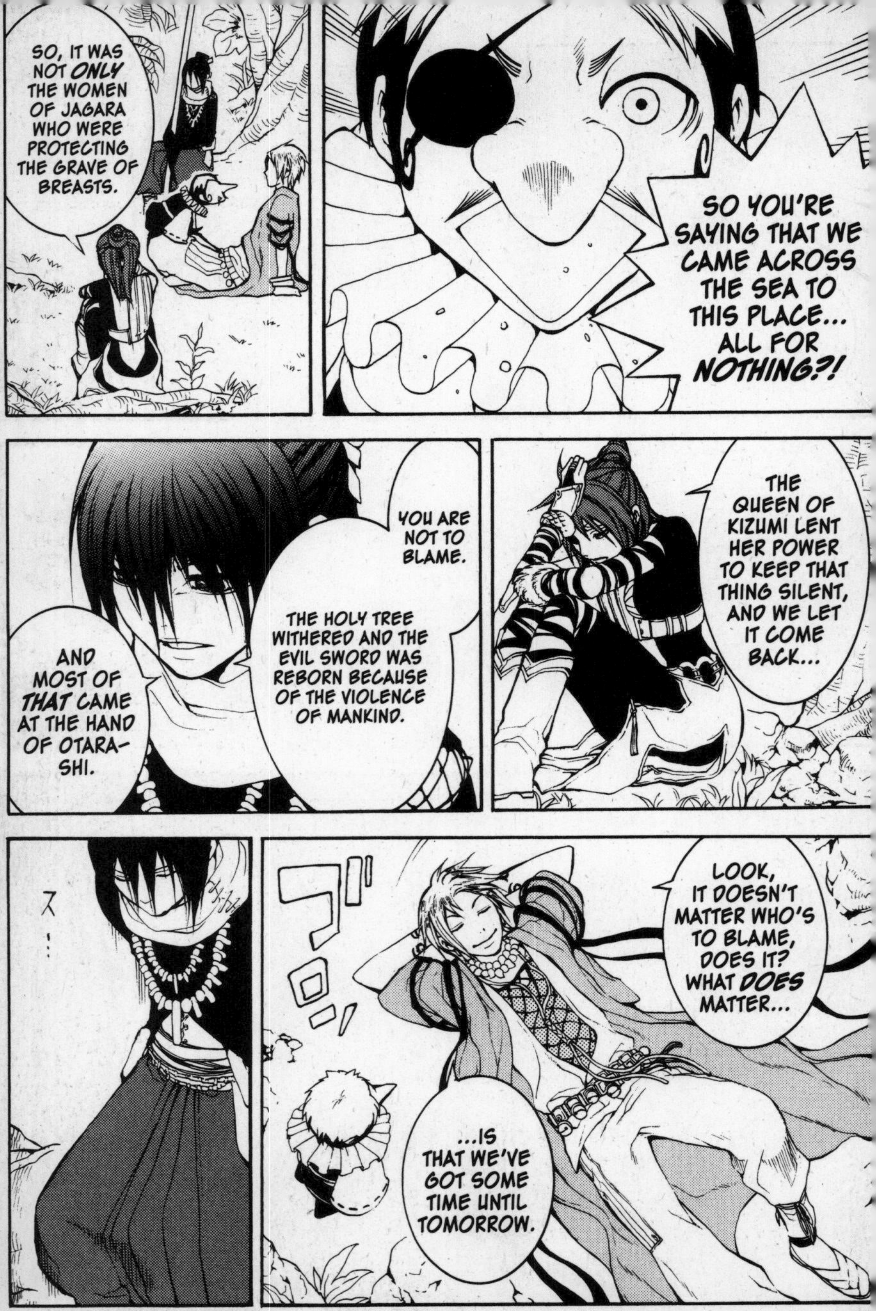
SO YOU'RE SAYING THAT WE CAME ACROSS THE SEA TO THIS PLACE... ALL FOR NOTHING?!
SO, IT WAS NOT ONLY THE WOMEN OF JAGARA WHO WERE PROTECTING THE GRAVE OF BREASTS.
THE QUEEN OF KIZUMI LENT HER POWER TO KEEP THAT THING SILENT, AND WE LET IT COME BACK...
YOU ARE NOT TO BLAME.
THE HOLY TREE WITHERED AND THE EVIL SWORD WAS REBORN BECAUSE OF THE VIOLENCE OF MANKIND.
AND MOST OF THAT CAME AT THE HAND OF OTARA-SHI.
LOOK, IT DOESN'T MATTER WHO'S TO BLAME, DOES IT? WHAT DOES MATTER...
...IS THAT WE'VE GOT SOME TIME UNTIL TOMORROW.
ゴロン
ス…!

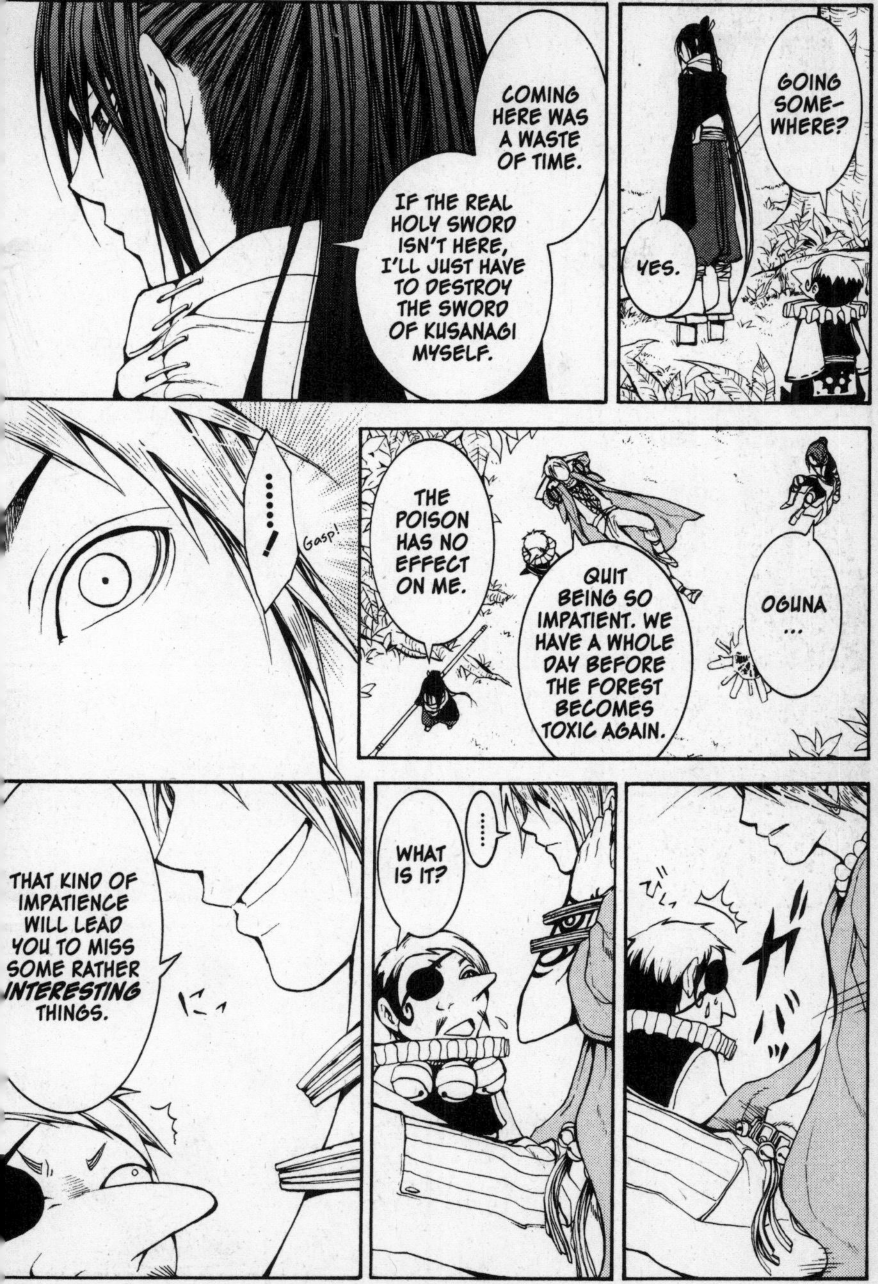
GOING SOME-WHERE?
YES.
COMING HERE WAS A WASTE OF TIME.
IF THE REAL HOLY SWORD ISN'T HERE, I'LL JUST HAVE TO DESTROY THE SWORD OF KUSANAGI MYSELF.
OGUNA ...
QUIT BEING SO IMPATIENT. WE HAVE A WHOLE DAY BEFORE THE FOREST BECOMES TOXIC AGAIN.
THE POISON HAS NO EFFECT ON ME.
......!
Gasp!
......
WHAT IS IT?
THAT KIND OF IMPATIENCE WILL LEAD YOU TO MISS SOME RATHER ***INTERESTING*** THINGS.

WHAT?

PERHAPS I CAN MEET YOUR EXPEC- TATIONS, AFTER ALL.

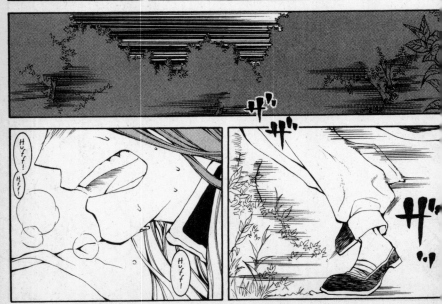

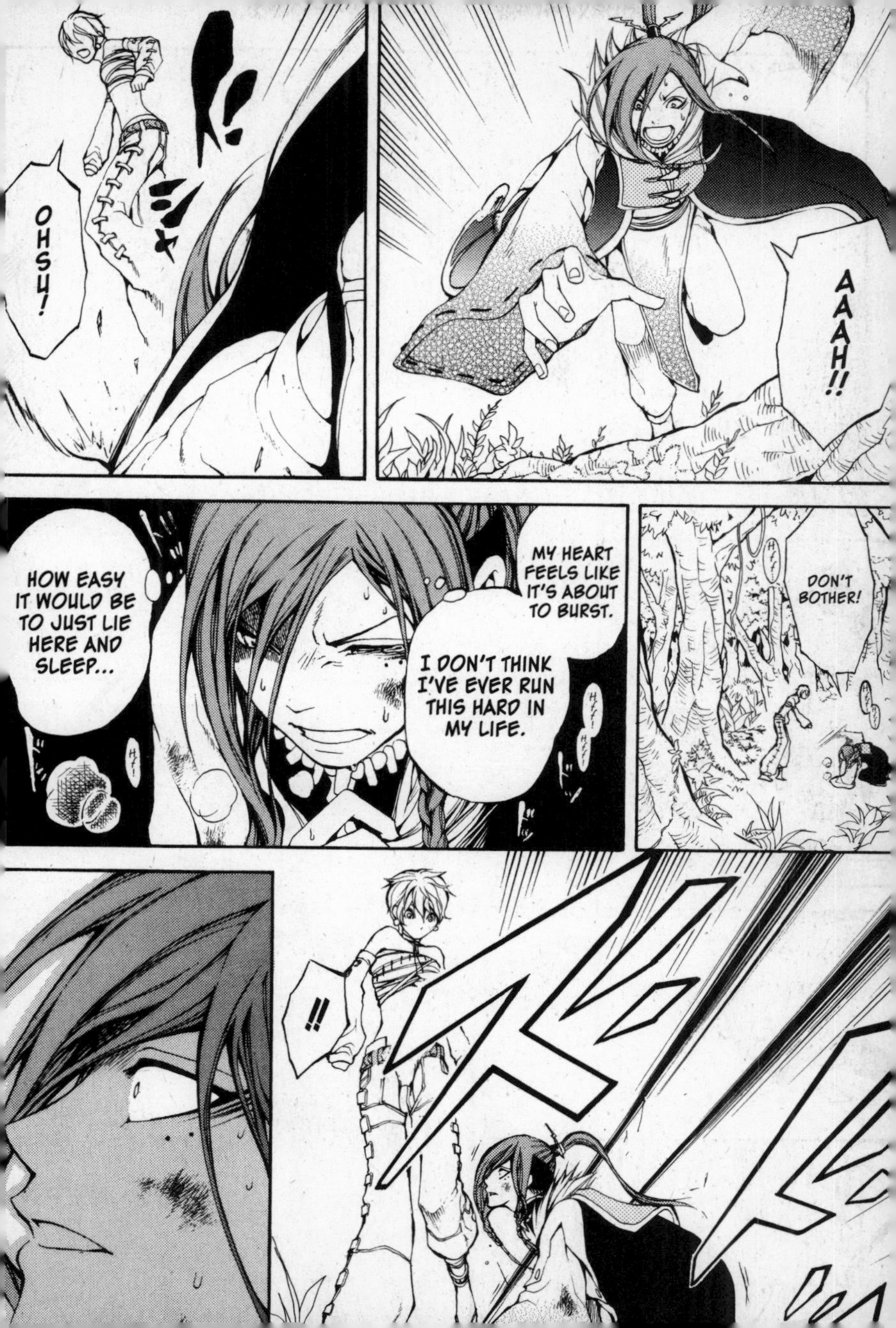
AAAH!!
OHSU!
DON'T BOTHER!
MY HEART FEELS LIKE IT'S ABOUT TO BURST.
I DON'T THINK I'VE EVER RUN THIS HARD IN MY LIFE.
HOW EASY IT WOULD BE TO JUST LIE HERE AND SLEEP...
!!

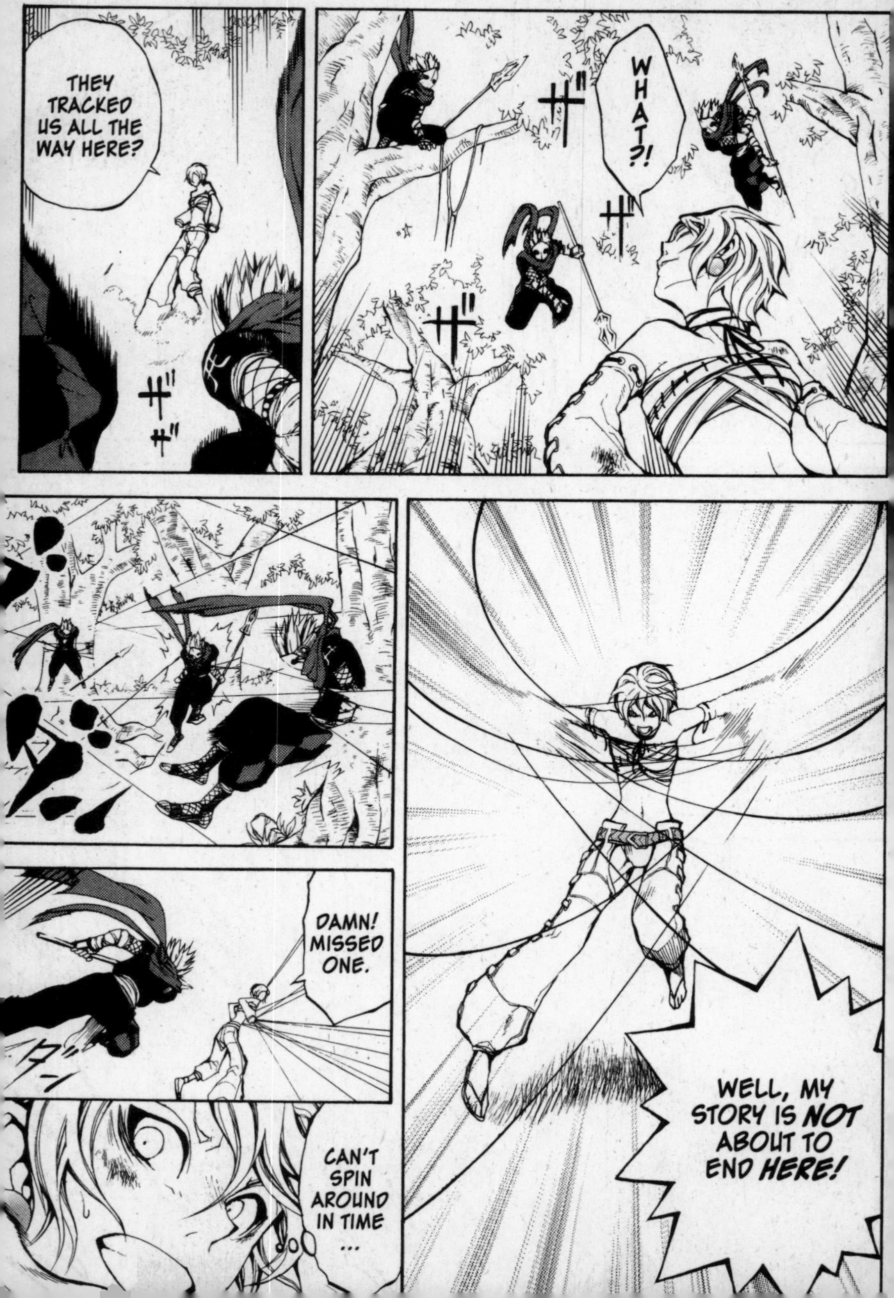
WHAT?!
THEY TRACKED US ALL THE WAY HERE?
WELL, MY STORY IS ***NOT*** ABOUT TO END ***HERE!***
DAMN! MISSED ONE.
CAN'T SPIN AROUND IN TIME ...

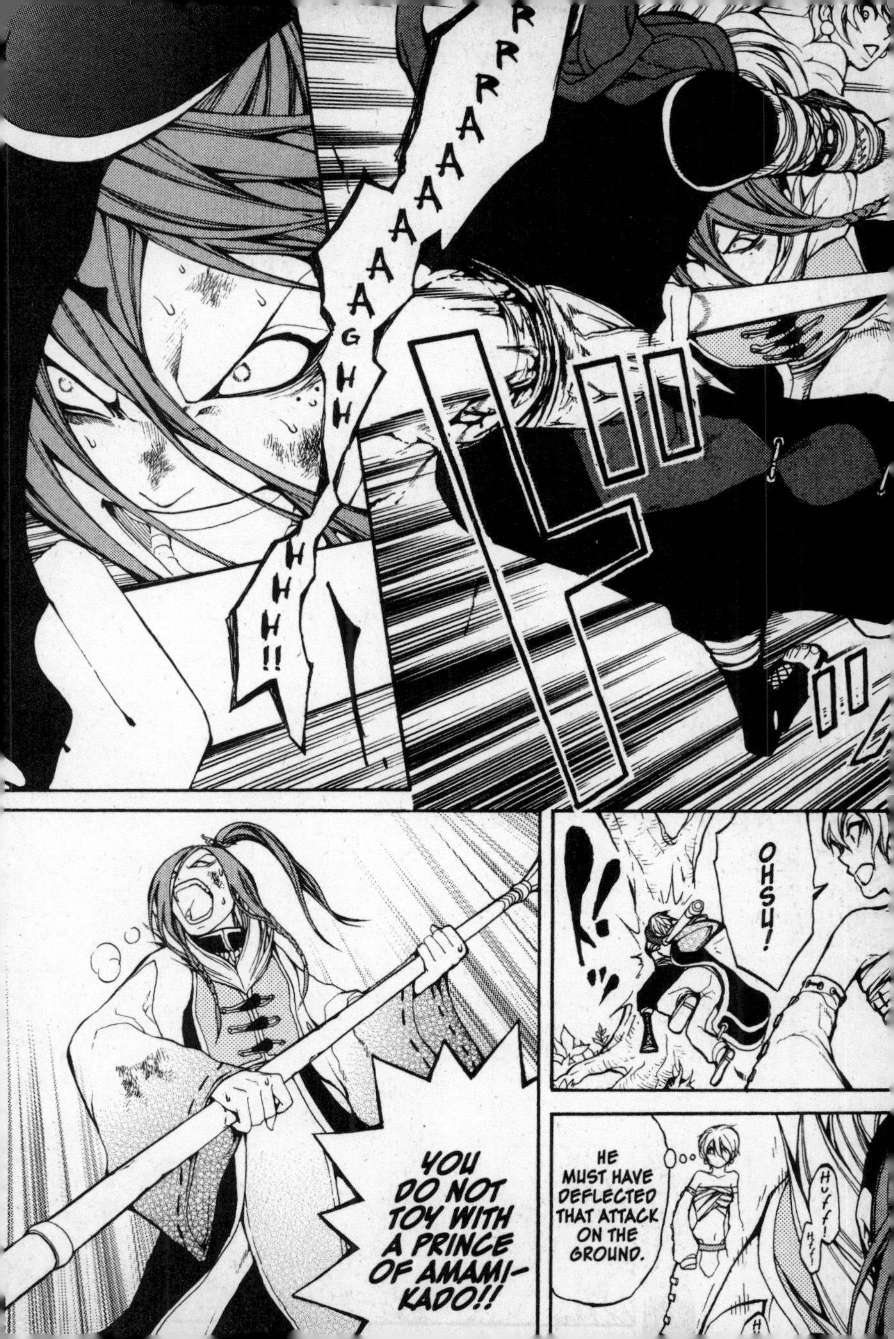
RRRAAAAAAGHHHHH!!
OHSU!
HE MUST HAVE DEFLECTED THAT ATTACK ON THE GROUND.
Huff! Huff!
YOU DO NOT TOY WITH A PRINCE OF AMAMI-KADO!!

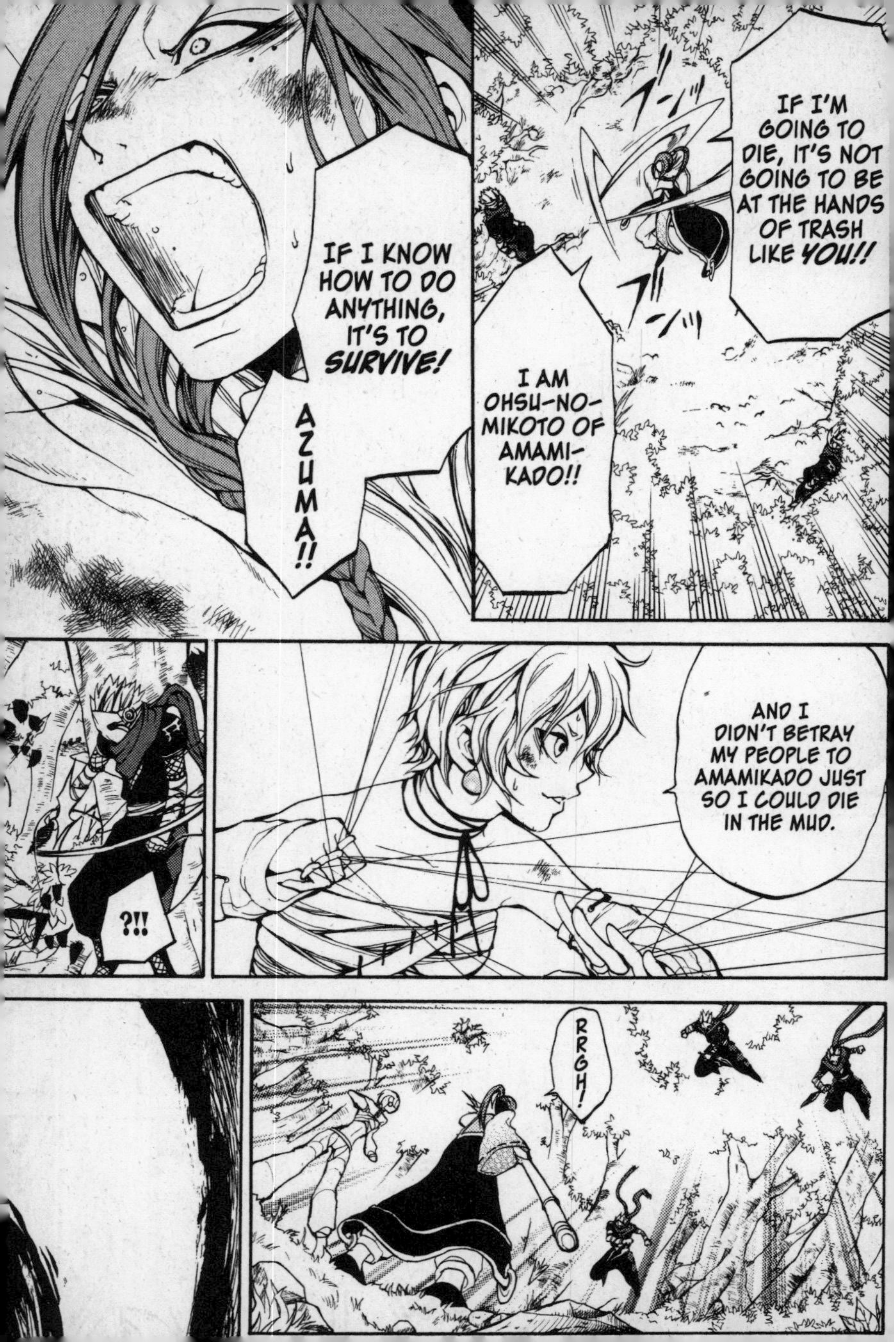
IF I'M GOING TO DIE, IT'S NOT GOING TO BE AT THE HANDS OF TRASH LIKE *YOU!!*
I AM OHSU-NO-MIKOTO OF AMAMI-KADO!!
IF I KNOW HOW TO DO ANYTHING, IT'S TO *SURVIVE!*
AZUMA!!
AND I DIDN'T BETRAY MY PEOPLE TO AMAMIKADO JUST SO I COULD DIE IN THE MUD.
?!!
RRGH!

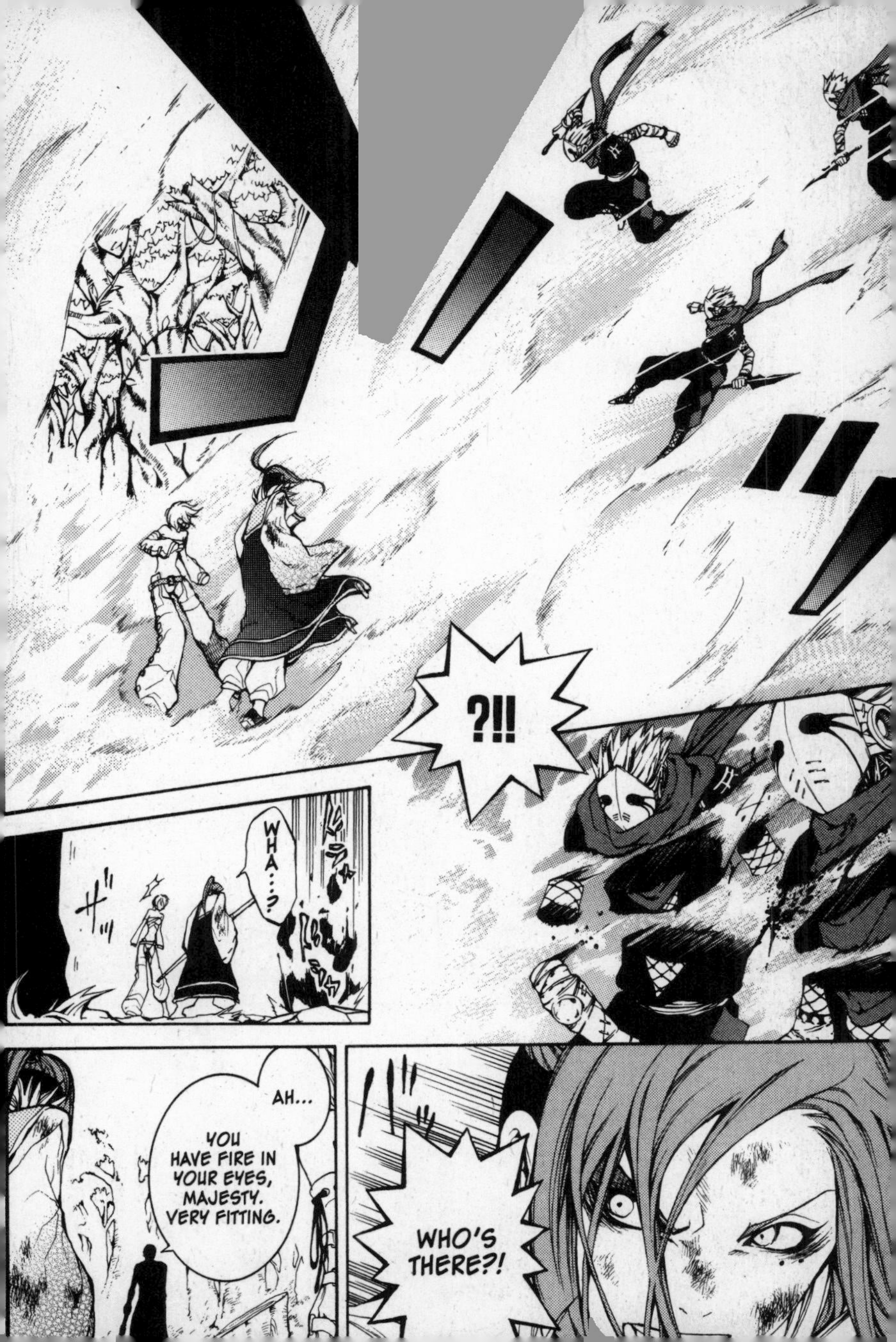
?!!
WHA...?
WHO'S THERE?!
AH...
YOU HAVE FIRE IN YOUR EYES, MAJESTY. VERY FITTING.

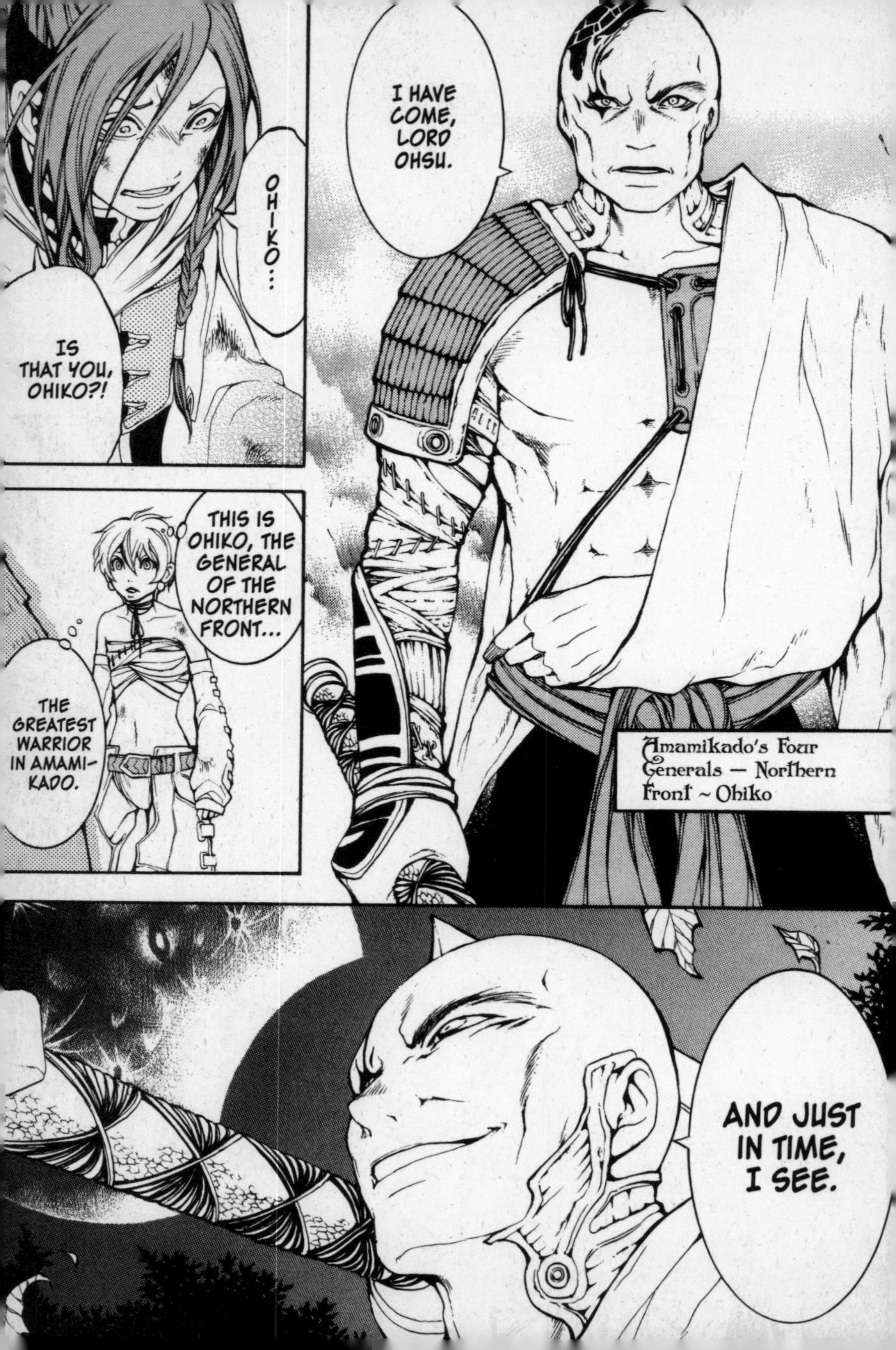
I HAVE COME, LORD OHSU.
Amamikado's Four Generals — Northern Front ~ Ohiko
OHIKO...
IS THAT YOU, OHIKO?!
THIS IS OHIKO, THE GENERAL OF THE NORTHERN FRONT...
THE GREATEST WARRIOR IN AMAMIKADO.
AND JUST IN TIME, I SEE.

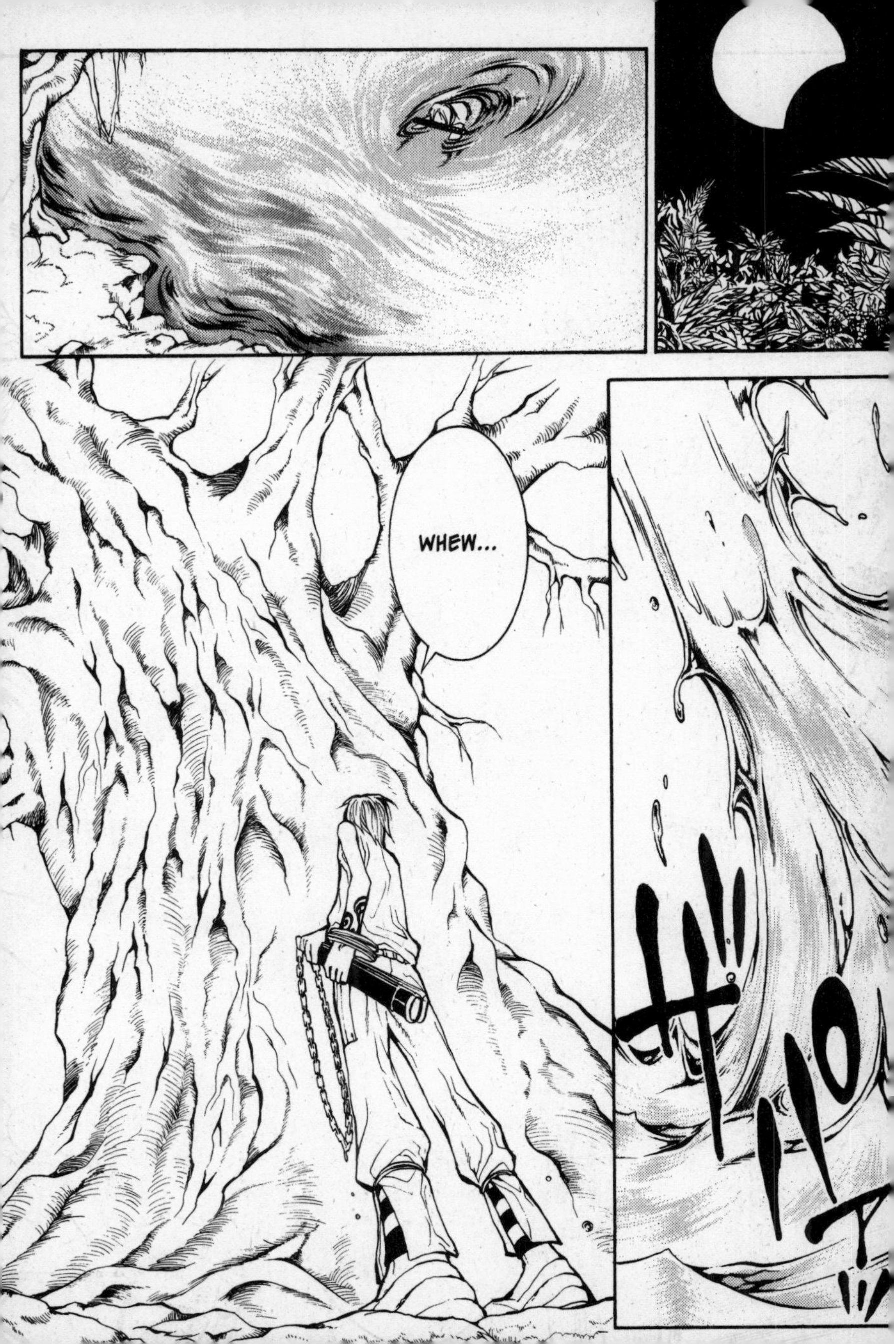
WHEW...

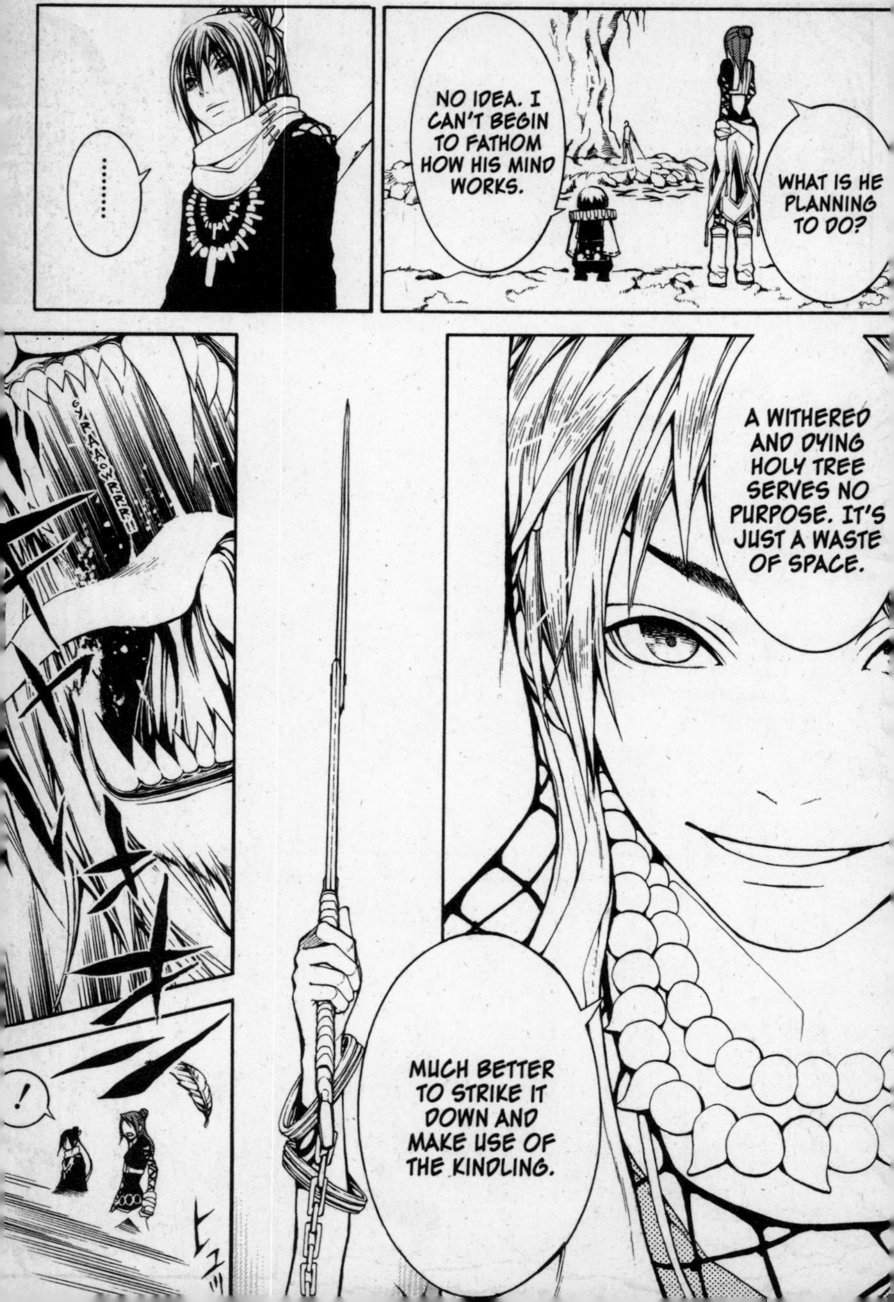
WHAT IS HE PLANNING TO DO?
NO IDEA. I CAN'T BEGIN TO FATHOM HOW HIS MIND WORKS.
......
A WITHERED AND DYING HOLY TREE SERVES NO PURPOSE. IT'S JUST A WASTE OF SPACE.
MUCH BETTER TO STRIKE IT DOWN AND MAKE USE OF THE KINDLING.
GYRAAAOWRRR!!
!

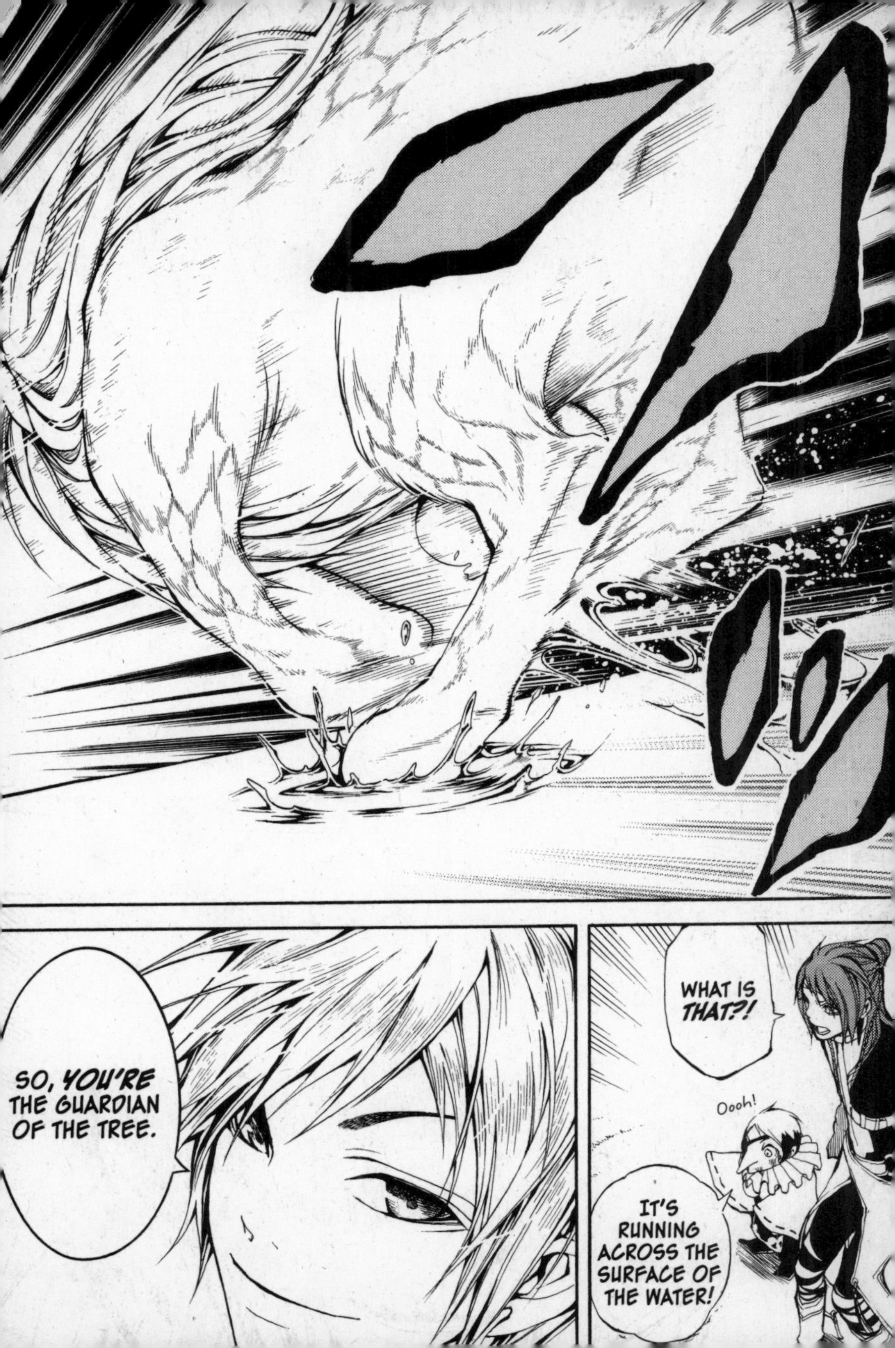
WHAT IS THAT?!
Oooh!
IT'S RUNNING ACROSS THE SURFACE OF THE WATER!
SO, YOU'RE THE GUARDIAN OF THE TREE.

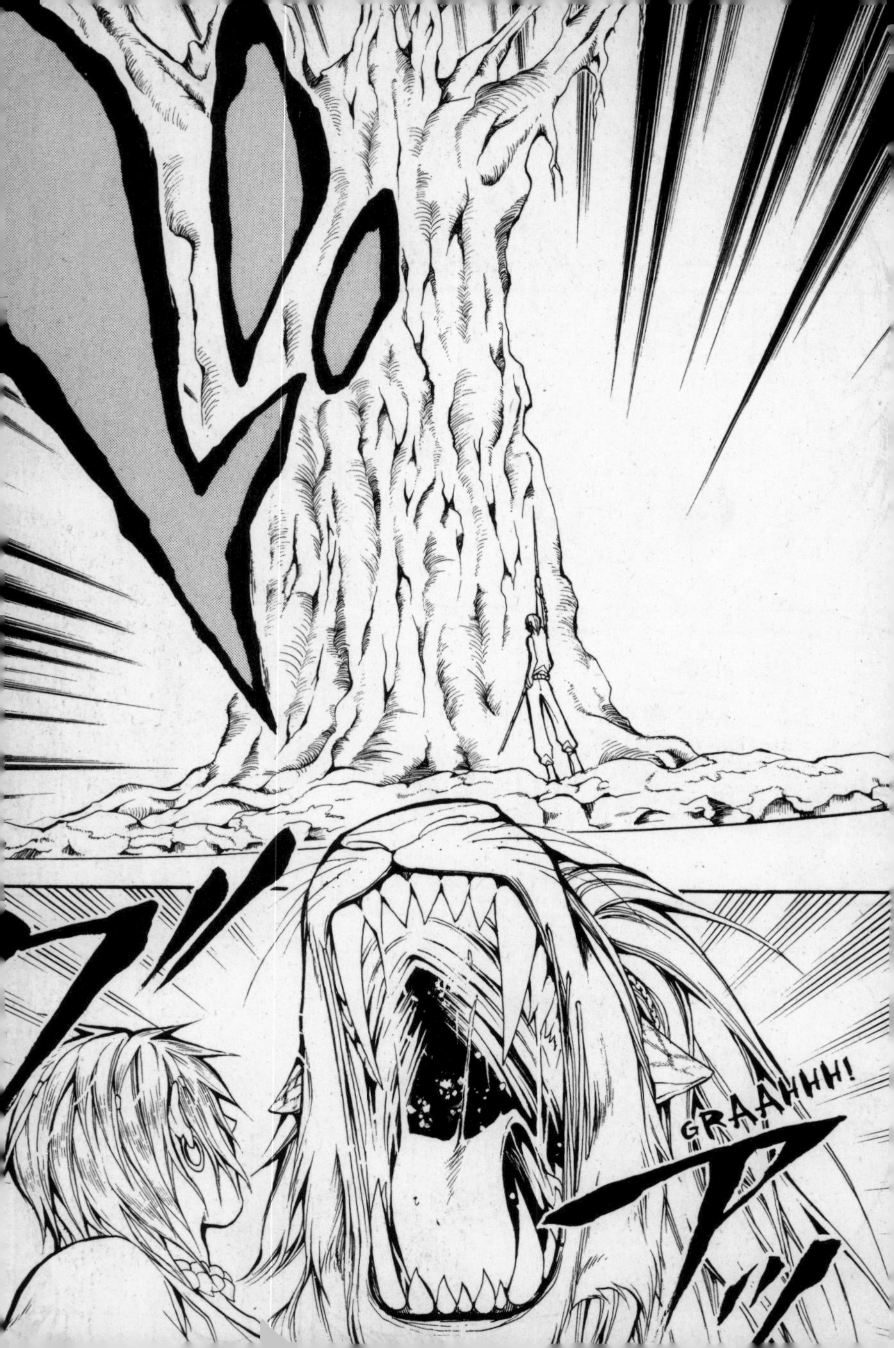
GRAAHHH!

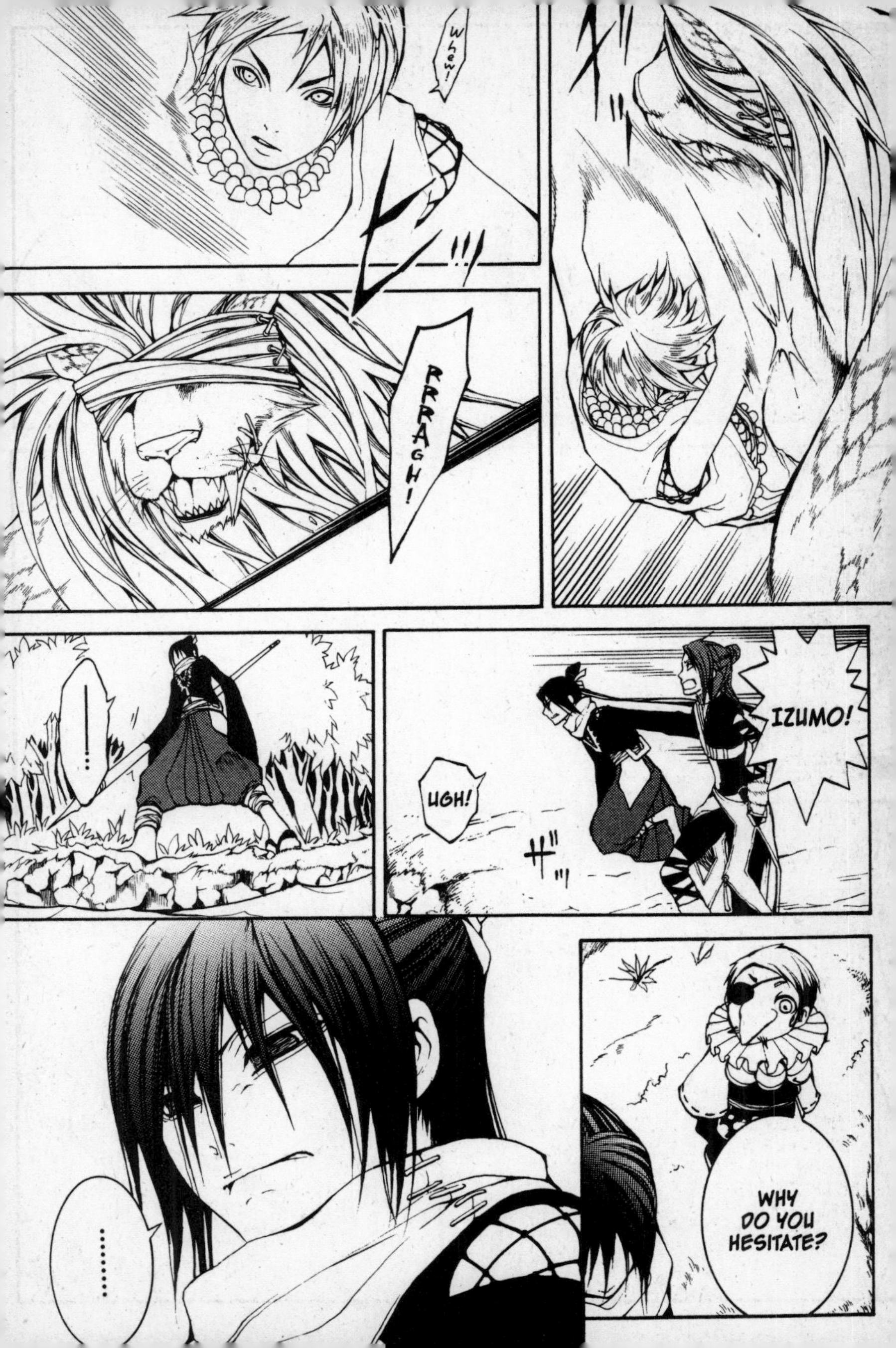
Whew!
RRRAGH!
IZUMO!
UGH!
!......
WHY DO YOU HESITATE?
......

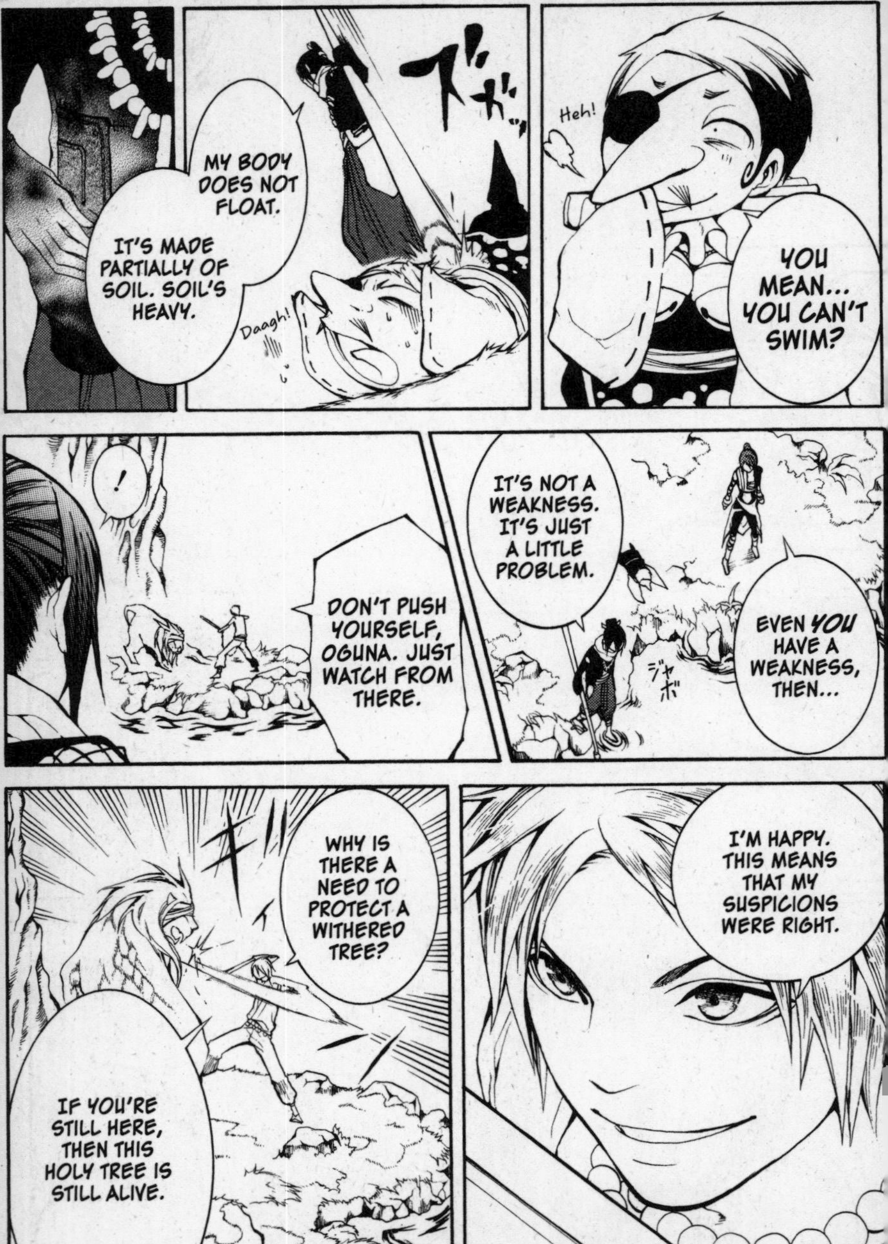
Heh!
YOU MEAN... YOU CAN'T SWIM?
Daagh!
MY BODY DOES NOT FLOAT.
IT'S MADE PARTIALLY OF SOIL. SOIL'S HEAVY.
EVEN YOU HAVE A WEAKNESS, THEN...
IT'S NOT A WEAKNESS. IT'S JUST A LITTLE PROBLEM.
ジャボ
!
DON'T PUSH YOURSELF, OGUNA. JUST WATCH FROM THERE.
I'M HAPPY. THIS MEANS THAT MY SUSPICIONS WERE RIGHT.
WHY IS THERE A NEED TO PROTECT A WITHERED TREE?
IF YOU'RE STILL HERE, THEN THIS HOLY TREE IS STILL ALIVE.

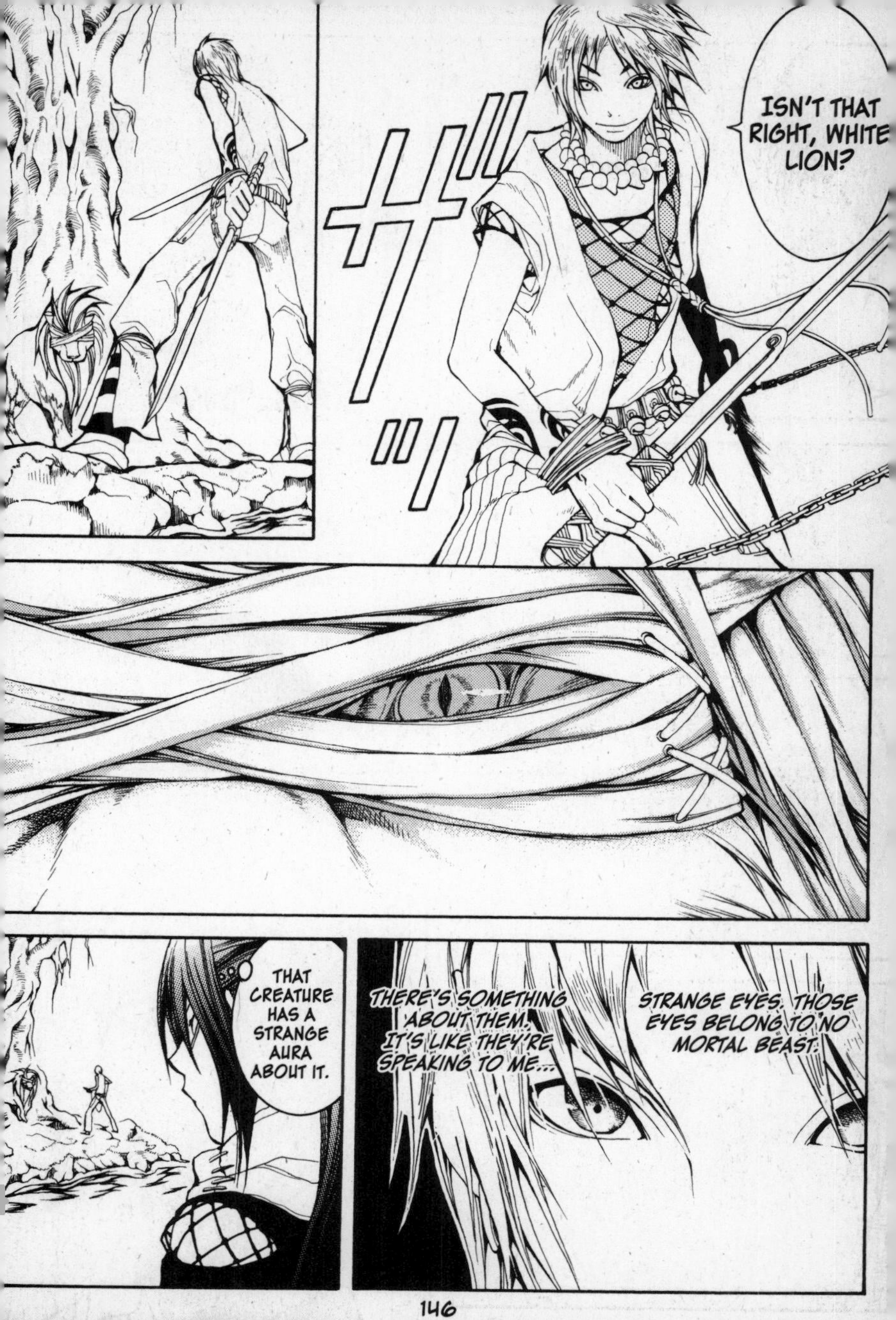
ISN'T THAT RIGHT, WHITE LION?
ザッ
STRANGE EYES. THOSE EYES BELONG TO NO MORTAL BEAST.
THERE'S SOMETHING ABOUT THEM. IT'S LIKE THEY'RE SPEAKING TO ME...
THAT CREATURE HAS A STRANGE AURA ABOUT IT.

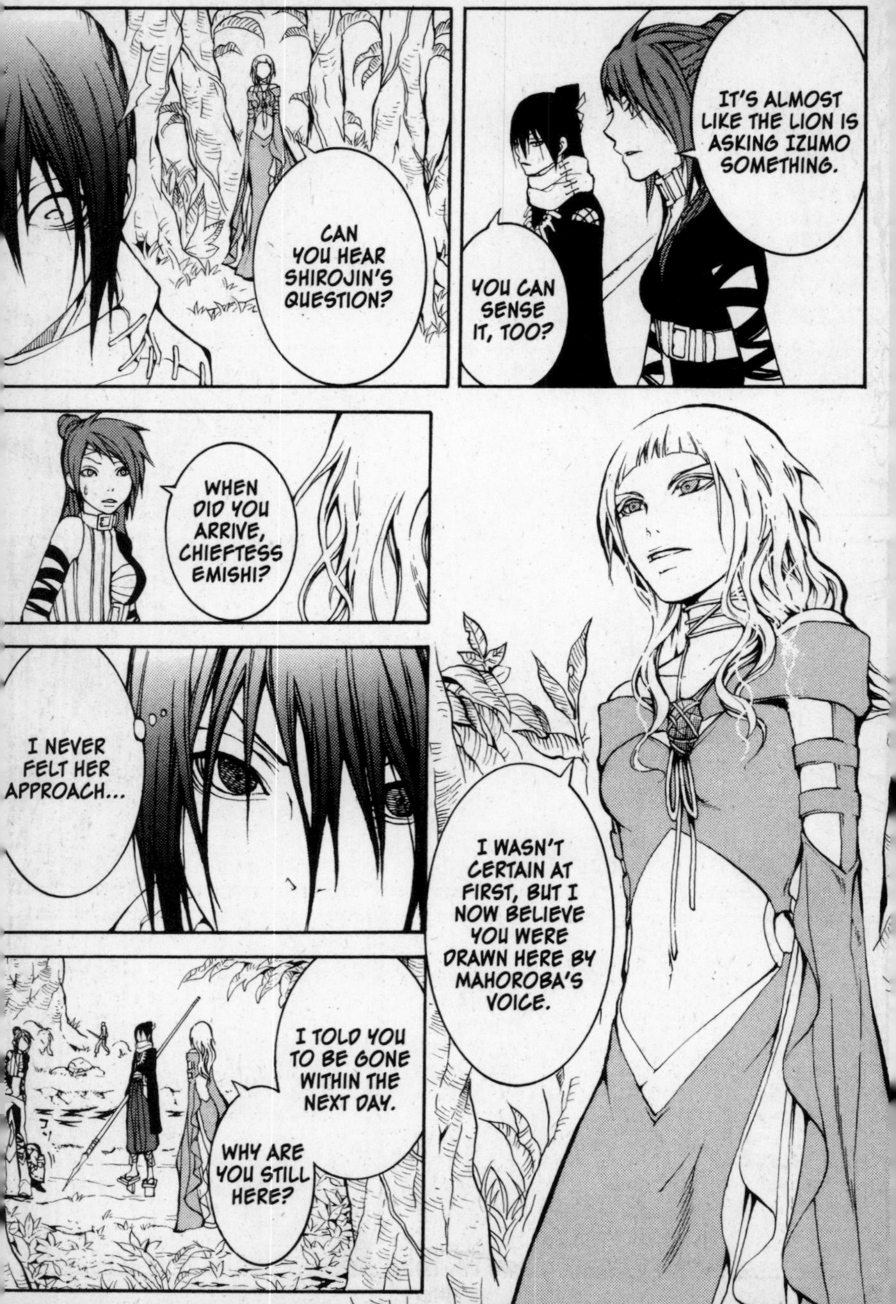
IT'S ALMOST LIKE THE LION IS ASKING IZUMO SOMETHING.
YOU CAN SENSE IT, TOO?
CAN YOU HEAR SHIROJIN'S QUESTION?
I WASN'T CERTAIN AT FIRST, BUT I NOW BELIEVE YOU WERE DRAWN HERE BY MAHOROBA'S VOICE.
WHEN DID YOU ARRIVE, CHIEFTESS EMISHI?
I NEVER FELT HER APPROACH...
I TOLD YOU TO BE GONE WITHIN THE NEXT DAY.
WHY ARE YOU STILL HERE?

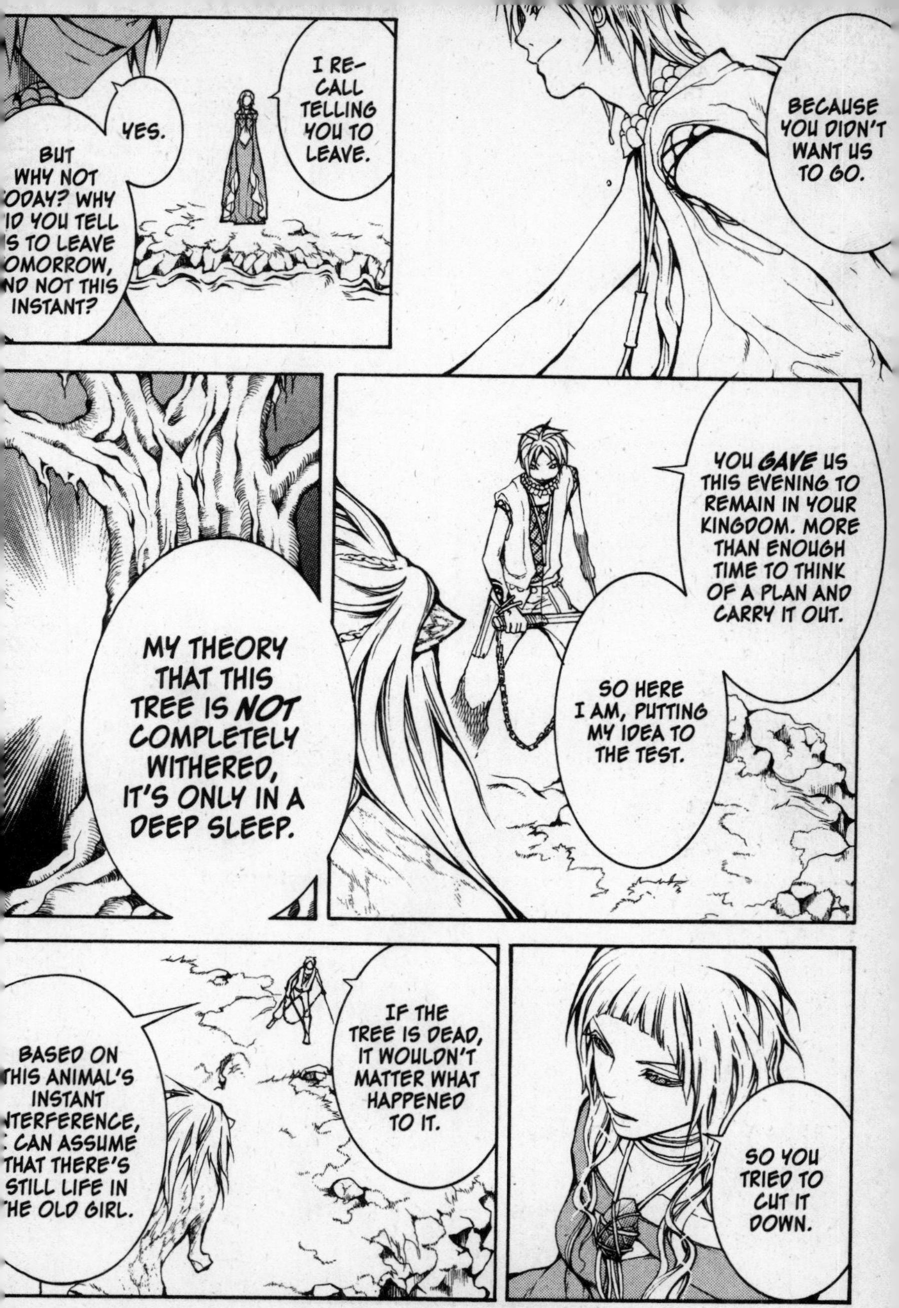
BECAUSE YOU DIDN'T WANT US TO GO.
I RE-CALL TELLING YOU TO LEAVE.
YES.
BUT WHY NOT ODAY? WHY ID YOU TELL S TO LEAVE OMORROW, ND NOT THIS INSTANT?
YOU *GAVE* US THIS EVENING TO REMAIN IN YOUR KINGDOM. MORE THAN ENOUGH TIME TO THINK OF A PLAN AND CARRY IT OUT.
SO HERE I AM, PUTTING MY IDEA TO THE TEST.
MY THEORY THAT THIS TREE IS *NOT* COMPLETELY WITHERED, IT'S ONLY IN A DEEP SLEEP.
SO YOU TRIED TO CUT IT DOWN.
IF THE TREE IS DEAD, IT WOULDN'T MATTER WHAT HAPPENED TO IT.
BASED ON THIS ANIMAL'S INSTANT NTERFERENCE, CAN ASSUME THAT THERE'S STILL LIFE IN HE OLD GIRL.

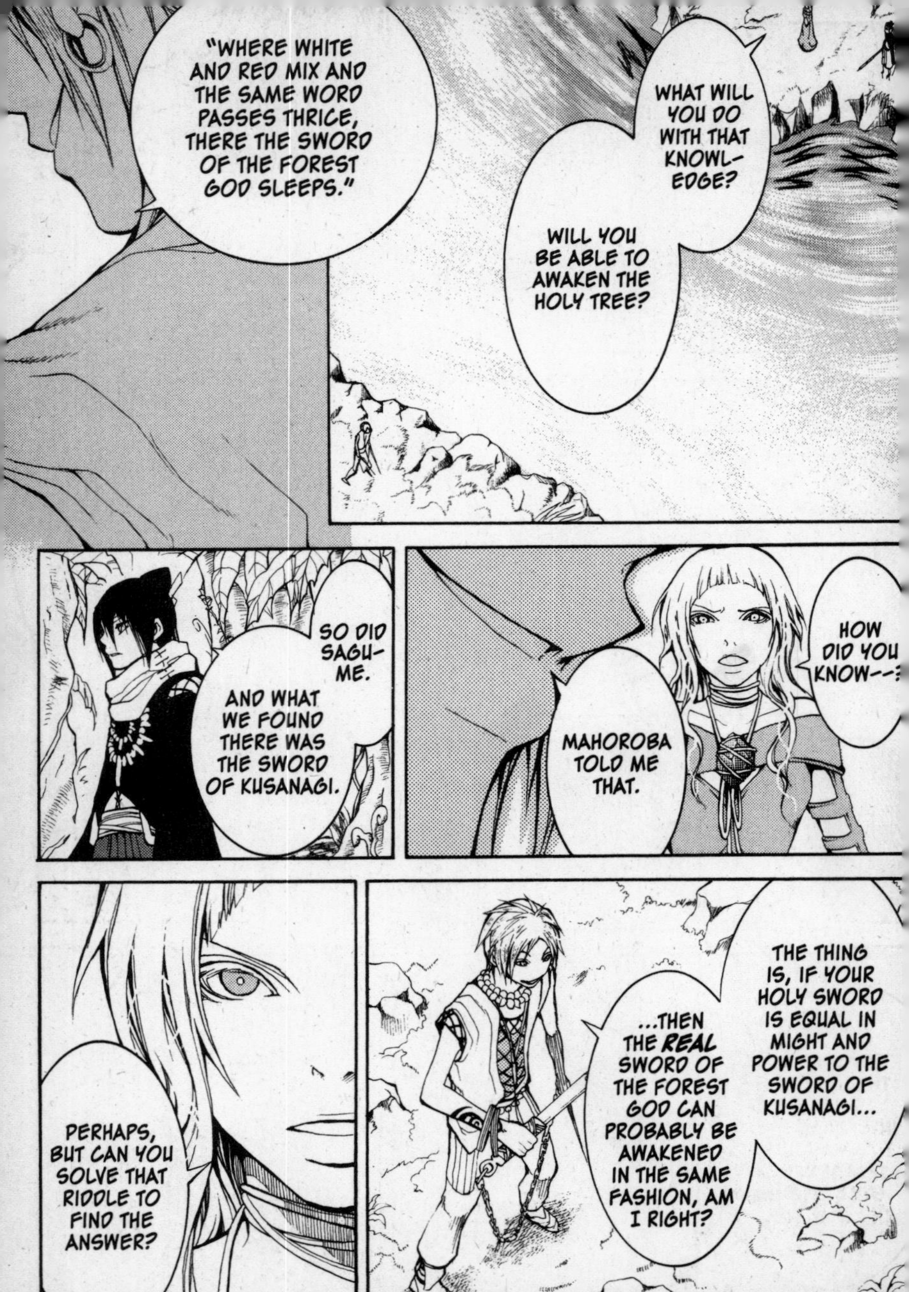
WHAT WILL YOU DO WITH THAT KNOWL-EDGE?
WILL YOU BE ABLE TO AWAKEN THE HOLY TREE?
"WHERE WHITE AND RED MIX AND THE SAME WORD PASSES THRICE, THERE THE SWORD OF THE FOREST GOD SLEEPS."
HOW DID YOU KNOW--?
MAHOROBA TOLD ME THAT.
SO DID SAGU-ME.
AND WHAT WE FOUND THERE WAS THE SWORD OF KUSANAGI.
THE THING IS, IF YOUR HOLY SWORD IS EQUAL IN MIGHT AND POWER TO THE SWORD OF KUSANAGI...
...THEN THE *REAL* SWORD OF THE FOREST GOD CAN PROBABLY BE AWAKENED IN THE SAME FASHION, AM I RIGHT?
PERHAPS, BUT CAN YOU SOLVE THAT RIDDLE TO FIND THE ANSWER?

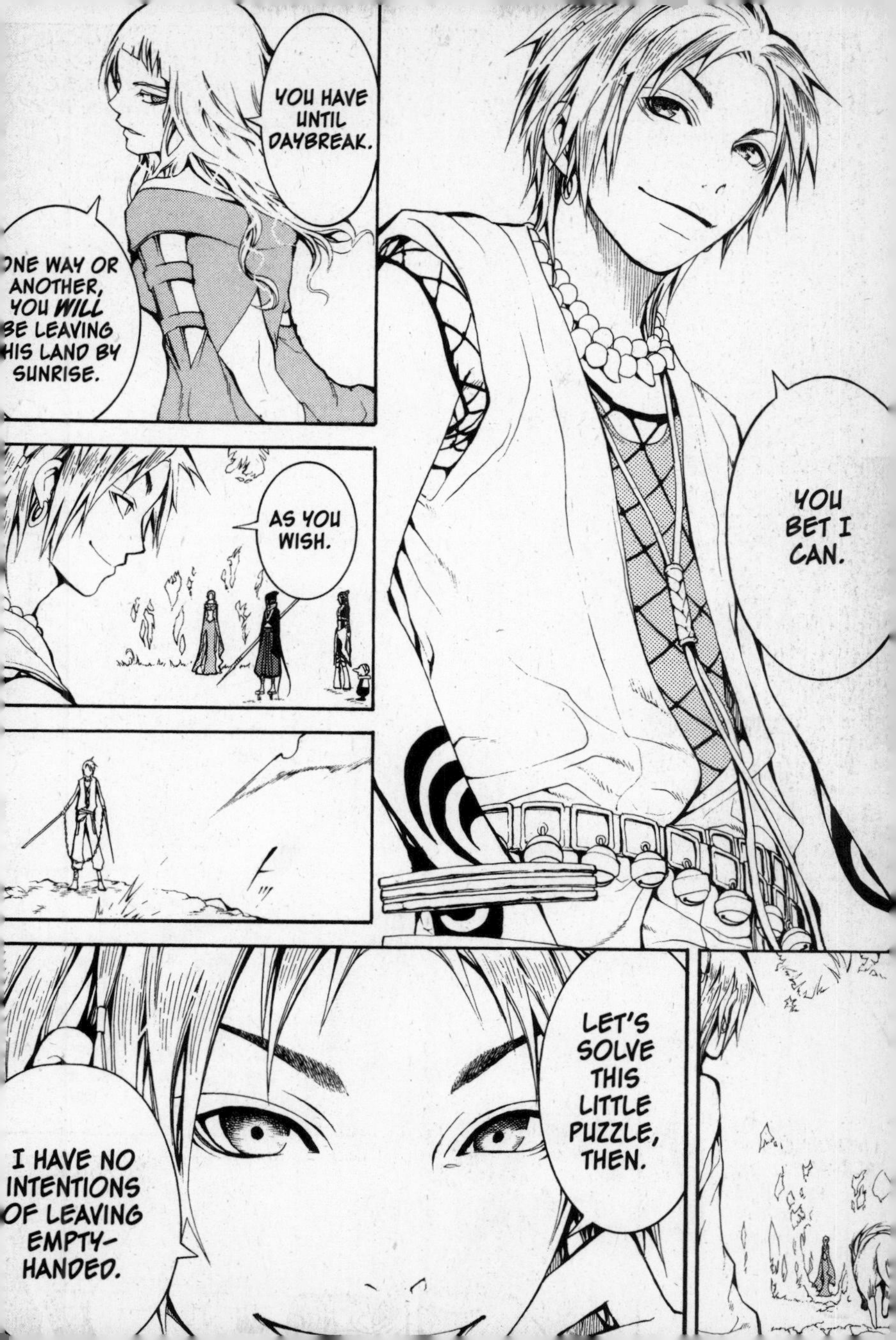
YOU BET I CAN.
YOU HAVE UNTIL DAYBREAK.
ONE WAY OR ANOTHER, YOU **WILL** BE LEAVING HIS LAND BY SUNRISE.
AS YOU WISH.
LET'S SOLVE THIS LITTLE PUZZLE, THEN.
I HAVE NO INTENTIONS OF LEAVING EMPTY-HANDED.

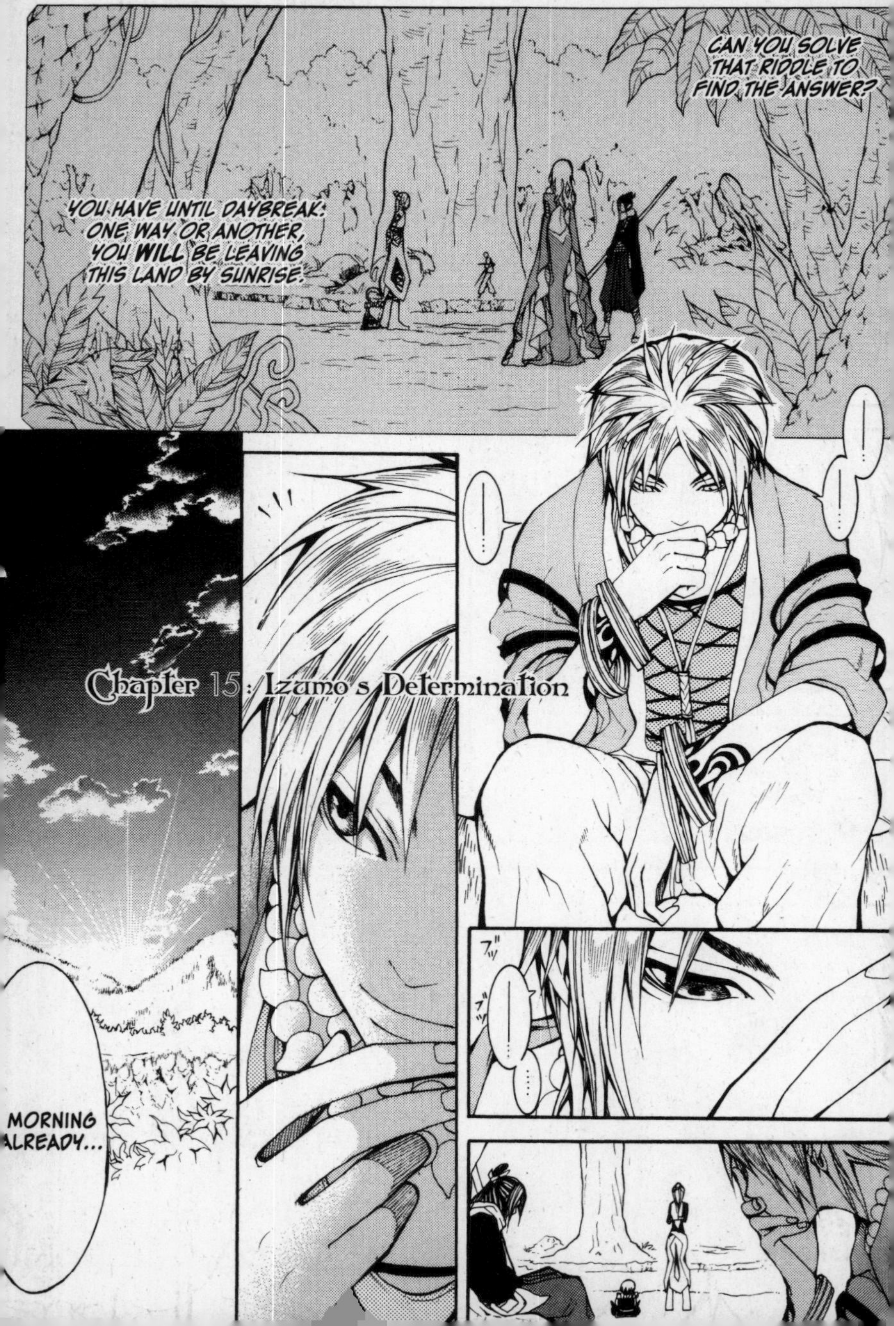
CAN YOU SOLVE THAT RIDDLE TO FIND THE ANSWER?
YOU HAVE UNTIL DAYBREAK: ONE WAY OR ANOTHER, YOU WILL BE LEAVING THIS LAND BY SUNRISE.
!...
!...
Chapter 15 : Izumo's Determination
!...
......
ブツ
ブツ
MORNING ALREADY...

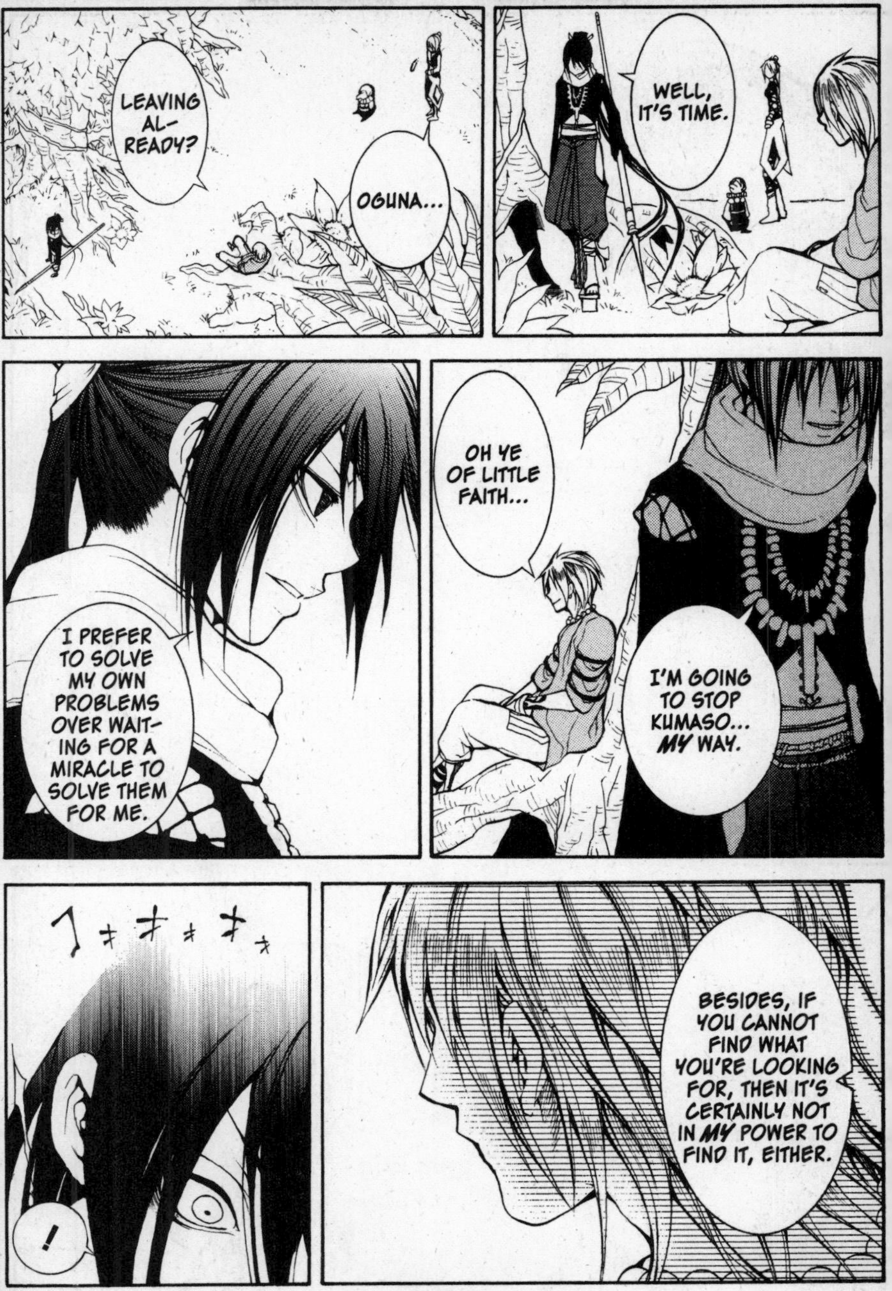
WELL, IT'S TIME.
OGUNA...
LEAVING ALREADY?
OH YE OF LITTLE FAITH...
I'M GOING TO STOP KUMASO... *MY* WAY.
I PREFER TO SOLVE MY OWN PROBLEMS OVER WAITING FOR A MIRACLE TO SOLVE THEM FOR ME.
BESIDES, IF YOU CANNOT FIND WHAT YOU'RE LOOKING FOR, THEN IT'S CERTAINLY NOT IN *MY* POWER TO FIND IT, EITHER.
フォオォオォ
!

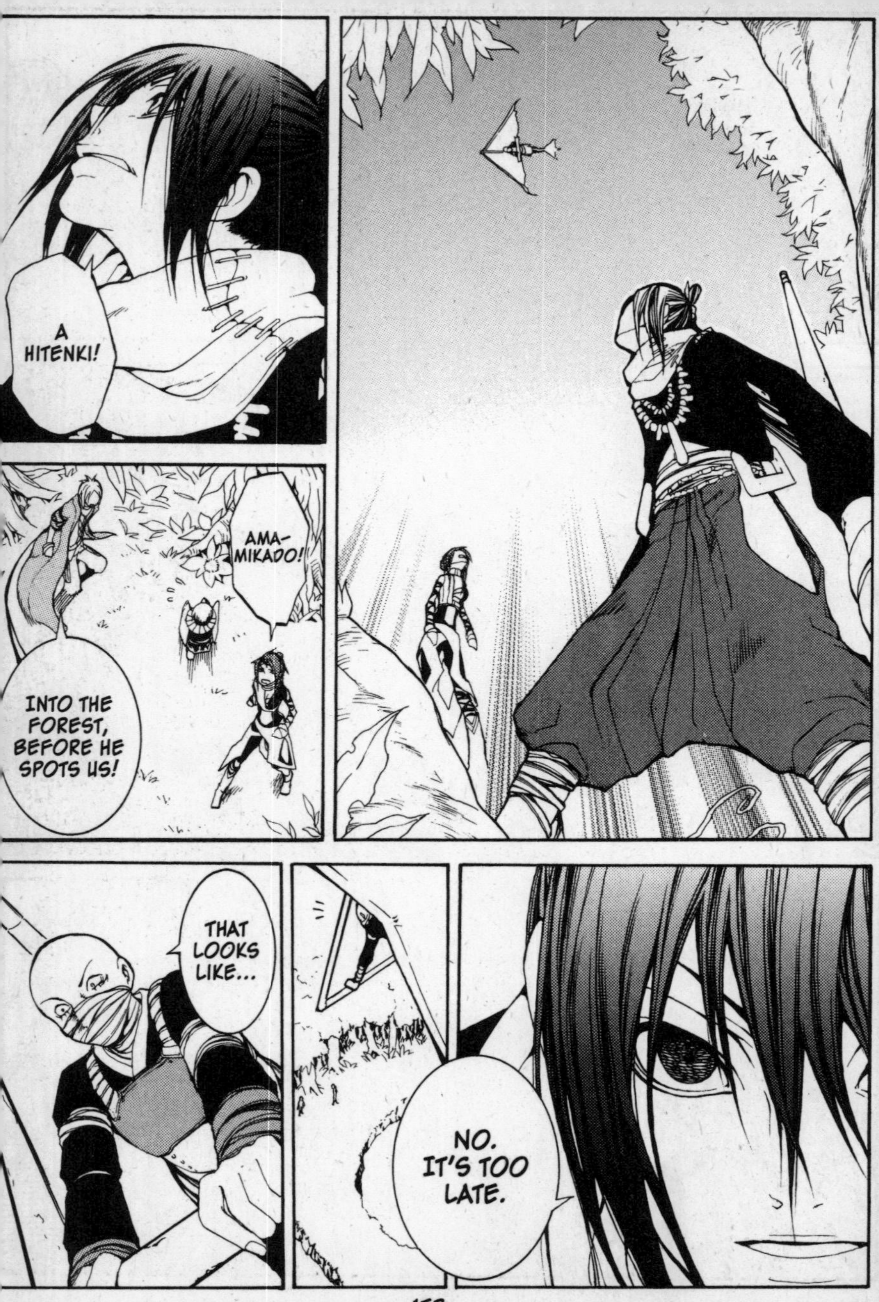
A HITENKI!
AMA-MIKADO!
INTO THE FOREST, BEFORE HE SPOTS US!
NO. IT'S TOO LATE.
THAT LOOKS LIKE...

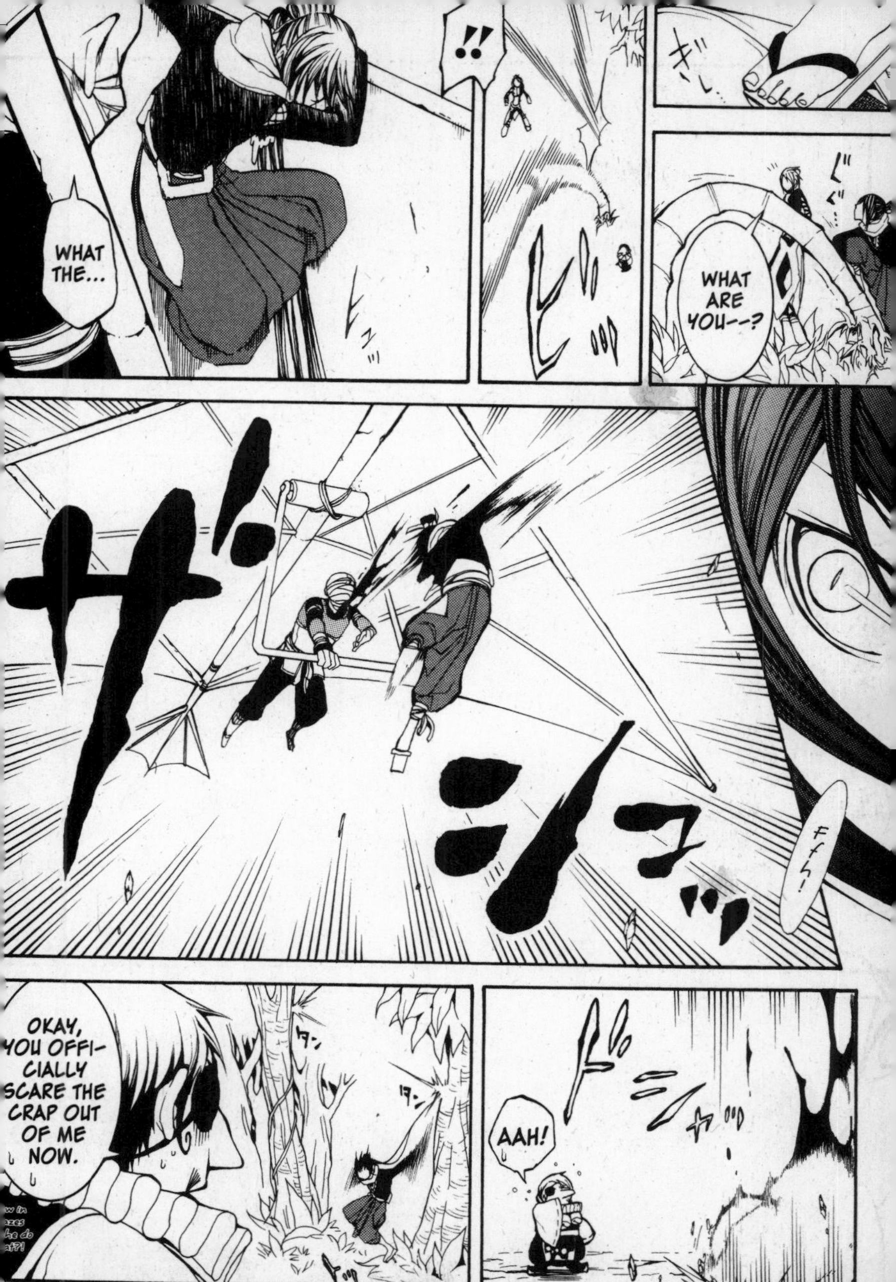

WHAT ARE YOU--?
!!
WHAT THE...
AAH!
OKAY, YOU OFFI-CIALLY SCARE THE CRAP OUT OF ME NOW.

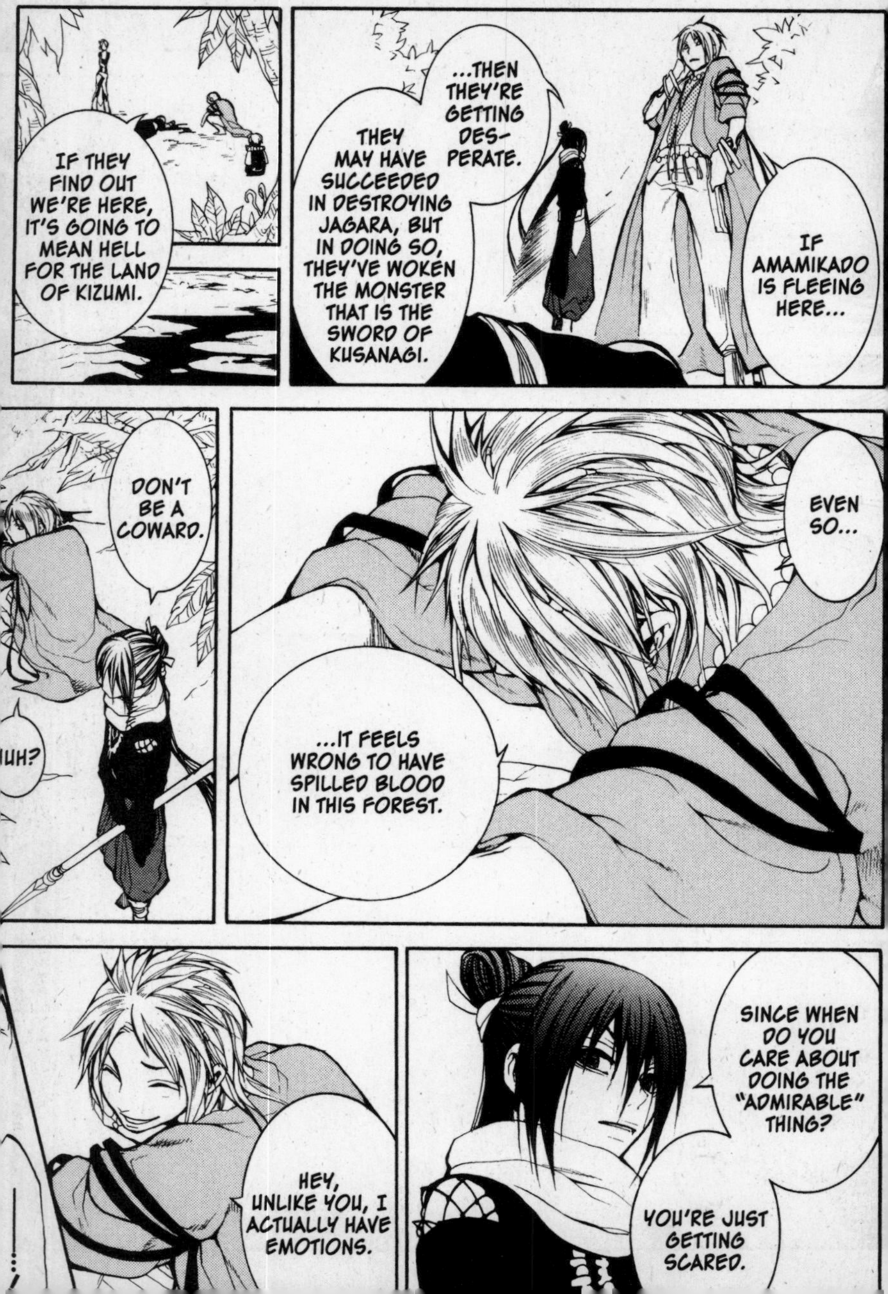
IF AMAMIKADO IS FLEEING HERE...
...THEN THEY'RE GETTING DES-PERATE.
THEY MAY HAVE SUCCEEDED IN DESTROYING JAGARA, BUT IN DOING SO, THEY'VE WOKEN THE MONSTER THAT IS THE SWORD OF KUSANAGI.
IF THEY FIND OUT WE'RE HERE, IT'S GOING TO MEAN HELL FOR THE LAND OF KIZUMI.
EVEN SO...
...IT FEELS WRONG TO HAVE SPILLED BLOOD IN THIS FOREST.
DON'T BE A COWARD.
UH?
SINCE WHEN DO YOU CARE ABOUT DOING THE "ADMIRABLE" THING?
YOU'RE JUST GETTING SCARED.
HEY, UNLIKE YOU, I ACTUALLY HAVE EMOTIONS.

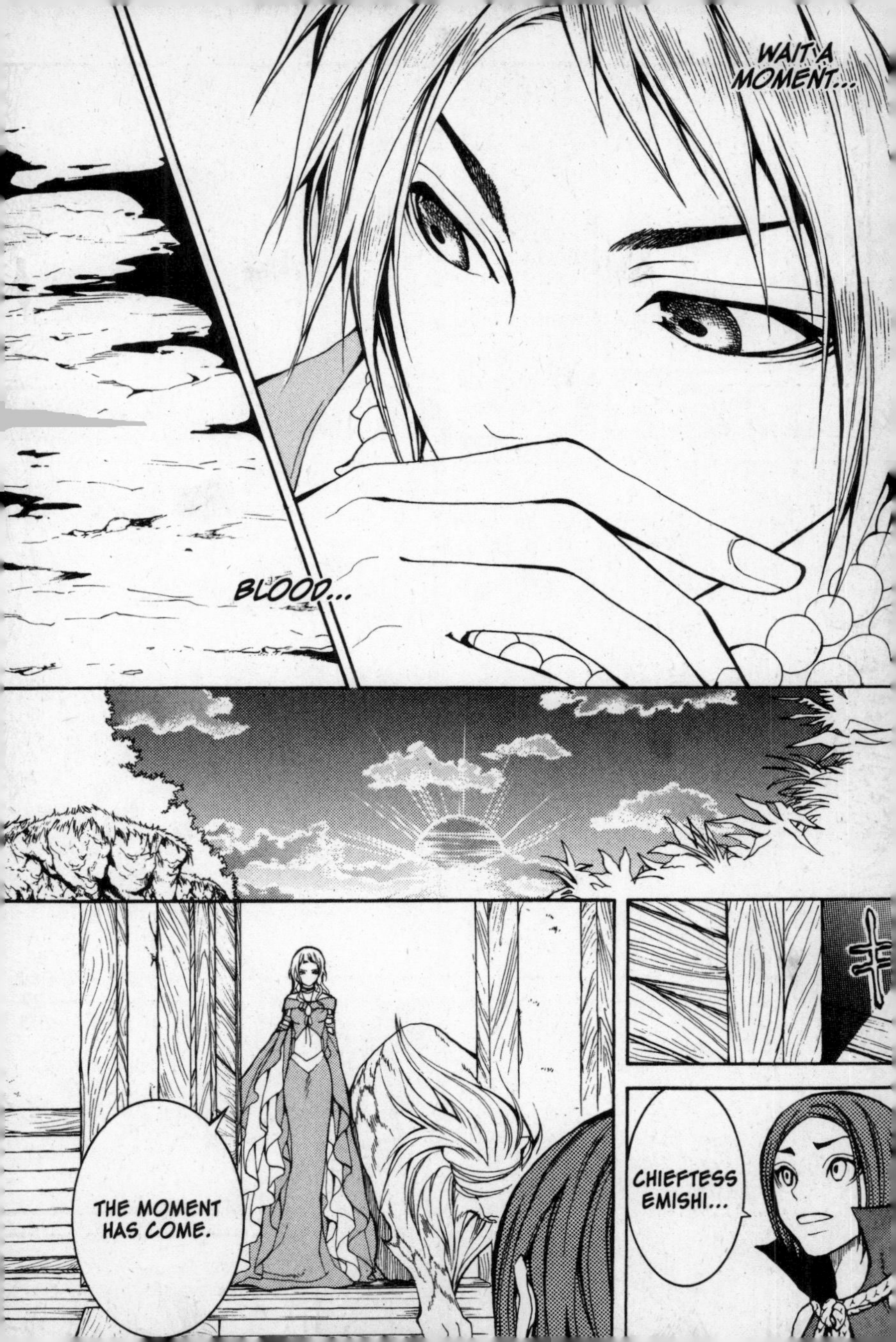
WAIT A MOMENT...
BLOOD...
CHIEFTESS EMISHI...
THE MOMENT HAS COME.

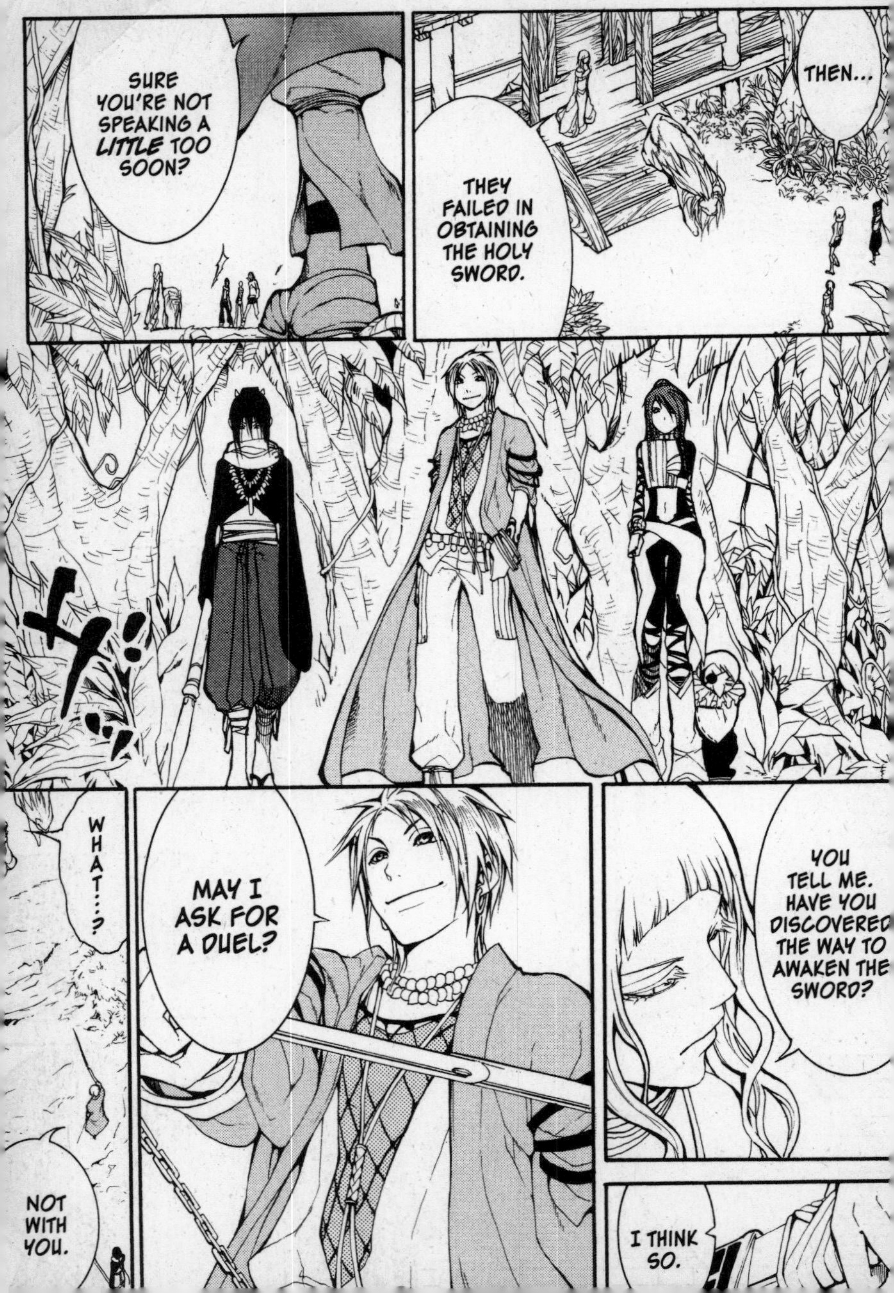
THEN...
THEY FAILED IN OBTAINING THE HOLY SWORD.
SURE YOU'RE NOT SPEAKING A *LITTLE* TOO SOON?
YOU TELL ME. HAVE YOU DISCOVERED THE WAY TO AWAKEN THE SWORD?
I THINK SO.
MAY I ASK FOR A DUEL?
WHAT...?
NOT WITH YOU.

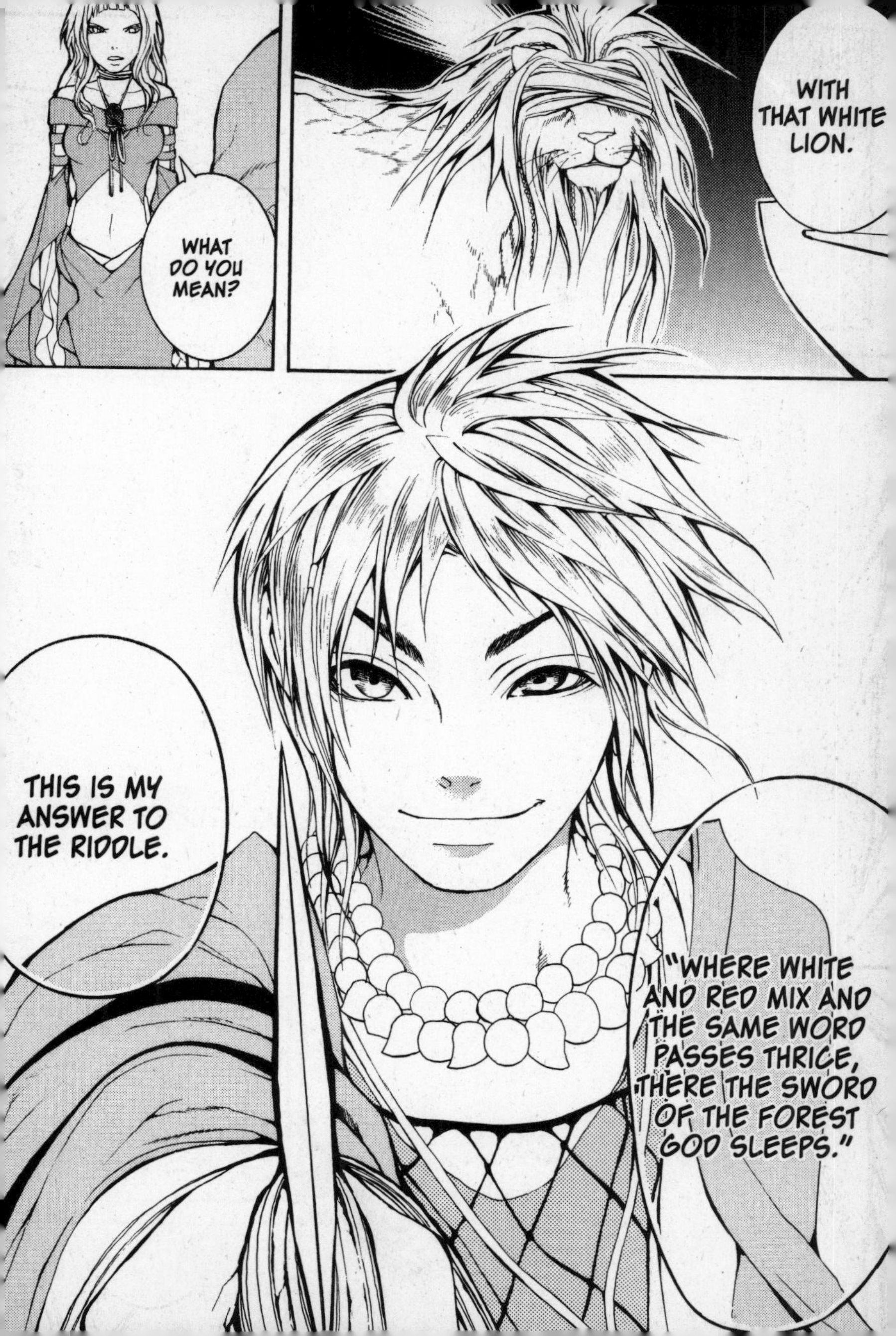
WITH THAT WHITE LION.
WHAT DO YOU MEAN?
THIS IS MY ANSWER TO THE RIDDLE.
"WHERE WHITE AND RED MIX AND THE SAME WORD PASSES THRICE, THERE THE SWORD OF THE FOREST GOD SLEEPS."

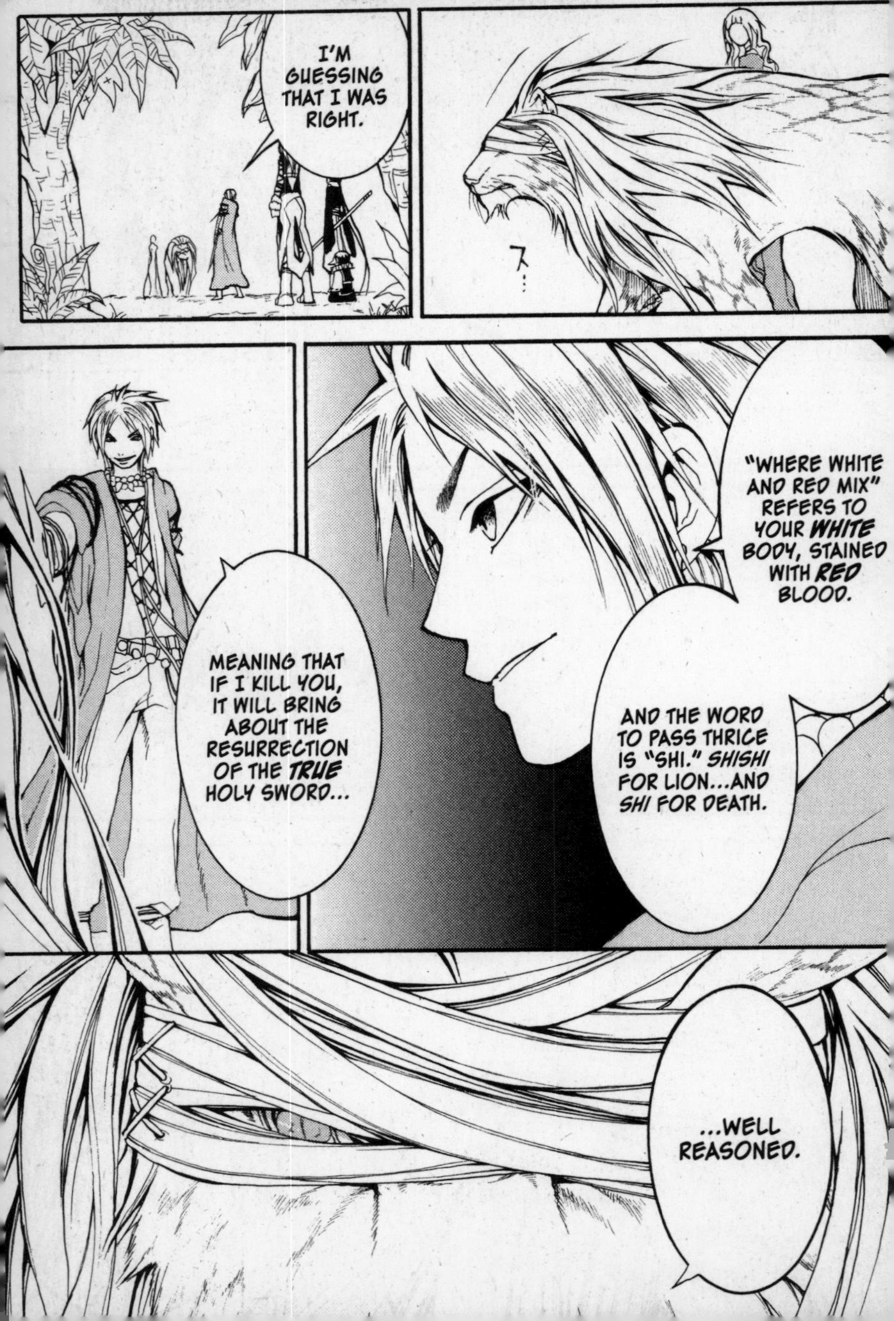
フ…
I'M GUESSING THAT I WAS RIGHT.
"WHERE WHITE AND RED MIX" REFERS TO YOUR *WHITE* BODY, STAINED WITH *RED* BLOOD.
AND THE WORD TO PASS THRICE IS "SHI." *SHISHI* FOR LION...AND *SHI* FOR DEATH.
MEANING THAT IF I KILL YOU, IT WILL BRING ABOUT THE RESURRECTION OF THE *TRUE* HOLY SWORD...
...WELL REASONED.

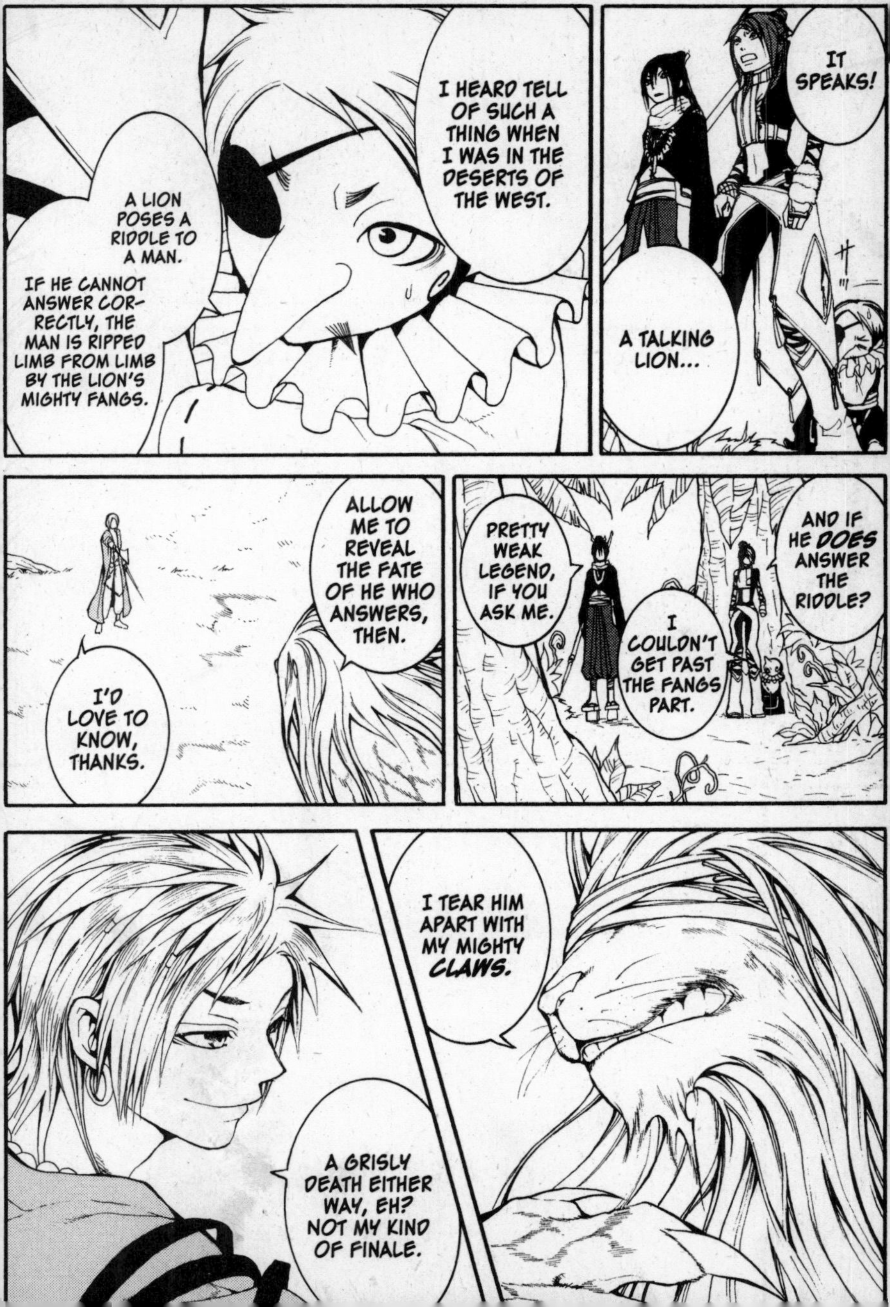
IT SPEAKS!
A TALKING LION...
I HEARD TELL OF SUCH A THING WHEN I WAS IN THE DESERTS OF THE WEST.
A LION POSES A RIDDLE TO A MAN.
IF HE CANNOT ANSWER CORRECTLY, THE MAN IS RIPPED LIMB FROM LIMB BY THE LION'S MIGHTY FANGS.
AND IF HE *DOES* ANSWER THE RIDDLE?
PRETTY WEAK LEGEND, IF YOU ASK ME.
I COULDN'T GET PAST THE FANGS PART.
ALLOW ME TO REVEAL THE FATE OF HE WHO ANSWERS, THEN.
I'D LOVE TO KNOW, THANKS.
I TEAR HIM APART WITH MY MIGHTY *CLAWS.*
A GRISLY DEATH EITHER WAY, EH? NOT MY KIND OF FINALE.

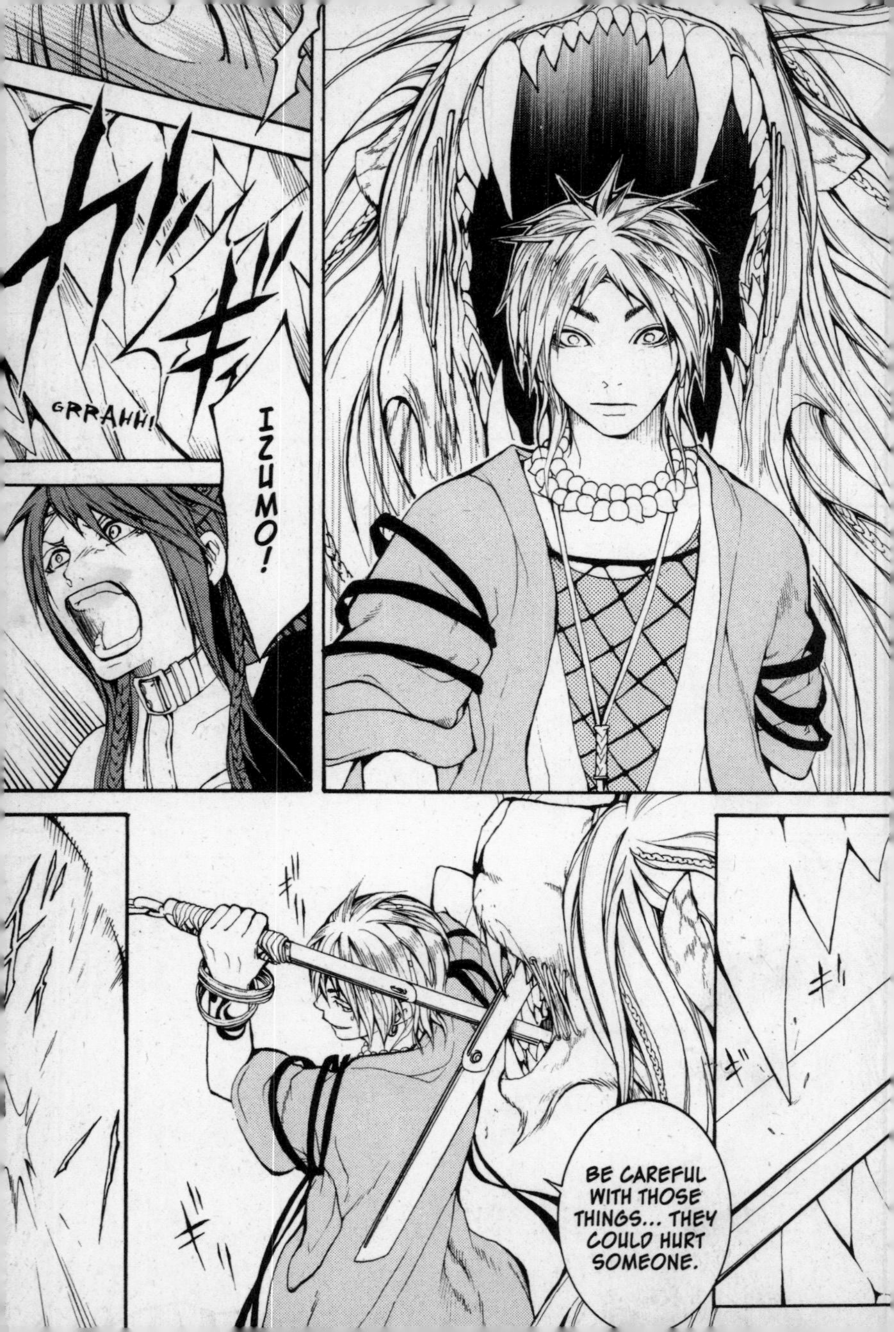
GRRAHH!
IZUMO!
BE CAREFUL WITH THOSE THINGS... THEY COULD HURT SOMEONE.

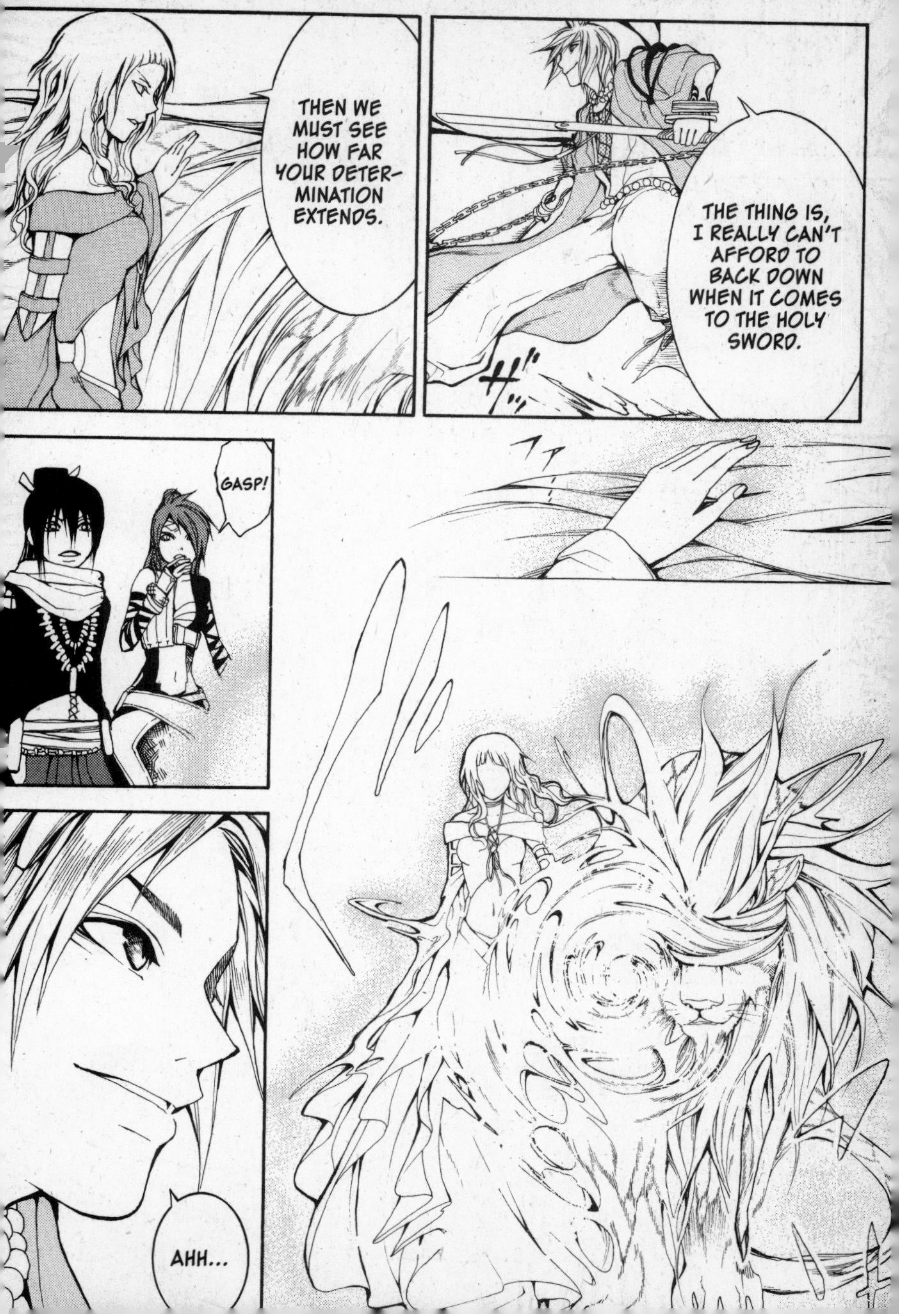
THE THING IS, I REALLY CAN'T AFFORD TO BACK DOWN WHEN IT COMES TO THE HOLY SWORD.
THEN WE MUST SEE HOW FAR YOUR DETER-MINATION EXTENDS.
GASP!
AHH...

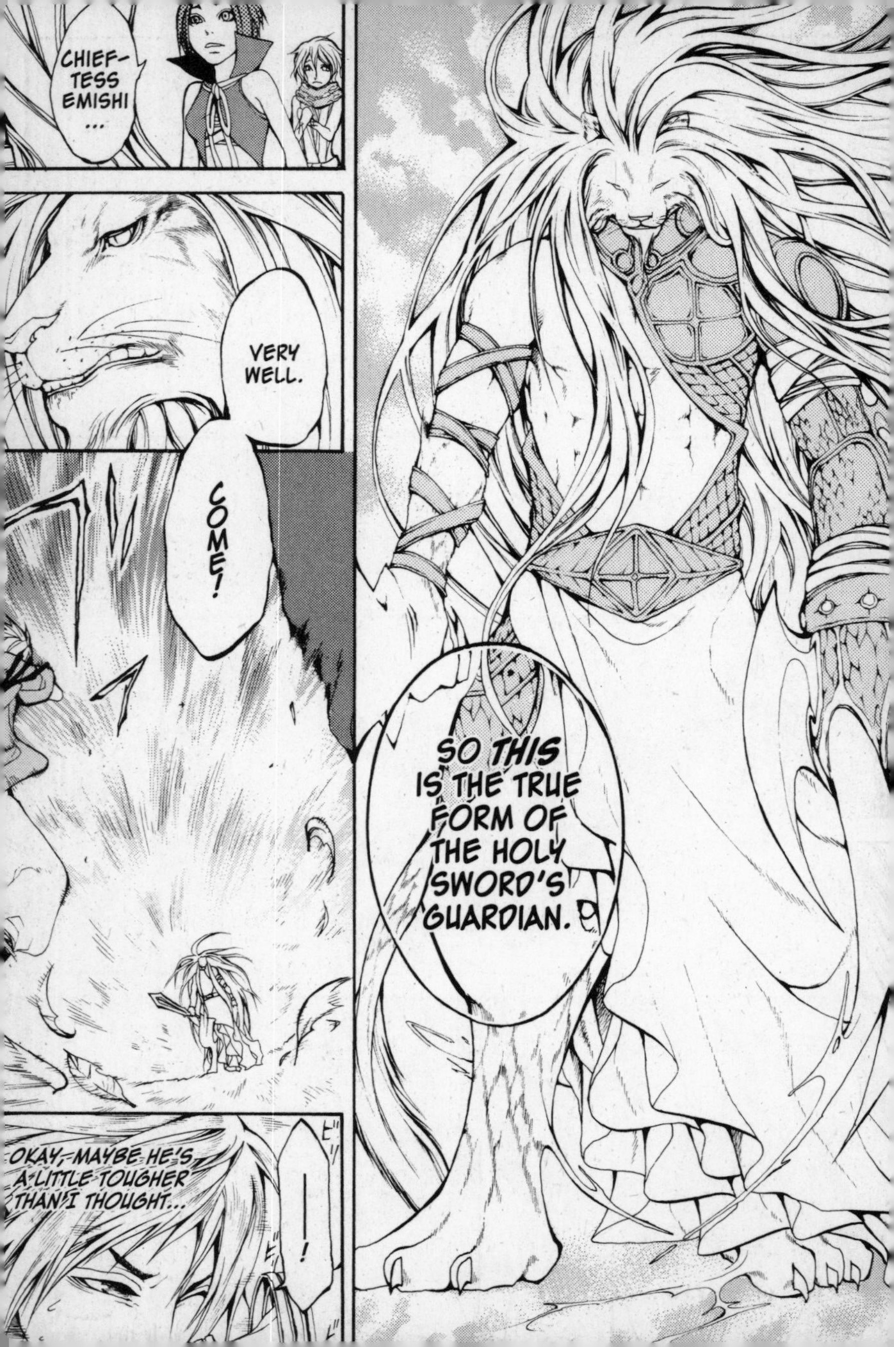
SO THIS IS THE TRUE FORM OF THE HOLY SWORD'S GUARDIAN.
CHIEF-TESS EMISHI ...
VERY WELL.
COME!
!
OKAY, MAYBE HE'S A LITTLE TOUGHER THAN I THOUGHT...

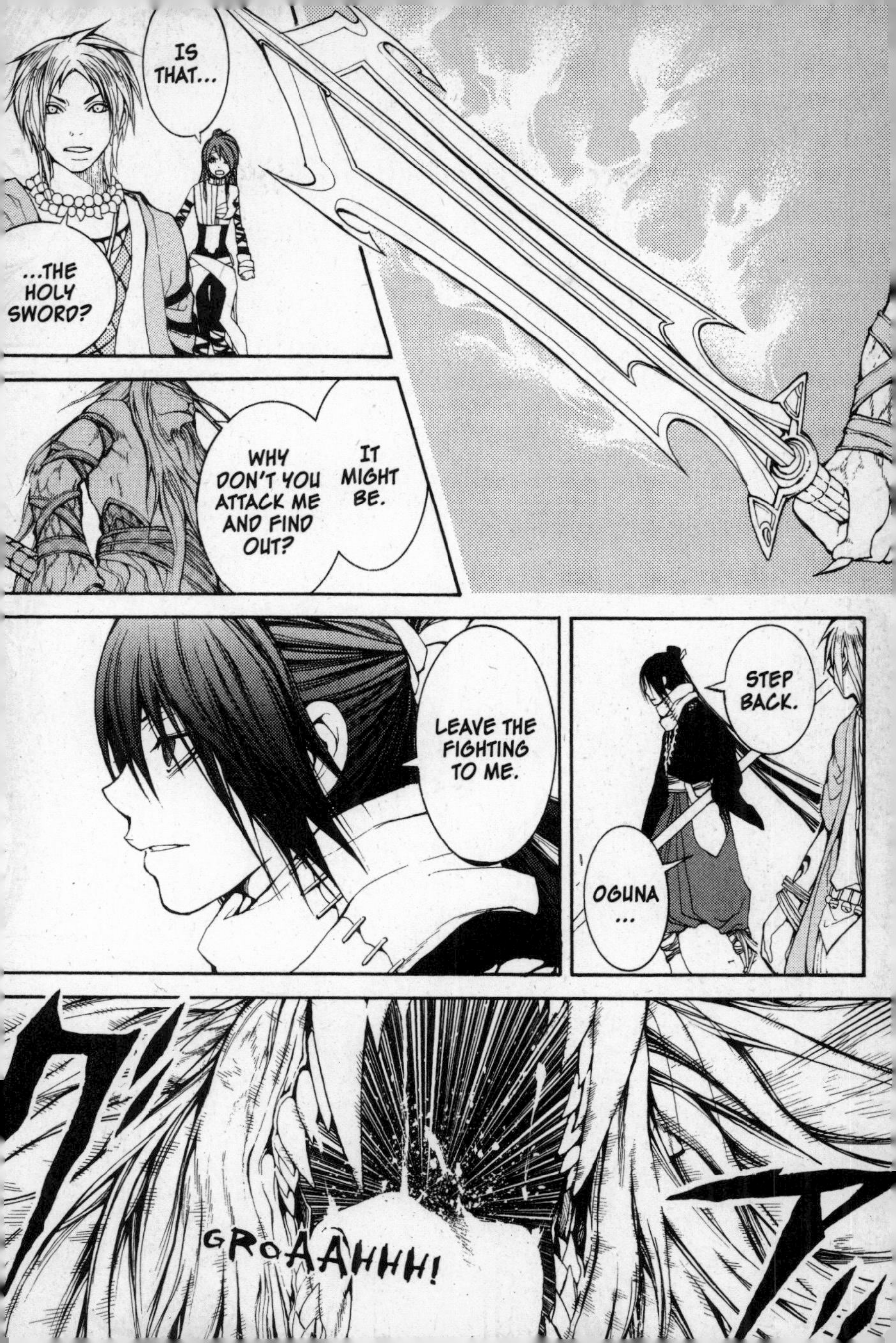
IS THAT...
...THE HOLY SWORD?
IT MIGHT BE.
WHY DON'T YOU ATTACK ME AND FIND OUT?
STEP BACK.
OGUNA ...
LEAVE THE FIGHTING TO ME.
GROAAHHH!

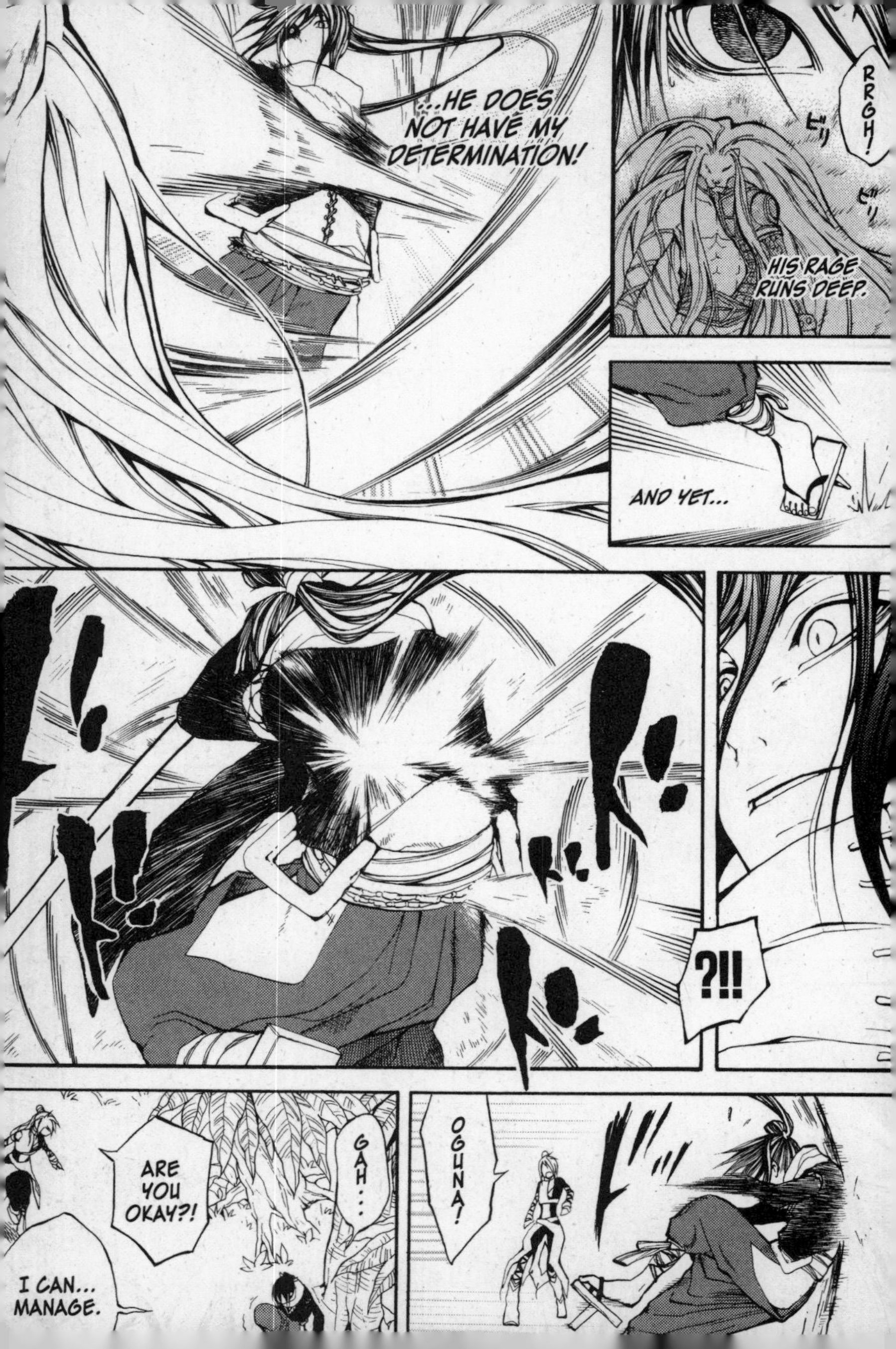

RRGH!
ビリ
ビリ
HIS RAGE RUNS DEEP.
AND YET...
...HE DOES NOT HAVE MY DETERMINATION!
?!!
OGUNA!
GAH...
ARE YOU OKAY?!
I CAN... MANAGE.

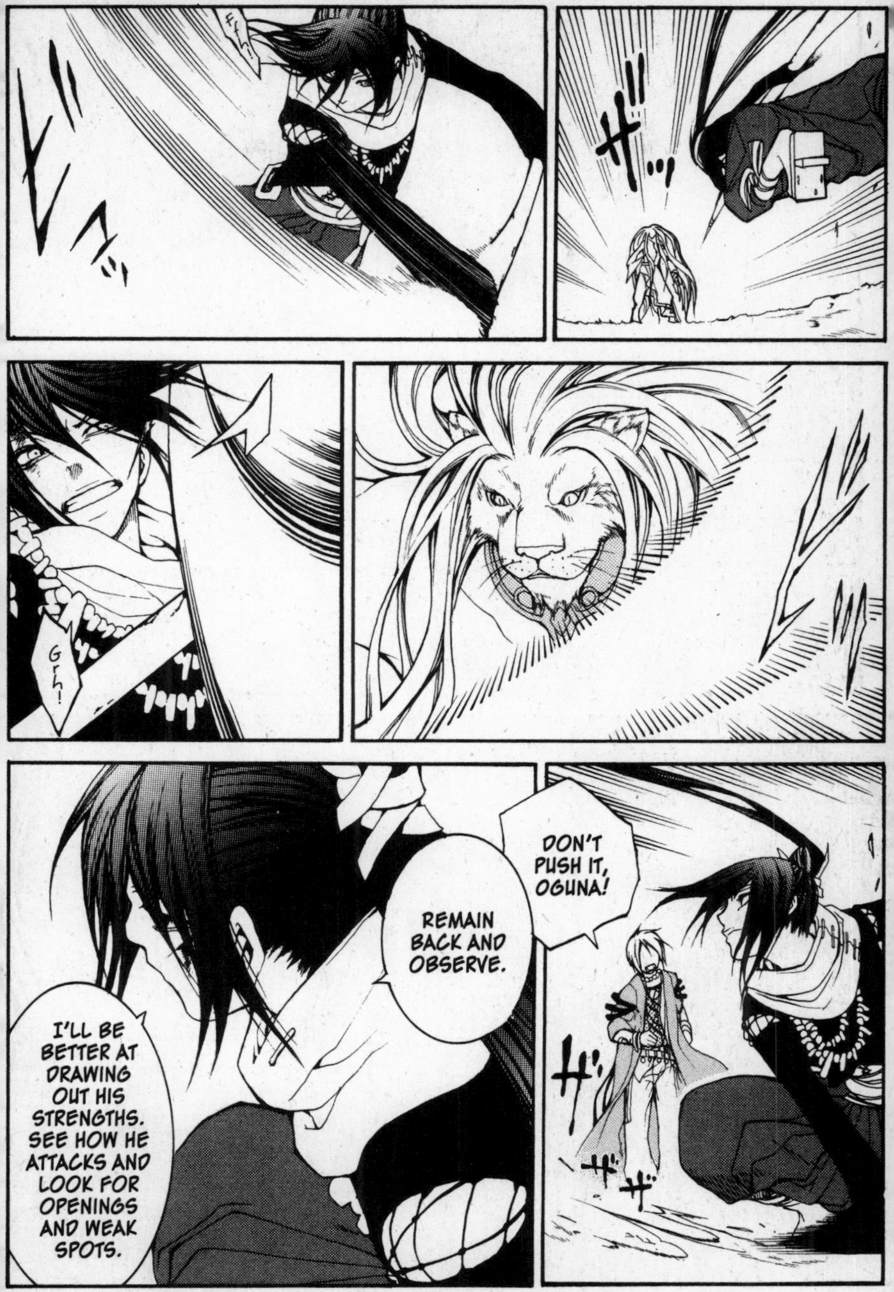
Ffh!
Grh!
DON'T PUSH IT, OGUNA!
REMAIN BACK AND OBSERVE.
I'LL BE BETTER AT DRAWING OUT HIS STRENGTHS. SEE HOW HE ATTACKS AND LOOK FOR OPENINGS AND WEAK SPOTS.

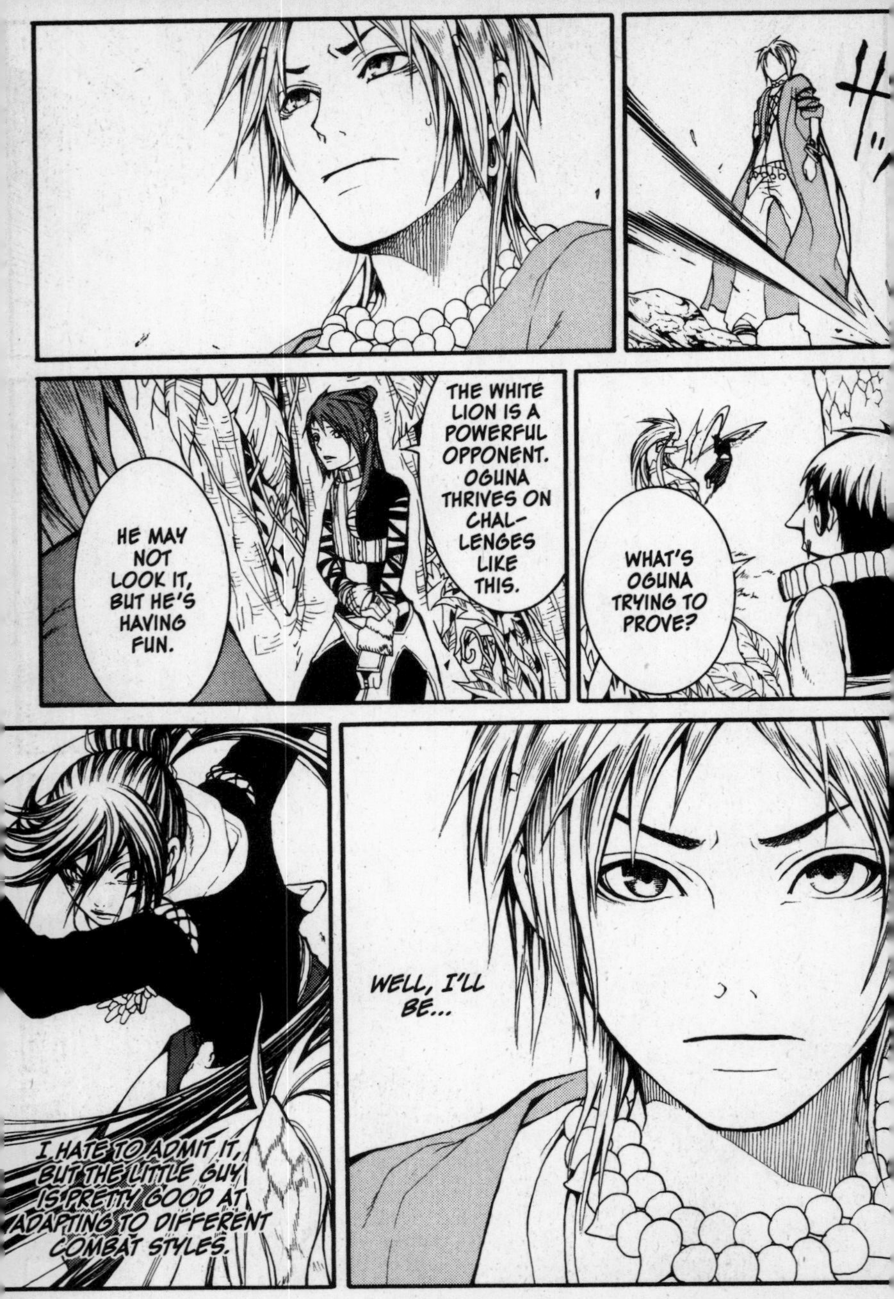
WHAT'S OGUNA TRYING TO PROVE?
THE WHITE LION IS A POWERFUL OPPONENT. OGUNA THRIVES ON CHALLENGES LIKE THIS.
HE MAY NOT LOOK IT, BUT HE'S HAVING FUN.
WELL, I'LL BE...
I HATE TO ADMIT IT, BUT THE LITTLE GUY IS PRETTY GOOD AT ADAPTING TO DIFFERENT COMBAT STYLES.

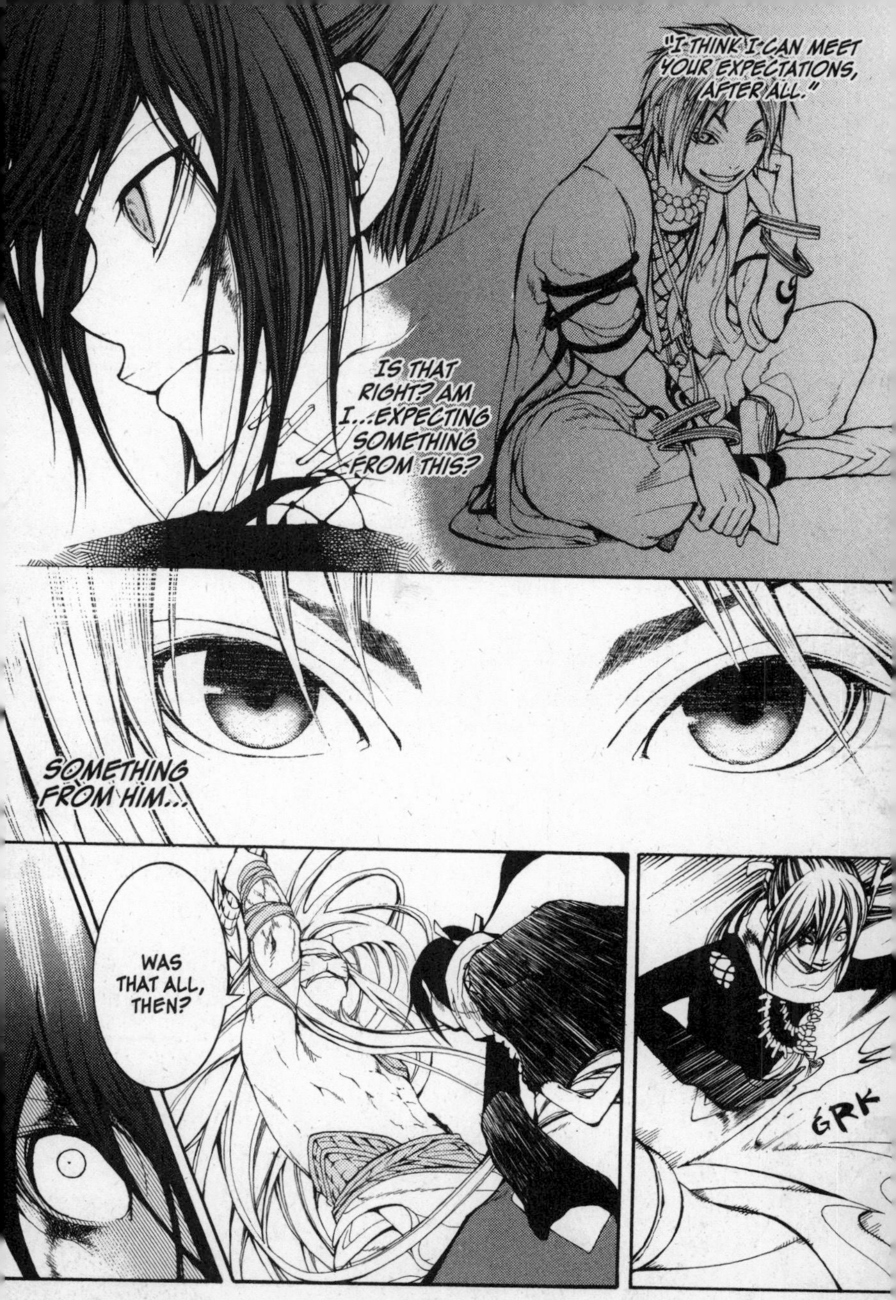
"I THINK I CAN MEET YOUR EXPECTATIONS, AFTER ALL."
IS THAT RIGHT? AM I...EXPECTING SOMETHING FROM THIS?
SOMETHING FROM HIM...
GRK
WAS THAT ALL, THEN?

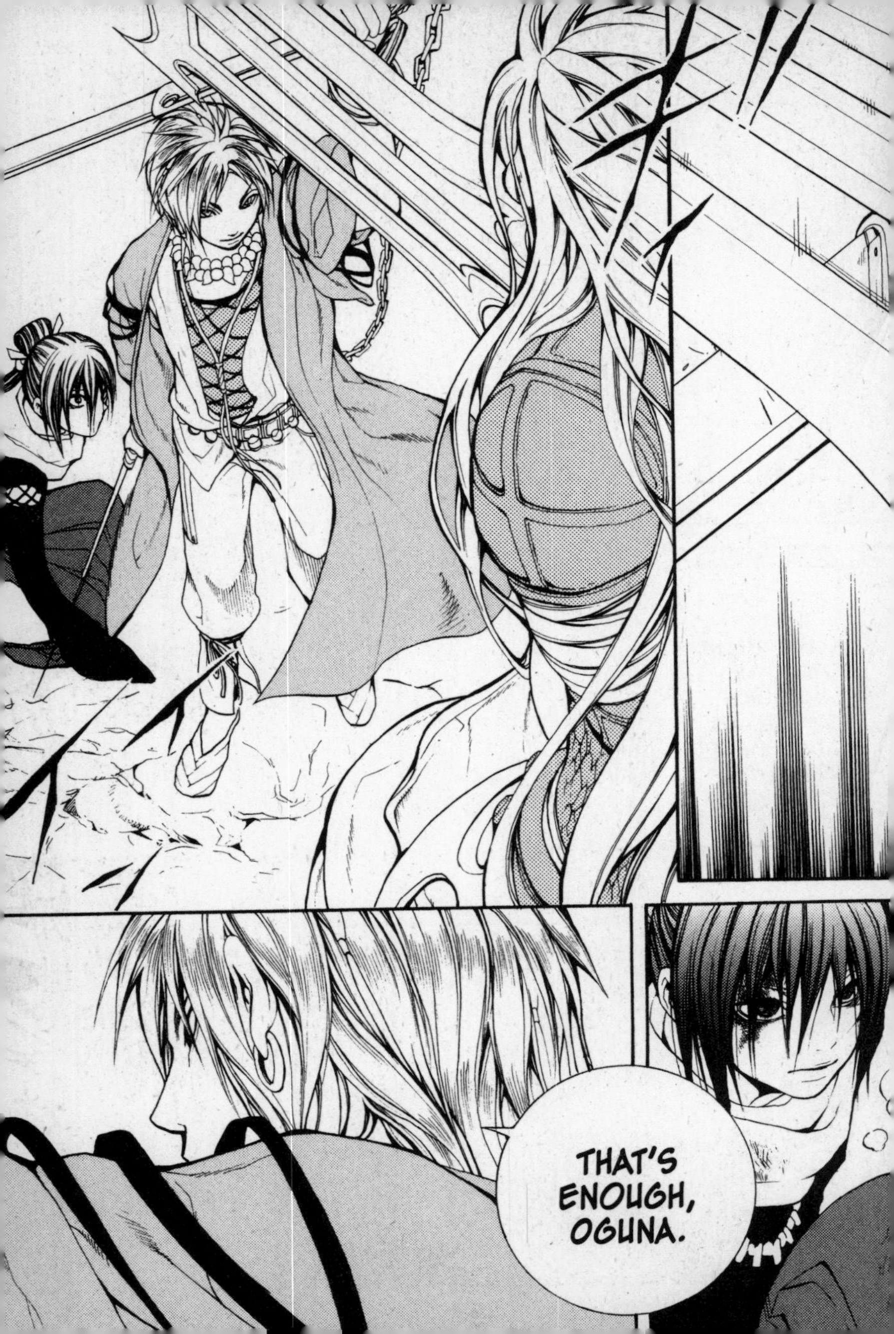
THAT'S ENOUGH, OGUNA.

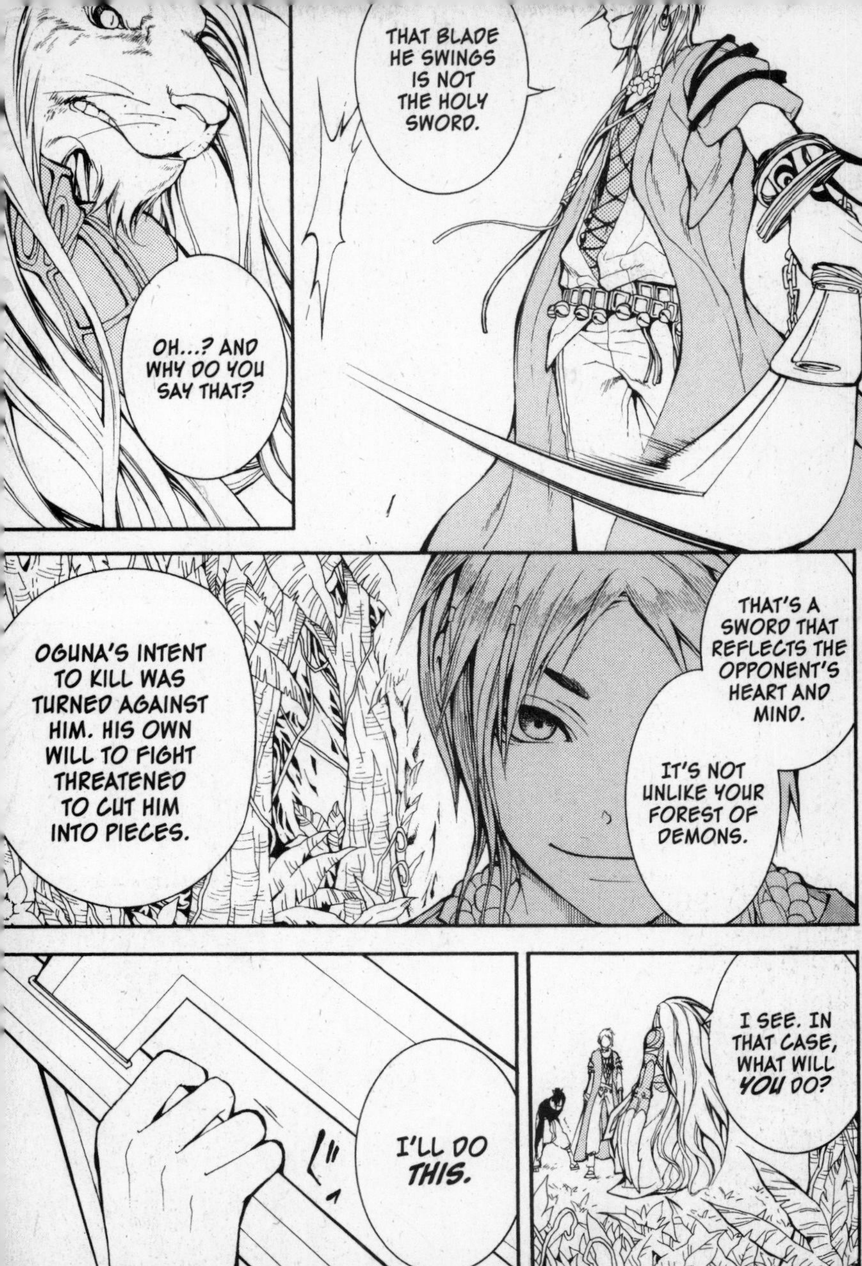

THAT BLADE HE SWINGS IS NOT THE HOLY SWORD.
OH...? AND WHY DO YOU SAY THAT?
THAT'S A SWORD THAT REFLECTS THE OPPONENT'S HEART AND MIND.
IT'S NOT UNLIKE YOUR FOREST OF DEMONS.
OGUNA'S INTENT TO KILL WAS TURNED AGAINST HIM. HIS OWN WILL TO FIGHT THREATENED TO CUT HIM INTO PIECES.
I SEE. IN THAT CASE, WHAT WILL *YOU* DO?
I'LL DO *THIS.*

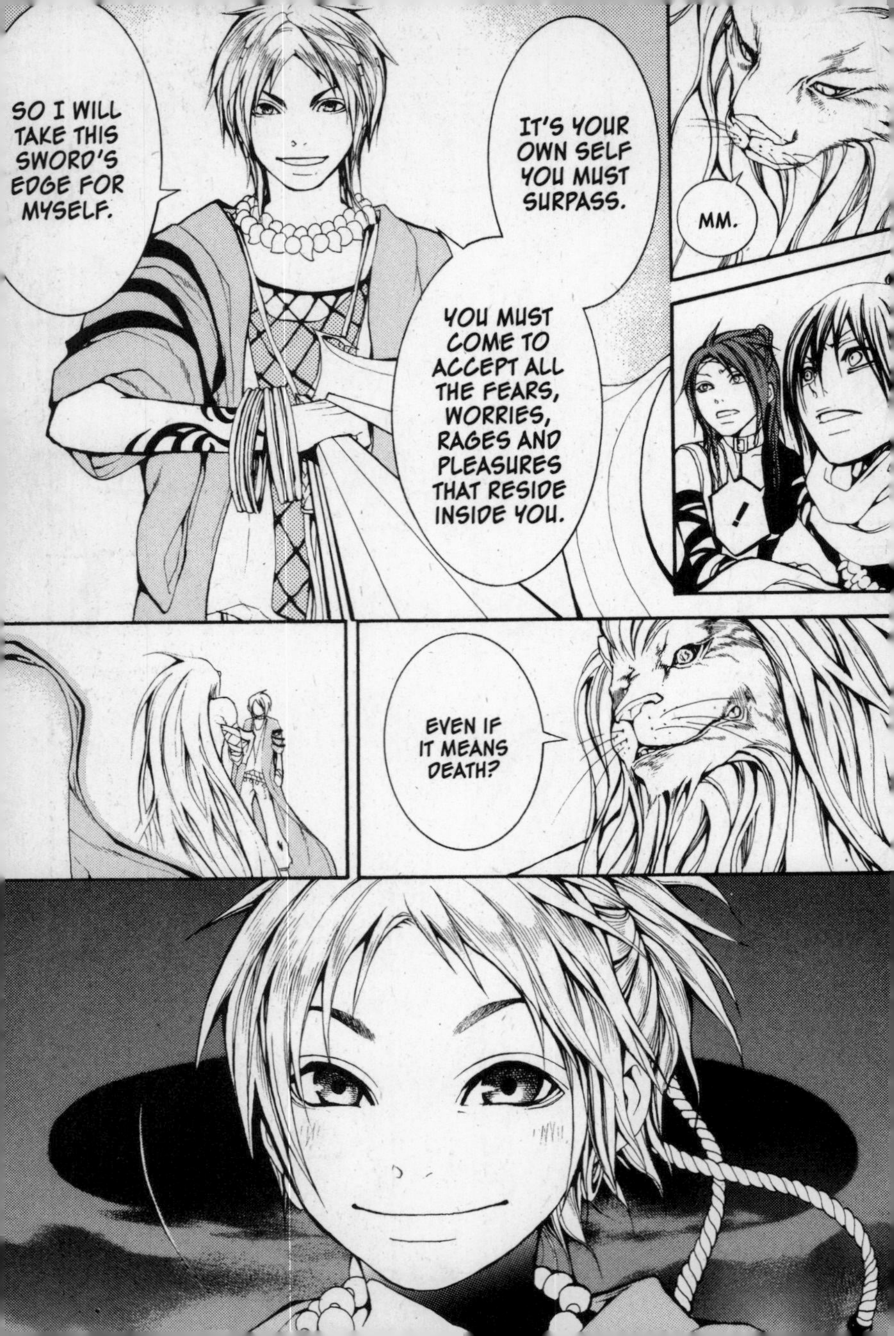
MM.
!
IT'S YOUR OWN SELF YOU MUST SURPASS.
YOU MUST COME TO ACCEPT ALL THE FEARS, WORRIES, RAGES AND PLEASURES THAT RESIDE INSIDE YOU.
SO I WILL TAKE THIS SWORD'S EDGE FOR MYSELF.
EVEN IF IT MEANS DEATH?

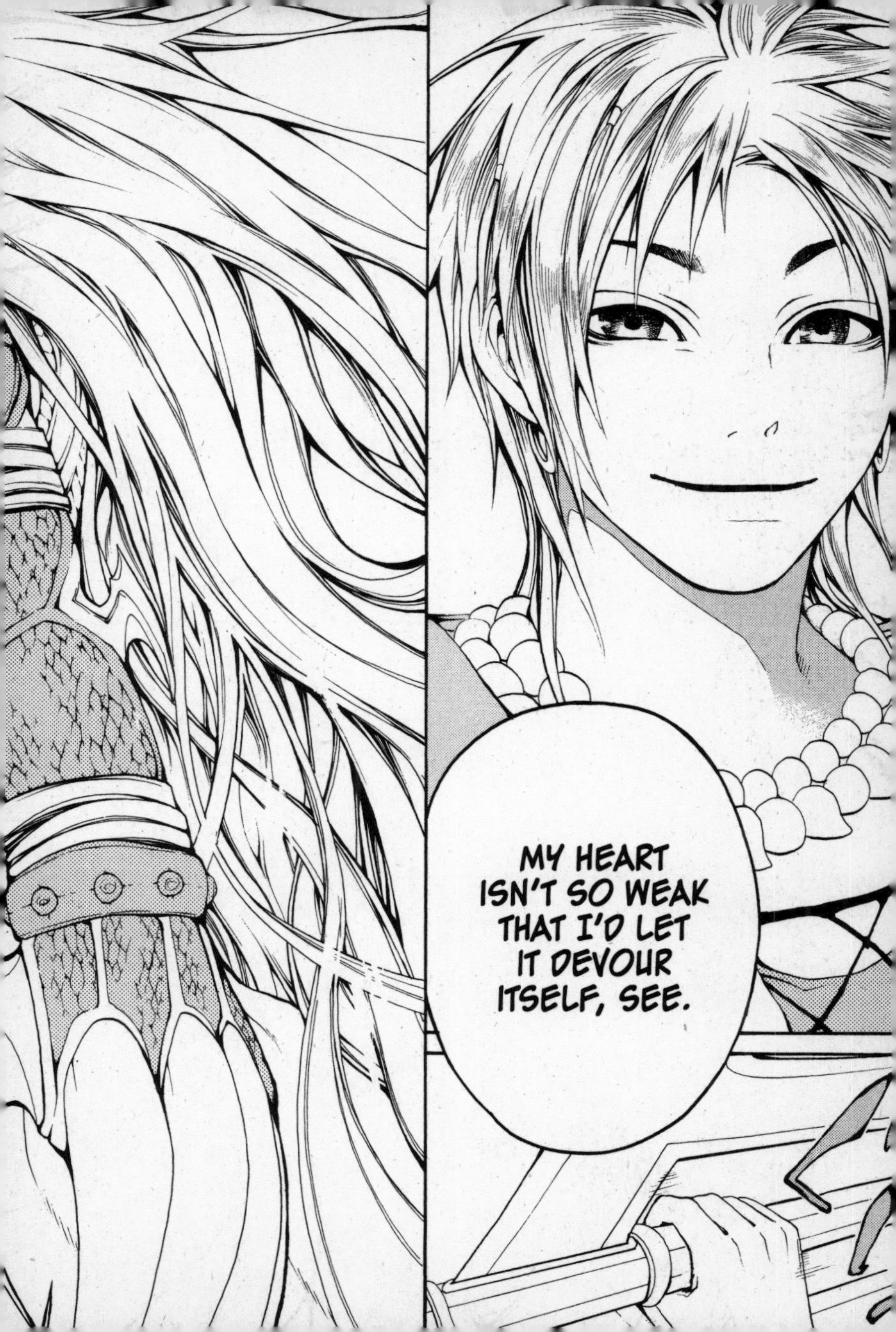
MY HEART ISN'T SO WEAK THAT I'D LET IT DEVOUR ITSELF, SEE.

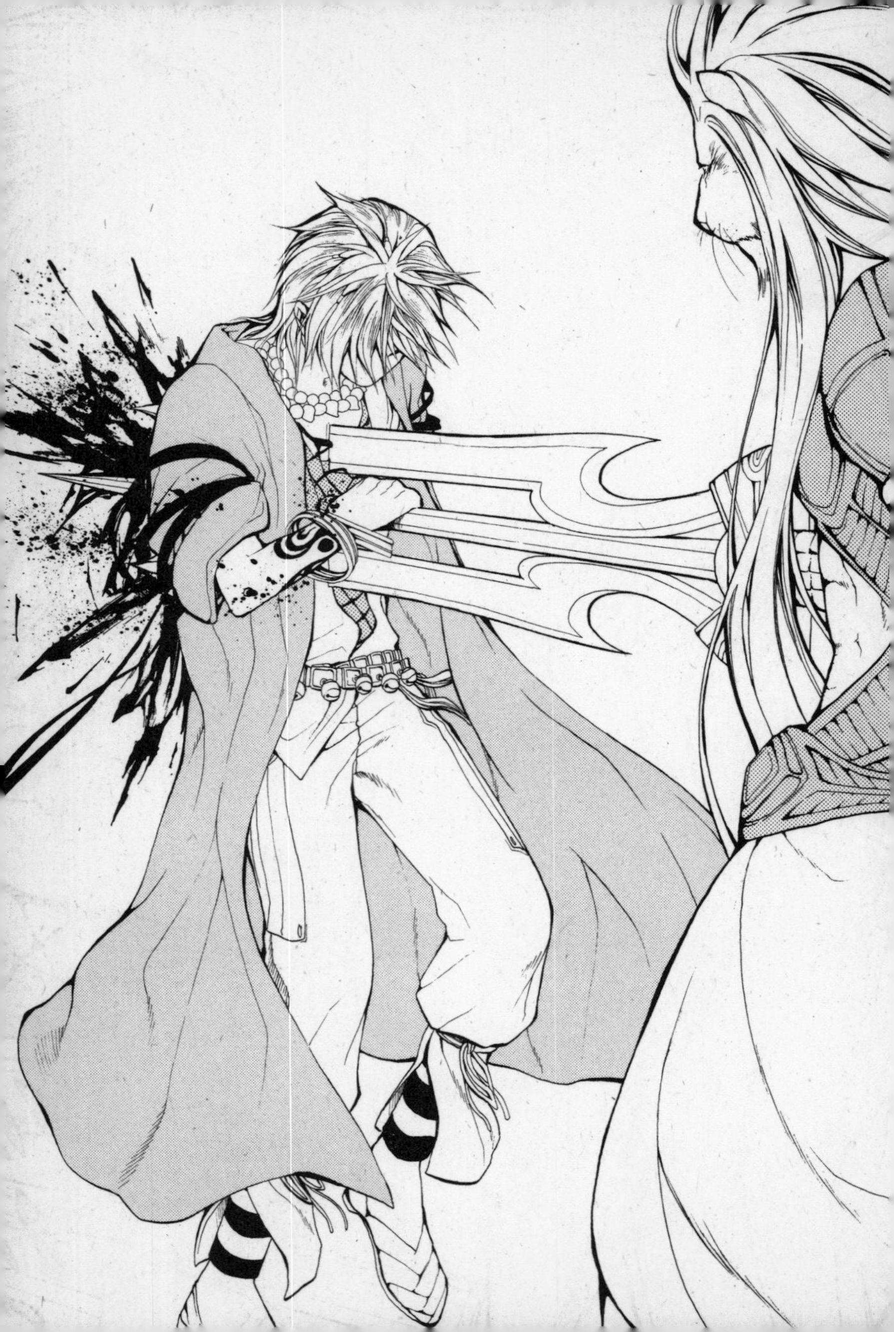

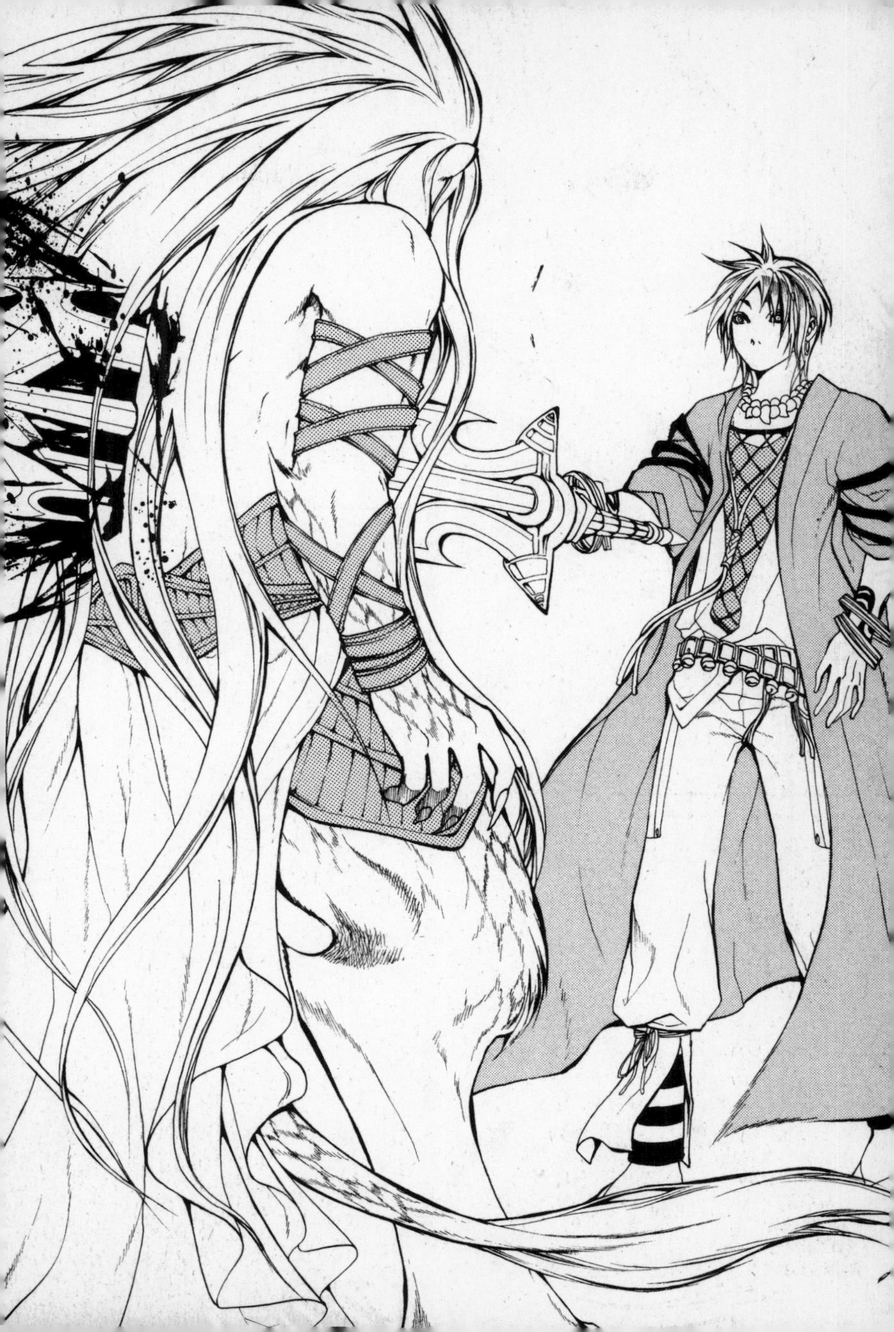

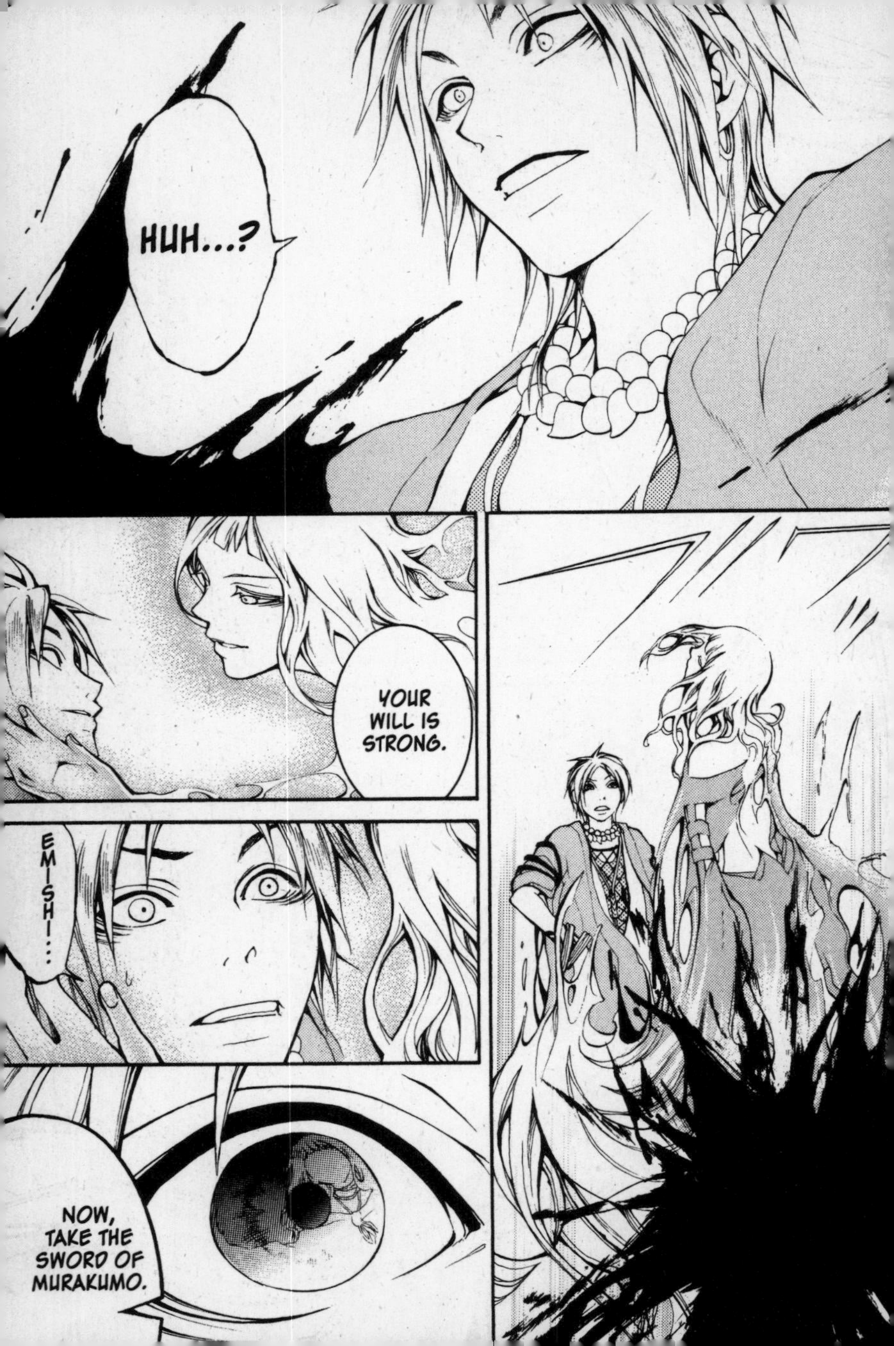
HUH...?
YOUR WILL IS STRONG.
EMISHI...
NOW, TAKE THE SWORD OF MURAKUMO.

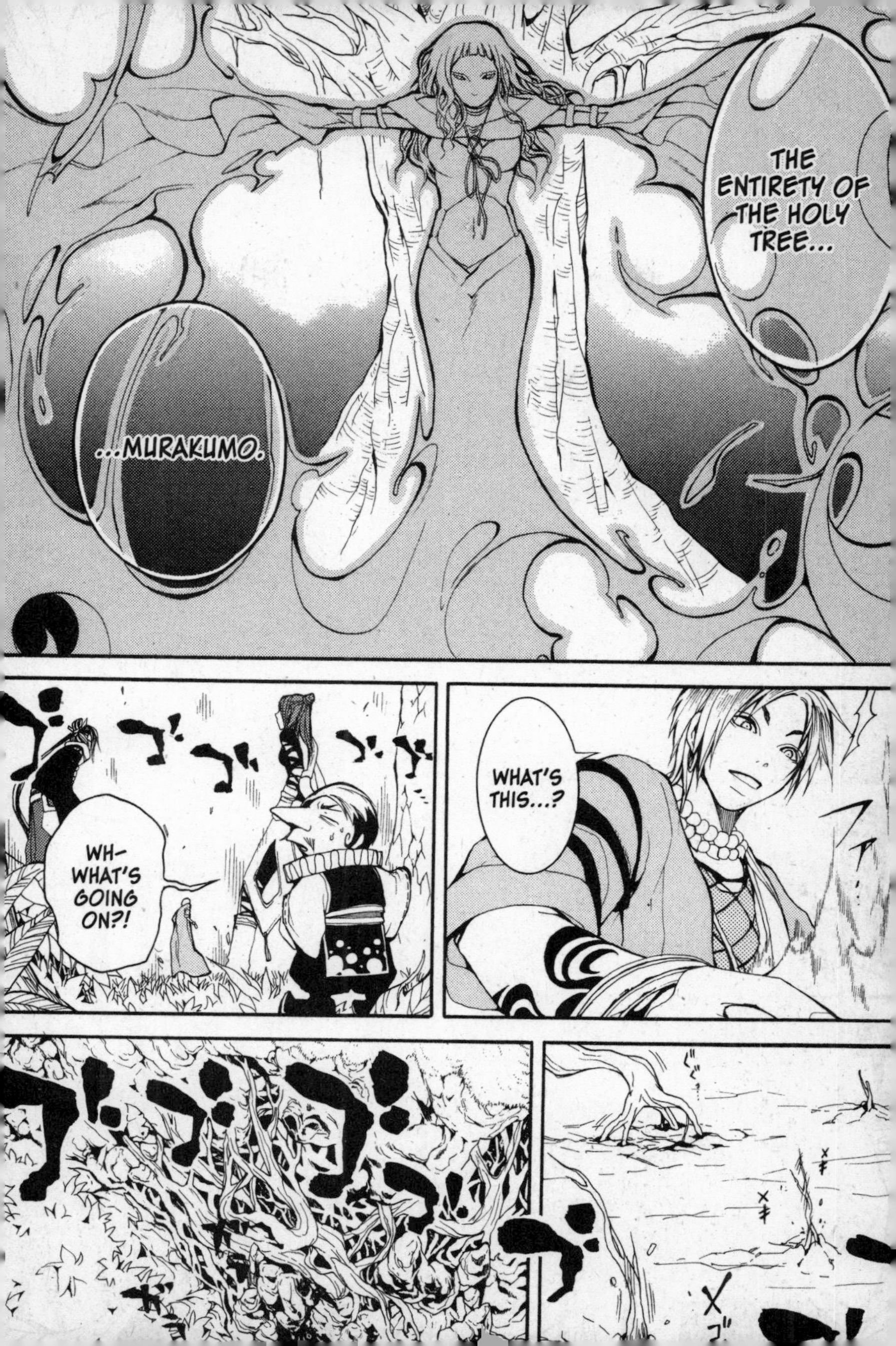
THE ENTIRETY OF THE HOLY TREE...
...MURAKUMO.
WHAT'S THIS...?
WH- WHAT'S GOING ON?!

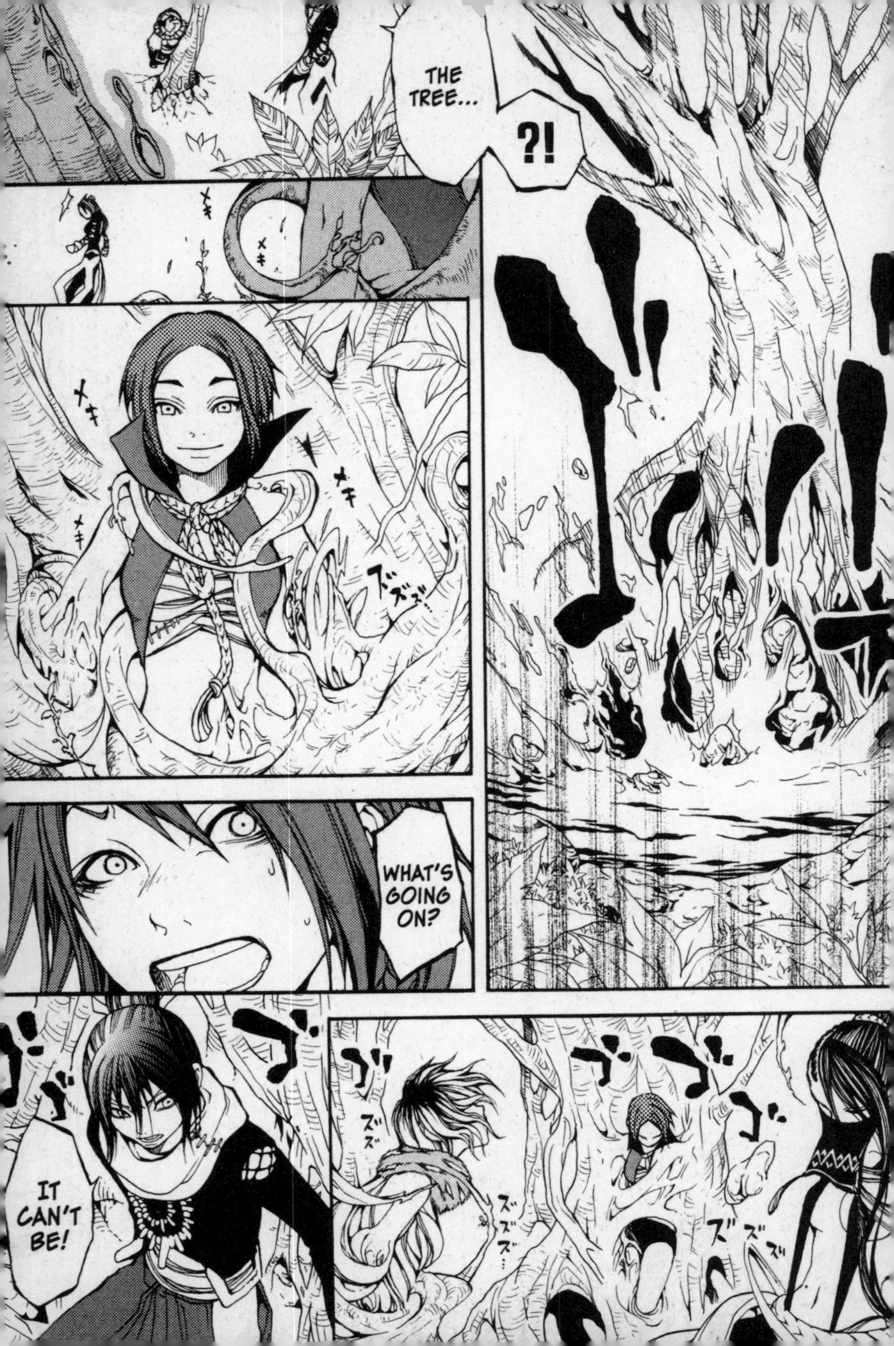
THE TREE...
?!
WHAT'S GOING ON?
IT CAN'T BE!

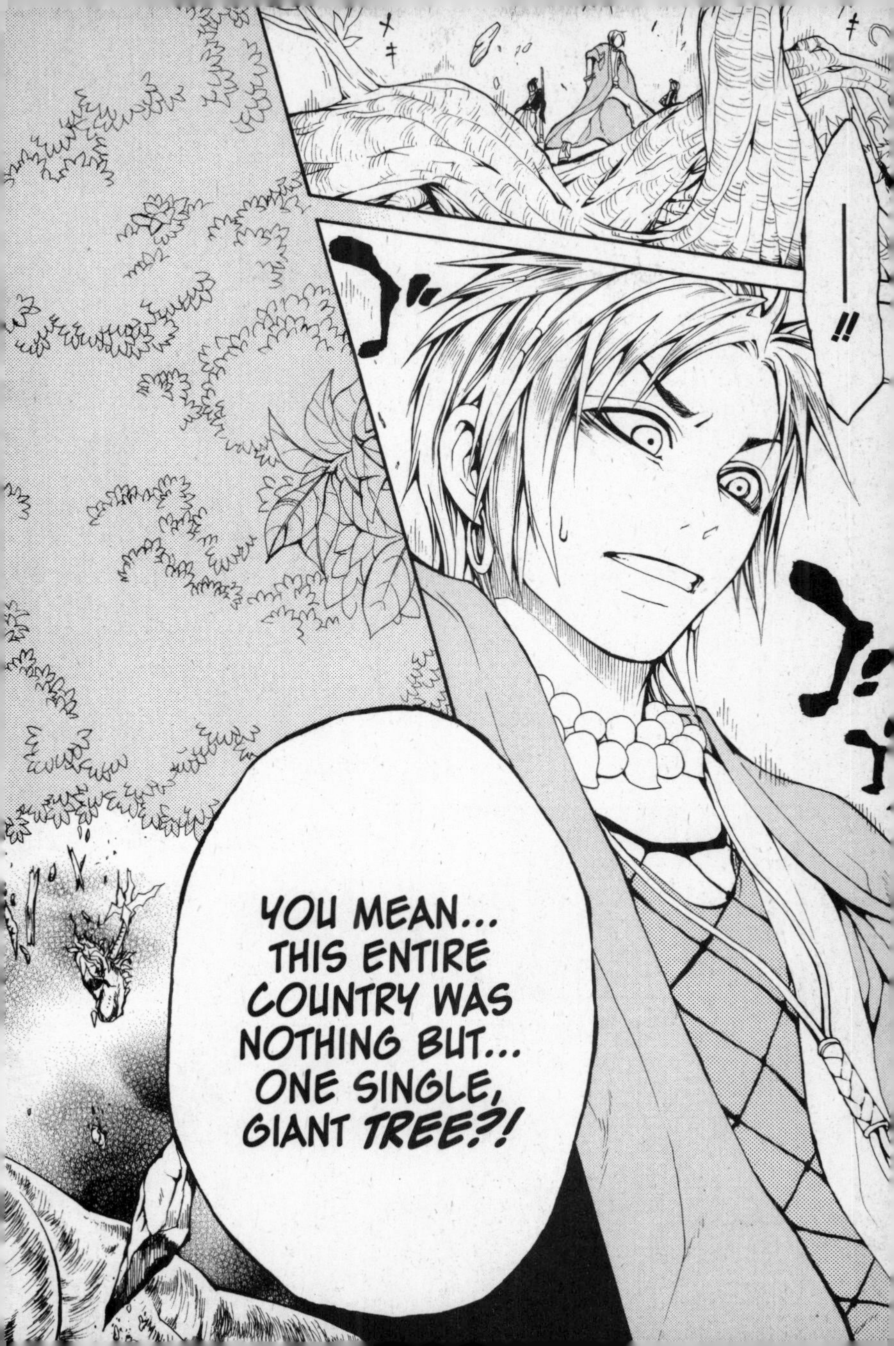
YOU MEAN... THIS ENTIRE COUNTRY WAS NOTHING BUT... ONE SINGLE, GIANT TREE?!

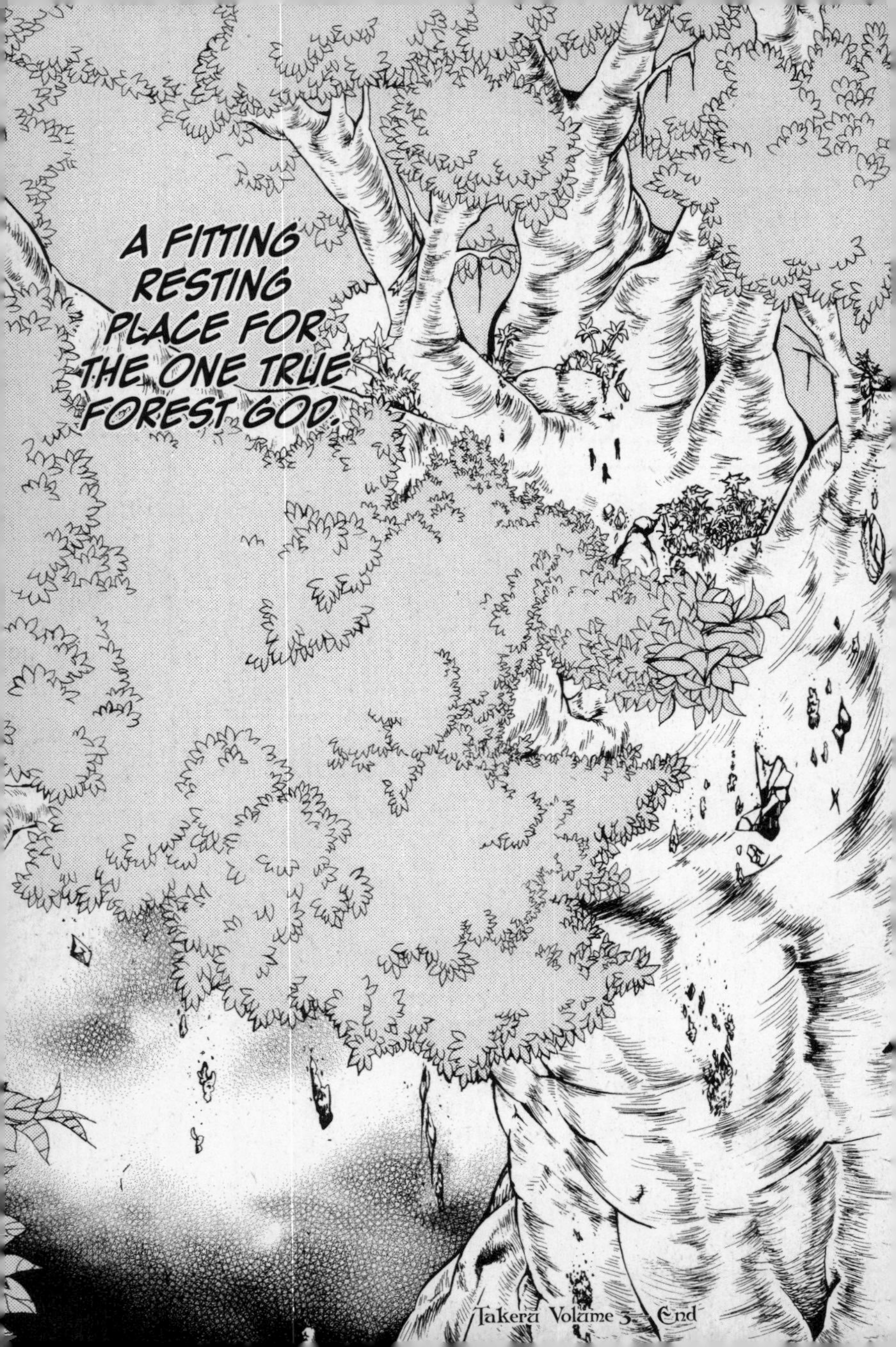
A FITTING RESTING PLACE FOR THE ONE TRUE FOREST GOD.
Takeru Volume 3 End

Special Thanks

Kazuki Nakashima

The readers

Kitano
Takubo
Akao
Uenakai
Ume
Yoshimine

Ichii (for the erasers)
Fujiwara
Ida
Fuchi
H-mori
Y-da
Family

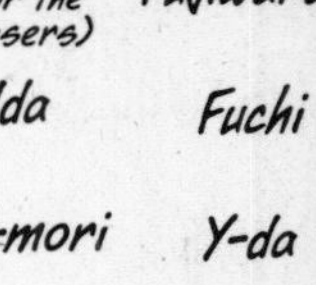

Genes

Hmmm ...
Father
+
Son
=
40 years later
Wh- What was that for?!
I just felt like it.

Flowers

My flower has finally bloomed!
Ha ha ha ha!
...
Well, I certainly see a resemblance.
They say a flower changes depending how you raise it.
Best to let it grow within the harsh reality of nature...
Father, your weeds seem to be outgrowing the flower.
Ohiko
Heh! Flowers are delicate. I'm keeping it away from sunlight and strong breezes...
That's good. I'd hate to see it, y'know, GROW!
Kibitsu
What happened, Kawa-wake?!
It wasn't my fault.
Nothing ...
by Kawa-wake

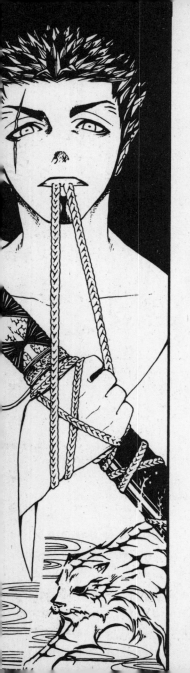

Baa.

FRoM UNDER THE oRIGINAL COVER

What, for real?

Once there is a legend of a sword.
It says that the sword of a rude god was
sealed up in "JAGARA-MOGARA".
When spilit of these tree,Light,Water and Earth,
meet together,the seal will break then the sword
was immortalize.
That is the sword of SUSANOH.
This is a tale who was fascinated by the
sword of SUSANOH.

中島かずき×唐々煙
kazuki nakashima×*karakarakemuri presents*

ダ ケ ル ―SUSANOH〜魔性の剣〔劇団☆新感線〕より―

takeru

OPERA SUSANOH SWORD OF THE DEVIL

The forces controlled by the evil Sword of Kusanagi have reached the gates of the Kingdom of Amamikado, led by the possessed hero Kumaso. But while the armies of Amamikado rally to protect their lands and their lives, is it possible that the arrival of the sword and its wave of destruction is exactly what Otarashi-no-Mikoto truly desires? And if so, then it's up to Izumo and Oguna return to Amamikado in time, armed with the one weapon powerful enough to defeat Otarashi's horrific scheme.

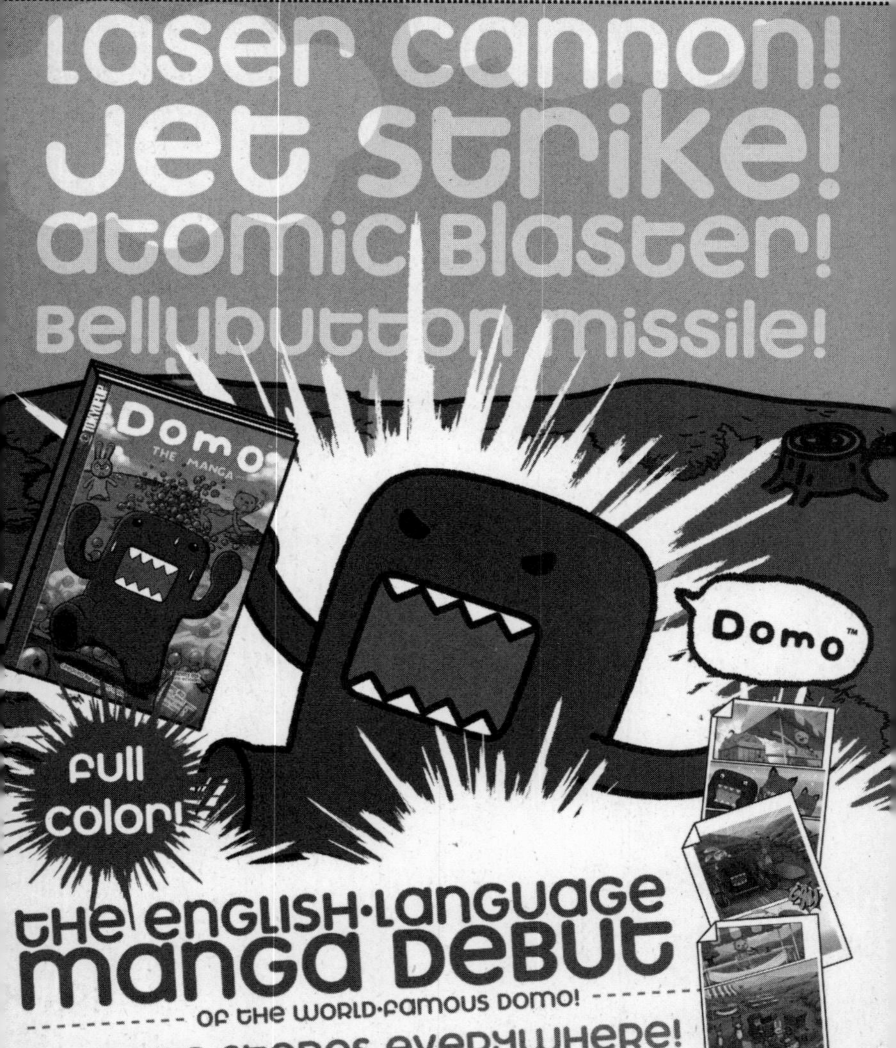
Laser Cannon!
Jet Strike!
atomic Blaster!
Bellybutton missile!
Domo THE MANGA
Domo™
full color!
the english-language manga debut
of the world-famous Domo!
invading stores everywhere!
PREVIEWS, CONTESTS, AND MORE AT WWW.TOKYOPOP.COM/DOMO_MANGA
DOMO © NHK-TYO 1998-2009. DOMO ANIMATION © DOMO PRODUCTION COMMITTEE. ALL RIGHTS RESERVED. WWW.DOMONATION.COM

A dark, Gothic tale from the artist of *Trinity Bloo*

A mysterious drug, known only as "Zone-00," seems to be causing demons all over Tokyo to lose control and revert their old, violent ways. Enter two young students who sta opposite sides of an ageless conflict. One a demon, the o an exorcist, they must now join forces to uncover the sec of "Zone-00" before it's too late!

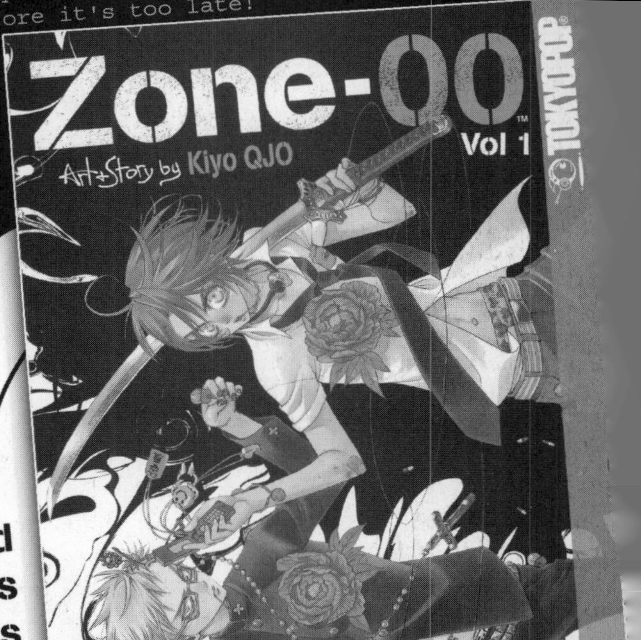
Zone-00™
Vol 1
Art+Story by Kiyo QJO
TOKYOPOP
From the artist of
TRINITY BLOOD

**In a world
here humans
and demons
coexist under
a fragile
peace, change
is coming...**

BE SURE TO VISIT WWW.TOKYOPOP.COM/SHOP FOR EVERYTHING YOU COULD EVER WANT!

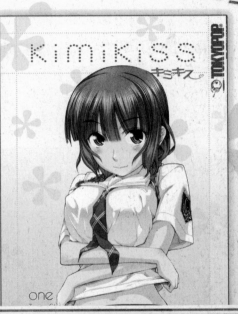

You wou... ...ding!

This book is printed "manga-style," in the authentic Japanese right-to-left format. Since none of the artwork has been flipped or altered, readers get to experience the story just as the creator intended. You've been asking for it, so TOKYOPOP® delivered: authentic, hot-off-the-press, and far more fun!

DIRECTIONS

If this is your first time reading manga-style, here's a quick guide to help you understand how it works.

It's easy... just start in the top right panel and follow the numbers. Have fun, and look for more 100% authentic manga from TOKYOPOP®!

漫画革命

LEADING THE MANGA REVOLUTION · LEADING THE MANGA REVOLUTION